# BLACK
# ATLANTIC
# POLITICS

SUNY series in Afro-American Studies
John R. Howard and Robert C. Smith, editors

# BLACK
# ATLANTIC
# POLITICS

Dilemmas of Political Empowerment
in
Boston and Liverpool

William E. Nelson Jr.

State University of New York Press

Published by
State University of New York Press, Albany

For information, address State University of New York Press,
State University Plaza, Albany, NY, 12246

Production by Marilyn Semerad
Marketing by Anne M. Valentine

**Library of Congress Cataloging-in-Publication Data**

Nelson, William E., 1941–
    Black Atlantic politics : dilemmas of political empowerment in Boston
    and Liverpool /
    William E. Nelson, Jr.
        p. cm. — (SUNY series in Afro-American studies)
    Includes index.
    ISBN 0–7914–4671–9 (alk. paper) — ISBN 0–7914–4672–7 (pbk. : alk. paper)
        1. Afro-Americans—Massachusetts—Boston—Politics and government. 2.
    Blacks—England—Liverpool—Politics and government. 3. Boston (Mass.)—
    Politics and government. 4. Liverpool (England)—Politics and government.
    I. Title. II. Series.

F73.9.N4 N45 2000
323.1′196041′0942753—dc21                                    00–020247

10  9  8  7  6  5  4  3  2  1

*This book is dedicated to my wife, Della J. Nelson, my son, Nicholas F. Nelson, my parents, William E. Nelson and Mildred E. Nelson and in memory of my dear friends Dr. Clyde W. Franklin and Thelma Clark*

# Contents

viii    CONTENTS

# Illustrations

# ILLUSTRATIONS

# Foreword

This is one of the most important books available for understanding race and class and urban politics within a comparative framework. Professor Nelson has utilized his own social and activist experiences and impressive scholarship of urban politics to identify several key variables that explain the substance, style, and contours of Black politics in the cities of the United States and England. Professor Nelson's book helps us, here, to see our struggles, including victories and temporary defeats, as part and parcel of the struggles there. This is a powerful realization for those interested in social and racial justice in both places.

This book will stand as a model for future comparative studies involving issues of race, class, and methodologies for studying these issues. This claim is based on several observations. First, the study represents a systematic investigation and analysis of the demographic, economic and institutional factors that mold urban racial politics in cities in the United States and England. Nelson discusses similar historical and class dynamics in both settings. Second, the author focuses on the political activism and agendas of grassroots sectors in the cities of Boston and Liverpool. By doing this he overcomes the weakness of many studies of Black political behavior ensconced conceptually in the definition of such as merely *voting* and *nonvoting*. Third, this book helps to bridge a gap of information about Black political and activist experiences in the international arena. This gap was identified by Malcolm X as a major explanation for the political weakness of Black America and the consequent social backwardness of the nation. To quip him, "We cannot straighten out Mississippi, unless we straighten out the Congo; and we cannot straighten out the Congo, unless we straighten out Mississippi." This remains a powerful observation for the contemporary period, albeit with different names and players. The essential problem in advancing social justice and alluded to by Malcolm X is that political consciousness and understanding of political history is incomplete if confined by national boundaries. This book will help us to break our intellectual confinement and realize how significant are international issues and connections in explaining the social and economic status of the Black community in the United States, as well as other places.

JAMES JENNINGS

The Trotter Institute
University of Massachusetts Boston

# Acknowledgments

The debts I owe to individuals and institutions who have supported my scholarly efforts are legion. My greatest debt is to my wife Della J. Nelson, and my son, Nicholas F. Nelson, two of the individuals to whom this book is dedicated, who tolerated my long absences from home and long hours marooned in my study, with grace and extraordinary human affection. I shall be eternally grateful for the many sacrifices they have made out of their love for me. I am also indebted to the Centre for Urban Studies at the University of Liverpool, the European Institute for Urban Affairs at Liverpool John Moores University, and the William Monroe Trotter Institute at the University of Massachusetts Boston. All of these institutions provided warm and supportive environments for my work. They provided for me essential technical support; I benefited greatly from the wisdom and knowledge I received from the scholars in residence at these institutions. The clerical and staff assistance I received at these institutions was unbelievable. I came away from my visits at the Centre for Urban Studies, the European Institute for Urban Affairs, and the William Monroe Trotter Institute with a new appreciation for the importance of the development of institutional centers for the study of race, ethnicity, and urban change. I consider myself extremely lucky to have had an opportunity to spend productive times at these superb institutions of research. The debt that I owe Michael Parkinson, director of the Centre for Urban Studies and the European Institute for Urban Affairs, and James Jennings, director of the William Monroe Trotter Institute, is more than I can ever repay. I shall be eternally grateful to both of them. I wish to also extend thanks to Donald Brown of Boston College for providing essential logistical support.

Two funding sources were critical to this research undertaking. I am indebted to the Fulbright Foundation for the award of a Foreign

Research Fellowship. The Fulbright Fellowship funded my initial research visit to Liverpool. Without this fellowship support, my long stay in Britain would not have been possible. I also received travel support for trips to Liverpool and Boston from the College of Social and Behavioral Sciences at The Ohio State University. I am grateful both to the college and to the Department of Political Science for answering my requests for assistance with positive responses. The Department of African American and African Studies at The Ohio State University has remained a source of technical and professional support; many of the material and psychological resources I have relied upon to see this project to completion have emanated from that department.

The list of individuals who have assisted me in the production of this volume is very long. I can only name a few. Randall Ripley, dean of the College of Social and Behavioral Sciences; Paul Beck, chair of the Department of Political Science; William T. McDaniel, former chair of the Department of Black Studies; John Roberts, chair of the Department of African American and African Studies; and Graylyn Swilley, director of the African American and African Studies Community Extension Center, all colleagues at The Ohio State University, have consistently supported my work strongly and enthusiastically. I deeply appreciate their efforts on my behalf. I received invaluable clerical and administrative assistance from Jean Parry of the Centre for Urban Studies, University of Liverpool; Eva Hendricks and Muriel Ridley of the William Monroe Trotter Institute, University of Massachusetts Boston; and Jeanne Boykins, Shirley Turner, Jacqueline Craig, and Carla Wilks of the Department of African American and African Studies, The Ohio State University. I am especially grateful to Jeanne Boykins for the time and effort she devoted to helping me prepare this manuscript for publication. I am also grateful for the extraordinary editorial assistance provided by Barbara DeSalvo. Graduate students have been the life blood of this project. I have received incredible assistance from Kendra King, Laurel Elder, Shelly Anderson, Daniel Gutierrez, Jessica Perez-Monforti, and Michele Cushnie. Their labors have been invaluable, both in the transcription of the tapes and in the preparation of the figures.

In pursuing research strategies, I have been guided by the wisdom of a number of key individuals. In Liverpool I profited from the assistance and counsel of Gideon Ben-Tovim, Sam Semoff, Irene Loh Lynn, Mark Christian, June Henfry, Alan Harding, Noel Boaden, Rashid Mufti, Linda Loy, Protasia Torkington, Hilary

Russell, John Hamilton, Nigel Mellor, Sonia Bassey, Ruby Dixon, Manneh Brown, Maria O'Reilly, Dave Clay, Michael Parkinson, Alex Bennett, Adam Hussein, Carleton Benjamin, Estelle Newman, Chief Ben Agwuna, Kathryn Dixon, and Dorothy Kuyu. In Boston I received major assistance and counsel from Harold Horton, James Jennings, Regina Rodriguez-Mitchell, Russell Williams, Jamdari Kamara, Paul Parks, Jean McGuire, Tyrone dePass, Phillip Hart, Hubie Jones, Bill Owens, Shirley Owens-Hicks, Charles Yancey, Robert Dentler, Anthony Van Der Meer, Gareth Saunders, Dianne Wilkerson, Byron Rushing, Leonard Alkins, Bruce Bolling, Robert C. Hayden, Martin Kilson, Wilbur Rich, Eugene Rivers III, and Angela Paige Cook.

A number of individuals have read all or portions of the manuscript and given me the benefit of their feedback. These individuals include Samuel Patterson, Phillip Hart, Mark Christian, Sam Semoff, Paulette Pierce, June Henfry, Yasmeen Abu-Laban, Verna Okali, Viola Newton, Daniel Gutierrez, Noel Boaden, Gideon Ben-Tovim, Dennis Judd, Kendra King, Stefanie Torphy, Michele Cushnie, Jelanie Favors, Lewis Randolph, James Upton, Anthony Affigne, Hanes Walton Jr., Ronald Walters, Cedric Johnson, Wilbur Rich, Randall Ripley, James Jennings, Robert Smith, Toni-Michelle C. Travis, Michael Preston and Harold Horton.

Finally, I wish to acknowledge the contributions paid to my intellectual development by two brilliant former teachers, Samuel DuBois Cook and Ray F. Russell.

# Introduction

Officially this project has been almost a decade in the making. In reality it has deeper roots. The sequence of events leading to the completion of this book began with a phone call in the spring of 1986 from Dennis Judd, my former classmate at the University of Illinois, inquiring into my interest in speaking at a conference in Liverpool. My experience in Britain having been confined to London, the name *Liverpool* evoked immediate interest. I formally accepted an invitation from Michael Parkinson, director of the Centre for Urban Studies at the University of Liverpool, to speak at a conference in Liverpool sponsored by the Centre entitled "Liverpool in Context." In my talk I traced the historic struggle by Blacks in the United States to obtain social and economic rights through political action, including electoral mobilization and public protests.

I found the visit to Liverpool uniquely stimulating. The visit brought me in contact with a range of British scholars, public administrators, and community activists. Through my conversations with these individuals, I began to get a crash course on British local government and politics. The most profoundly illuminating aspect of my visit were the discussions I had with representatives of the local Black community. These individuals were eager to talk about their ongoing struggles for democratic rights and social justice in Liverpool and questioned me closely about the experiences of Blacks in America around the same issues. Much of what they said had a familiar ring. I found the parallels between Liverpool's Black community's struggles and those of Blacks in major American cities quite startling. I learned during my talks that no fully comprehensive study of the Black political experience in Liverpool had been done. I made a vow, both to myself and the Black activists I met, to return to Liverpool one day to conduct such a comprehensive study.

The opportunity to return to Liverpool came in 1990 in the form of a Fulbright Research Fellowship to conduct scholarly research in Britain. I received an appointment as a research fellow at the Centre for Urban Studies at the University of Liverpool, thanks in large measure to the support of Michael Parkinson and Gideon Ben-Tovim, Senior Lecturer in Sociology at the University of Liverpool and head of the University's Race and Social Policy unit. I remained in Liverpool continuously for almost five months. During that time I conducted interviews with community activists, academicians, professional politicians, and members of the city bureaucracy. I collected enough data to write a comprehensive study of Black politics in Liverpool. I wrote several draft chapters and circulated them among scholars and community activists in Liverpool before returning home to the United States.

With the idea of a single city study still etched in my consciousness, I returned to Liverpool in the spring of 1993 to update my data set. During this visit I increased my list of completed interviews and compared the material I collected with the data collected in 1990. The conclusion I reached was that little had changed in the political posture of the Black community since my last visit. The basic value of my visit in 1993 was the reaffirmation of the main line of the analytical impressions I had forged during my initial research visit. By 1994 the notion of a single city case study had grown stale. A trip to Boston in 1995 to lecture at a community forum entitled the "Black Agenda Project," organized by James Jennings of the University of Massachusetts Boston, convinced me that the Liverpool study should be pursued in a broader analytical context. A conversation I had in Boston with my longtime friend from Ohio State Harold Horton, a faculty member at the University of Massachusetts Boston, gave me the conceptual anchor for my research. Professor Horton described a history of struggle by Blacks in Boston that sounded remarkably like the taped conversations emanating from my Liverpool research. This conversation inspired me to read again the extraordinary comparative study on immigration and racial politics written by Ira Katznelson entitled *Black Men, White Cities*. Out of a close reading of Katznelson and related works, including Paul Gilroy's *The Black Atlantic*, emerged the germinal idea of this book, *Black Atlantic Politics*. When this background work was complete, it was clear to me that my analytical goals required that I pursue a comparative study of Black politics in Boston and Liverpool. In the service of this objective, I traveled to Boston to conduct interviews on subjects comparable to the ones I researched in Liverpool. This work was generously supported by my appointment in the spring of 1996 as a Visiting Research Scholar at the William Monroe Trotter Institute at the University of Massachusetts Boston. Using the Trotter Institute as a base of operation, I conducted interviews with community activists, scholars, professional politicians, and members of the Boston city bureaucracy. I made follow-up visits to Liverpool in the summer of 1996 and to Boston in the spring of 1997. This study tracks the shifting sands of Black politics in an important American city and an important British city over a period of nearly three decades.

The data base for this study is massive. During my research visits to Liverpool between 1990 and 1996, I conducted 105 formal interviews. I began with an initial list of names of possible respondents supplied by scholars at the University of Liverpool. As the interviewing process progressed, I added names to the list based on suggestions I received from a number of informed sources. Through this research methodology, I was able to hold in-depth conversations with a broad range of political activists, academicians, politicians, and public administrators in Liverpool. I adopted a similar research strategy in Boston. Scholars at the University of Massachusetts Boston provided me with an initial list of possible respondents. I arranged appointments for a first round of interviews from my home base in Columbus, Ohio. Additional interviews were set up in Boston through the help of the staff of the William Monroe Trotter Institute at the University of Massachusetts Boston. In total, 56 formal interviews were conducted in Boston in the spring of 1996 and spring of 1997. The Boston interviews also consisted of in-depth conversations with a broad range of political activists, scholars, politicians, and public administrators.

Interviews in Boston and Liverpool were recorded on tape (some individuals were interviewed more than once) and ranged from one to three hours. Several short interviews were also conducted over the telephone and summarized through written notes. Direct quotations from the interviews have been provided to strengthen the scholarly analysis and to allow the people of Boston and Liverpool to speak for themselves on critical issues. In keeping with promises to the respondents, most of the quotations are cited anonymously. Names are attached only to interviews with prominent administrators and politicians. These individuals are personally cited only when identification is essential to understanding the meaning and context of the insights provided by their interviews. The research methodology has included an extensive examination of special reports, books, articles, and newspaper files. These data ( both the interviews and the complementary sources) serve as the pivotal cornerstones of this comparative analysis of the political and social development of Black communities in two of the Atlantic world's most important cities.

# PART ONE

# Black Atlantic Politics

# 1

## The Black Atlantic:
## Race and Local Politics

### The Black Atlantic

The fifteenth-century explorations of Portuguese ships carrying their mysterious cargo from Africa to Europe set in motion a chain of events that would envelop the Atlantic world and forever change the course of African history. For four hundred years, the Atlantic slave trade forcibly removed Africans from their homelands and repositioned them as enslaved noncitizens in Europe, the Caribbean, Latin America, and North America. These were the pivotal building blocks of the Black Atlantic.

We must be careful not to confuse the concept "Black Atlantic" with the term *African Diaspora*. The Black Atlantic stands as only one facet of the African Diasporian experience. The concept "African Diaspora," in its fullness, encompasses the worldwide migration of Black people out of Africa long before the commencement of the Atlantic slave trade. This migration is well documented. Research on the international history of African people confirms that ancient Africans traveled throughout Europe, the Middle East, and Asia as merchants and sailors.[1] When European crusaders traveled to Rome, Florence, Portugal, and Spain, they were accompanied by Ethiopian monks and missionaries devoted to the sacred cause of spreading the gospel of Christianity and Islam around the world.[2] Arab slavery preceded European slavery by fifteen hundred years. At the end of this experience, Black communities were left behind in Iran, Iraq, India, and the northern Mediterranean coast.[3] Africans were world travelers, leaving a rich cultural legacy in North America long before the arrival of Columbus.[4] When Balboa,

Columbus, and Panfilo de Alvarado landed in North America, they were not alone: great seamen of African descent served as key members of their exploration parties.[5]

The humanistic reach of the African Diaspora has been worldwide. No province on earth has been unaffected by the transcontinental migration of African people. The conceptual boundaries of the Black Atlantic fall within well-defined parameters of the broader concept of the African Diaspora. When we speak of the Black Atlantic, we refer to the complex of new world forces ushered into existence by the Atlantic slave trade. European penetration of Africa produced a tidal wave of human migration. The Atlantic slave trade created both a new world order and new world communities. In the wake of its destructive impulses, the African world, at home and abroad, would never be the same. Blacks in the new Diaspora would be transplanted from rational, well organized, culturally fulfilling, psychologically uplifting environments to strange societies where the mosaic of primary institutions would be largely alien, remote, unpredictable, atomistic, and irrational. Out of the experience of their human oppression, they were compelled to undertake the arduous task of recasting their lives and building new, functional communities—and they had to do so with no guideposts and few economic resources. The Black Atlantic emerged in the fifteenth century as a compelling human phenomenon and continued to develop over five subsequent centuries. Spread out over several continents, Blacks would search for the meaning of life in music, dance, song, extended family ties, and militant political action. Everywhere they traveled, they would leave the indelible marks of Africa. The old world would become the new world transfigured by the perennial storms of cultural interaction. Rising above it all would be an irrepressible hunger for human liberation.

### The Racial Hierarchy: Piercing the Conceptual Veil

Contemporary students of the African Diaspora have searched for a plethora of operational concepts to distill the essence of the Black Atlantic. When viewed through the intellectual prism of postmodernist critic Paul Gilroy, the Black Atlantic becomes a metaphor for transnational cultural linkages that bind Blacks together in a cohesive rhythm of spiritual awareness and internal self-expression.[6] Gilroy rails against the narrow identification of Black culture with nationalism. This approach, according to Gilroy, leads to the articulation of forms of cultural absolutism that elevate parochial national interests above the universal cultural artifacts produced by the intermixture of ideas and artistic creations flowing out of the totality of the new world experiences of African people. Gilroy suggests that Black culture has been made anew by the emergence of a transnational Black community that draws its energy and substance from disparate sources.[7] This "vernacular culture" is not American, Caribbean, Latin, or European, but represents the reconfiguration of the culture of all of these places into a unique cultural form. According to Gilroy, this is not a new phenomenon; it is poignantly reflected in the writings of towering intellectuals such as W. E. B. Du Bois, C. L. R. James, and Richard Wright and in the political works of Martin Delany, Ida. B. Wells, William Wells Brown, and Marcus Garvey.[8] Although based in the United States, the Garvey movement, Gilroy contends, should properly be viewed as a transcontinental movement, elevating the struggle for Black freedom to new levels of consciousness and conviction all across the Black Atlantic.[9] This is the fundamental meaning of Du Bois's concept of double consciousness: to be aware of one's existence in a particular nation while embracing transnational values and constructs and imbibing polymorphic cultural spirits that link one's human commitment to the struggles of Black people everywhere.

Gilroy's vision of the Black Atlantic is at once revealing and concealing. His work makes an extremely important contribution to our understanding of the limits and distortions of modernist cultural history and criticism. This genre of scholarly work has been exceedingly myopic in its refusal to move the analysis of Black culture beyond the restricted box of neo-Americanism. The value of Gilroy's intervention is diminished by his unwillingness to give credence to the importance of nationalism as a strategic factor in the actions of Black artists, intellectuals, and political leaders. Existing evidence shows that the transnational actions of these individuals have been guided by a keen awareness of their duties and obligations as citizens of the nation. Transnational connections have often been used by political leaders to serve the goals of primordial national causes. Thus, Frederick Douglass traveled to England not to bolster the cause of international antiracism but to mobilize support for the abolitionist campaign in the United States.[10] Beyond the question by whom are you influenced is the deeper question for whom do you act and speak—what is your primary significant other? Du Bois's dilemma of double consciousness is real and can serve to weaken as well as strengthen one's commitment to transnational struggle.

Gilroy also cannot elude the criticism that transcultural identities have tended to be the exclusive possessions of the elite. How much do grassroots Blacks in Newark know, or care to know, about the struggles of Blacks in Bristol? The analysis is long on the illumination of elite to elite connections but short on identifying grassroots organizational connections across the Atlantic world.

Clearly, the illumination of transnational cultural connections cannot tell us much that we need to know about human strivings in the Black Atlantic. The full import of the cultural dimension can only be understood in the context of race and power relations that have served to relegate Black people to subordinate positions in every sector of the Atlantic world. Postmodernist thought does not give sufficient recognition to the fact that the struggle to rescue and transnationalize Black culture is a political struggle with inextricable ties to a deeper struggle for human rights and personal freedom. From the perspective of politics, the Black Atlantic can be seen as the array of forces that bring Black people together to fight for justice, representation, and power within hierarchical political systems based on white domination and Black subordination.

The institutionalization of White dominance and Black subordination within hierarchical political systems is a continuing legacy of the European slave experience. Realization of the goals of European capitalist expansion required the establishment of processes of human bondage that sought to maximize White control over every aspect of Black life. In the United states, efforts were made to exercise sufficient physical and psychological control over enslaved Africans that their journey to freedom would become an insurmountable task. The objective was not only to make Africans stand in fear but also to unhinge their psychological balance.[11] To accomplish this goal, legal codes were enacted that reduced the status of Blacks to the position of chattel slaves—human property. As early as the 1640s leaders of the Virginia colony were engaged in legal maneuvers to create a system of racial subordination reserved for Blacks only.[12] The legal enslavement of Blacks was codified full blown in Virginia law in 1705 with the passage of legislation that classified African slaves as personal property rather than real estate.[13] These steps toward legal subordination were undergirded by a racial ideology that dehumanized Black life and ruled Black people out of the human family. Audrey Smedley contends that the racist ideology developed by American colonists to justify slavery was an extension of ideological positions fashioned by the English to rationalize the brutal suppression of Irish human rights in the sixteenth century.[14] The reduction of the enslaved African from a person to a thing became one of the pivotal touchstones and defining characteristics of American slavery. In the words of Joel Kovel, White slave owners told their slaves in effect:

> While I own much, much more than my body, you own not even your body: your body shall be detached from your self and your self shall thereby be reduced to subhuman status. And being detached and kept alive, your body shall serve me in many ways: by work on my capitalist plantations to extract the most that can be taken from the land in the cheapest and therefore most rational manner; as a means to my bodily pleasure—both as nurse to my children and a female body for sexual use (for my own women are somehow deficient in this regard); and as medium of exchange, salable like any other commodity of exchange along with or separate from the bodies of your family. For in fact you have no family, since a family is a system that pertains to human beings, and you are not human. And since I, being a man of the West, value things which are owned above all else, I hold you—or, rather, the owned part of you, your body— in very high regard and wish to retain you as my property forever. On the other hand, since I have a certain horror of what I am doing, and since you are a living reminder of this horror and are subhuman to boot, I am horrified by you, disgusted by you, and wish to have nothing to do with you, wish, in fact to be rid of you. And since this set of ideas is inconsistent and will stand neither the test of reason nor of my better values, I am going to distort it, split it up and otherwise defend myself against the realization.[15]

This process of rationalizing and justifying human oppression reached its apogee when enslaved Africans came to believe in their own inferiority and the inevitability of their debasement, degradation, and subjugation.

The demise of slavery in the Americas in the nineteenth century did not destroy the system of hierarchical power. Reconstruction politics in the United States embraced the electoral disfranchisement of the Black population in the South and the institutionalization of wage slavery and social segregation. Falling to the weight of raging white supremacy, African Americans marched into the twentieth century largely poverty stricken and powerless.[16] The results were not significantly different in Latin America and the Caribbean.

In the post-emancipation period of the nineteenth century in Brazil, efforts at economic modernization produced a huge influx of foreign immigrants to major cities. Blacks were victimized by this process. Their strategic position in the economy was supplanted by foreigners and rural migrants, pushing Blacks into marginal sectors of society and transforming them into a subproletariat.[17] From its inception, the process of economic modernization in Brazil was a revolution for Whites only. Under the guise of racial democracy and color-blindness, a system of racial privilege continued in Brazil that largely ignored the plight of Blacks at the bottom of the social and economic order. Race relations in Brazil have taken on a profoundly Orwellian cast:

> The Whites do not victimize the Negroes and Mulattos consciously and willfully. The normal and indirect effects of the functions of color prejudice do that, without racial tensions and social unrest. Because they restrict the economic, educational, social and political opportunities of the Negro and the Mulatto, maintaining them 'out of the system' or at the margin and periphery of the competitive social order, color prejudice and discrimination impedes the existence and the emergence of a racial democracy in Brazil.[18]

Racial bias and hierarchical relationships have frozen the subordinate status of Blacks into the social fabric of Venezuela and other Latin American countries.[19] Social conditions in the Black community in Colon City in Panama, for example, have been characterized by escalating poverty, homelessness, and violence. Militant demonstrations led by the Movement of the Unemployed of Colon (MODE-SCO), founded under Black leadership in 1992, have sought to radically reduce unemployment, upgrade health services, and halt the eviction of tenants occupying houses reverted by the United States government to Panamanian authorities.[20] Parallel demonstrations by Black protest groups in El Chorrillo, led by Hector Avila, have attempted to block the entrance to Puente de las Americas (Bridge of the Americas), the major link between Panama City and the central and western provinces of Panama.[21] In the 1990s, the institutionalization of hierarchical racial relations remains a crucial source of social tension and political conflict throughout the Americas.[22]

The footloose character of twentieth-century capitalism has reinforced the racially exploitative predilections of hierarchical political systems. Throughout the Black Atlantic, the massive flow of capital from the West to the Pacific Rim has left Black communities socially marginalized and economically shattered. The endless and ruthless search for profits by American corporations has triggered the decentralization of jobs outside of cities with large Black concentrations (See figure 1.1).[23] This pattern has produced depressionlike conditions in

**Figure 1.1. Black/White Central City Unemployment Rates, 1990**

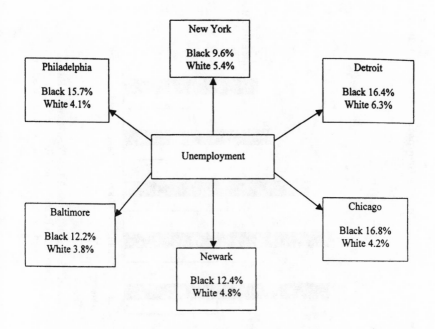

Source: U.S. Department of Labor—Bureau of Labor Statistics, June 1991.

central cities, while the economies of the suburbs have flourished. Processes of racial subordination have stifled the ascension of Blacks into entrepreneurial roles required to rebuild the economic foundations of America's most depressed urban communities.[24] Similar results have obtained in Britain where Black males in the 1980s earned 10 to 15 percent less than their White counterparts and were largely locked out of positions in the top sectors of the British economy.[25] The concentration of Black workers in Britain in declining industrial sectors of the economy has produced high unemployment and poverty in the Black community. From 1983 through 1987, unemployment rates among ethnic minorities in Britain hovered at the level of 20 percent; among African Caribbeans aged sixteen–twenty-four, the unemployment rate exceeded 30 percent.[26] Although the gap between Black and White unemployment dropped after 1989 because of improvement in the British economy, high unemployment remained a major problem for the Black community (See figure 1.2). High unemployment has spawned extraordinary tension between Black youth

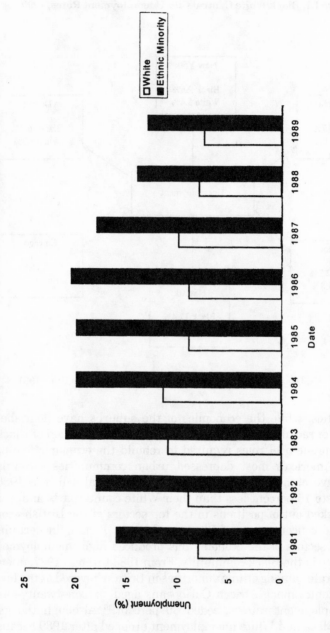

**Figure 1.2. Unemployment Rates for Whites and Ethnic Minority Groups in Britain, 1981–1989**

Source: Adapted from statistical data included in Colin Brown "'Same Difference': The Persistence of Racial Disadvantage in the British Employment Market," in Peter Braham, Ali Rattansi, and Richard Skellington (eds.), *Racism and Anti-Racism: Inequalities, Opportunities and Policies* (London: Sage Publications Ltd., 1992), pp 58–59.

and the police in Britain. Commenting on the response of the dominant power structure to rising social unrest in British Black communities in the 1970s, A. Sivanandan notes:

> Black youths could not walk the street outside the ghetto or hang around streets within it without courting arrest. And apart from individual arrests, whole communities were subjected to roadblocks, stop and search and mass arrests. In Brixton in 1975 the para-military Special Patrol Group (SPG) cruised the streets in force, made arbitrary arrests and generally terrorized the community. In Lewisham the same year the SPG stopped 14,000 people on the streets and made 400 arrests. The pattern was repeated by similar police units in other parts of the country.[27]

The search for justice, power, and representation in racially hierarchical political systems constitutes the fundamental mission, method, orientation, and motivation of Black politics in the Black Atlantic. Mack H. Jones has correctly called attention to the critical need to frame the analysis of Black politics in the context of the struggle for power between dominant and subordinate groups in society.[28] Racial politics in the Black Atlantic illuminate important power relationships in society. Throughout the Atlantic world, Whites have occupied privileged positions and used their positions to keep Blacks locked out of key domains of policy making and resource distribution. A realistic and insightful frame of reference for Black politics must shed penetrating light on the barriers to Black empowerment in society and the dilemmas faced by Blacks in their efforts to fundamentally alter the power equation. Black political empowerment involves the reallocation of power in ways that enhance or favor the policy preferences of the Black community.[29] Three critical benchmarks of Black political empowerment are the capturing of high-status elected offices by socially conscious and racially committed Black politicians, expansion of significant and effective Black representation in public-sector jobs, and major enhancement of Black influence and control over governmental agenda setting and decision making.[30] Black political activities that do not achieve a reallocation of power reinforce subordination rather than promote empowerment.[31]

An essential element in the analysis of Black political empowerment is the examination of strategies adopted by Black activists to create effective resource bases and mobilize collective power in the political system.[32] One key starting point in this analysis is the history of protest that has served as the crucial foundation for efforts by Blacks to respond to the dominant White power forces arrayed against them.[33] The vision of the Black Atlantic as a warrior community united in protest against structures and processes of racial domination represents a conception of the Atlantic world deserving of probing investigation and analysis. Protest politics, of course, constitutes only one dimension of the struggle for Black freedom and liberation. This volume will meticulously assess a medley of instruments in the strategic armor of Black communities struggling for justice, power, and representation in the political process.

## Theories of Race in Local Politics

More than twenty years ago, Ira Katznelson called for extensive comparative research on the local politics of race.[34] This volume attempts to speak to many of the issues raised by Katznelson by analyzing the dilemmas of political empowerment faced by Black Atlantic communities in Boston and Liverpool. Since the publication of Katznelson's book, the literature on the local politics of race in the United States and Britain has continued to ignore or misconstrue important dimensions of dominant-subordinate group relations. Despite the pioneering work of W. E. B. Du Bois, Carter G. Woodson, Oliver Cox, and John Rex underscoring the centrality of race in the policy-making process, mainstream studies in political science and sociology have often failed to address the implications of dominant-subordinate relationships in racially hierarchical political systems. On this score, Hanes Walton Jr. has observed that behavioral studies of American politics have routinely rendered Black challenges to the prevailing political system invisible.[35] These studies lodge the source of Black behavioral action in sociopsychological and intrapsychic forces emanating internally from the Black environment rather than structural power arrangements that artificially limit Black access to important arenas of public and private decision making.[36]

Following the groundbreaking theories advanced by American sociologist Robert Park, scholars writing on race in the cities have tended to discount the importance of race in the policy process because of what they view as the unfailing capacity on the part of the political system to assimilate racial minorities and address their needs within traditional channels of the political and governmental process. The Park school of social analysis views race relations as a

process that evolves through four stages: contact, conflict, accommodation, and assimilation.[37] The pivotal underlying assumption of
studies of racial attitudes, prejudice, and discrimination, based on
this model, is the existence of societal consensus on major racial
issues and the infinite capacity on the part of the political system to
promote racial harmony and conciliation. This pattern of analysis
has been a central motif of scholarly studies on race in Britain as
well as the United States. Assessing the orientation of scholarly
studies on the politics of race in Britain, John Solomos concludes
that the dominant focus of these studies has been on "a set of limited
issues relating only to some aspects of the integration of black
minorities in the established political institutions."[38]

A logical extension of the Park theory of assimilation is the theory
of pluralism. Pluralist analysis is the dominant theoretical para-
digm for the description and evaluation of decision making in the
United States and Britain. The key assumptions of pluralist analysis present immense difficulties for the realistic examination of
dominant-subordinate race relations in society.[39] Pluralist theory
also discounts the importance of race as a barrier to the exercise of
effective influence over policy making by minority citizens. Claims
are made that in Western democracies the political process is sufficiently open that all citizens who wish to have an impact on policy
can do so with great effect.[40] Interest groups in these societies have
developed a multitude of techniques for influencing government policy.[41] The rules and procedures of democracy guarantee that the
needs and concerns of minority groups will be accommodated by the
agencies of government and the instumentalities of the wider political system.

Robert Dahl's study of decision making in New Haven, *Who
Governs?* represents the classic statement of the pluralist position.[42]
Dahl paints a picture of local politics characterized by multilateral
conflict between an array of interest groups. He disputes the existence of a power elite, contending that the political influence of economic notables in New Haven has been limited mainly to the area of
urban redevelopment.[43] This analysis underscores one of the guiding assumptions of pluralism: that power in local communities is so
decentralized, and the influence of political actors so specialized,
that racial and economic hierarchies cannot take root and do not
serve as impediments to the full flowering of minority political influence in the governing process. Dahl contends that the ballot stands
as the ultimate instrument of power in democratic polities. For the
sake of survival, elected officials are compelled to anticipate the

needs of grassroots citizens and to address their policy concerns, even if they are not formally organized as permanent interest groups.[44] The promises of democratic representation and influence are preserved through a two-step decision-making process linking leaders and subleaders to their grassroots constituents.[45]

Pluralism does not stand up as a valid theoretical model for understanding and evaluating the impact of the race factor in local politics. As Marguerite Ross Barnett has cogently observed, the racial status of Blacks in America has not been characterized by democratic inclusiveness; the objective reality for Blacks has been one of exclusion based on color and the continuing production of discriminatory policy outcomes by a permanent racial hierarchy.[46] Pluralist analysis does not acknowledge the fact that lower-strata Black communities have often been disconnected from the policy process of local government.[47] In an extremely revealing case study of community politics in Newark, New Jersey, Michael Parenti found that for lower-strata Blacks in Newark, there was only the world of the rulers and the world of the ruled. Black activists seeking to promote community goals in Newark ran up against an intractable urban power structure that flatly refused to recognize the legitimacy of their claims or provide access to the basic resources of local government.[48] The primary political world of Blacks in Newark analyzed by Parenti was far removed from the pluralist republic described by Robert Dahl.

Theories of pluralist democracy are flawed because they do not take into account nondecision making: the capacity of powerful groups to prevent issues relating to the needs of lower-strata groups from penetrating the policy arena.[49] Black issues often become nonissues; they exist as long-standing grievances but are never addressed in any meaningful sense by policy-making institutions.[50] The political impact of these issues is muted by a "mobilization of bias" that firmly insulates the policy preferences of the poor from the arena of governance and decision making where the policy interests of affluent actors are systematically endorsed and implemented by the prevailing racial hierarchy.[51] This reality has lead E. E. Schattschneider to remark: "The flaw in the pluralist heaven is that the heavenly chorus sings with a strong upper-class accent."[52] Schattschneider concludes that the system of pressure group politics is a highly selective process "ill designed to serve diffuse interests."[53]

In a major theoretical work, Rufus P. Browning, Dale Rogers Marshall, and David H. Tabb have suggested that Black communities can overcome the constraints produced by the racial hierarchy by adopting strategies designed to promote Black political incorporation. By *political incorporation*, they mean significant access by racial minorities to the key policy-making processes and resources of city government.[54] In this sense, *political incorporation* is a term used to signify the extent to which a group's interests are effectively represented in the policy making process. Effective representation requires not only the formal representation of a group in the governing process by members of that group, but also the substantive involvement of the group in a coalition that dominates city policy making on issues of greatest concern to the group.[55] Browning, Marshall, and Tabb contend that substantive participation in a dominant coalition will enhance a group's control over policy making and secure its position as an influential participant in the prevailing city governing coalition.

As a measure of political power, political incorporation can range from no representation in city government to the position of a group as an equal or leading force in a dominant coalition strongly committed to minority interests.[56] The logic of the theoretical model presented by Browning, Marshall, and Tabb suggests that strong Black political incorporation would strengthen Black governmental control and endow Black politicians with the power to promote Black community development by radically altering the policy priorities and basic programs of city government. To achieve these results, they recommend that Black political strategies focus on the formation of biracial and multiracial coalitions. Browning, Marshall, and Tabb's study of minority politics in ten California cities found that strong Black incorporation was directly related to Black involvement in biracial and multiracial coalitions. Their study revealed that when Blacks joined forces with liberal Whites to form majority governing coalitions, the responsiveness to Black community policy objectives greatly increased. Black political incorporation in California meant that the social and economic policy preferences of the Black community could no longer be ignored: senior citizen centers were located in Black neighborhoods; minority health projects were launched; parks were developed or improved in minority districts; and a host of community-based programs were given increased financial support.[57]

While the Browning, Marshall, and Tabb theoretical perspective provides interesting insights into the possible impact of minority coalition politics, there are major drawbacks. First, biracial and multiracial coalitions are difficult to develop and maintain. Long histories of cross-racial antagonisms in many cities have made it difficult or impossible for Black and White political activists to arrive upon a community of interests and hammer out a workable common agenda. Often Whites will only join coalitions with Blacks if Blacks agree to serve as junior partners. Kwame Ture ( Stokely Carmichael ) and Charles V. Hamilton have vividly pointed out the dangers such coalitions pose for the Black community.[58] When forged, many biracial and multiracial coalitions are short-lived. Interestingly, in the California case, biracial and multiracial coalitions were undermined by the decision by city administrations to drop funding for minority programs in the wake of shrinking federal support for community-based initiatives.[59] The deterioration of Black-Jewish relations precipitated by the visit to Los Angeles in 1985 by Louis Farrakhan of the Nation of Islam created major cracks in the liberal coalition that dominated city politics during the twenty-year reign of Black mayor Tom Bradley. The defeat of Michael Woo, a progressive Chinese American city councilman and a protégé of Bradley, in the 1993 mayoral election by Republican businessman Richard Riordan, brought to a precipitous end the long march of strong minority incorporation in Los Angeles.[60]

A serious rollback of minority gains has occurred in big cities with the defeat of Black mayoral candidates in New York, Chicago, and Philadelphia. These defeats reflect dramatic shifts in racial ideologies by liberal Whites whose support for minority concerns has substantially eroded; they also reflect the emergence of White-led centrist coalitions with broad appeals to Whites and Latinos who formerly served as backbones of Black-led coalitions.[61] The increasing racial diversification of the urban population has meant that Latinos are no longer satisfied with serving as junior partners in Black-led coalitions. The changing attitude of Latinos is underscored by the fact that coalitions between Blacks and Latinos established in Black mayoral campaigns in New York and Chicago have crumbled in the months after the elections on the back of sharp disagreements across racial lines regarding leadership, the distribution of patronage benefits, and the direction of the minority policy agenda.[62] In Britain, the gap between the ideological and policy orientation of African Caribbeans and Asians has been quite large.[63] Disputes between these two groups over a range of issues, including protest and electoral strategies, has made it extraordinarily difficult to build effective minority-based coalitions in Britain. Second, it should be noted that biracial and multiracial coalitions do not challenge the racial hierarchy; they result in the replacing of all White power structures with new power arrangements without altering the prevailing institutionalized hierarchical structure that systematically produces Black subordination and exclusion. Third, biracial and multiracial coalitions only make sense where Black numbers are large enough to assure that Blacks will have meaningful representation and power in key areas of coalitional decision making. In cities such as Boston and Liverpool where Blacks are vastly outnumbered, the utility of the coalition strategy as a power strategy is, to say the least, problematic.

Clarence Stone has extended the discussion of political incorporation beyond the analysis of city coalitions to embrace the interplay of political and economic forces that establish the foundation for the operation of urban regimes. In Stone's analysis, urban policies are pursued through an array of forces impacting on the electoral process as well as the broader political economy in which elections take place. Minority incorporation requires that minorities not only join dominant coalitions but become a part of the governing coalition that controls decision making in the public arena.[64] The analysis of urban politics must therefore entail the identification of private and public actors involved in the making of public policy and an understanding of the relationship of these actors to one another, as well as the specific resources and strategies they bring to the governing process.

Stone posits the existence of informal linkages among public officials, business leaders, and politically active groups representing the interests of important segments of the urban electorate. Like the pluralists, Stone fails to give adequate attention to the hierarchical racial structures and relations that systematically screen Blacks out of the arena of informal bargaining and therefore blunt Black incorporation into local governing coalitions. Penn Kimball has confirmed the existence of systematic biases in the political system that keep broad sectors of the Black community disconnected from the political process.[65] Stone's urban regime acquires its legitimacy and power not from the consent of the governed but from the ability of urban elites to manipulate the resources of politics to their advantage. Black elites involved in the process (especially Black business elites) rarely represent the interests of grassroots Black citizens and provide little leverage for the Black community in the decision-making process. To the extent that grassroots Black community interests are represented in the process, they are represented by community-based organizations, an arena of politics basically ignored by regime theory.[66] This failing is especially noteworthy since divisions over racial issues by community-based organizations constitute a major source of political pressure that must be constantly managed by public and private elites.[67]

Regime theory has only limited utility for cross-national comparative research. The process of informal bargaining described by Stone is muted in the British context by the ability of the central government to set the local agenda and define the ground rules for political interaction. In Britain, private business leaders have fewer targets of opportunity. Because local officials are not permitted by the unitary system to operate autonomously, the ability of business interests to use mobile wealth to garner tax breaks and other benefits from local officials is significantly constrained.

The growing concentration of Blacks in major cities in Europe and North America has drawn attention to electoral mobilization strategies as instruments for Black empowerment. Clearly, the resources of numbers and concentration have given Blacks strategic advantages in the electoral process. In the United States, Blacks hold electoral majorities or near majorities in some of the country's largest and most important cities.[68] The strong representation of Blacks in the populations of northeastern states has meant that Blacks have often played decisive roles in the outcome of presidential elections.[69] Although Blacks in Britain are only 5 percent of the national population, their concentration in important boroughs in London has given them considerable political clout in local and parliamentary elections. In many localities outside of London, Black electoral potential is not insignificant. Blacks constitute at least 15 percent of the population in sixty parliamentary constituencies.[70] Since 1987, nine Blacks have held elected seats in Parliament (including four of African descent and five of Asian descent). To what extent have Black electoral resources promoted political incorporation? The greatest political breakthrough for the Black community has been at the local level in the United States. Since the passage of the 1965 Voting Rights Act, Black electoral mobilization has resulted in the election of an impressive array of local Black officials; among the most important have been Black mayors of major American cities.

While the record of achievement of Black mayors has been outstanding, one goal that they have not been able to accomplish is Black political incorporation.[71] Problems of economic decline, physical deterioration, unemployment, and social instability have continued to multiply in cities governed by Black mayors. Black representation in city hall has not lead to Black control over the

mainsprings of policy making in central cities. Despite the election
of Black mayors, the core defining ingredients of the racial hierarchy remain firmly in place. Black mayoral leadership has not significantly challenged the institutional arrangements that produce
Black subordination but has concentrated on shifting the social and
economic priorities of city government within the confines of the
prevailing racial hierarchy.[72]

## Obstacles to Political Incorporation

The explanation for the failure of the electoral strategy to achieve
Black political incorporation is rather complex. First, we know, in
retrospect, that high-pitched Black mayoral campaigns represent a
two-edged sword. On the one hand, these campaigns produce high
racial consciousness and electoral turnout; they also provide valuable lessons in community organizing and resource management.[73]
On the other hand, Black mayoral campaigns tend to become so all
consuming they damage or destroy other important avenues for
political mobilization, including neighborhood organizations and
organizational networks linking citizen action groups with
churches, civil rights organizations, and educational institutions.
When the election is over, all eyes are on city hall to provide leadership for the entire Black community. Hindsight also teaches us that
it is extremely difficult to sustain Black mayoral coalitions beyond
the election campaign. Many Black mayors have discouraged the
continuation of their campaign organizations on the grounds that
these organizations are unwieldy and get in the way of day-to-day
policy implementation.[74] The continuity of electoral organization
has also been stifled by the dissipation of insurgency politics in the
Black community.[75] Many second-generation Black mayoral candidates have abandoned grassroots Black community strategies
designed to challenge the prevailing order; they have preferred to
run deracialized campaigns incorporating the extensive involvement of nonBlack community residents and a phalanx of public relations consultants.[76] This new approach to political campaigning has
had the effect of demobilizing grassroots participation.

Issues of resources and leadership have been at the center of the
dilemma of political incorporation. The capacity of Black mayors to
serve as effective urban managers has been severely circumscribed
by the massive withdrawal of strategic funds to local communities
by the federal government. Direct federal aid to cities fell from 26

percent of the cities' own-source revenues in 1978 to 14.5 percent of own-source revenues in 1984.[77] Among the cities hardest hit by this drop have been those governed by Black mayors. City resources have also been reduced by the flight of middle-class taxpayers to the suburbs and the disinvestment in cities by factories and corporations.

Black mayors have been restrained in their capacity to deliver redistributive benefits to their Black constituents by the competition for mobile wealth in metropolitan areas. Facing diminishing tax bases, Black mayors have had to place the search for corporate and industrial development at the top of their programmatic agendas. Like their White counterparts, Black mayors have become strategically dependent on businesses and corporations to assist them in their efforts to achieve their administrative goals.[78] This dependent relationship has helped to foster White corporate dominance over the policy-making processes of Black mayoral governed cities.[79] The opportunity costs for Black organizations are so great, they cannot compete with White businesses and corporations (with lower opportunity costs) for the time, attention, and support of Black mayors. Economic pressures have compelled Black mayors to be prudent fiscal managers. This has often meant that issues of social and economic development in the Black community have been reduced to secondary importance in their agenda-setting priorities. Shifts in policy priorities at the local level have been reinforced by parallel moves by state and national officials. President Clinton has made it clear that affirmative action and welfare programs will not receive priority attention in his second term. Britain's historic commitment to color-blind urban policies has been expanded since the days of Margaret Thatcher to include the defunding of programs for urban minorities and the transfer of major urban projects from public to private agencies.

Obstacles to Black political incorporation also emanate from the milieu of community politics. The achievement of political empowerment by minority groups requires the cultivation and effective utilization of indigenous resources such as social institutions, communications networks, an experienced leadership corps, organized groups, and money.[80] Black Atlantic communities are suffering from a paucity of these resources. The disappearance of neighborhood civic associations and community development groups is especially troubling. Black protest movements of the 1960s relied heavily on indigenous resources to build movement centers to coordinate and strategically manage a broad range of essential political activities.[81] The loss of these resources means that the community's capacity to defend its interests through the formation of viable movement centers has been seriously weakened.

The internal politics of the Black community has created a number of class problems. Postcivil rights developments in the Black community in the United States have created segmented opportunity markets that have pushed some Blacks up the class ladder while keeping others permanently fixed in the lower strata.[82] These patterns have produced social class tensions. In some communities class divisions run so deep that avenues for discussion have totally broken down. Many middle-class Blacks have walked away from their community responsibilities. Lucrative business deals have fostered political alliances between Black and White entrepreneurs that threaten to abolish important sources of Black community leadership.[83]

African Caribbeans in Britain have been able to avoid serious class problems because, except in London, no major middle class has emerged among this group. Blacks in the United States and Britain (African Caribbeans) share the problem of leadership co-optation. Both societies have seen the emergence of buffer organizations and arrangements designed to thwart efforts to build and maintain independent Black institutions.[84] The buffering problem has been especially severe in Britain where community relations councils (CRCs ) and the Commission for Racial Equality (CRE), have used government resources to co-opt and neutralize community organizations.[85] This phenomenon lead A. Sivanandan to charge: "The CRE took up the Black cause and killed it."[86]

Competition for scarce resources and leadership recognition has played havoc with the mounting of common Black agendas and the uniting of community organizations in collective political struggle. Frequent calls for Black unity in the United States and Britain have fallen on deaf ears. There were many in the United States who hoped that the Million Man March would have the lasting effect of quelling internal rivalries and disputes.[87] This goal of the march has not been realized. Internal friction appears to be a common currency of Black Atlantic communities. Ironically, internal divisions are continuing in a political atmosphere that has produced mounting White hostility to the aims and objectives of the Black community's quest for justice, power, and representation. In the United States both major political parties have used the issues of rights and taxes to polarize the electorate and create a conservative backlash against Black social and economic advancement[88] In Britain the passage of anti-immigration legislation in 1968 signaled the emergence of a political strategy endorsed by both parties to bring the issue of race to the center of the electoral process.[89] On the heels of the provocative "Rivers of Blood" speech delivered by Tory politician Enoch Powell and the warning by Margaret Thatcher that Britain ran the risk of being "swamped" by foreign immigrants, the race card became a staple of British politics.[90] In the United States and Britain, the politics of racial liberalism has been abandoned. This fact was underscored by presidential candidate Bill Clinton's shunning of active political support by Jesse Jackson and the Rainbow Coalition in the 1992 and 1996 presidential campaigns and the absolute refusal by the Labour Party to approve petitions by Black political activists to establish a Black section of the party equivalent to those in effect for women and young people.[91]

How have Black Atlantic communities in the United States and Britain attempted to grapple with the dilemmas of political empowerment? What success have they enjoyed in forging effective structural linkages to dominant decision-making forces in local government? To what extent does the racial hierarchy operate as a major impediment to the realization of Black social, economic, and political objectives? These questions serve to establish the analytical parameters of our examination of Black politics in Boston and Liverpool.

## Comparative Black Politics

Research presented in this volume ventures into the uncharted waters of comparative racial politics. The comparison is between two historically Irish port cities: Boston and Liverpool. Blacks in Boston and Liverpool live in Atlantic world cities with long histories of racial conflict and institutional discrimination. The barriers to Black political incorporation in these cities are unusually high. Blacks in Boston and Liverpool are compelled to fight deeply entrenched racial hierarchies without the advantage of majority numerical concentration. In addition to the liability of a relatively limited numerical base, Blacks have faced in these cities dominant White forces that have been exceptionally resistant to Black demands for justice, representation, and power.

Our essential task is to spell out the precise ways political systems in Boston and Liverpool produce structured inequality for the Black community; we will also examine the consequences of these power arrangements for the exercise of effective political power by the historic victims of institutionalized racial subordination. Central to our analysis will be a comparison of the structure of political and governmental power in Boston and Liverpool. This analysis will be guided by Katznelson's injunction that an assessment of structural factors should be the starting point of comparative racial research. Katznelson notes that the examination of structural factors is key because structured political linkages shape and limit the choices of racial groups.[92] The central focus of our study will be on the power dimensions of racial politics. Again, Katznelson provides a compelling rationale for a concentration on power in comparative race relations research: "[T]he relative power of racial groups to make and carry out decisions and non-decisions—institutionally expressed and organized—is the most significant independent variable for the student of race politics."[93] This study probes multiple dimensions of racial power relations through the analysis of structural factors as independent variables and group behavioral patterns (e.g., protests, electoral participation ) as dependent variables. The fundamental objective of this analysis is to illuminate key factors that shape and limit choice in the decision-making process; we will be especially concerned with identifying the crucial factors that facilitate or block access by racial minorities to key resources and important arenas of decision making in the process of local politics and governance. Among the factors analyzed in this regard will be the direction of power relations between prominent racial groups. As Katznelson has noted, the direction of power relations has a major impact on the capacity of racial minorities to gain access to the mainsprings of decision making in the political system. Unidirectional relations, involving decisional domination by a racially dominant group, tend to promote and institutionalize minority exclusion and powerlessness, while bidirectional relations, involving decisional parity, facilitate bargaining and minority inclusion and empowerment. Since buffer groups often play important mediating roles in race relations, our analysis will include an examination of buffering as a factor in local racial politics.

Thus, a major focus of our study will be on the character and impact of political linkage between the Black community and local government in Boston and Liverpool. To what extent have Blacks in these cities been able to overcome the disadvantages of nondecision making by establishing primary functional links with the formal policy-making institutions of local government? How important has the issue of linkage been in determining the character and utilitarian impact of Black representation and incorporation?

The discussion of linkage will focus, in part, on the Liverpool City Council. Local authorities in Britain play a crucial role in the policymaking process. These authorities exercise both extensive legislative and executive powers. They are not only pivotal sources of policy initiatives but regulate and provide a framework for policies and administrative practices beyond their formal domain.[94] Research on the policy-making behavior of local authorities in Britain suggests that they have used a variety of strategies to avoid accommodating the demands of minority groups. Some authorities have rejected race demands on the grounds that such demands divide the working class and retard the transformation of Britain into a socialist society.[95] This position is articulated within the broader framework of traditional British attachments to the pursuit of color-blind policy objectives and the narrow vision of the scope of the policy arena produced by adherence to the fundamental canons of British nationalism.[96] Authorities have also capitalized on the central government's ambivalence on race issues, refusing to use the broad discretionary authority they are given under law and party policies to embrace race policy initiatives.[97] Local authorities have attempted to undermine collective action by community groups by establishing grievance mechanisms that only accommodate individual complaints.[98] Minority group power in the policymaking process has also been diluted through the consignment of group representatives to symbolic consultation roles in local government.[99] The upshot of these policies has been to reinforce the racial biases of the prevailing political order and to create a profound sense of alienation, hopelessness, and demoralization among minority citizens seeking redress and positive action through the local governing process. To what extent has the city council in Liverpool been willing to accommodate the policy demands of the Black community? How has the relationship between the council and the central government facilitated or thwarted the formation of policy initiatives to address the urgent social and economic problems of Blacks in Liverpool? Has the fusion of legislative and executive authority limited the number of effective access points for minority groups seeking to advance their interests through council action? What success have Blacks enjoyed in forging a relationship of strategic dependency with the city council; how have they handled the factor of opportunity costs? What assessment can be made of the effectiveness of Black leaders as authentic representatives of Black community interests in the linkage process between the community and the council?

In Boston we will focus on the governing authority and policy direction of both the mayor's office and the city council. Since the Boston system is a strong mayor system, the structuring of linkages between the local government and the Black community is driven, in large measure, by mayoral initiatives and power. How have these relationships evolved over time, and what have been the implications of these changes for Black justice, representation, and power in Boston? Irish machine politics has historically played a preeminent role in Boston in the structuring of power relationships and the distribution of policy benefits. What has been the relationship between the machine and the Black community? How has machine politics affected the articulation of Black demands, unity, and division in the internal politics of the Black community and the effective penetration by Blacks of the innercircles of policy making and authority in city politics? Is there hard evidence that the Boston City Council has adopted strategies of minority demand avoidance analogous to those widely practiced by local authorities in Britain?

A key issue in the analysis of racial linkage is the location of Black policy interests in the policy process. Ben-Tovim, Gabriel, Law, and Stredder tell us that Black political groups in Britain have had to consistently fight the marginalization of race issues in the policy process.[100] This issue is also relevant to the political status of Blacks in Boston. In the current climate of attack against race policy initiatives in the United States and Britain, how do Black political activists take effective steps to assure that programs for the Black community are placed at the center rather than the periphery of the urban policy process? This question draws attention to the role of Black elected officials and the leaders of key community organizations. We will examine the leadership roles and challenges of Black elected officials in Boston. Has the election of Blacks to state and local offices resulted in the redistribution of policy benefits across class lines in the Black community? Although no parallel group of actors exists in Liverpool, it is possible to look at efforts by Black organizational representatives in that city to fill in the leadership breach. The analysis will illuminate factors impacting on the capacity of Black political leaders to provide substantive rather than mere symbolic leadership for the Black community.

Both Boston and Liverpool have been the target of major urban regeneration schemes fueled by national and local efforts to halt the spiral of decay in central cities. We will examine the role of the

Black communities in Boston and Liverpool in the design and implementation of these regeneration programs. How have these policies affected the physical boundaries, housing stock, racial diversity, psychic bearing, economic status, and political orientation of Black communities in these cities? On the basis of the information at hand, what projections can we make for the future?

Terri Sewell has underscored the need for Black activists in Britain to play duel roles, working within and outside of mainstream politics.[101] The role of the strategic insider is an immensely important one because it relates to the ongoing need for Black communities to establish modes of effective representation, communication, and interest articulation within the pivotal core of governing coalitions. Institutionalization of patterns of inside power aggregation constitutes an absolute prerequisite for the cementing and fortification of bidirectional power relationships. But authentic political incorporation must also entail the development of prodigious external resources. Specifically, Black political activists must cultivate an extensive storehouse of indigenous resources, including strong organizational networks beyond the effective control of mainstream politicians and political institutions. Underscoring the importance of independent variables as explanatory factors, a major focus of our study will be on the difficulties encountered by Black political activists in Boston and Liverpool in their efforts to establish and maintain independent organizational networks and to cultivate politically potent indigenous resources. We will closely examine processes of racial co-optation in both cities. The buffering roles played by Black organizations on multiple sides of the political spectrum will be highlighted. Our analysis will look at the structure of Black organizational relations. An important element of this analysis will be the illumination of factors that promote both unity and division across organizational lines. We will also assess the value and impact of electoral and protest strategies as instruments for the achievement of justice, representation, and power for Black citizens in Boston and Liverpool.

Careful attention is given to the comparative perspective throughout this volume. We will illuminate similarities and differences in the character of race politics in the United States and Britain emanating from factors such as the procedures and rules of legislative bodies, the centralization and fragmentation of governing authority, and the political ideologies and policies of political parties. Since, as Robert C. Liberman observes, racial divisions in society are socially and politically constructed, differences in the social and political environments of the United States and Britain can be expected to produce different approaches to the structuring and management of racial issues.[102]

In the United States racial issues have been embedded in the country's primary institutions from its very inception; over the years racial politics has permeated every facet of American life, infusing itself into the policy priorities of national, state, and local institutions.[103] The forging of racial policies in the United States has passed through the vortex of transformative upheavals such as the Civil War and the Civil Rights movement. In the twentieth century, racial issues and racial politics in America have occupied center stage of the social policy environment, shaping the character and institutional operation of the American political system in profound ways.

Racial issues and racial politics in Britain are of relatively recent origin; they have emerged in the context of long-standing, preexisting policy-making bureaucracies and governing institutions. Liberman has hypothesized that the difference in the sequence of race and policy development in the United States and Britain has had a major impact on the salience, scope, and organic expression of racial politics in these societies:

> If national political institutions—the state—are relatively underdeveloped when racial division becomes a salient political, social, and economic cleavage, then institutions, as they do develop, will be constructed so as to maintain the dominance of the ruling racial group and pose barriers to racial assimilation. The result is likely to be a politics in which racial conflict is pervasive and omnipresent, infecting nearly every element of political life. Conversely, if a country's political institutions are more highly developed, more "mature," then the introduction of racial division into political life should have a more subtle, less calamitous impact. More mature political institutions may be more resilient, more resistant to change, than less developed institutions that are at an earlier stage of formation. Rather than politics adapting itself to racial domination and conflict, racial groups will be more apt to adapt to the political arrangements in which they find themselves. Thus the pervasiveness and virulence of such a society's racial politics are likely to be more variable, and to echo the preexisting characteristics of the country's politics.[104]

Liberman's analysis helps to account for the fact that, historically, racial politics has been less pervasive in Britain than in the United States. The long-term development of the British state prior to its transformation into a multiracial society meant that the fault lines of national politics had already been forged, permitting racial politics to become institutionalized within the existing terrain of class and party struggle. The more mature institutions of the British state were in a better position to manage and suppress racial conflict. The British pattern, in contrast to the American pattern, has been to (1) to give only grudging recognition to the existence of racial politics; (2) deny the applicability of racial issues across a wide range of policy domains; (3) confine bureaucratic responses to one or two special departments of the central government; and (4) decentralize responsibility for the implementation of race policy objectives to local organizations in the race industry, especially community relations councils.[105] In view of these differences in the American and British approaches, the key question to be asked is what impact have these approaches had on the quest for political empowerment and incorporation by Black communities in Boston and Liverpool?

# 2

## Boston and Liverpool: A Tale of Two Cities

### The Policy Context of Racial Politics

Across the Atlantic Black communities have been compelled to grapple with dilemmas produced by hierarchical systems of racial domination. Black communities in Boston and Liverpool have not escaped the impact of White racial domination and control. In both cities, the Black community faces dilemmas of political empowerment. These dilemmas can best be understood in the context of policy environments that establish, maintain, and reinforce inequality on the basis of race.

Urban political systems in the United States and Britain are racial benefit systems; they function through policy networks that are extremely sensitive and responsive to the preferential claims of dominant White interests. Racial discrimination has been an endemic and enduring feature of the social systems of Boston and Liverpool. The outcomes of the policy process in these communities impose enormous burdens on Black citizens who are deprived of a multitude of opportunities and benefits because of the color of their skin and the character of their cultural heritage. While the lives and fortunes of Black and White citizens in Boston and Liverpool intersect in many ways, they diverge in others. In both cities Black citizens do not enjoy the protection from police harassment or the chances for unfettered upward mobility that are so often taken for granted as facts of life by the White majority. It has been this pattern of institutional discrimination that has been the primary catalyst for Black political action in these prominent Atlantic world cities.

Black politics in Britain and the United States has its roots planted principally in the soil of local politics.[1] The policy context for Black politics varies widely from city to city, producing a medley of forms and strategies of Black political action. Each city has its own set of demands, values norms, and rules of behavior. These differences notwithstanding, the policy context for Black politics in both countries is framed by a set of interrelated factors that establish the fundamental foundation for comparative analysis. Among the most important of these factors are:

1.    The economic environment of the local government as measured by the size and flexibility of its budget, levels of employment and unemployment, the financial health of citizens, and the performance and character of primary financial institutions.

2.    The legal and political relationship between the local government and central government.

3.    The prevailing ideological attitude regarding the authority and responsibility of government to take ameliorative action to combat the effects of racism and social disadvantage on the Black community.

4.    The balance of party power, the governing capacity of city administrations, and the responsiveness of parties and other governing institutions to the needs and aspirations of the Black community.

5.    The existence in the Black community of the resources requisite for effective political action, including numbers (size of population) and effective leadership and organization.

6.    The ability of the Black community to consolidate its potential power and mobilize sufficiently in the political process to place Black concerns on the public agenda and obtain benefits from the political system to satisfy Black needs and promote Black progress.

This chapter analyzes the social, economic, and political environments in Boston and Liverpool in which fundamental policies relating to Black political empowerment are debated, evaluated, and implemented.

Politics and Policy in Boston

For many years, Blacks in Boston have struggled to overcome the liabilities of racial disadvantage. One of the most formidable barriers they have faced on the road to equality and political empowerment has been the enormous control over the governing process exercised by a ruling elite that can, in great measure, trace its roots to the wealth and power of an eighteenth-century business class known as the "Boston Brahmins." The high social standing and great wealth of the Brahmins translated into superior political power and governmental control. Brahmin influence permeated every sector of local government in Boston in the eighteenth century.[2] Operating chiefly through the Federalist Party, Brahmin leaders controlled the election of mayors and city councillors and dominated the process of decision making in local government. Under the guiding hand of premier Brahmin politicians such as Josiah Quincy, who served five one-year terms as mayor, Boston successfully made the transition from town to city during the second decade of the nineteenth century. An activist mayor, Quincy stimulated economic growth through the revamping of police, fire, and sanitation services and the construction of a downtown public market.[3]

Boston politics today remains under the firm control (although not exclusively) of an economic elite composed of members of many of the old Brahmin families.[4] Preserving their class status through financial trusts and intermarriage, Boston's Yankee elites continue to play a major role in the setting of the public agenda and the implementation of important policy decisions.

Brahmin power has not gone unchallenged. Irish immigrants, seeking to escape from poverty and political upheaval, settled in Boston in significant numbers in the middle years of the nineteenth century and used their ethnic representation in the electorate to compete for public offices. Victims of wholesale discrimination and assaults, including political attacks by the Know-Nothing Party and the American Protective Association, the Irish turned to the political arena as a major avenue of power and upward mobility.

Within a decade of their arrival, the Irish strategy of ethnic bloc voting began to have a profound impact on the Boston political system. Between 1850 and 1855 the number of registered Irish voters tripled; by the latter year the Irish had become one-fifth of the eligible electorate.[5] Capitalizing on the key political resources of numbers and group consciousness, the Irish began to translate

their power at the ballot into control of key public offices. The first
Irish common councillor in Boston was elected in 1857; this victory
was followed by the election of the first Irish alderman in 1870.[6]
These were the opening scenes in an urban drama that would witness an incredible shift of governing authority from Yankee to
Irish politicians. In 1882, the Commonwealth of Massachusetts
elected its first Irish congressman. Of even greater political signif-
icance was the election of Hugh O'Brien in 1884 as the first Irish-
born mayor of Boston. Relying heavily on grassroots Irish support,
Patrick A. Collins became the second Irish-born mayor of Boston
in 1901.

O'Brien and Collins manifested leadership styles that sought to
build bridges of cooperation between Irish and Yankee politicians.
The turn of the twentieth century witnessed the emergence of a new
breed of Irish mayoral leadership. John Fitzgerald's election as
mayor in 1905 signaled the arrival to power of the quintessential
neighborhood Irish politician. Fitzgerald broke the grip of Brahmin
control over city hall by installing a system of patronage that decentralized the distribution of benefits to the neighborhoods. Key Irish
ward politicians were placed in charge of major city departments.[7]
The decentralization of benefits and the dethroning of Brahmin
administrators by Fitzgerald threatened to seriously alter the balance of ethnic power in the city. Fitzgerald became a salient target
for the chief political instrument of Yankee power, the Good
Government Association. The *Boston Herald*, also a handmaiden of
Brahmin power, denounced the new Irish politicians in control of
city hall as "wanton mercenaries."[8]

The next Irish mayor of Boston posed an even greater threat to
Brahmin power and control. James Michael Curley was a seasoned
Irish ward politician with a flamboyant personality and a passionate commitment to grassroots Irish empowerment. Elected mayor of
Boston for the first time in 1914, Curley exercised a commanding
presence in Boston politics for over four decades. His public service
career included four terms as mayor (1914–17, 1922–25, 1930–33,
and 1946–49), election to the city council in 1908, to Congress in
1910 and 1912, governor in 1934, and Congress again in 1942 and
1944. Curley represented Brahmin leadership's worst nightmare.
Describing himself as a man of the people, Curley taxed banks and
other businesses heavily to pay for patronage-rich public works projects. Shortly upon arriving in city hall after his first election as
mayor, he sent out to his Brahmin critics a blunt message: "[T]he
New England of the Puritans, and the Boston of rum, codfish and

slaves are as dead as Julius Ceasar."[9] The Yankee elite responded by withdrawing from formal participation in local electoral politics and withholding financial support for the physical reconstruction of the downtown core.

The Boston Brahmins were able to endure the political storm and return to power after Curley's final defeat in the mayoral contest of 1949. This fact underscores both the durability of Brahmin financial influence and the policy limitations of Irish machine politics. Despite the longevity of Irish rule, the Irish were relatively ineffective in translating control over elective office into representation in the dominant financial institutions of the city. Evidence of this fact can be found in the failure of the Irish by the end of the 1920s to capture a major leadership position in the Boston Chamber of Commerce.[10] Brahmin investments in insurance companies and banking trusts in the years between the world wars effectively preserved their base of power in the Boston economy. In Chicago, the power of the business class was threatened by the development of highly centralized, well-oiled Irish machines. No such machines were constructed in Boston. Fitzgerald and Curley were able to amass tremendous amounts of personal power through the centralization of patronage in the mayor's office. Their efforts to build citywide machines, however, were undermined by the noncooperation of state officials and the continuing control of neighborhood bosses over their own political empires.[11] Some scholars have suggested that the Irish patronage system stifled rather than promoted Irish social and economic mobility. J. Brian Sheehan and Steven Erie, for example, attribute the slow occupational mobility of the Irish, relative to other European ethnic groups, to the tendency of the Irish patronage system to concentrate Irish employment in low-wage city jobs and in manual labor positions in declining sectors of the industrial economy.[12]

Boston politics in the post World War II years has been marked by a resurgence of Yankee business elite power and control. The business community engineered the defeat of Curley in 1949 and replaced him with John B. Haynes, a conservative bureaucrat, former city clerk, and former acting mayor, with no base of power in the Irish neighborhood wards. Yankee business leaders took advantage of the changed governmental environment to move the agenda of the business community to the center of the policy-making process. Their premier goal was to build a "New Boston" through the massive redevelopment of the downtown business center. The political arm of this effort was the New Boston Committee (NBC).

Formed in 1950 as an outgrowth of the Haynes election, the NBC sought to insure the election of a new breed of business-oriented elected officials through public forums, fundraising, endorsements, and voter mobilization.[13] The political impact of the NBC was powerful and immediate; in 1951 its candidates won a majority of the seats on the city council and school committee.

With the enthusiastic support of the mayor's office and external federal funding, Boston's business elite began to implement development strategies that dramatically changed the face of the urban landscape. A massive urban renewal project removed seven thousand people from the West End to make way for luxury apartments, office buildings, parking garages, and medical research facilities. Additional land was cleared to facilitate construction of a new government center. The pivotal anchor of the march towards redevelopment was the clearance of twenty-eight acres of Back Bay property to accommodate plans by Prudential Insurance to build a regional office and $75 million commercial complex.[14]

Urban redevelopment strategies materialized out of marathon brainstorming sessions sponsored by business leaders at Boston College. To spearhead and guide economic recovery, a new business group was formed in 1959 officially named the "Coordinating Committee" but popularly known as the "Vault" because its initial meetings were held in the board room of a safe deposit and trust company.

Since the early 1950s, the construction of a new Boston under the guidance of the business community has continued unabated. John Collins, who succeeded John Haynes as mayor in 1959, defined city politics as a partnership between the business community and local government. In concert with this philosophy, he placed the merchants of Boston, through the Retail Trade Board, in charge of planning changes for the central city.[15] Under Collins, billions of dollars poured into Boston to fund major renewal projects, among them the extensive reconstruction of the downtown water district.[16] Collins's successor, Kevin White, fully embraced the strategy of corporate-centered downtown development. During his first term, White enthusiastically pushed community-centered empowerment and development projects. Upon gaining reelection, White shifted gears and tied his future ambitions to the implementation of a strategic business-oriented action agenda.

Power and Policy Making in Liverpool

Like Boston, Liverpool is a heavily Irish city with a long history of ethnic tension and conflict. For more than a hundred years, party politics in Liverpool was based on sectarian conflict stemming from social competition between Irish Catholics and Protestants. Heavy Irish immigration into Liverpool after the potato famine in the nineteenth century gave Liverpool politics a peculiar ethnic flavor. Physical confrontations and overt displays of ethnic loyalty such as St. Patrick's Day or Orange Day parades were transferred into the political arena and resulted in sharp divisions between the Irish who were strongly working class (and Catholic) and constituted the backbone of the Labour Party and working-class Protestants, who supported the Conservative Party. Into the decade of the 1950s, Liverpool politics was marked by strong two-party competition between the Conservative and Labour parties. Party politics was strongly ward oriented and took on the character of the American brand of machine politics.[17] Since 1955, the city government of Liverpool has mainly been under the formal control of the Labour Party.

The structure of political decision making in Liverpool diverges sharply from the structure in Boston. Under the British unitary system, final authority for the administration of local affairs rests with the central government. According to the doctrine of ultra vires, local authorities can only execute functions that fall within the purview of national statues. In practical terms, this means that the central government in Britain plays a much larger role in the structuring of policy relations in Liverpool than the federal government in the United States in the structuring of policy relations in Boston. Control of Liverpool City Government by the Labour Party inspired the Conservative-controlled central government under Margaret Thatcher and John Major to take extraordinary steps to circumscribe the participation of the Liverpool authority in key areas of local decision making.

To preserve its power at the local level and limit the reach of council authorities, Britain's Conservative government promoted the use of public private partnerships as local policy making and administrative agencies. Labour first introduced inner-city partnerships in the 1970s. They were designed to forge functional links among the central government, local authorities, and community groups in cooperative efforts to develop innovative solutions to a myriad of social and economic problems in the cities. Under the Conservatives, the emphasis of the partnership program shifted from community to private partnerships.[18] These government-initiated agencies, or "quangoes," are separately funded administrative units empowered to execute a range of important functions at the local level.

In Liverpool, a great deal of the money appropriated for urban redevelopment and regeneration has been given to the Merseyside Development Corporation. This corporation is structurally and legally disconnected from local government. It functions as an autonomous central government agent with planning authority, capital to purchase land, and power to initiate its own projects. Run by a small staff because it contracts out for basic services, its primary objective is to mobilize private-sector initiative in the process of urban regeneration. The Liverpool City Council has no oversight authority in the expenditure of funds by the Development Corporation. Similarly, money to promote housing redevelopment regularly bypasses the city council and goes directly into the coffers of housing associations. Another important independent agency is the Merseyside Docks and Harbor Company, which controls the Port of Liverpool. The central government has established a permanent office in Merseyside to coordinate the work of its local partnerships.

In the wake of the creation of these central government agencies, the importance of the Liverpool City Council as a key policy agency has been reduced. Liverpool City Council has ninety-nine members and has the power to execute a broad range of administrative and legislative functions. The chief executive, the Lord Mayor, is a ceremonial position with no formal policy-making power or authority. In contrast to Boston, representatives of private business interests in Liverpool do not consistently play a major role in setting the civic agenda. The most important private players come from the world of banking, insurance, and retail sales (especially Royal Insurance Company and Littlewoods Department Stores). Liverpool has no parallel to the Vault to provide a coordinated approach to leveraging policy influence for the business community in the political process.

In Liverpool, economic issues are paramount. Over the past thirty years, the policy environment of Liverpool has been centrally focused on one major problem: the city of Liverpool, by any yardstick, is one of the poorest in Europe. Not only are Liverpool's financial problems massive, but they have, over several decades, defied reasonable solution.

The structure of Liverpool's economy has made it extremely vulnerable to shifting economic and demographic forces. As a consequence of its involvement in the transatlantic slave trade, Liverpool, in the eighteenth and nineteenth centuries, became one of the richest cities in Europe. Slavery transformed Liverpool from an insignificant seaport to an eighteenth-century thriving boom town. Vast fortunes were made by Liverpool merchants through their participation in the slave trade. A number of the individuals who reaped the greatest profits from the slave trade were prominent figures in Liverpool government and politics.

A list, compiled in 1752, of 101 Liverpool merchants trading to Africa included 12 who had been, or were to become, mayor of the town, and 15 who were pew holders in the fashionable Benn's Garden Presbyterian chapel. At least 26 of Liverpool's mayors, holding office for 35 of the years from 1700 to1820, were or had been slave-merchants or close relatives.[19]

Liverpool's prominence as an industrial center also stemmed from its location as a shipping route for the flourishing cotton industry in Lancashire, Manchester, and Yorkshire. The port in Liverpool provided the easiest access to these inland locales from the Atlantic Ocean. In addition, the shape of the river around Liverpool made it a very fast, deep outlet that could easily and efficiently accommodate large ocean-going ships. Eventually, Liverpool would become a major transportation route for transatlantic steamships and the home of one of the most important ship-building industries in Europe. In the early decades of the twentieth century, Liverpool remained a major English seaport, standing second only to London in capacity and importance. According to Michael Parkinson, in 1914 one-third of all British exports and one-quarter of all imports traveled through the Liverpool Port.[20]

The present economic difficulties experienced by Liverpool are directly linked to the collapse of the shipping industry in Liverpool after World War II. Liverpool's Port was gravely injured by the death of the cotton industry in Britain and the transfer of transatlantic passenger shipping to Southampton. When the docks collapsed, no new manufacturing concerns, except for small-scale food processing, were established to replace them. The upshot was a massive decline in dock-related employment from 45,000 jobs in 1945, to 3000 jobs in 1977.[21] As the following respondent notes, the impact of the port's decline on the overall economy of Liverpool was devastating. "If this had been a mining area it would have gone as

well. It just so happens that mining areas were not as densely popu-
lated. We've got villages that close down because the mine goes.
When the port goes the sequence of related calamities are irre-
versible."[22]

In the case of Liverpool, the related calamities were multitudinous. The decline of the port meant the folding under of dockland
repair shops that had been used as support units for dock-related
activities. Because dock work is casual labor, dockworkers were
mainly unskilled, making them unattractive as potential employees
for industries that might contemplate moving into Merseyside.
Advances in shipping technology rendered the skills possessed by
dockworkers totally obsolete.

## Black Atlantic Communities in Transition

Blacks are not newcomers to the Atlantic world societies of
Boston and Liverpool. The first Blacks landed in Boston in 1638,
just eight years after the establishment of the Massachusetts Bay
Colony by John Winthrop and the Puritans.[23] Blacks were brought
to Boston in the seventeenth century to work as slaves for wealthy
White merchant families. Their position as slaves remained fixed
until the waning years of the eighteenth century. The path to freedom was opened in 1777 when Blacks petitioned the Massachusetts
legislature to provide for Black people, "in common with all other
men," the inalienable right to freedom.[24] Although the petition was
rejected by the legislature, Black freedom fighters, led by Prince
Hall, persisted in their demand that Blacks be given personal and
human rights. A major victory for the Black community was won in
1783 when the Massachusetts courts declared that the clause in the
new state constitution declaring "all men are born free and equal,
and have certain natural, essential and unalienable rights," had the
legal effect of abolishing slavery in the state forever.[25] The ranks of
Blacks in Boston were expanded by the migration of southern
Blacks to Massachusetts in search of freedom and economic opportunity. When the first census of the United States was taken in
1790, 766 African Americans were counted (4 percent of the population). In 1800 some 1,100 Blacks in Boston constituted one of the
largest free African American communities in North America.[26]

The original area of settlement for Blacks was Charlestown in the
far North where Blacks worked as servants for rich Whites. In the
post-Revolutionary War period, Blacks moved en mass to the West

End on the north slope of Beacon Hill. Between 1800 and the end of the Civil War, a robust Black intellectual and political community emerged on Beacon Hill. Many of the Black leaders of the northern abolitionist campaign, including firebrand David Walker, were residents of this community. Barbershops owned by Peter Howard and John J. Smith located at the foot of Beacon Hill were important meeting places for antislavery forces and served as stations of the underground railroad.[27] The Black community continued to grow. In 1865, there were 2,348 Blacks in Boston; by 1880, the number had climbed to 5,873.[28] After the Civil War Blacks began to be displaced on Beacon Hill by White immigrants, especially the Irish and Italians. Beginning in 1865 small numbers of Blacks began to trickle into the lower South End, where houses were being abandoned by upwardly mobile Yankees on their way to the suburbs. As Beacon Hill became overcrowded between 1870 and 1890, Blacks moved into the South End in heavy numbers. In the first two decades of the twentieth century, the Black movement southward continued, spreading from the South End into Roxbury, North Dorchester, and Mattapan.

The Black community in Liverpool is one of the oldest in Britain. The roots of the Liverpool Black community date back to at least the eighteenth century. Some members of Liverpool's Black community entered as slaves. Evidence that Blacks were sold as slaves in Liverpool can be found in advertisements that appeared in local newspapers from 1750 through 1790.[29] Slave auctions continued to be held in Liverpool up to 1780 despite the formal abolition of slavery in Great Britain in 1772.[30]

A number of Blacks who found their way to Liverpool in the eighteenth century were runaways and students from Africa and the Caribbean. By the turn of the nineteenth century, the appearance of Blacks on the streets of Liverpool was commonplace. Many Blacks worked as servants; increasingly, Black seamen attached to merchant ships began to make their permanent homes in Liverpool. A substantial Black community emerged in Liverpool after 1870 when the Elder Dempster Shipping Line began to employ Africans on ships traveling between Liverpool and West Africa. Africans were especially drawn to the Elder Dempster Line because of the company's policy of giving Africans a virtual monopoly on firemen's and trimmer's jobs.[31] Many of the African seamen working for the Elder Dempster Line settled in Liverpool and intermarried with local women.

Government policies during World War I also contributed to the growth of the Black community in Liverpool. As a part of the war effort, many merchant ships containing Black seamen were transformed into government transports. Black crews on these ships were replaced with White crews. Many of the African seamen who lost their jobs in this action found jobs in war-related industries on Merseyside and made homes in the local Black community.[32]

Blacks in Boston and Liverpool encountered enormous racial problems in their search for freedom and equality in the nineteenth and early twentieth centuries. By 1919, the size of the Black community in Liverpool had grown to approximately 5,000. The rapid expansion of the Black population sparked by postwar demobilization created tremendous racial tension between Black and White workers who were in competition for a limited number of jobs. White resistance to Black employment led to the firing in one week alone of 120 Back workers in Liverpool sugar refineries and oilcake mills.[33] Conflicts between Black and White workers culminated in the death of one Black man and the wounding of four policemen. The Black man killed was a former navy serviceman named Charles Wootton. Before the fury ended, 800 Black people were taken into protective custody and hundreds of homes in the Black community were destroyed.

Long after the riots were over, Blacks continued to suffer from racial persecution in Liverpool. A major depression meant that many Blacks lost their jobs at sea and found themselves among the list of unemployed in Liverpool. White trade unions refused to admit Blacks because they considered them immigrants who were "keeping white seamen out of work" and forcing down their standard of living.[34] In 1925 a Coloured Alien Seaman's Order was passed that applied to all Black seamen, regardless of nationality, unless they could provide irrefutable proof that they were British. This order required Black seamen to carry special credentials at all times and subjected them to continuous threat of deportation.

Social and political conditions were equally difficult for Blacks in Boston. The size of the Black population continued to grow after the turn of the twentieth century, from 12,000 in 1900 to 16,350 by 1920. Blacks moving into the expanding communities of the South End and Roxbury were subjected to virulent racism and extensive social segregation. Employment discrimination confined Blacks to unskilled low-wage jobs in the railroad yards and station of the South End. Black workers demonstrated very little occupational mobility during the first half of the twentieth century. In 1900, 56 percent of Black workers were unskilled laborers, servants, waiters, and porters; in 1940 53 percent of Black workers held such positions.[35] The percentage of Blacks in white-collar jobs grew from 8 percent in 1890 to only 11 percent in 1940.[36] Racial discrimination allowed the Irish to move rapidly ahead of Blacks in occupational mobility. First-generation immigrants ranked far ahead of Blacks in occupational mobility in 1890, 1910, and 1930. Throughout these years, half as many Blacks as first-generation immigrants held middle-class jobs and twice as many were unskilled or semiskilled laborers.[37] Second-generation immigrants had a middle class four times the size of the middle class in the Black community.[38] Disparities in the treatment of Black workers and other ethnic workers were defining characteristics of the social life of Boston in the first half of the twentieth century. These developments had deep historical roots; they illuminated a system of racial discrimination that appeared to be impervious to change over many decades. On this subject, one prominent historian of social relations in Boston notes:

> In 1850 the majority of employed Black men and women, those who were working, were in low paying menial jobs; you had the same percentage in low paying menial jobs in the 1870s, 1880s. Nothing changed, even though my understanding is that those Blacks who were in the city schools in the first three or four decades of the 1900s had a level of completion in school right along with Whites. But their occupational opportunities were not equivalent. You had second and third generation Irish and Italian Americans who were far above Blacks, native born Blacks.[39]

The demographic character of Black communities in Boston and Liverpool has changed in dramatic ways since World War II. In Boston, the continued movement southward of the Black population has resulted in the concentration of Black residents in Roxbury and Mattapan. Blacks constituted the overwhelming majority of residents in both of these communities in 1990, 72 percent in Roxbury, and 82 percent in Mattapan.[40] Population shifts in recent years have resulted in Black penetration into North Dorchester (see figure 2.1). As Blacks have moved south, newly arrived immigrants, especially Latinos, Haitians, and South Asians, have moved in significant numbers into the resulting vacated areas.

Boston's racial composition is changing at a rapid clip. The predominant trend is the decline of the White population and the remarkable growth of Black and immigrant populations. Between

**Figure 2.1. Pattern of Boston's African American Community
Neighborhood Settlement**

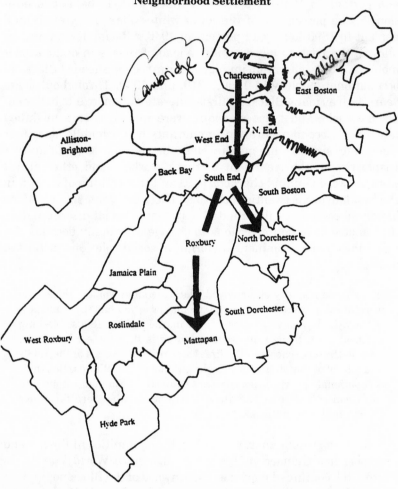

Source: Adapted from data distributed by the Boston Redevelopment Authority
Research Department

1950 and 1980, Boston's White population declined from 95 percent
to 70 percent; across these same years, the Black and minority population climbed from 5 percent to 30 percent.[41] Latinos and Asian
Americans are the fastest growing population groups. From 1980 to
1990 Latinos showed a 69 percent increase (from 6.4 percent to 10.8
percent) while Asian representation grew by 83 percent (from 2.7
percent to 5.3 percent).[42]

The Black community is now highly ethnically diverse. Haitians, Cape Verdeans, Ethiopians, Somalians, and Nigerians represent growing segments of the Black population. It is interesting to note in this regard that Boston's Haitian population is ranked in size only behind the Haitian populations in Miami and New York.[43] Today over 40 percent of Boston's population is Black, Latino, or Asian. Taking giant steps to maintain their race and class homogeneity, four major Boston communities remain 90 percent or more White: Back Bay/Beacon Hill, Charlestown, West Roxbury, and South Boston.[44]

The Black community in Liverpool has also experienced significant demographic change since World War II. To solve its manpower shortage during the war, Britain vigorously recruited skilled and semiskilled workers from the West Indies. Some 345 West Indian workers arrived in Liverpool between 1941 land 1943. This immigration experiment was the dress rehearsal for a process that would bring thousands of Blacks from the Caribbean to Liverpool to work on the docks and in the factories.

As the size of the Black community grew, its residential location shifted. At the turn of the twentieth century, the Black community was concentrated in the Pitt Street area by the docks. During World War I, many dockside dwellings were badly damaged by the German blitz, compelling Blacks living in the dock area to move inland. Initially, the bulk of the Black community moved from the docks into Abercromby Square near the University of Liverpool.[45] Land development policies by the university in the 1960s drove Black residents into the Toxteth Granby area (See figure 2.2). Black movement into this area has been so intense that the Black community in Liverpool is the most concentrated in Britain.

Granby shares Liverpool 8 with most of the Dingle Ward, part of the Abercromby Ward, and part of the Arundel Ward. Geographically, Granby resides in a triangle bounded by Lodge Lane, Upper Parliament Street, and Princess Road. Black citizens are unevenly distributed in ward polling districts with the largest concentration of Blacks occurring in district 148. It is interesting to note that the Black communities in Boston and Liverpool are both located only a few miles south of the downtown city core.

The Black community in Liverpool does not match the proportionate size of the Black community in Boston. Presently, no method has been devised to accurately gauge the size of the Black community. An analysis of the 1991 census published by the Granby Toxteth Community Project reported the Black population to be 3.8

**Figure 2.2. Pattern of Liverpool's Black Community Neighborhood Settlement**

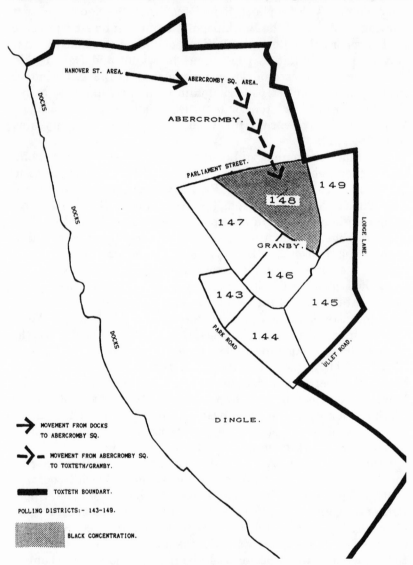

Source: Adapted from data distributed by Liverpool City Council.

percent of the total population.[46] This figure is widely believed to represent a substantial undercount. The undercount is explained, in part, by legal entanglements emanating from the immigration process. In addition, a number of mixed race people in Liverpool prefer to be categorized as White or other. Gideon Ben-Tovim, director of the Race and Social Policy Unit at the University of Liverpool, suggests that the most realistic estimate of the size of the Black community in Liverpool is 8 percent.[47] This figure is, of course, still substantially below Black representation in Boston—a figure that was almost 24 percent in 1990.

The Black community in Liverpool is ethnically diverse. Classifying by race is a far more complicated process in Liverpool than in Boston. In the United States, the term *Black* is used to refer to individuals of African and African Caribbean heritage. By tradition, the term *Black* in Britain is used to refer to all nonWhite minorities, including a host of individuals from the South Asian subcontinent.[48] Liverpool-born Blacks make up the largest proportion of the Black community. Blacks from the Caribbean and the African continent, especially Nigeria, Somalia, and Sierra Leone, continue to settle in the Black community in significant numbers.

## The Black Economy

Blacks in Boston and Liverpool are caught in a web of racism that sharply limits their access to fundamental social, economic, and political resources. The economic base of the Black community in both cities is enormously weak. Discrimination against Blacks in Boston in the realm of economics is pervasive; its overall effect is to rob Blacks of the resources they need to be competitive in the economic market place. Black neighborhoods in Boston are the poorest in the city. In 1990 Roxbury had the lowest mean family income in Boston: $28,979 as compared to $136,764 for Back Bay/Beacon Hill and $57,162 for West Roxbury.[49] Poverty is exceptionally high in Boston's Black community. While the overall family poverty rate for the city was 15 percent in 1990, the rate for Black families was 22 percent.[50] Black children in Boston are the special victims of poverty. In the city as a whole, 28 percent of children lived in poverty in 1990; for Blacks the percentage was 33 percent (See figure 2.3).[51] Per capita incomes also show important racial disparities. Black per capita income in 1990 was $9,406.00 while White per capita income was $18,939.[52]

The income figures cited above reflect continuing patterns of discrimination in the areas of employment and occupational mobility. Black unemployment in Boston remains consistently twice as high

Figure 2.3. Percentage of Children and Families Living Under the Poverty Level, Boston 1990

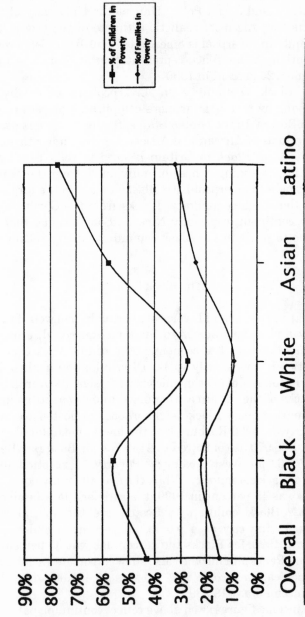

*Source:* Adapted from statistical data included in Paul Wantanabe, *A Dream Deferred: Changing Demographics, Challenges and New Opportunities for Boston* (Boston: Institute for Asian American Studies, University of Massachusetts, Boston, 1996).

as White unemployment. Black unemployment in 1990 was 13.5 percent, more than double the rate of White unemployment of 6.3 percent.[53] Although Black labor force participation rates are comparable to those of Whites, the jobs held by Blacks are more unstable, leading to higher rates of Black unemployment. Evaluating the tenuous employment circumstances of Blacks, one reporter for the *Boston Globe* concluded in 1983, "Boston is the most difficult city in the United States for a Black person to hold a job or earn a promotion."[54] In the world of high finance, Blacks are almost totally invisible. Although the Boston metropolitan area is the center of a booming technology industry, Blacks have been significantly shut out of positions in the field of technology. Thus, a study conducted by the EEOC showed that Blacks made up only 3.6 percent of the 225,000 employees in the high technology industry in Massachusetts.[55] The overwhelming preponderance of Blacks holding high tech jobs were found to be concentrated in lower-level, lower-paying positions.[56] Underutilization and exclusion of Blacks is the standard practice of businesses in the private sector in a rich variety of fields: banking, education, printing and publishing, communications, and retail sales. Indeed, it is quite startling that in a city the size of Boston, very few Blacks are employed in the downtown shopping and business center. The hard reality is that approximately 80 percent of the jobs in the downtown area are held by White nonresidents who commute into Boston on a daily basis from the suburbs.[57] It should also be noted that the process of Black exclusion is not limited to the private sector. Both municipal departments and state departments have been guilty of overlooking Blacks in their hiring practices or consigning Blacks to lower-level, lower-paying positions.[58]

Discrimination by White employers has not been offset by Black business development. Blacks own only about 4 percent of the proprietorships, partnerships, and 1120S corporations in the Boston metropolitan area.[59] Of the existing minority businesses, the distribution is skewed toward services and retail trade and away from construction, finance, insurance, wholesale trade, and real estate. Only 10 percent of Black businesses are in retail trade, while 61 percent are located in the service industry.[60] Black businesses in Boston tend to be small, undercapitalized, hire relatively few persons, and often have a difficult time surviving for more than 3 years.[61]

Boston has a highly visible and thriving Black middle class consisting of lawyers, account executives, scientists, and engineers associated with its burgeoning high tech corporate community. The Black middle class is not a socially functional class since most of its members live in the suburbs and play almost no role in the social and civic affairs of the Black community.

The Black community in Liverpool has also exhibited a marked pattern of economic underdevelopment. For decades, the city of Liverpool has refused to make major economic investments in Liverpool 8. The meager funds allocated to this area by the city have been recycled out so that no pattern of capital accumulation has taken root over several generations.

Unemployment reigns as an omnipresent menace to economic development in the Black community (See figure 2.4). Estimates of adult Black unemployment range from 26.7 to 60 percent.[62] Precise calculations of Black adult unemployment are difficult to make because of poor government record keeping and because many Black workers—as a consequence of dock employment and one-year government work schemes—are only part-time laborers.

There is little question that for many Black adults, unemployment has become a way of life. From 1971 to 1981, unemployment in the Granby Ward increased 100 percent for men and 95 percent for women.[63] A survey of the Toxteth area conducted by the Liverpool City Council in 1982 found that 52 percent of all households in the area had no wage earner. The 1991 census analysis conducted by the Granby Toxteth Community Project placed total Black unemployment at 26.7 percent as compared to 21.6 percent for the total city workforce.[64] Unemployment by Blacks in the three wards where Blacks are most significantly concentrated was uniformly higher for Blacks than non-Blacks.[65] The unemployment picture for Black teenagers is alarming. Unemployment among males sixteen to nineteen in Liverpool was found by the Toxteth Survey to be at the astronomical level of 73 percent.[66] A survey of Black youth between seventeen and nineteen conducted by researchers in the Sociology Department at the University of Liverpool found that only 17 of 134 (12.7 percent) of young Blacks interviewed were engaged in full-time employment.[67] The Granby Toxteth Community Project's 1991 census analysis found Black youth unemployment to be 40.2 percent compared to a total youth unemployment rate of 31.2 percent.[68]

A number of factors—all associated with the practice and process of racial discrimination—account for the reality of high unemployment in the Black community. The high degree of economic distress in Liverpool has meant that Blacks have been the chief victims in the search for employment opportunities in Liverpool. Trade unions

49

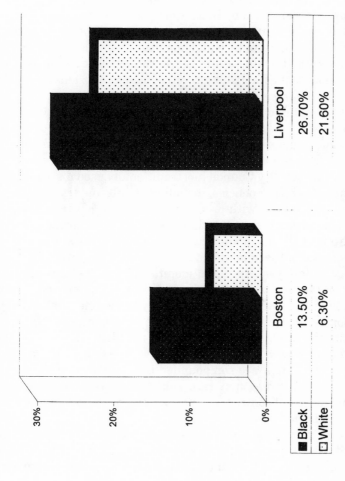

**Figure 2.4. Unemployment Rates by Race in Boston (1990) and Liverpool (1991)**

Source: Adapted from statistical data included in the Granby Toxteth Community Project *Statistical Analysis of the 1991 Census* (Liverpool: Poverty 3, 1994); and Paul Watanabe, *A Dream Deferred: Changing Demographics, Challenges, and New Opportunities for Boston* (Boston: Institute for Asian American Studies, University of Massachusetts Boston, 1996).

have operated as closed shops, keeping the bulk of available jobs in union families. Heavily unemployed, Blacks have had little representation and clout in the unions and therefore have been left out of the job procurement process. The position of Blacks in the labor market has been further undermined by the stress by employers on color-blind approaches that do not take into account the special deprivation experienced by Black workers.

Private-sector employers have been guilty of overt discrimination. While claiming to be equal opportunity employers, they have refused to recruit, train, or hire Black workers or to seriously entertain the notion of establishing positive action programs that might increase the representation of Blacks in their workforce in the long term. One notable exception in this regard is the Littlewoods Company, which has established a minority employment target of 5 percent and appointed race relations specialists to improve the company's recruitment and training record.[69]

The Liverpool City Council has traditionally used discriminatory methods in its hiring policies, including an internal trawl (a system that provides unions with preferential access to job vacancies) and union nomination rights, that have resulted in the gross underrepresentation of Blacks in all areas of the council's workforce. Council intransigence in the adoption of positive action programs, including minority training schemes and monitoring, has had a devastating impact on the employment profile of the Black community.[70] While abandoning the internal trawl, the City Department of Personnel has adopted procedures for announcing job vacancies to the public that continue to leave large segments of the Black community out of the effective flow of communication. Weaknesses in the council's employment system are compounded by the failure of the central government to strengthen race relations statues to compel the implementation of contract compliance and nondiscriminatory policies by public and private agencies.

Finally, frequent encounters by Black youth with the police, coupled with the negative attitude of employers, have served to undermine the quest for permanent employment by a sizable proportion of the Black community's potential workforce.

> We [Black youth] are given a police record before we are 15. When you are given a police record, employers find it easy to discriminate against you for being Black. If they want to discriminate against you because of your color, this record will come of age. And if that's not the case, they'll just turn around and say, we're not hiring anyone today. You say it's in the paper. They'll say someone else just came before

you. So you go through the motion of interviewing. But you know you're not going to get the job. A Black person has a feeling when he or she is being discriminated against. You just get that feeling.[71]

Decades of unemployment and the absence of a substantial business and professional sector have left the economy of the Black community crippled. Measures to develop a viable economic base for the Black community have been slow to materialize. The city council has been reluctant to invest in Black employment and business development schemes. Millions of pounds in urban regeneration funds spent by the central government have bypassed the Black community. Relying on their instincts for survival, many Blacks have had no choice but to marshal government benefits and the profits of the informal economy as staples of their financial resource networks.

## The Social Context of Racial Policy

Social policy networks and institutions in Boston and Liverpool have also promoted institutionalized discrimination against the Black community. Blacks in Boston have been victimized by an educational system that has failed to prepare them to compete in the broader society. Historically, the Boston School Committee has been firmly committed to the operation of a highly segregated school system that has produced unequal treatment and results on the basis of race. The extent of school segregation was documented by the Massachusetts State Advisory Committee to the United States Commission on Civil Rights in a report published in January 1965. This report showed that nine of seventeen high schools in Boston served geographic areas. Of the nine schools, five located in East Boston and South Boston had no Black students.[72] In the citywide schools, Girls' High School was 70.4 percent Black and the Black percentage in the remaining schools ranged from 5.36 percent to 21.49 percent.[73] Segregation made the practice of racial discrimination routine and acceptable. Black schools were uniformly more overcrowded, the dropout rate for Black students was higher, and the performance by Black students on standardized tests was weaker.[74] The negative impact of public school education on Black children was so severe that many parents believed that they had no choice but to place their children in private school.

Initially my older daughter went to public school in pre-kindergarten. The next year about thirty parents made the decision to take their children out of the school system. We just did a walkout because nothing substantively was happening there. That was during a time in the late 60s when Boston was divided as it relates to the distribution of resources and the schools in the Black neighborhoods were disproportionately allocated resources. We just decided it didn't make sense. My daughter who had gone to kindergarten knew how to write and spell some and to do some reading. She regressed the first year she was there. And though she was only in kindergarten, I knew enough to know that this was not working for her. We eventually sent our children to an independent school funded by the federal government—it was what you would call today a charter school. It was called Highland Park Free School.[75]

The educational experiences of Black students in Liverpool parallel those of Black students in Boston. Numerous studies have documented the underachievement of Black students in Liverpool in the educational process. Much of the blame for the low achievement of Black students can be placed at the doorstep of the local Education Authority. Decisions by the authority to close and consolidate comprehensive schools have compelled Black students to attend schools away from their families, churches, and other supportive community institutions.[76] Teachers assigned to teach Black students by the authority are often not competently trained or sensitive to the special needs of Black students. Black youngsters in Liverpool schools are subjected to social abuse from both professional staff persons and other students.[77] Respondents in this study contend that it is not unusual for Black students to be singled out for special punishment. The collective tapestry of experiences faced by Black students in school—negative relations with teachers and students, the development of a low sense of self-esteem and confidence—robs them of the basic tools they need to succeed in school. In too many instances Black students find education irrelevant to their needs and drop out of school at an early age without marketable skills.

Unless a Black child has a strong home background that can raise his sense of self-esteem, he's got a war by the time he's sixteen or maybe even thirteen. You can go out on the street at any time and find Black kids from nine upwards roaming the streets. Their parents rarely get to know them in school. They're not at school. They're ignored. But what can you expect, they're Black. It's their family background. That's what we are told.[78]

Relations between the Black community and the police have been on a downward spiral in Boston and Liverpool since the 1960s. For years, Blacks in both cities have complained about the heavy use of police power. Police practices in the Black community are based on the general perception of the Black community by the police as a hotbed of criminality that can only be controlled through "physical policing." In Liverpool, the concept of physical policing has been translated into the heavy patrolling of the Black community via police vans and the liberal use of stop-and-frisk techniques. These policies have produced a long history of conflict between the police and citizens in the Black community, particularly Black youth.

> Patrolling the Black community in Liverpool is like having your own safari park so far as the police are concerned. You go riding in with tanks and your guns and anything is game. If you can get somebody or something then you get them. Over a period of time, twenty, thirty years or so, it effectively means a large portion of the population has got some form of criminal record or something. There were all those by-laws about vagrancy and possession that gave the police free reign to stop and frisk. It may well be that a person was not in possession of anything, but the process of intimidation quite often led to confrontational situations where the original reason for the stop and search perpetuated a later offense.[79]

Confrontations between the police and Black citizens in Boston have become almost routine. Blacks in Boston still talk with great emotion about the heavyhanded tactics used by the police to break up a protest by Black welfare mothers in 1967 and to put down Black reaction to the slaying of Dr. Martin Luther King, Jr. in 1968. The most sensational incident occurred in 1989 when Charles Stuart, a White store clerk, filed a false report that a Black man had invaded his car in the Mission Hill District, killed his wife, and shot him in the abdomen from the backseat.[80] On the basis of this report, the police launched an all-out assault on the Black community, stopping Black men at random and hauling them to jail to participate in police line-ups. When it was discovered that Stuart had killed his own wife (he later committed suicide), the Black community was outraged.

> The city went crazy. The mayor got on the radio and television and said he was going to use all the resources of the city to find the culprit. We were struck by the intensity of the mayor's position, pulling police out of all other areas and running roughshod over the community in Mission Hill, banging down doors with sledge hammers, destroying

property as they were searching for evidence. They were totally disrespectful of the community. During that same evening, unfortunately, there was a Black woman killed. There was hardly a report. This simply reinforced the notion that the lives of African Americans are not as valuable as the lives of European Americans.[81]

Blacks in Boston and Liverpool experience major disadvantage in the areas of health and housing. Despite the existence in Boston of one of the most comprehensive and technically advanced health systems in the world, many Blacks find themselves effectively locked out of the health care delivery process. One respondent assessed the health status of Blacks in Boston in the following manner:

Blacks in Boston have fared poorly in the area of health. Their situation in 1996 is worse than it was in 1986. We have the highest negative indicators in every disease category you can name in this city: highest incidence of heart disease, highest incidence of high blood pressure, highest incidence of respiratory problems in children in particular because of the toxins they inhale every day in the communities they live in, the air they breathe. Six years ago we were second only to Washington D.C. in the highest infant mortality rate in the country.[82]

Discriminatory policies leading to social and economic deprivation have also cut the Black community in Liverpool off from a variety of health services. The decision to close down most of the services provided at Myrtle Street Children's Hospital and to transfer these services to Alder Hey Hospital substantially reduced the availability of medical services for the Black community. This decision did not take into account the fact that Myrtle Street Hospital was within blocks of the Black community, while the transfer to Alder Hey Hospital placed it beyond the physical and financial reach of Black parents who would be required to pay nearly 7 pounds a week to visit their children.[83]

The search for quality, affordable housing by Blacks in Boston became an issue of monumental importance for the Black community in the 1980s; in the 1990s the housing crisis of the Black community continued to escalate. Little growth in housing opportunities for Blacks took place over these decades.[84] The basic trend in housing has been the construction of luxury rental units, condo conversions, and abandonment of low-rent units. This pattern has meant that new housing opportunities have moved far beyond the financial reach of low- and moderate-income Black citizens.[85] Programs emphasizing the construction of public and subsidized housing have ground to a halt and are unlikely to be reactivated in the foreseeable future. The age and condition of Black housing and the continuing expansion of the Black population have increased the need for new, affordable housing in the Black community; this need has gone largely unmet. Critical losses to the Black housing stock continue in the face of pressure placed on the Black community from upscale redevelopment, speculation, and disinvestment.[86]

The housing market for Blacks in Liverpool has also limited Black access to quality accommodations. Limited economic resources have forced Blacks mainly into large multiple family houses and housing estates built and managed by the city council. Public housing in the inner city has become hard to let as entire buildings have been abandoned by former tenants. Boarded up council flats can be found throughout Liverpool 8. These dwellings have become uninhabitable as vandals have moved in to strip them of copper tubes, sinks, and other basic materials within hours after they have become vacant. Over the years, the council has found these dwellings too expensive to repair; it has been forced to either leave them standing as vacant shells or target them for demolition. Some public housing demolished in recent years was built as late as the early 1970s. In the Baumont/Falkner/ Entwistle area alone, 865 dwellings have been demolished, including the entire Falkner Estate and two multistory blocks.[87] Thus in Boston and Liverpool social disadvantage has served well the cause of White domination and control.

## Dilemmas of Political Empowerment

Social, economic and political arrangements in Boston and Liverpool have presented formidable dilemmas for Black political activists in search of the keys to Black freedom and equality. Boston's business-dominated governing coalition has, for many years, operated without meaningful Black representation or input. Positions in the top echelons of power and decision making are uniformly occupied by wealthy White businessmen. The power of the business community is reinforced by business ownership of the media, banking institutions, major corporations, and prominent law firms. Business control over the governing process is promoted by structural arrangements that give extensive decision making powers to the mayor while substantially limiting the scope of countervailing power that can be exercised by the council.

The Black community in Boston is disadvantaged by its relatively low numerical representation of approximately 24 percent. With these numbers, Blacks do not have the basic resources required to capture city hall, control the council, and break the critical ties existing between city government and business elites. Under these circumstances, policy linkage and bidirectional influence become difficult political strategies to execute. Blacks are further disadvantaged by the fact that channels of upward mobility in the Democratic Party are blocked by the continuing control by the Irish over neighborhood ward organizations—control that the Irish have been very reluctant to relinquish. Active involvement by the media in the shaping of values and opinions supportive of the prevailing political culture has served to assure that the policy-making process in Boston will remain well beyond the effective management and control of the Black community.

Blacks have been systematically shut out of the politics of this city. They have been shut out of major power positions in the world of employment. There are few Blacks on major corporate boards in this city. The few that are there have arrived in the last decade. There is a kind of informal governance that goes on in Boston that has a hell of a lot of power—almost as much power as elected official governance. It is the power of cultural institutions, the power of universities, the power of the media. The people in these positions play a big role around the choices that are made by mayors, by governors, by city councillors. We [Black people] are not a part of that official governance since we do not have a toehold in the corporate institutions, in the major universities. Because we do not have that kind of clout, we are cut out of the informal governance of the city.[88]

Roadblocks to effective Black penetration of the policy process have also emerged from the terrain of ethnic politics. Black political leaders Bal and Shag Taylor initiated a tradition of delivering Black votes to machine politicians in the 1950s that has continued to bedevil the efforts of Black candidates seeking to run progressive, independent campaigns.[89] Black electoral efforts seeking to challenge the power of the dominant policy making coalitions have been extremely difficult to mount. Multiracial alliances have been unable to surmount the extraordinary level of racism in Boston that keeps ethnic groups involved in perpetual conflict.[90] Boston is a city of ethnic enclaves where citizens view the world through the lens of their own urban villages.[91] Social separation has been a potent breeding ground for ethnic conflict and racial antagonism. Beneath the city's public facade of liberty and democracy lurks a seedbed of racial animosity. Respondents in this study agreed that race relations in Boston were among the worst in the nation.

> I am invited to speak in Boston all the time about race relations, and the first thing I tell my audiences is that we don't have any. There is this superficial discussion going on that has nothing to do with the people who live here every day, who live in Roxbury, who live in Dorchester, who live in South Boston, who are standing down on Dudley. These people have no idea and no concept of any improvement in race relations because they are not talking to any more White folk today than they were talking to ten years ago. This is still one of the most segregated cities in the country. And the segregation is encouraged and accommodated in every imaginable way. I think that White people think of Boston as the last bastion. Even the politicians talk about neighborhoods. They were the first gangbangers so far as I am concerned. They talk about turf and neighborhoods. We have a housing system that is implemented in such a way that there are certain parts of the city where certain people can't go. That is gang mentality. That is what we criticize young people for doing in their turf battles. That's what we do here.[92]

Blacks in Boston have experienced a mobilization of bias in the policy process that has produced a continuing parade of social and economic results detrimental to the welfare and progress of the Black community. The first major urban renewal project implemented by the Haynes administration was New York Streets, which devastated a South End Black community. This project alone displaced hundreds of Black families. The decision to target this community for demolition was made without Black input. This was the beginning of a process that would lead to widespread gentrification in the Black community.[93] The list of further misdeeds is quite long: redlining by banks and other financial institutions; abrogation of Black housing rights; discrimination in job recruitment and training programs; the siphoning off of federal funds for downtown development intended for Black community revitalization.[94] The capacity on the part of the Black community to effectively respond to these negative policy results has been constrained by external factors emanating from the broader political environment and internal factors that have undermined the uniting of political interests in the Black community into a cohesive and enduring base of competitive power.

Although the political dilemmas faced by Blacks in Liverpool do not precisely replicate the Boston model, the consequences of racial subordination and control have been remarkably similar. The tremendous financial problems experienced by Liverpool have made it exceedingly difficult to get issues relating to the social and economic needs of the Black community placed on the public agenda. Budgetary limitations have placed severe restrictions on the ability of city administrations to launch massive programs of social and economic reconstruction for the Black community. In circumstances of gross fiscal decline, programs involving major resource allocations for minority communities become difficult to defend politically. "Had we been in a growth budget, we might have seen some gestures to deal with major housing and employment problems in the Black community. In a declining budget, the redistributive implications of dealing with negative discrimination based on race are really pretty severe."[95]

Program targeting for the Black community has also been complicated by the existence of massive unemployment among members of the White working class. Indeed, many government, business and educational leaders in Liverpool argue that economic conditions for Blacks are no worse than those for Whites. These individuals believe that social policymakers would be well advised to design policies that do not seek to give special relief to Blacks but to improve economic and social conditions for all members of the working class, Black or White.

> Many of the problems that the Black community has are actually, as far as one can see, statistically hardly any worse than the poor, uneducated Whites living on the same streets. Racism compounds the problem to the extent that it is compoundable, but if you've got a situation where 75 to 80 percent of all youth are unemployed anyway in a city like Liverpool, where school leavers in those areas do not have any school exam qualification whatsoever, then it is very difficult to make it worse. The situation of all youngsters is so bad that undoubtedly if Blacks applied for jobs, there would be discrimination, but given the fact there are no jobs for White kids either, this makes it difficult to deal with the problem of race discrimination. That explains the view held by many that the solutions to the problems have to be socio-economic ones rather than race and racism.[96]

The pivotal policy dilemma for the Black community in Liverpool is that Blacks are in direct competition for government support with members of the White working class whose social and economic progress has also been affected by widespread unemployment and poverty in the city's economic system.

The best end of Liverpool service is not bad; the worst end is awful. The Black community would be at the worst end. But there are many other people who are at the bad end who are not Black. That is the dilemma for the Black community. In identifying themselves as particular, they find themselves at odds with many others who share their situation other than their blackness. The blackness is the compounding factor. It is not the explanatory factor because there are far too many other people who find themselves in that deprived position.[97]

Political dilemmas faced by Blacks in Boston and Liverpool raise immensely important questions regarding the capacity of Black Atlantic leaders and institutions to mobilize the resources required to address and resolve urgent survival issues facing their communities as they march rapidly toward the twenty-first century.

If you said to me "you're discriminating against me, you've got to let me in the door." I'd say I am not. Therefore, I can't open the door for you. The minute you say to me discriminate in favor of me, I say I can't do that because I wasn't discriminating in the first place. The system doesn't accept that it is discriminatory, and until it does, it will not address the question of racial inequality.[98]

Blacks in Liverpool are more disadvantaged in the electoral process than Blacks in Boston because of their low numerical representation in the total population. The liability of numbers is reinforced by internal organizational conflict in the Black community and the debilitating impact of racial buffering.

PART TWO

# Black Politics in Boston

# 3

---

# Boston: City Governance and Black Political Empowerment

## Formal Structure and City Governance

Any meaningful analysis of Black political power in Boston must begin with an examination of the formal governmental structure. The present structure of Boston City Government was first spelled out in a new city charter adopted in 1949 that incorporated many of the elements of the Model City Charter promoted by the National Municipal League. Among the most notable provisions of this charter was the creation of a strong mayoral form of government. Under this arrangement the mayor functioned as the city's chief executive. The charter concentrated extensive governing authority in the hands of the mayor, giving to the chief executive the power to appoint and remove all major department heads. The mayor was also provided with legislative veto power as well as broad authority in the budget-making process. Compared to the power of the mayor, the power of the city council was significantly constrained. Mayors were given four-year terms, while councillors were required to run for office every two years. A two-thirds majority vote in the council was needed to override a mayoral veto. The council was given the power to reduce or reject a budget originating in the mayor's office but had no power to add to or increase mayoral budget proposals.[1]

Across the years, since the adoption of the 1949 Charter, important modifications have been made in the structure of Boston City Government. A city referendum passed in 1981 changed the structure of the city council from nine councillors elected at-large to a thirteen-person council, with nine councillors elected from districts and four councillors elected at-large. The requirements of urban leadership have vastly expanded the power and authority of the mayor's office. Despite the existence of a comprehensive civil service system, the patronage resources of the mayor's office are so great that Mayor Kevin White was able to bolster his campaigns for re-election in 1975 and 1979 by hiring up to two thousand temporary city workers.[2] In Boston, the appointment powers of the chief executive are extensive, giving the mayor dominion over every major department of local government except the city council, the clerk's office, the Finance Commission, the Licensing Board, the Registry of Deeds, and the Suffolk County Sheriff's Office (See figure 3.1). Recent mayors have aggressively sought to expand their formal powers by taking legal control over departments and agencies that have traditionally operated independently.[3] The extensive administrative and political reach of the mayor's office means that the formal organization of city government changes significantly with each new administration. Current mayor Thomas Menino has reduced the size of the city bureaucracy by consolidating a number of formerly free-standing departments; surviving departmental units have been clustered in eight cabinet departments, each headed by a chief cabinet officer ( See figure 3.1).

## Political Culture and Environment

The formal structures of Boston City Government do not stand alone but operate within the context of a broader social, economic, and political milieu. Boston's political environment is marked, in part, by a political party system that has been substantially weakened by the decentralization of political organizations and resources into highly parochial ethnic enclaves. The neighborhood-centered character of the political process has inspired the development of a political culture that emphasizes the unvarnished pursuit of material benefits. Bread-and-butter issues rather than the achievement of civic virtue represent the crucial program materials of Boston politics.[4] An accent on ethnic chauvinism has given to Boston politics a peculiar conservative cast. White ethnics in Boston have manifested little sympathy for the plight of people of color, making the formation of biracial alliances a difficult objective to achieve. The pursuit of benefits along ethnic lines has produced a virulent form of zero sum logic. Elected officials wishing to retain their positions have had, in their minds, little choice but to succumb to the conservative imperatives of Boston's urban villagers.[5]

**Figure 3.1. City of Boston Cabinet Structure**

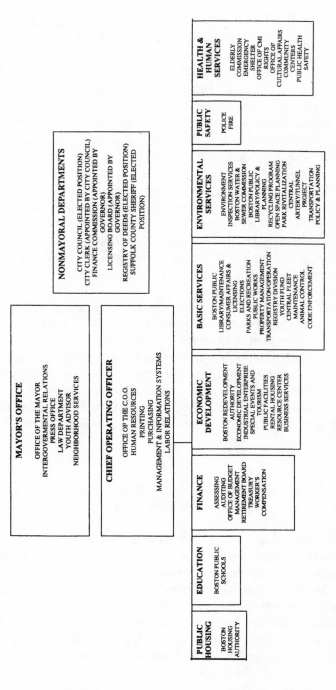

Source: Adapted from data included in *The Organization of the City of Boston*, 1996, distributed by Boston City Hall.

The evolution of a conservative political culture and weak party system has produced in Boston a salient brand of personality politics. Political campaigns have become the battle grounds of strong personalities. The relatively modest role of parties in bankrolling campaigns means that financial and political support must be mobilized through high-powered public relations campaigns. These political and financial requirements have elevated the importance of the media and business groups in the electoral process. The capacity of the media to shape public opinion and provide access to important avenues of political support means that the media, especially the major daily newspapers, stand at the very center of the public power nexus.[6] Business groups constitute a crucial source of campaign funding. Since the early days of urban renewal and downtown redevelopment, business groups have played a critical role in the setting and implementation of the public agenda. While Martha W. Weinberg may be accurate in her assessment that the business community in Boston does not speak in a single voice, the multiple voices that it projects have become transformed into a powerful chorus.[7] Compared to business, the role of labor in Boston politics is far less visible and powerful. Operating in what is deemed to be a favorable political climate, public unions in Boston have been far less willing to mount confrontational campaigns than in strong union cities like New York and Detroit. The weakness of labor is also a by-product of political culture—a culture where politics rather than union membership determines one's worth in the economic marketplace.[8]

## From Curley to Collins: Mayoral Leadership and Black Political Influence

The commanding role played by the mayor in Boston City Government renders the mayor's office a prime target for political actors interested in promoting Black access and incorporation. In Boston, the reality of access is dependent on the values, personality, philosophy, and political priorities of the individual mayor. Boston's Black community has been consistently ineffective in using the power, resources, and prerogatives of the mayor's office to advance its social, economic, and political objectives. Measured by its linkage to mayoral power, the direction of Black political influence in Boston has been toward a weak form of political incorporation.

During the first half of the twentieth century, effective linkage between the Black community and mayoral administrations was nonexistent. Under mayors Curley, Haynes, and Collins, Blacks were thoroughly locked out of the key corridors of urban power and influence. Curley's style of ward-based politics precluded the reallocation of policy benefits, or decentralization of decision making authority, to the Black community. Bal and Shag Taylor, the owners of Lincoln Pharmacy on Tremont Street, coordinated the Curley organization in the Black community. Using the patronage resources of the city organization and their special connections to Black citizens, the Taylor brothers were very effective in delivering the Black vote to the Curley forces in elections. Bal and Shag Taylor were perfect buffers for the downtown power structure. The political relationship they helped to forge between the Curley administration and the Black community was entirely unidirectional. Lacking an independent base of political power, the Black community was able to obtain little from the Curley administration beyond a few judgeships and the election in 1958 of Lincoln Pope to the state legislature.[9]

The administrations of John Haynes and John Collins were characterized by a commitment to the construction of a "New Boston" through urban renewal. In support of this objective, a new "downtown" governing coalition was formed, consisting of bankers, corporate executives, politicians, technocrats, and academicians.[10] Positive social and economic development for the Black community did not fit into the emergent definition of a "New Boston." Haynes and Collins implemented massive urban renewal campaigns leading to the destruction of Black neighborhoods in the West End and the South End and their redevelopment in the form of office complexes and apartment buildings to satisfy the demands of corporate entrepreneurs, developers, and the White gentry. Irish and Italian city councillors were able to mitigate the impact of the urban bulldozer in White ethnic neighborhoods; the absence of Black representation on the city council left the Black community completely vulnerable to development schemes designed to radically alter the physical and economic face of the central city.[11] Under the hammer of urban renewal, Black families were evicted from their homes and compelled to fend for themselves. The exclusion of Black representation in the urban renewal decision making process and the failure of the Haynes and Collins administrations to intervene in this process in behalf of its Black victims eventually precipitated a firestorm of militant Black protests.

The White Administration: The Politics of Personality

Kevin White considered himself to be the ultimate urban statesman. His ascension to the mayor's office of Boston in 1967 raised the
intriguing prospect that the insulation of the Black community from
key policy-making arenas in city government would be broken.
White brought to the mayor's office credentials as a progressive liberal from a well-established political family.[12] Running against several arch conservatives, including Louise Day Hicks, leader of the
Boston anti-busing movement, White positioned himself to the left,
embracing the struggle for civil rights and promising to focus his
administrative policies on neighborhood development. Kevin
White's liberal pronouncements were greeted with great enthusi-
asm in the Black community and by liberal Whites whose support
would be essential to the realization of his higher aspirations in
state and national politics. In the final election White beat Hicks by
12,429 votes. Support for White in Black wards was extraordinarily
strong; he received 84 percent of the vote in Ward 9, 94. 5 percent of
the vote in Ward 12, and 53. 8 percent of the vote in Ward 11.[13]

The race policy agenda adopted by White during his first term
appeared to justify the strong support he received from the Black
community in the mayoral contest. White made conscientious
efforts to place Blacks in highly visible positions in his administration. Among the most notable Black appointments was the selection
of Reginald Eaves to head the Office of Human Rights and Paul
Parks to serve as director of the Model Cities Program. White also
promoted Herbert Craigwell Jr., a Black police detective, to the position of deputy superintendent of police. White's race policy agenda
provided for the Black community much more than symbolic reassurance. After the death of Dr. Martin Luther King Jr., White began
paying regular visits to the Black community, mingling with neighborhood residents, answering their questions, and responding to
their concerns. Under the orders of the mayor, Franklin Park, the
major green space in the Black community was refurbished; the
mayor also initiated a mobile program called "Summerthing" to provide music and entertainment for young people during hot summer
days. In the area of substantive policy changes, White hired more
Black policemen to patrol the Black community, initiated an in-fill
housing program to construct low-income housing units on vacant
city land, and introduced reforms to the Boston Housing Authority
(BHA) to make it more responsive to tenant demands.[14] Responding
to the crisis in Black unemployment, White negotiated the appoint-

ment of Blacks to jobs in federally funded programs. White also opened up the city bureaucracy to Black employment. During White's sixteen years in office, Black employment in city government increased from 6 percent to 20 percent.[15]

Kevin White's campaign promises to stimulate development in the neighborhoods began to bear fruit with the introduction of his Little City Hall program. The primary goal of this program was to decentralize the service delivery process by establishing service centers in the neighborhoods. In 1968 a total of eighteen such service centers were placed in inner-city neighborhoods. From the perspective of the White administration, little city halls provided a means by which city officials could help citizens transact business, file complaints, receive information, and receive emergency assistance. For many Black citizens, little city halls appeared to be ideal vehicles for strengthening community ties to city hall and gaining access to badly needed housing, health, and employment benefits.

Unfortunately, many of the promises of Kevin White's race policy agenda were delivered with smoke and mirrors. Long before the conclusion of his first term in office, White's commitment to a progressive race policy agenda dramatically waned. The formal shift in White's perspective on the race issue occurred in the aftermath of his defeat for governor in 1970. In this race, White was beaten not only statewide by his Republican opponent Francis Sargent but also in Boston, where he won the Black community but lost by significant margins in White ethnic communities. The vote in Boston was a clear indication of White ethnic disaffection from the White administration in the wake of White's aggressive efforts to redistribute benefits to the Black community, a policy perspective that led many White ethnics to refer to him derisively as "Mayor Black."[16] The outcome of the governor's race suggested to White that his reelection would depend heavily on his ability to win major support in Boston's White ethnic neighborhoods. During the balance of his career in public office, White would divest himself of all trappings of liberalism, including his intellectual advisers and his racially progressive policy agenda.[17] In the process, Kevin White's political style changed from that of an urbane liberal activist to that of a consummate machine politician.

The White machine was not a party machine but a personal machine. After his 1971 reelection, White made every effort to centralize the power and authority of city government in his hands. In doing so, he expanded the role of the mayor far beyond that originally envisioned by the city charter. For example, White used his authority to appoint the commissioner of the Assessing Department to reward his friends and punish his enemies by manipulating the assigning of assessments and the distribution of abatements. He also used the power of his office to award multimillion-dollar contracts and licenses to clients ranging from cable television operators to the architects and builders of the downtown Faneuil Hall Marketplace.[18] The use of the mayor's official and discretionary powers in this way allowed him to undermine the legal authority of the council and collect hundreds of thousands of dollars in campaign contributions from politically connected donors. White was able to maximize his control over the city bureaucracy by maintaining a fluid institutional structure in city hall.[19] This structure was characterized by the shifting of personnel from place to place at the whim of the mayor, the making of duplicate assignments, and the assignment of identical tasks to different persons or institutions.[20] White discovered that the creation of a deliberate state of confusion was one way he could keep the heads of city bureaucracies at bay, thwart their efforts to amass autonomous power, and expand the scope of his authority to encompass even the most remote sectors of governmental operations.[21]

The heart of the machine was the political organization. During his second term, White decided that he needed to build a separate political organization to assure his victory in future campaigns. To accomplish this objective, White used the patronage resources of city hall to recruit a permanent staff of political activists to occupy key positions in his political organization. The formal organization consisted of a central committee of five, ward coordinators, precinct captains, and an army of "volunteers." All coordinators and many precinct captains were on the city payroll. Using sophisticated computer technology and lists compiled from a constant canvassing of wards and precincts, organization leaders would meet daily in city hall to "measure the rate of successful interventions on the part of each volunteer and the number of votes which Kevin White—or another member of the party— received in the area of the volunteer's responsibility at the time of elections."[22]

Through careful organization and planning, Kevin White was able to bring all the various neighborhood organizations scattered across Boston under his singular umbrella. The tentacles of the White machine reached far into the Black community. Little city halls in the Black community became convenient mechanisms for controlling the Black vote through the distribution of divisible benefits. These institutions served not as instruments of empowerment but obstacles to empowerment.[23] Thus, while little city halls decentralized services, they did not decentralize power. One of the cardinal rules of the Little City Hall program was that the head of all neighborhood units had to be noncommunity appointees of the downtown organization, a classic model of domestic colonialism and indirect rule.[24] In the final analysis, little city halls became vehicles for suppressing community demands and keeping community issues away from line departments, the city council, and the mayor's office. Because of the little city halls, a formidable administrative wedge was created between Black community leadership and city government. On this subject one Boston respondent commented:

> The White administration seemed to structure more within the city apparatus and therefore did not have to deal with community leaders because it set up this decentralized facade of city governance. It channeled the community's interests through these little city halls which really didn't have the power but created the facade administratively.[25]

White shrewdly used the patronage resources of city hall to prevent the emergence of an independent base of electoral power in the Black community. Acceptance of a city job, or a job in a federal program, became an iron-clad contract to work as an active participant in the White campaign organization. Careful records were kept of city workers that did not fulfill their political obligations. The requirement of political commitment extended to high-level Black appointees in the White administration. Individuals like Clarence "Jeep" Jones, deputy mayor during White's second term, were often called upon to serve as diplomats from the mayor's office to the Black community.[26] Selected Black ministers were used as political buffers in exchange for financial grants and appointments. Memberships on prestigious boards and commissions were used as inducements to obtain the cooperation of key Black leaders. Noncooperation could produce harsh results.[27]

Black community interests were also undermined by the White administration through nondecision making. The most glaring example of this phenomenon was the refusal of the mayor to intervene on the side of the Black community in the school desegregation controversy. Despite the eruption of widespread violence provoked by White reaction to court-ordered racial busing, Mayor White refused to use the power of his office to quell the violence or the moral authority of his office to counsel against lawlessness and civil disobedience.

We did not have political leadership that stood up against White violence and said this [school desegregation] is being done in the interest
of education, we will not tolerate violence. Kevin White never got up
in the middle of this and deplored violence or chastised folk, never
took a moral position. He believed for political reasons it was not in
his interest to do so. The Black community had pitched battles with
Kevin White at Freedom House, asking him what are you going to
say? Are you going to stand up and provide moral leadership as mayor
of this city? He got huffy and walked out. "I don't have to take this
stuff. You know what I've done for you folk." There simply was not the
use of the bully-pulpit of the mayoralty here to set a tone and make it
clear where political officials stood.[28]

White's official position on the school desegregation controversy was
that responsibility for implementing school policy was lodged in the
elected school committee, not the mayor's office.

During his last two terms in office, White erased race policy
issues almost totally from his governing agenda. Seeking to permanently establish his place in urban history, White embarked on a
vigorous campaign to complete the process of downtown development. This approach assured the political incorporation of business
interests in city politics while simultaneously seriously undermining prospects for Black incorporation and empowerment.

### The Flynn Administration: The Limits of Urban Populism

Sensing probable political disaster, White decided not to run for
reelection in 1983, ending his sixteen-year reign over city hall.
White was succeeded in the mayor's office by Ray Flynn. The 1983
election was historic, pitting Flynn against Mel King, the first Black
politician to win enough votes in the preliminary race to run as a
candidate in the final mayoral contest.

Ray Flynn came to prominence as a highly visible leader of the
antibusing fight in South Boston. He was a former state representative and served three terms on the Boston City Council. Flynn ran
for mayor in 1983 as an urban populist, promoting issues starkly
reminiscent of those pushed by Kevin White in 1967. At the center of
his electoral appeal was a promise to balance downtown renaissance
with a renaissance in the neighborhoods. Flynn promised to give
Boston neighborhoods a greater share of the city's governing authority as well as its economic resources.[29]

Upon assuming the duties of mayor, Flynn embraced a highly progressive agenda. To spur development in the neighborhoods, he created the Mayor's Office of Neighborhood Services. This agency hired individuals to act as liaisons to ethnic communities and facilitated the formation of neighborhood councils as basic service units in the neighborhoods. A Mayor's Hunger Commission was also created to coordinate the distribution of food through private and public agencies.[30]

Flynn made a conscious effort to reach out to the Black community. At considerable cost to his standing in working-class White communities, he supported a demand by the federal Department of Housing and Urban Development that a program of public housing integration be vigorously pursued in Boston. Flynn also expressed his willingness to comply with federal court rulings supporting Boston school desegregation. And it is illuminating to note that Flynn took unprecedented steps to rainbow his administration by appointing Blacks to high positions in city government. George Russell was appointed by Flynn as the first Black Boston city treasurer, a post that managed over $1 billion in funds. Russell was succeeded by the second Black city treasurer, also appointed by Flynn, Lee Jackson. Other African Americans occupying high positions in Flynn administrations were Doris Bunte, director of the Boston Housing Authority, and Leon Stamps, city auditor. Flynn's efforts to promote neighborhood development, school desegregation, and minority access to key positions in city government generated glowing assessments by academicians and liberal progressives of his pioneering role as an innovative urban entrepreneur. In this regard Professor Robert Dentler of the University of Massachusetts Boston observed of Flynn:

> I see him as the vehicle for the realization of the post-segregation era. He was ideal for it; it was like Nixon going to China. This man had been such a vigorous opponent of desegregation that the changeover was dramatic. He never stopped materializing in the middle of Roxbury and the middle of Mattapan for every tragedy that occurred, every accident. My heart went out to him.[31]

Flynn's agenda of progressive reforms did not reverse the subordinate status of the Black community in the political and governmental process. Like White, Flynn used the patronage resources of the mayor's office to exercise tight control over the process of decision making in the Black community. The appointment decisions of the mayor, while providing access to government for the Black community, had the concomitant effect of robbing key Black agencies of their leaders. Mayoral appointments to major city boards and commissions came from the ranks of agency heads identified as leaders in the Black community. Not only did this process create a vacuum in community leadership, but also it installed in city hall a new network of buffers to carry the mayor's programs to the Black community and stifle the emergence of independent community insurgency groups that might threaten mayoral power from below. Flynn's control over the budgetary process, maximized by the strategy of releasing fragmentary information on key items to the council, depressed the development of independent social programming agencies in the Black community. Decisions regarding the distribution of city and federal dollars for social programming in the Black community served to keep Black agencies in dependent positions within Flynn's governing coalition and limited their administrative and political impact principally to issues that did not reach beyond the restricted boundaries of the Black community. "The process under Flynn was very segregated. Black folks could rule as long as it was in Black neighborhoods and touched on issues that White folks felt reflected our community: crime, drug issues, civil rights. But in general policy areas such as development and planning, we were not permitted to play a meaningful role."[32]

Black political interests remained marginalized in the executive office of the mayor under Flynn. No Black person operated within the inner circle of senior advisers to the mayor. Black influence in sensitive areas, such as the staffing and management of the police department, was virtually nonexistent. On this subject City Councillor Charles Yancey observed:

> Under Flynn the police continued to serve as a hostile force in the Black community. The most important battles we had with the Flynn administration were over police accountability and the distribution of police services. I did not see it as inconsistent to ask that the police be accountable to the community while offering a greater measure of services. Mayor Flynn did not agree. This debate finally came to a head with the arrival of the Charles Stuart incident.[33]

It can be said that the Charles Stuart case created major disruptions in effective linkage between the Flynn administration and the Black community. Black citizens found Flynn's hard-nosed law and order reaction to the initial reports of a Black perpetrator appalling. More than anything else, Flynn's position on police-community relations issues underscored the limits of his populist agenda and the continuing isolation of the Black community from the inner core of governance and political decision making in crucial local arenas of power. In the minds of many Black citizens, Flynn's response in the Stuart case brought back painful memories of his role in the crusade to block the movement of school buses from Roxbury to South Boston.

> All I use to see on television during those busing days was that man, Flynn, standing in the school door with those evil looking eyes trying to keep Black kids from going into that school. I remember that. And that look on his face will never, ever fade from my memory. It will always be there. I never trusted Flynn, never. I don't care how nice a guy they said he was as mayor. There was always something inside of me that stopped me just inches from trusting that guy. I never trusted him. A lot of people forgot that, but I didn't. Even when he was mayor I wouldn't vote for that guy.[34]

In the world of reality, political trust is a fragile commodity that sometimes cannot be retrieved, once lost, even in the face of what appears to be a sincere and sacred burning bush conversion.

## The Menino Administration: Racial Buffering and Political Subordination

Thomas Menino took the reins as the first mayor of Italian heritage in the history of Boston on 18 January 1994. Menino was appointed by the city council as acting mayor upon the resignation of Ray Flynn to become United States Ambassador to the Vatican in July 1993. Menino prevailed in a special preliminary election in September 1993 and a final election in November 1993. Before his elevation to the mayor's office Menino had served on the city council for nine years as a representative of the Hyde Park area. He was elected president of the council in 1993.

Menino has brought a low-keyed, blue-collar style to the mayor's office. One respondent suggested that his style was in the Mediterranean rather than Northern European Irish tradition. Another respondent described him as a "don't talk well, lunch bucket, pot hole fixing, democratic pragmatist." Menino's commitment to democratic pragmatism has been marked by a willingness to engage in bargaining and to bend to pressure and persuasion. "Tom's policies for the day depend on the last person that advised him and told him what to do that day."[35] Menino's political instincts are those of a quintessential ward politician. An energetic campaigner, he has worked hard to preserve and expand his electoral base in the Irish community, the Italian community, and the Black community. Billing himself as the education mayor, he has devoted a considerable amount of time to issues of educational reform and school governance. Has Menino's election promoted Black linkage and incorporation? On this subject the verdict is quite mixed. His relationship to the Black community has been fraught with tension, conflict and ambivalence. He appears to be extremely comfortable in Black community settings and has made efforts to maintain a high profile in the Black community through attendance at important Black events. Menino's record of appointment of Blacks to high positions has been impressive. Key Black appointments have included Allyce Lee as Chief of Staff (now a consultant to the mayor's office), and Juanita Wade to the cabinet-level position of Commissioner of Basic Services. Other key Black appointments are Diane Lopes, Commissioner of Elder Services; Charles T. Grigsby, Director of the Department of Neighborhood Development; Victoria Williams, Member of the Fair Housing Commission; and Reginald Nunnally, Director of the Boston Empowerment Center.

Steps toward Black representation and linkage initiated by the Menino administration have been offset by Menino's bold attempt to co-opt Black leadership and control the Black social and economic policy agenda. As mayor, Menino has consistently identified a special set of Black leaders with whom he believes he can work and used these leaders as buffers between the Black community and the city administration. "It is clear that the city has selectively identified a corps of people who have been identified and put forward to represent the interests of the Black community that are willing to accommodate the interests of the Menino administration."[36] Three sets of Black leaders have been the central targets of Menino's buffering strategy: (1) Black administrators holding top positions in city government; (2) Black ministers; (3) leaders of Black community organizations, especially those involved in economic development activities. The role of Black leaders in the implementation of the race policy agenda of the Menino administration has been the source of considerable controversy in the Black community.

> Menino operatives are being paid off by appointments to various committees. They won't say anything or do anything. The mayor has bought off the ministers. He courts them with appointments as city chaplains. If the mayor was Black he wouldn't even get on the ballot. Have you heard him talk? "He be pitiful." When he was on the city

council he voted down every budget the school committee sent forward. And now he's trying to pose himself as the education mayor. I
can't stand it. He's got his key Blacks that are co-opted. They know
how to buy them off with a few baubles and beads. It is hard to pin-
point why some people do certain things. They don't read the stuff
they need to read to be politically aware of what's going on.[37]

Critics of Menino in the Black community note that while he has
appointed a number of Blacks to high-profile positions, he has done
very little to increase Black representation in middle and upper levels of the city bureaucracy. These individuals observe that Black
city workers remain concentrated in entry-level positions that offer
low wages and weak job security. Few effective steps have been
taken by the Menino administration to lift the glass ceiling on the
promotion of people of color within the ranks of major city departments and agencies.

Mayor Menino's decision to force Black School Superintendent
Lois Harrison-Jones to resign and replace her with a White
Superintendent, Thomas Payzant, has been an additional source of
tension in his relationship with the Black community. Harrison-
Jones was very popular in the Black community because of her progressive educational ideas and her deep involvement in the work of
community organizations. In contrast to former Black Superintendent Laval Wilson, who was viewed as estranged from the Black
community, Lois Harrison-Jones was viewed as a dynamic and committed community worker. Menino's decision to ask her to resign in
the middle of her contract set off widespread protests by her supporters in the Black community. Many Blacks have also been
unhappy with Menino's decision to turn over ownership of Boston
State Hospital land to a private firm. This decision ran contrary to a
bill sponsored by State Representative Shirley Owens-Hicks to
transfer this state-owned property to the City of Boston to promote
neighborhood revitalization activities in Roxbury and Mattapan.
Although no final assessments can be made of the race policy
agenda of the Menino administration, it can be said that no dramatic breakthroughs in Black political linkage and incorporation
have taken place or are on the horizon. The proclivities toward
Black leadership co-optation and annihilation exhibited by the
administration suggest that the institutional subordination of the
Black community in the political process will not be reversed by the
leadership instincts and policy preferences of the present occupant
of the mayor's office.

People who work in city hall are often called upon to do the political
bidding of the mayor because he hires them indirectly. The mayor
uses African Americans to soften the criticisms of his efforts. The
mayor very adeptly uses people of color as his front people so that criticisms will be weakened when it comes to the question of impact on
the city and impact on people of color of some of the reactionary positions he has taken and policies, especially school policies, he has tried
to implement.[38]

The formal, public face of the racial hierarchy in Boston reaches its
summit in the mayor's office and is firmly rooted in the soil of Black
political subordination. In this sense the political relationship
between the Black community and the mayor's office is emblematic,
in microcosm, of a number of the broader dilemmas faced by Black
communities struggling for power across the Black Atlantic.

### The City Council and the Representation of Black Interests

Rufus P. Browning, Dale Rogers Marshall, and David H. Tabb
have correctly identified city councils as important arenas of opportunity for minority groups seeking political incorporation in local
political systems in the United States. They stipulate that preconditions for incorporation include minority group control of the council
or effective participation in a dominant coalition supportive of the
policy preferences of minority communities.[39] In Boston, structural
and demographic constraints have prevented the Black community
from satisfying these preconditions for minority incorporation
through city council action. We should note in this regard that the
structural allocation of council seats, four at-large and nine in districts, presents formidable barriers to Black political incorporation.
Because of its size and concentration, the Black community constitutes an electoral majority in only two districts—District 4
(Mattapan and North Dorchester ) and District 7 (Roxbury and the
South End). This fact has tended to limit Black representation on
the council to two seats.

Before the switch from a nine-seat at-large council to a thirteen-
seat council with a combination of at-large and district seats, the
hurdles to Black representation on the council were exceptionally
high. The first Black politician to surmount the at-large obstacle
was Thomas Atkins, a lawyer and president of the Boston branch of
the NAACP. Atkins was elected to the council in 1967. He remained
on the council for two terms, leaving the council permanently in

1971. For a full decade after Atkins's departure, no Black candidate was able to mobilize enough votes to win a council seat. For example, Bruce Bolling, son of state representative Royal Bolling, ran for the council in 1977 and lost in the preliminary election by a substantial margin. In 1981 Bruce Bolling ran for the council again and won, while Charles Yancey ran in the same election and lost by 2 percent of the vote. The switch to district elections in 1983 made possible the election of Bolling and Yancey from two newly created Black districts; Bolling represented District 7, and Yancey represented District 4. Bruce Bolling became the first Black president of the city council in 1986 when six White councilmen asked him to join their voting bloc to form a councilmanic majority with the power to select the council president. Bolling ran for an at-large seat on the council in 1991 and lost. He was succeeded as District 7 councillor by Tony Crayton. Bolling returned to the council in 1992 when he was appointed to an at-large seat upon the death of councillor Christopher Ianella. This time his term on the council lasted only a year; in 1993 Bolling resigned from the council to run for mayor of Boston. Political representation for District 7 changed again in 1993 as Tony Crayton was defeated by Gareth Saunders. Currently, Saunders and Yancey serve as Boston councillors representing Districts 7 (Roxbury and the South End) and 4 (Mattapan and North Dorchester ) (see figure 3.2).

Racial politics has prevented the Black community from translating its control over two council seats into effective access and power. Boston City Council is ruled by a dominant White coalition that is extraordinarily conservative and largely unresponsive to the policy preferences of the Black community. The council president, James Kelly, was a vocal and influential leader of the anti-busing campaign in South Boston in the 1970s. One prominent Black leader has described him as the David Duke of Boston politics.

White district councillors represent White neighborhoods that are in direct competition with Black neighborhoods for benefits, services, and resources; they normally make no effort to sponsor or support legislation to provide services or assistance to the Black community. At-large White councillors have demonstrated no inclinations to substantively represent Black interests in council deliberations. Thus, the two Black councillors have had to shoulder the responsibility of representing the interests of the Black community on the council by themselves. Given the conservative character of the council, this has been, to say the least, a herculean task. Black councillors have found it virtually impossible to form enduring coali-

## Figure 3.2. City of Boston Elected Officials–1997

---

### Thomas M. Menino, Mayor

---

### James M. Kelly, Council President

---

| Margaret Davis-Mullen | Stephen J. Murphy | Albert L. O'Neil | Francis M. Roache |
|---|---|---|---|
| *At-Large City Councillor* | *At-Large City Councillor* | *At-Large City Councillor* | *At-Large City Councillor* |

**DISTRICT 1**
Diane J. Modica
East Boston: Ward 1, Pct 1–14
Charlestown: Ward 2, Pct 1–7
North End/Waterfront: Ward 3, Pct 1–6*

**DISTRICT 2**
James M. Kelly
Downtown/Chinatown: Ward 3, Pct 7–8
South Boston: Ward 6, Pct 1–9
Ward 7, Pct 1–9
South End: Ward 4, Pct 1–4, Ward 5, Pct 1
Ward 8, Pct 1–2, Ward 9, Pct 1–2

**DISTRICT 3**
Maureen E. Feeney
Dorchester: Ward 13, Pct 3, 6–10
Ward 15, Pct 1–9, Ward 16, Pct
1–12, Ward 17, Pct 4, 11–14*

**DISTRICT 4**
Charles C. Yancey
Mattapan/North Dorchester: Ward 14, Pct
2–14, Ward 17, Pct 1–3, 5–10, Ward 18, Pct
1–5.21

**DISTRICT 5**
Daniel F. Conley
Hyde Park/Roslindale/West Roxbury:
Ward 18, Pct 6–20, 22–23, Ward 19, Pct
7, 10–13, Ward 20, Pct 1–4, 7-9

**DISTRICT 6**
Maura A. Hennigan
Jamaica Plain: Ward 10, Pct
6–9, Ward 11, Pct 4–10, Ward 19,
Pct 1–6, 8, 9
West Roxbury: Ward 20, Pct
5.6. 10–20

**DISTRICT 7**
Gareth R. Saunders
South End/Roxbury: Ward 4, Pct 8, 9,
Ward 7, Pct 10, Ward 8, Pct 3–7, Ward 9,
Pct 3–5, Ward 10, Pct 1, Ward 11, Pct 1–3,
Ward 12, Pct 1–9, Ward 13, Pct 1, 2, 4, 5,
Ward 14, Pct 1

**DISTRICT 8**
Thomas M. Keane, Jr.
Back Bay/Beacon Hill: Ward 5, 3-9,
Fenway/Kenmore: Ward 4, Pct 5–7, 10,
Ward 5, Pct 2, 10, Ward 21, Pct 1–3,
Mission Hill: Ward 10, Pct 2-5

**DISTRICT 9**
Brian J. Honan
Allston/Brighton: War 21, Pct
4–16, Ward 22, Pct 1-13

\* Harbor Islands are a part of District 3, except Deer island which is part of District 1.
Source: Adapted from data distributed by the Boston City Council, 1997

tions with White councillors. They have found little ideological congruence with White councillors who, although officially members of the Democratic Party, hold positions on issues more akin to those of conservative Republicans. Even the four women on the council are exceptionally conservative, providing strong support for the policy agenda articulated by President Kelly.

Black councillors have found it difficult to get their White colleagues to embrace race policy issues in a positive fashion, even when the issues have been mainly symbolic. Thus, Councillor Yancey could generate little support in the council for a resolution condemning Black church bombings in the South. In leading the vote against this resolution, President Kelly contended that the issue was irrelevant since no such incidents had occurred in Boston. The council also voted down a resolution by councillors Yancey and

Saunders asking that the city compensate the family of Reverend Accelynne Williams, an elderly Black man who died of a heart attack when the Boston police violently entered his home by mistake in search of a suspected drug dealer.

Ordinances sponsored by Black councillors and engineered through the mine field of the council chambers have sometimes not been able to escape the wrath of a mayoral veto. Councillor Yancey learned this lesson when he negotiated a unanimous vote on an ordinance to equip school buses with monitors, seat belts, and crossing gates. Mayor Menino vetoed the legislation on the grounds that these safety devices were too expensive and were unnecessary. Yancey found it impossible to muster enough votes in the council to override the mayor's veto.

The enormity of the challenge of garnering majority votes in the council for race policy issues has meant that Black councillors have sometimes had to concentrate on issues with broad public appeal rather than issues narrowly targeted to Black concerns. Councillor Yancey's legislative agenda, for example, has included issues such as a ban on the public distribution of cigarette samples, the regulation of cigarette vending machines, visitation rights for parents during school hours, the banning of assault weapons, the confiscating of funds from drug busts for use in crime watch programs, and the location of temporary homes for Haitian refugees. Councillor Bruce Bolling commented candidly on the challenges faced by Black city councillors seeking to achieve at least a modicum of success in the Boston legislative process.

> My legislative career was built on the ability to look at common areas of interest and concern and get beyond the politics of ideology, of neighborhood, of philosophical bent, and be able to work with councillors and get them to support my initiatives to the point that I got a majority of the vote. I was looked upon as someone who was somewhat cooler, more deliberate, because I was in the legislative body. As far as I saw it, the measure of your effectiveness is the ability for you to generate legislative initiatives that proved to be timely and appropriate to addressing a myriad of issues and concerns impacting the city and be able to raise them and to lobby for them and to politic for them and get them passed substantially intact. That was my forte. I did it well.[40]

Utilizing immense parliamentary and political skills, Black councillors, often against the odds, have been able to move helpful race policy legislation through the council. The first ordinance passed by

Bruce Bolling as a councillor was a fair housing initiative affecting the sale and rental of housing to minorities. Bolling was also the principal sponsor of the link development program established during the Flynn administration. In 1985 Councillor Yancey pushed through the council the Minority and Women's Business Enterprise Program. This legislation mandated that 15 percent of all city contracts go to minorities and 5 percent to women.

Councillor Yancey has used his position on the council to promote the equitable distribution of services and resources to the Black community. He has successfully injected rules in the budgetary process that require that every department head submit information regarding the employment of minorities and women, sign a statement agreeing to the vigorous pursuit of affirmative action objectives, and provide the council with an annual plan for the concrete achievement of affirmative action hiring objectives. Councillor Yancey has also been responsible for an ordinance requiring the mayor's office to provide weekly statistics on the deployment of police services. This legislation was developed in response to the fact that, in the past, high crime areas in the Black community had been underserviced by the police while a disproportionate amount of police services were distributed to low crime areas in the White community. Councillor Yancey has found a reliable ally in Councillor Saunders. Among Councillor Saunders's legislative activities, one of the most important has been his efforts to amend the Boston jobs ordinance to increase the residency requirements for workers on city projects from 50 percent to 75 percent. A corollary to this action is the requirement he has introduced that workers on city projects be drawn from specific neighborhoods rather than the city as a whole. Councillor Saunders has also sponsored legislation that would allow a percentage of development contract dollars to be invested in job training, academic, and recreational programs for minority youth.

The overwhelming disadvantages faced by the Black community in the legislative process have limited the capacity of Black city councillors to pursue major redistributive objectives in behalf of the Black community. Blacks in Boston are victimized by persistent councilmanic nondecision making. The structure of the legislative process is clearly unidirectional. Key factors that shape and limit choice in the policy making process are well beyond the grasp, or influence, of the Black community. Decisions regarding the distribution of services, for example, are often made at the level of individual departments. Boston's Black community does not have

sufficient influence on the decision making process at the departmental level to guarantee it will receive its fair share of services. At
this juncture in the decision making process, the primary political
linkage is between department heads and the mayor's office.

Mayoral control over the budget process assures that department heads will be highly responsive to mayoral initiatives and
preferences. City departments also maintain ongoing political and
administrative relations with non-Black constituent groups whose
superior political and economic resource bases place them in a position to block Black demands for priority consideration in the policy
making process. Black city councillors represent one set of multiple
actors involved in the agenda-setting and policy-implementation
activities of the city council. Because they are outnumbered, and frequently outvoted, their most useful role often takes the form of dra-
matizing the concerns of the Black community through speeches on
the council floor. They are also valuable as guardians of the Black
community's interests in the service delivery process; however,
their ability to effectively intervene in this process in behalf of their
Black constituents is greatly circumscribed by their limited
resource base within the council and within the broader arena of
city government.

Black influence in the policy-making activities of the city council
is undermined by the fact that the Black community's linkage to the
council's policy process is unsystematic and discontinuous. One
objective of the Boston Black Political Assembly, founded in the
1970s as a response to the 1972 Gary Black Political Convention,
was the establishment of a local Black political organization that
would lobby the city council in a systematic and continuous way in
behalf of the Black community. Although strenuous efforts were
made to achieve this objective, no structures to promote institutionalized lobbying before the city council for the Black community were
ever fully developed. The upshot has been the development of a pattern of Black interest articulation that focuses on individual issues
rather than the institutionalization of Black influence across a
range of policy areas. Further, formal interaction between the council and the Black community is weakened by the failure of the Black
community to systematically monitor council deliberations and to
lobby for Black issues on a continuous basis. Bruce Bolling commented on the impact of this pattern of Black community linkage on
the legislative process during the 12 years he served as a member of
the Boston City Council.

Lobbying by the Black community before the council varied, depending on the issue and the concern. There were organized efforts that were obviously in support of many initiatives I put forward that were progressive. I would say that there was a lack of consistency; it would vary from time to time in terms of the depth and breadth of that support or opposition when that was required. That's something that councillors clearly looked at to see how many people would come to the hearing. That would be a determining factor in terms of whether or not a councillor would or would not support a particular legislative initiative. I would say that is an area where the community has fallen down considerably. That level of organizational consistency required to make a difference simply has not been there.[41]

One of the lessons that Black councillors have learned is that they cannot carry the weight of the Black community in the legislative process by themselves. Black incorporation requires the development of collective interests and the consolidation of disparate organizational resources. Black councillors are now playing leadership roles in the building of external networks critical to the mobilization of Black community interests in the legislative process. A major step in this direction has been taken by the formation of the District 7 Leadership Council by Councillor Gareth Saunders. The Leadership Council is a "family" network of businesses, churches, and community organizations that meet with Councillor Saunders on a regular basis to discuss issues and plan strategies for policy implementation. These kind of efforts are essential if the fundamental building blocks for power are to be forged through rational, instrumental action in the political process by Boston's Black community.

## Black Political Dilemmas

Clearly the structural design of Boston City Government has served to marginalize the interests of the Black community in the local decision-making process. Centralization of governing authority in the mayor's office has meant that the flow of decision making has been mainly unidirectional. The legacy of mayoral leadership in Boston has given the mayor an extraordinary capacity to limit the impact of the Black community on the crucial choices made by city officials in the distribution of benefits. Mayoral authority in this regard is reinforced by the formal strictures of the city charter, the control of party organizations over the electoral process, and the pivotal influence wielded by private interests in the process of local government.

Black political incorporation and empowerment are stifled by the inability of the Black community to exercise countervailing power through the city bureaucracy and the city council. The absence of major Black representation in the city bureaucracy and the city council represents a crucial obstacle to Black linkage. In this regard it should be underscored that the structure of council representation and the prevailing political culture effectively limit Black access to the levers of power in the council to the offices of the two Black councillors. Strong pressures on the council emanating from White ethnic communities to avoid the construction of a comprehensive race policy agenda have produced a pattern of council nondecision making that deflects Black issues from the center of local government policy construction and implementation. The racially conservative bent of the Boston political environment prevents the serious discussion of the development of race units within the council or the broader city bureaucracy of the kind established by Liverpool to provide special avenues of access for Black policy interests (see chapter 8).

Blacks in Boston have only a limited capacity to reverse the dominant pattern of race policy decision making by assuming the roles of strategic insiders. The ability of Boston mayors to co-opt some Black leaders and use them as political buffers has served as a potent mechanism for suppressing Black demands, undermining Black linkage, and channeling policy benefits to powerful sectors of the dominant governing coalition. In the face of the prevailing structure of power, the Black community is compelled to confront a powerful dilemma: the identification of major sources of competitive power beyond the reach of the mayor's office. This dilemma represents a formidable political challenge for an urban community whose historic roots are not embedded in the fundamental institutions and processes of local government.

# 4

## Black Political Linkage: The Search for Alternative Sources of Power

### The Boston School Committee

The mayor's office and the city council do not represent exclusive potential reservoirs of power for the Black community in Boston City Government. Relatively weak incorporation of the Black community in the central units of local government has lead to a search for alternative sources of public power. One important alternative target of opportunity for the Black community has been the Boston School Committee. For many decades the issue of public education has been a driving force in Boston politics. Much of that politics has focused on the policy-making authority and power of the Boston School Committee, a publicly financed administrative unit whose origins can be traced to the organization of public education in Boston in the late eighteenth century.[1] Functioning as an important source of political patronage as well as policy control, the school committee became, by the turn of the twentieth century, a crucial cog in the wheel of Irish dominance of Boston politics. In the 1930s, Boss Curley seized control of a "reformed" five-member school committee that principally serviced the needs of middle-class and lower middle-class Irish Catholics seeking to use the public schools as a lever of upward mobility in the local economy. The school committee remained under Irish control during the turbulent 1960s. School committee policies in the 1960s reflected the fears of grassroots Irish voters that the Civil Rights movement would profoundly alter the social fabric of Boston society and stifle the flow of social and economic benefits to Irish communities. The hot button issue of the decade was school desegregation. Under the leadership of its chair,

Louise Day Hicks, the school committee established and maintained a posture of overt opposition to school desegregation. Symbolic of its defiant stand, the school committee, on several occasions, rejected the demand by the Boston branch of the NAACP that it acknowledge the existence of de facto school segregation in Boston and eliminate discrimination in the hiring of teachers. The school committee's implacable position was that it was not guilty of discrimination and could not solve problems that did not exist.[2]

School committee opposition to desegregation was also expressed by its refusal to comply with the Racial Imbalance Law passed by the Massachusetts General Court in 1965. This law required that all cities in Massachusetts take giant steps toward the elimination of dual public school systems. In the wake of school committee intransigence, Black parents filed a lawsuit in federal court to force the city of Boston to desegregate its public schools. A 1974 ruling by federal judge W. Arthur Garrity ordering the city to desegregate through the institutionalization of a comprehensive school busing program was met with widespread resistance and violence in the White community. Boston school committee members took the lead in denouncing Judge Garrity's ruling as inappropriate, undemocratic, and oppressive.

The power exercised by the school committee over school policy, and its reactionary role in the school desegregation controversy, made it a strategic target for insurgency action by Black political activists. For many years Black candidates campaigned for seats on the school committee but could not overcome obstacles produced by at-large election procedures that required that candidates mobilize votes from across the city. In 1959, NAACP education committee chair Ruth Batson became the first Black candidate to run for the school committee in the modern era. Although Batson received strong support in the Black community, she was not able to generate enough White votes citywide to win. Another Black politician, community activist Mel King, ran strong campaigns for the school committee in 1961, 1963, and 1965 but fell short of receiving the votes needed for election each time. John O'Bryant, a former Boston public school teacher, scored a landmark victory for the Black community in 1975 by winning a seat on the school committee, becoming the first Black person in the twentieth century to officially serve on this body. O'Bryant's victory was given a boost by his Irish-sounding name and the use of bullet voting techniques by Black voters who voted only for O'Bryant in the election.[3] O'Bryant was followed on the school committee in 1981 by Jean McGuire, a Black community activist with an Irish-sounding name who had been recruited to run for the school committee by O'Bryant in 1979 and had missed being elected in the earlier race by seventy-five votes.[4] In 1981 a massive citizen campaign to reform the electoral process resulted in a change in the structure of the school committee through a public referendum from a five-member at-large body, to a thirteen-member body with nine members elected from districts and four members elected at-large. One major consequence of the reform process was the election of two Black community representatives to the school committee in 1983, Shirley Owens-Hicks in District 4 and Grace Romero in District 7.[5] In later years, Juanita Wade and Gerald Anderson would also serve as representatives of the Black community on the school committee.

In the 1980s the school committee became an important source of reciprocal bargaining for the Black community. School committee members representing the Black community became high-profile, vocal advocates for policy innovations that would move the quest for Black progress to the center of the city's decision making processes. As a result of the active lobbying of its Black members, the school committee voted to hire, on separate occasions, two Black school superintendents, Laval Wilson and Lois Harrison-Jones. Over time, the center of gravity for Black policy action began to shift decisively in the direction of Black members of the school committee. Through their actions, the school committee became a major sounding board for the articulation of Black grievances across the entire spectrum of the political system. Here it should be noted that, in some respects, Black school committee members were in a better position to represent the interests of the Black community than Black city councillors because their policy priorities were more focused and their bases of political support were more independent of direct party control. Educational issues tend to be highly personal, establishing a uniquely sensitive relationship between elected educational officials and individual citizens in the Black community. As one respondent explained, "The school committee meeting is Wednesday. There is a forum for the debate of the issues. That leadership [of the school committee] was more immediate. It affects my daughter who goes to the Hernandez School. That leadership of the elected members of the school committee was most important."[6]

Apparently, Black citizens were not the only ones who recognized the pivotal linkage role played by elected Black school committee members. In the wake of escalating Black influence, major steps were taken by the downtown establishment to change the school committee from an elected to an appointed body. The campaign to change the committee in this fashion was initially led by Mayor Ray Flynn. Frustrated with his administration's efforts to control school policy indirectly, Flynn petitioned the state legislature to give the Mayor of Boston the power to appoint all thirteen members of the Boston School Committee. The petition was approved by the Massachusetts General Court in 1990, with the proviso that the issue would have to be revisited by the voters of Boston in the form of a referendum in six years. In keeping with the governing conditions of the legislation, a referendum on the structure of the school committee was held in November 1996. Mayor Menino strongly endorsed the idea of an appointed school committee and campaigned vigorously in its behalf. Despite strong countermobilization against the mayor's position in the Black community, citizens across the city voted to retain the appointed school committee structure.

> Many Black people were confused. The wording on the ballot made it difficult to determine if one was voting for or against the issue. The administration was also effective in making the point that six years was not long enough to assess the impact of the appointed committee's policies. Their argument was that school policies during the Menino administration were still in the experimental stage.[7]

In reality, the policy as well as the political consequences of the shift to an appointed school committee have substantially crystallized. One notable policy consequence, according to a number of respondents, has been the removal of progressive voices from the school committee devoted to policies of educational uplift for minority students.

> Our schools are not doing well. The school budget has not kept pace with the needs of our children. Except for the Latin School which is still the sacred preserve of the White privileged class, we do not have quality programs in fine arts, music, and language. Our children's test scores are down. We still have old line teachers that hated busing. The mayor [Menino] has refused to put liberals on the school committee with an agenda to save our schools from what Jonathan Kozol calls "savage inequality." He only picks people he can control—people who will dance to his music.[8]

Politically, structural reform has meant a reduction in the number of elected Black city officials from six to two, and the total elimination of Black officials elected citywide. A primary consequence of this reduction has been the elimination of a crucial source of community-based leadership and policy influence. Another significant consequence has been the consolidation and further centralization of mayoral authority and power over the Black public agenda. Mayoral appointment of the school committee has had the effect of creating a new contingent of Black political buffers. In addition, the boundary maintenance capabilities of the mayor's office have been greatly enhanced. By taking control of the school committee, the mayor has, at once, curtailed the boundaries of effective Black political action and sharply reduced the potency and salience of the school committee as a source of symbolic resonance, policy influence, and collective struggle.

Deep scars of division and rancor have been left in the Black community by the campaigns for and against the appointed school committee. The role of Black ministers in this controversy has been especially contentious. Black ministers were present in significant numbers to support the petition by Ray Flynn in the General Court to abolish the elected school committee. The campaign in the Black community by the Menino administration to retain the appointed school committee was also spearheaded by Black ministers working in close collaboration with top Black Mineno appointees. These actions by Black ministers have cemented their reputations as political buffers and stimulated continuing conflict and disunity in vital sectors of the Black political establishment. Commenting on the role of Black ministers in the school committee controversy during the Flynn administration, one respondent observed:

> In the pitch of the battle we had a referendum on the ballot concerning whether or not to abolish the elected school committee. It lost. Most people in the African American community wanted to keep it [the elected committee]. The mayor at that point went to the clergy. Fifteen Black clergy stood on the steps of the statehouse and held a press conference in 1990 and said "we want an appointed school committee." And one week later the legislature took a vote and abolished the elected school committee for the city of Boston. That's the kind of backwards, anticommunity role the Black clergy plays here.[9]

## The Massachusetts Black Legislative Caucus

In Boston, the Massachusetts Black Legislative Caucus constitutes another important potential source of alternative power for the Black community. The election of Blacks to the Massachusetts

state legislature dates back to 1867, the year Edwin Walker, a
Boston attorney and Charles Mitchell, a Boston printer, were
elected to serve one-year terms.[10] Since that time over thirty Black
persons have held seats in the Massachusetts General Court.

Black state legislators have played highly visible roles in Boston
politics. For many years political representation for the Black community in Boston rested exclusively in the hands of Black state legislators. While the at-large system consistently defeated Black
candidates for city offices, Black legislative candidates, running in
districts, were swept into office by majority Black constituencies.
This historic pattern carved out for Black state legislators the
unique role of being representatives of the Black community in state
and local affairs. Of this role of Black state legislators, State
Representative Byron Rushing noted:

> We didn't have Black city councillors because of at-large elections.
> Black people would call on Black state representatives to solve their
> problems rather than White councillors. Also, because of redistrict-
> ing, many of the Black voters that live in my district are from the
> same council district as South Boston. And since they are in a minor-
> ity [their city councillor will always come from South Boston] they call
> me up.[11]

The high visibility of Black state legislators was enhanced by the
reputations as political activists of several notable members of the
Boston delegation. Mel King's election to the legislature in 1972 was
achieved, in part, by his involvement in a number of protest actions
against racism in Boston.[12] Bill Owens, elected to the Massachusetts State Senate in 1972, gained his political spurs through the
Massachusetts Black Political Assembly and was a chief organizer
of school desegregation protest rallies in the 1960s.

Black state legislators have exhibited a positive orientation
toward community struggle and empowerment. In 1972 the
Massachusetts Black Legislative Caucus was formed to fight for
Black advancement in the wake of the election of five Black politicians to the state legislature: Doris Bunte, Bill Owens, Royal
Bolling Sr., Royal Bolling Jr., and Mel King (see figure 4.1). The legislative agenda of the caucus recognized the crucial intersection of
Black interests at the state and local level of governmental administration and politics.

The political and legislative accomplishments of the Black caucus have been impressive. It has fought relentlessly to obtain state
funding for education, housing, and health care programs for inner-

Figure 4.1. Massachusetts Black Legislative Caucus Members–1997

## SENATE

Dianne Wilkerson
2nd Suffolk District
*Committees:* Ways and Means, Insurance (Chairperson),
Local Affairs (Vice-Chairperson)

## HOUSE OF REPRESENTATIVES

Charlotte Golar-Richie
5th Suffolk District
*Committees:* Housing and Urban
Development (Chairperson)

Shirley Owens-Hicks
6th Suffolk District
*Committees:* Ways and Means,
Election Laws

Gloria Fox
7th Suffolk District
*Committees:* Ways and Means, Personnel
and Administration (Vice-Chairperson),
Public Service

Byron Rushing
9th Suffolk District
*Committees:* Ways and Means,
Personnel and Administration,
Transportation

Benjamin Swain
12th Hampden District
*Committees:* State Administration, Taxation

Alvin E. Thompson
28th Middlesex District
*Committees:* Rules (Vice-
Chairperson), Federal Financial
Assistance

Source: Adapted from data provided by the Massachusetts Black Legislative Caucus
Office.

city communities. Aggressive and creative lobbying by the caucus
resulted in the appropriation of state funds to build a new campus
for Roxbury Community College. Through its central office, located
in the statehouse in Boston, it has published research reports detail-
ing the voting records of members of the General Court on issues
relevant to the interests of the Black community. Legislative campaigns waged by the caucus have attempted to roll back redlining
practices in the Black community and block deep cuts in welfare
benefits for Black mothers.

To what extent have members of the Massachusetts Black
Legislative Caucus been able to transfer their power, authority, and
political skills to the arena of local governance? The data from this

study suggest that the lines of demarcation between city government and state government are too great to allow Black caucus
members to play more than a marginal role in the local linkage
process. Effective linkage in this sense requires that Black state legislators penetrate the arena of local decision making, disrupt the
usual flow of benefits, and activate the redistribution of social and
economic resources to the Black community. There is no evidence
that their bills or lobbying campaigns have achieved these results; it
is also clear that these political actions have not significantly
enhanced the ability of Black citizens to function as participant
equals in the policy making process. Despite laudable representational efforts by the caucus, Blacks in Boston remain largely disconnected from local arenas of power dominated by the "competitive
establishment."[13]

The institutional practice of home rule operates as a formidable
barrier to the transfer of state legislative power to the local arena. If
Black city councillors are often insulated from the central domains
of local power, Black state legislators encounter layers of insulation
that are immeasurably higher and thicker than those encountered
by city-based Black elected officials. Structural barriers inherent in
the concept of home rule means that mayors and city councils are
not legally obligated to consult with members of the legislature
before a multitude of major policy decisions are made. Although
technically these barriers can be contravened through informal
interaction, the racial character of the Boston city regime virtually
rules out the forging of these sorts of informal links with Black state
legislators on anything more than an ad hoc and superficial basis.
Effective linkage would also require that Black state legislators construct multiracial coalitions that would provide entree to the Black
community into the local governing coalition operating beyond the
mayor's office and the city council. The limited political base of their
legislative offices makes the construction of such coalitions an
impossible task.

> Black state representatives in Boston are prominent, but I don't see
> them having a lot of power. That's a problem in general here in
> Massachusetts. I grew up in Denver. We do not have a significant
> Black population relative to Boston. Two guys I grew up with,
> Wellington Webb is the mayor of Denver and now Norm Rice is the
> mayor of Seattle. Both these cities have relatively small Black popula-
> tions. But somehow both these individuals were able to cross  racial
> lines in terms of attracting voters to their campaigns. And I don't
> think those cities have a history of segregation that is as severe and
> restrictive as is Boston's. It's just difficult for candidates  to reach
> across lines here.[14]

Internal difficulties have impaired the ability of the Black legislative caucus to operate as a linkage agent in local politics. Caucus members have refused to consolidate their campaign resources into one umbrella organization; rather, they continue to run separate campaigns and to maintain their own campaign organizations. Although the caucus maintains a professional staff, staff activities rarely move beyond the central office to the broader Black community. A number of respondents blamed the limited outreach efforts of the caucus on the elected members. In this regard, one respondent observed:

> Very seldom do they [Black legislators] meet in the Black community to discuss the welfare of the people. They are nice people, but it appears to me they don't have what it takes to make the city do what needs to be done in the Black community. I have not seen them take the initiative to keep the Black community organized. It may happen sometime if someone is brutally beaten by the police, but after a point that will die down. I do not see on a regular, continuous basis Black state representative leadership here taking the type of leadership role they have been elected to do, even though they are some very nice people.[15]

Major components of the linkage process are missing from the political armor of Black state legislators. A meticulous look at their political history suggests that they have not—except on rare occasions—provided their local Black constituents with access to scarce resources. They also have not built indigenous organizational networks or substantially contributed to the growth of cognitive liberation and insurgency politics in the Black community. Hopeful signs in these directions have begun to emerge in the work of Representative Charlotte Golar-Richie, who is organizing community advising councils, and Shirley Owens-Hicks, who is organizing grassroots input into public education. Until these efforts become formally institutionalized into the routines of city governance, considerable power discrepancy between the Black community and downtown power elites will remain a key defining ingredient of the Boston political system.

## The Politics of Urban Regeneration

For the past fifty years the City of Boston has been caught up in a cycle of growth and development. Boston's regeneration history illuminates both the possibilities and the limitations of minority political linkage. The Boston story also provides a graphic illustration of the dire consequences that evolve when the benefits of regeneration are not shared with all sectors of the urban community.

From the very beginning, the central focus of regeneration policies in Boston has been on downtown development. The process has basically been managed by public officials and driven by the power, resources, convictions, and preferences of the business community. A central figure in the early regeneration process was Ed Logue, a professional administrator recruited by Mayor Collins from New Haven to head up the Boston Redevelopment Authority (BRA ). Logue used his connections inside the Ford Foundation to secure a grant under Ford's Gray Areas Program to establish Action for Boston Community Development, Inc. (ABCD).[16] This agency was designed to promote human development in the urban renewal process.[17] Missing from the strategic plans mounted by Logue's redevelopment machine were structural and political processes to promote and facilitate Black community linkage in the policy process. ABCD quickly became an urban bureaucracy controlled by elites in the interest of elites. With only one Black person, Melnea Cass, on its board, ABCD was in a poor position to understand or address the fundamental needs of low-income Black citizens.[18]

Under Logue, urban renewal became a synonym for Black removal. As Mel King has noted, a central tenet of the Boston Master Plan for development was the revitalization of inner-city residents out of their neighborhoods.[19] Thus the demolition of the South End became an essential element of the Master Plan, driving displaced Black citizens to affordable housing in Lower Roxbury. Blacks in Lower Roxbury would find this community to be only a temporary safe harbor. City development plans moved in concentric circles, transferring urban space from Black to White hands. A critical component of the Master Plan was the redevelopment of the Southwest Corridor. The initial proposal by the city called for an artery of connecting expressways that would run across the 128 technology corridor, connect with I 95, cut across the Melnea Cass connection, link up with I 93 and then swing directly into downtown. If implemented, this artery would run directly through the Black community, disrupting the lives of Black families in countless ways. Black community groups mounted energetic protests and successfully blocked the implementation of the redevelopment design.

A pivotal objective of the initial design was to force Blacks out of Lower Roxbury into Jamaica Plain and Roslindale. When the I 95 artery was blocked, this objective was not abandoned. The plan for Lower Roxbury was reconceptualized. Instead of an expressway, the public transportation system would be reconfigured to facilitate Black movement out of prime real estate in the heart of Boston. The crux of the new design was the movement of the rapid transit or "T" system off of the streets and onto existing Am Track rails. The following respondent explained the logic of this decision.

> They moved the tracks onto the Am Track lines. This is the current location of the Orange Line. This line became the feeder up the Southwest Corridor. It takes the traffic coming from downtown through Chinatown, Jackson Square, Ruggles, and into Jamaica Plain and Forest Park. The Orange Line parallels the direction I 95 was going to run before community protests. On the other side the Red Line goes through Quincy and splits off into Mattapan. This development of the transportation corridor has facilitated and encouraged the redistribution of the minority population into Jamaica Plain, Rosalindale, and Mattapan.[20]

The movement outward of the Black population has made Roxbury a primary focus of urban gentrification. For developers, Lower Roxbury has the advantage of being only two and one-half miles from the center of downtown Boston. Given the paucity of available land for development downtown, Roxbury stands as an ideal location for downtown expansion. Roxbury is also one of the few sites in the central city with large parcels of vacant land. The strategic position of Lower Roxbury has stimulated strenuous efforts by private developers to push Blacks out of this community. These efforts are buttressed by city policies that raise property taxes, encourage condominium conversions, and increase the price of rental units beyond the reach of low-income citizens[21]

> Many of the streets where Black people used to live in Roxbury are now all White. Black people are not allowed the opportunity to buy back into that community because of the cost of real estate in that area. Blacks have not only been displaced; the community has been divided. They have a lot of redlining going on where Black people are only allowed to buy in certain areas. Then they had this scam going on where these bankers along with these White real estate agents were going into Roxbury and getting these people to sign these papers to get their houses renovated, and they ended up losing their homes. They couldn't keep up the high mortgages. The interest rates fluctuated. Many people who lost their homes had owned them for generations. The real estate people would take the homes and resale them for a much higher price. A lot of people ended up as tenants in their own homes. Charles Yancey was real useful in stopping banks from foreclosing on a lot of people's homes in the area.[22]

The physical stability of the inner city is further threatened by the development policies of Boston-based colleges and universities. Northeastern University, which sits adjacent to Dudley Station—a key transportation zone in the Black community—has attempted to win the support of its Black neighbors by offering scholarships to neighborhood youth. The development programs of Harvard and MIT are far less benign.

> MIT's interest is mainly in Cambridge messing with the African American community there. Harvard goes both sides of the river. Nothing stops them. They are the ones who managed to make sure Mission Hill would turn out the way that it did by destroying housing that had been there. All that's gone because of the hospital expansion. That whole hospital area is their baby. Mission Main and Mission Extension is the place where they are going to warehouse poor folks. That development was their concession to the community; they would put up this stuff to house the people that were displaced. And what you wind up with is another warehousing situation. So Harvard's power is extremely important.[23]

The Black community's role in the regeneration process has been subordinate, discontinuous, and, for the most part, ineffectual. A middle-class Black group, led by Otto and Muriel Snowden, the founders of Freedom House, received limited incorporation during the Logue era when the BRA approved a plan by this group to launch a pilot urban renewal program in the Washington Park section of Roxbury.[24] Concessions to low-income Black groups were made only after bitter, hard struggle. In 1968 the Community Assembly for a United South End (CAUSE ) protested the BRA's demolition of Black homes by establishing a tent city on a municipal parking lot. Strong pressure by CAUSE led to the passage by the city council of legislation establishing an urban renewal committee that included membership by community residents. This legislation was later modified to insure continuing BRA control over the decision making process.[25]

## Ray Flynn: The Value of Public Intervention

Black community input into the urban regeneration process was maximized during the administration of Ray Flynn. Flynn embraced a progressive urban agenda that stressed balanced growth between downtown and the neighborhoods. Responding to pressure from housing activists and neighborhood associations, Flynn sponsored tenant protection legislation that attempted to re-institutionalize rent control.[26] This legislation sought to reverse the decontrol reforms of the White administration and directly address one of the most critical economic problems in the Black commu-nity—skyrocketing rents attributable to gentrification, condo con-versions, and a diminishing supply of quality housing.

Flynn also introduced a link development program requiring downtown office and institutional developers to pay $6.00 per square foot over a period of seven years into a pool of funds that would be used by the city to promote neighborhood development. This program produced $70 million in added housing revenue and resulted in the construction of over ten thousand units of affordable housing.[27] Flynn matched the link development program with an inclusionary housing initiative requiring developers of market rate housing to set aside a percentage of their units for occupancy by low- and moderate-income citizens. This initiative resulted in the con-struction of four hundred low- and moderate-income housing units that would not have materialized without the intervention of the Flynn administration.[28]

The policy innovations introduced by Flynn had political as well as social and economic implications. Flynn took steps to incorporate neighborhood organizations and housing activist groups into strate-gic positions in the urban regeneration process. Neighborhood coun-cils and planning/zoning advisory committees were established to participate directly in project planning, project review, and the making of zoning recommendations for neighborhoods to the BRA[29] Flynn also encouraged the formation of nonprofit groups to develop, manage, and maintain low- and moderate-income housing. This was a bold and pathbreaking move because it decentralized the process of inner-city housing development out of the BRA, the BHA, and city hall and placed it fundamentally in the hands of nonprofit commu-nity development corporations (CDCs).

Under Flynn, CDCs in Boston became major vehicles for the pro-motion of housing objectives and potential sources of reciprocal bar-gaining for the Black community.[30] CDCs became useful instruments for the promotion of inner-city housing objectives because of their unique ability to assemble funding from the variety of sources required to produce affordable housing in a competitive market place.[31] The emergence of CDCs in Boston was not a unique phenomenon but an integral part of a national movement that saw CDCs across the country fill in the void left by the strategic with-

drawal of federal dollars and technical assistance for the construction of low- and moderate-income housing in America's central
cities.[32]

For Flynn, CDCs served an avowedly political purpose: they crystallized and cemented his base of support in the neighborhoods and
among radical social activists by magnifying his image as a populist
mayor dedicated to giving "power to the people." To make the transfer
of power more than symbolic, Flynn made abandoned city property
available to CDCs at reduced costs, as low as one dollar, and assisted
them in securing mortgages and grants from the private market and
tax abatements and tax credits from public agencies. A number of
CDCs providing services to the Black community have been direct beneficiaries of Flynn's housing innovations. Among the most prominent
are Lena Park Community Development Corporation, Dorchester Bay
Development Corporation, Quincy-Geneva Housing Development
Corporation, Madison Park Community Development Corporation,
Grove Hall Neighborhood Development Corporation, Lower Roxbury
Community Development Corporation, Roxbury Multi-Service
Center, Jamaica Plain Development Corporation, and the Dudley
Street Neighborhood Initiative (DSNI ). Ties between the Flynn
administration and DSNI became permanently forged when Flynn
approved DSNI's request to the BRA for eminent domain authority.
Founded in 1984 through an initial grant from the Riley Foundation,
DSNI has become a national model for community development
through the marriage of public and private resources. DSNI has established Dudley Neighbors, Inc. (DNI), as a land trust to ensure ownership of land by the residents of the Dudley Triangle.[33] DNI purchases
land and then leases the land to residents over a ninety-nine-year
period. DSNI is involved in the construction and selling of affordable
housing, community organizing, the controlling of vacant land, and the
creation and implementation of a comprehensive plan.[34]

Did Flynn's policy innovations create effective political linkage
for the Black community? While the Black community's political
position was enhanced in the urban regeneration process by Flynn,
major power transfers or radical changes in policy direction did not
occur. Under Flynn, Blacks continued to operate at the substructure
of power. Only one Black person, Doris Bunte, head of the BHA, rose
to the summit of decision making authority in the arena of regeneration during the Flynn administration. Notably missing from the
linkage equation were organized Black political action groups capable of not only making demands but of participating in the policy
process in ways to assure that Black policy objectives would be real-

ized. In the absence of such organizations, Blacks were dependent on the good will and altruism of Flynn to develop distributional networks to deliver crucial social and economic benefits to the Black community.

At the community level, CDCs were poorly equipped to function as instruments of political power for the Black community in the policy-making process. The creative work of the Flynn administration did not drive real estate developers and corporate executives from the front ranks of the urban regeneration process. As political units, CDCs have been disadvantaged by the fact that their policy objectives run counter to the policy preferences of dominant business interests in Boston. CDCs operate most effectively in cities where a favorable business climate is supportive of their work.[35] Boston is not such a city. Decentralization of housing responsibilities into the hands of CDCs was achieved by Flynn against the wishes and over the staunch opposition of the business community.[36]

Because the scope of the activities of CDCs is usually limited to a particular geographic area, the ability of these enterprises to deliver political benefits for the entire community is innately circumscribed. It should be noted in this regard that in Boston, no cohesive citywide network of CDCs has materialized. Additional external obstacles to the political work of Black community CDCs arise from competition from a host of CDCs providing services to the Latino community. Indeed, the footprints of a CDC like Inquilinos Boricuas en Accion are very large and cannot be ignored. Since 1966 this Latino CDC has developed 850 units of housing, a small commercial center, a cultural center, a child development center, and a credit union.[37]

Another possible source of competition for Black community CDCs is the enterprise zone project operating in the Black community under the authority of the Boston Empowerment Center. The Black community enterprise zone project is one facet of a larger development program, an enhanced enterprise community. The comprehensive program encompasses seven communities in the central part of Boston ranging from Mattapan to China Town and the new industrial park in South Boston.[38] A grant from the federal government in 1995 gave Boston's enhanced enterprise community a total of $25 million–$22 million for economic development and $3 million for human services. An additional $22 million was generated under the Department of Housing and Urban Development's Section 108 program. A careful leveraging of federal dollars in the private market has elevated the total amount available for the enhanced enterprise community to $95 million. This process has resulted in the establishment of partnerships between the city and five major banks: the Bank of Boston, U.S. Trust, Fleet, Citizens, and State Street. All five primary bank partners have made commitments to contribute at least $1 million a year to economic development, with the Bank of Boston and Fleet agreeing to contribute $2 million annually.[39]

Successful CDCs must be able to obtain public support beyond their indigenous community base. The Menino administration has given no indication that it shares the Flynn administration's concern for decentralized regeneration initiatives. Since the Empowerment Center is, above all, an agency of city government and an instrument of city hall politics, important questions can be raised regarding its willingness to serve as a source or conduit of financial support for Black community-based CDCs. Thus far, the primary thrust of the Empowerment Center's work has been the establishment of viable links between private lenders and individual business entrepreneurs in the enhanced enterprise community. In cooperation with the Small Business Center of the University of Massachusetts Boston, the Empowerment Center is sponsoring a twenty-week course to train minority entrepreneurs to develop business plans that will meet the stringent requirements for funding by banks as well as the center itself. Primary start-up funds are secured from private lenders; the Empowerment Center provides subordinate or "mezzanine" funding to make proposals from minority clients more attractive to private lenders. The Empowerment Center also provides ongoing technical assistance to minority businesses seeking to reach the takeoff stage of development. Given its emphasis on business development, the activities of the Empowerment Center may well be largely incompatible with the housing-centered public agenda of community based CDCs.

### The Bias of Urban Regeneration

City-directed regeneration strategies have manifested a distinct class bias in the Black community. The primary beneficiaries of these strategies have been Black developers who have effectively positioned themselves to take advantage of link development programs created by the Flynn administration. A parcel-to-parcel program authored by Ricardo Millett, deputy director of the BRA under

Flynn, gave to Black developers a piece of the neighborhood redevelopment action. This program resulted in primary participation by Black developers in major construction projects in the Black community, such as the building of a site for the State Water Resources Department and Bureau of Motor Vehicle Registration in Lower Roxbury and the construction of a new police headquarters in the Dudley Triangle. Although these projects have favorably served the economic interests of Black developers, their impact on community development has been negligible.

> There is major confusion in the Black community over the issue of what constitutes development. Economic growth projects have been touted as vehicles for economic development. It is that confusion that has allowed the police headquarters to be moved to the middle of the Southwest Corridor in the name of community development. From my perspective, community development is about building the capacity and expanding the power of the community. I don't see how building the police headquarters there does any more than provide some workers short-term employment and some Black developers an opportunity to make a lot of money. The Water Resource Building is now vacant. The development of that parcel came as a result of Black elite support for a small cadre of people who worked for [Democratic Governor] Dukakis. As a residual of the Dukakis campaign they [Black developers] were able to leverage state contracts. That was the payoff. The city said in return for your support we will give you the police headquarters. Public-sector projects supporting elite developers, and a few Black workers get jobs. And what's the residual in terms of building the capacity for the community and real development? I suggest it's very little.[40]

At the grassroots level, community organizations like the Dudley Street Neighborhood Initiative have not provided the kind of comprehensive leadership required to reverse the mobilization of bias against low-income Black citizens endemic in the regeneration process. The following respondent commented on the limited organizational reach of DSNI:

> Persons who tend to be active in DSNI are folk who can afford to be active. They haven't done anything for folk who are renters. A lot of tenants are living in substandard housing conditions that everyone knows about. The organizing of that group by DSNI is not happening. DSNI is notorious; if its not in the Dudley Neighborhood, you don't see them. When we were doing mobilization around the [Reverend Accelynne] Williams's death, no one from DSNI was there; they were conspicuously absent. They have a three-part development agenda,

physical development, which is housing and infrastructure, economic development, and something they call "human development." This is where I have the strongest criticism. Anything that didn't fit into economic development or physical development that was still an issue got dropped into human development. So everything from family day care to doing a communitywide forum on the war on poverty became defined as human development The political work that was needed in Dudley never happened. We have nothing defending us.[41]

Serious efforts are now being undertaken to strengthen the functional impact of community organizations. These efforts are being spearheaded by Ken Wade, district director for New England of an organization called "Neighborhood Reinvestment." This agency specializes in providing technical and financial assistance and training to groups involved in the development of affordable housing. Created and funded by Congress in 1978, Neighborhood Reinvestment provides support for a network of 180 community groups nationwide. In Boston it has principally been involved with encouraging and facilitating the merger of the Quincy-Geneva Housing Development Corporation and the Grove Hall Neighborhood Development Corporation. The merger is designed to reduce competition by community organizations for external funding and to create a stronger organization that can better serve the community. Despite the important work of Neighborhood Reinvestment, a large gap in the political resources of community organizations remains. These organizations continue to search for the keys to translating their operational resources into political capital that can assist in lifting the Black community from its perpetual place at the bottom of Boston's power hierarchy.

Defense and promotion of community interests constitutes an important dimension of Black city politics. The dilemmas of the Black community in Boston in the urban regeneration process are, at bottom, reflections of the problem of weak linkage and weak incorporation in the political process. These issues run to the heart of the present and future status of the Black community in the Boston political system.

# 5

## Boston: Strategic Dimensions of Black Politics

### The Politics of Protest

In the preceding two chapters, we have discussed the structural dimensions of power in Boston. These structural factors, as independent variables, shed penetrating light on the continuing subordination of Blacks in Boston in the city's political and racial hierarchy. The direction and character of Black politics in Boston have been sharply defined by the behavioral responses of Black political actors to the isolation of the Black community from critical arenas of power and decision making. A careful reading of Black political history in Boston suggests quite firmly that Black Bostonians have not been passive in their responses to racial subordination and discrimination. As has been the case with Blacks in Liverpool and other Black Atlantic cities, Blacks in Boston have often adopted protest strategies in their efforts to overcome the burdens and tribulations of structured racial inequality. In the context of racial politics in Boston, protest has not only functioned as a political resource for the Black community, but has served as a vital force in the generation of other valuable political resources. Blacks in Boston have clearly understood the crucial political role of protest and have often resorted to this strategy in their quest for social and economic advancement.

Black protest politics has deep and venerable roots in Boston history. In the nineteenth century Boston was the locus of militant activities by Black abolitionists. William C. Nell and Benjamin Roberts spearheaded the effort in 1826 to form the Massachusetts General Colored Association, an organization devoted to the abolition of slavery.[1] This organization was the political home of David

105

Walker, a militant Black activist whose incendiary appeal for slave insurrections sent shock waves throughout the Southern slave empire.[2] A number of Black Boston leaders were members of the American Anti-slavery Society headed by William Lloyd Garrison. Among this group were Lewis and Harriet Hayden, John T. Hilton, John B. Vashon, Susan Paul, and William D. Logan.[3] Boston served as a terminus for the Underground Railroad. The downtown home of Lewis and Harriet Hayden was the best known rendezvous for runaway slaves in the Northeast.[4] Black churches such as Charles Street A.M.E. Church and Twelfth Street Baptist Church functioned as havens for runaway slaves. The hosting of antislavery meetings featuring nationally recognized speakers such as Frederick Douglass became a cardinal component of the religious and social mission of many Black Boston churches.[5]

Nineteenth-century Black protest politics embraced both local and national issues. A petition signed by Blacks in 1846 sought to abolish segregation in the Boston Public Schools. The petition was rejected by the Primary School Committee; the committee suggested that the maintenance of an all-Black school in Boston was not a violation of the constitutional rights of Black citizens. A second petition by 202 Black citizens in 1849 produced the same response. The refusal by the Supreme Judicial Court to overturn the position of the Primary School Committee precipitated community protest rallies led by William C. Nell. Responding, in part, to Black pressure, the Massachusetts State Legislature passed a law in 1855 making racially segregated schools in Boston illegal.[6]

The end of de jure segregation did not mean that policies of racial segregation would not continue to rob the Black community of its civil rights. During the second half of the nineteenth century, the cause of racial uplift would be taken up by Black ministers. Reverend Leonard A. Grimes of Twelfth Street Baptist Church moved decisively into the fight for civil rights through his campaign to secure the right for Black soldiers to join the Union Army.[7] At Charles Street A.M.E. Church, Reverend John T. Jennifer preached a strong brand of social gospel, one that encouraged militant protests, vigorously supported the passage of civil rights laws, and railed against the nullification of the Civil Rights Act of 1875 by the Supreme Court in 1883.[8] Similar progressive positions were taken by Reverend Matthew A. N. Shaw of Twelfth Street Baptist Church and Reverend Peter Randolph of Ebernezer Baptist Church.[9]

The turn of the twentieth century would witness the arrival on the Boston scene of a new contingent of civil rights leaders associated with the Niagara Movement.[10] Towering above this group was one of the twentieth century's most militant and important Black political activists: William Monroe Trotter. A native of Boston and a graduate of Harvard, Trotter was deeply committed to an agenda of racial equality. Obsessed with exposing Booker T. Washington as a traitor to Black people, Trotter used his newspaper, the *Guardian* (founded in 1901), as a vehicle to attack Washington and espouse a political program of social equality and racial democracy. He drew banner headlines in 1903 from an incident the White press labeled "The Boston Riot." Trotter and his supporters launched a verbal attack against Washington during a speech Washington gave at the Columbus Avenue A.M.E. Church. A general melee broke out when cayenne pepper was tossed up to the pulpit, causing Washington to cough and wheeze. In the aftermath, Trotter was fined $50.00 and given a thirty-day jail sentence.[11]

William Monroe Trotter's public career was permanently engraved in the soil of protest. In 1915 Trotter led nearly two thousand demonstrators to the State House to protest the showing in Boston of the racist movie *The Birth of a Nation*. Moving to the national level, Trotter led a group of Blacks to the White House in 1914 to protest the segregation of Black federal employees in government offices by President Woodrow Wilson. Trotter also campaigned in Washington in 1918, under the banner of the National Liberty Congress, to make Wilson's promises of "new freedom" a reality at home for Black soldiers who fought for the freedom of Whites in Europe.[12]

Trotter's influence on the struggle for civil rights in Boston waned in the wake of the founding of the National Association for the Advancement of Colored People (NAACP). The first branch of this historic organization was organized in Boston in 1911. For the next fifty years the campaign for Black equality in Boston would be dominated by the strategic and programmatic agenda of the NAACP. The Marcus Garvey movement did not provide significant competition for the NAACP in Boston. Although Garvey was very popular among West Indians in Boston, his movement failed to gain a formidable foothold among rank and file African Americans.[13] A. Phillip Randolph also failed to weaken the political influence of the NAACP in Boston. The Sleeping Car Porter's Union in Boston was one of the few in the nation to operate independently of Randolph's Brotherhood of Sleeping Car Porters.[14]

Control by the NAACP over nonelectoral Black political mobilization had a dampening effect on street-level protest politics. For the most part, street-level protests were limited to demonstrations over the issues of jobs and voter registration.[15] The principal focus of the action agenda of the Boston branch of the NAACP was legal representation of Black interests in the courts. This approach was in keeping with the primary political orientation of the national organization. It also reflected the neoconservative proclivities of the Black church, one of the main allies and financial supporters of the Boston branch. The agenda of the NAACP also provided a vivid indication of the immense control registered over the organization by Boston Black elites, sometimes referred to as the "Black Brahmins."

The Black elite in Boston functioned as a social gentry; many of its members could trace their ancestry back to the era of the first Black Boston settlers. For many years Boston's Black elite had served as brokers and peacemakers in the politics of race. They believed their interest and that of the community could best be served by the avoidance of controversy rather than the promotion of racial conflict. This belief motivated Black elites to maintain social, physical, and political distance from low-income Black immigrants moving into Boston in increasingly heavy numbers from the South and the West Indies. These concerns were reflected in the policy orientation of the NAACP. Members of the Black elite infiltrated the key policy committees of the NAACP, moving the political orientation of the organization in the direction of reconciliation rather than confrontation. This approach was compatible with the personal philosophy of Butler Wilson, who became president of the Boston branch in 1916 and remained in that position for twenty years. The concept of reconciliation translated into an inviolate commitment to integration. The commitment to integration was spawned by the alleged threat of a low-income Black invasion into elite neighborhoods. Black elites feared that middle- and upper-income Whites would move out of racially mixed neighborhoods, leaving Blacks who were well off vulnerable to a massive influx into their neighborhoods of poor Blacks from the South.[16] With this fear in mind, the Black elite prevailed upon the NAACP to push indefatigably for housing and school integration.

## The Movement for Civil Rights

The political hegemony of the NAACP could not withstand the decentralizing impact of the Civil Rights movement. This movement catapulted onto the political scene in Boston a host of grassroots actors with little reverence for the superior leadership role played by the NAACP over the previous fifty years. The Civil Rights movement brought to the Black community heightened political consciousness and a profound commitment to grassroots political activism. In the wake of these developments, the NAACP was compelled to relinquish its monopolistic control over the structuring and implementation of Black protest strategies.

The national campaign of militant Black protest in the 1960s found its political equivalent in Boston in the plethora of community-based struggles mounted by grassroots organizations during this turbulent decade. At the center of the storm was the Boston Urban League under the leadership of community activist Mel King. When he became executive director of the Urban League in 1967, King inherited an organization whose limited programmatic agenda was fixed principally on training unskilled Black workers for positions in local industries. Beyond this goal, the League focused on establishing links with a variety of public service institutions for the central purpose of enhancing the quality of their service responsiveness to the fundamental needs of the Black community.[17] King quickly concluded that the League needed to play a more decisive role in the lives of Black people. Within a few short months, King transformed the League into a political protest organization based on the philosophy of community development through community control.[18] This philosophy was the driving force behind the decision to move the League from downtown to the Black community and to change its name to "The New Urban League."

King's strategy was a product of a new political orientation by Black community activists that called for the hammering out of innovative strategies to place pressure on the downtown power structure for fundamental change. The specific objective of the new strategies was to use the mobilization resources of the Black community to promote Black advancement in economic development, housing, health, education, and other primary policy areas. It is important to note that the undergirding analysis viewed protest, not electoral mobilization, as the key agent in the process of change. Blacks in Boston watched as political activists in other northern cities brought the strategies of the southern Civil Rights movement home with great success. Given the wide gulf in the quality of life of Blacks and Whites in Boston, it made sense to use protest strategies perfected elsewhere to challenge the dominant governing regime in a city often dubbed the "cradle of liberty."

Black political activists began to make significant headway on many fronts. At the top of the political agenda was the issue of jobs. With the help of the New Urban League, a new Black union, United Community Construction Workers (UCCW), was formed. This action was taken following the mass firing of 100 Black workers recruited for a White construction firm by community agencies. The workers had been hired to participate in the rehabilitation of thirteen apartment blocks containing two-thousand units of low-income housing.[19]The Black worker recruitment effort was intended as a response to the unemployment crisis in the Black community and as a beginning step in the involvement of Blacks in the physical reconstruction of blighted areas in the Black community. UCCW was organized to fill the breach in the institutional foundation of the Black community in the areas of jobs, collective bargaining, and community representation in the building trades industry.[20]

Despite the influence wielded by UCCW, Blacks remained underrepresented on construction projects in the Boston area. To attack this problem, the New Urban League recruited college students to make demands on their schools that construction companies with projects on their campuses comply with federal guidelines relating to the employment of minority workers. Another campaign, led by community activist Chuck Turner, under the banner of a new organization called the "Boston Jobs Coalition," sought to reserve Boston jobs for Boston people. The following respondent commented on the central issues in this campaign:

> We wanted to say that at least 50 percent of the public jobs created in Boston should go to Boston people. That was actually an antiracist position because the building trades—which is one of the most racist unions in this area—though they may have Irish names, they are not living in Southie. They are living in Milton, Randolph; they are living way the hell out of the city, and they are the ones getting the jobs. So this policy was going to shake that up, getting Boston jobs for Boston residents. The jobs issue has been very important here.[21]

Mel King made the jobs issue a part of his platform during the preliminary contest for mayor in 1979. Incumbent Mayor Kevin White cut the ground from under King by issuing an executive order approving the job quota proposal advanced by the Boston Jobs Coalition.[22]

Strong Black protest also surfaced around the issue of police brutality. Black citizens still talk angrily about the "police riots" in 1967 when the police injured a number of community residents during a raid on the Grove Hall branch of the Welfare Department in Roxbury to break up a sit-in by welfare mothers protesting their treatment by welfare officials. In retaliation, community residents gutted the Grove Hall area, destroying a major commercial strip in the Black community. Black parents continue to complain about the strip searching by police of young Black men during the Charles Stuart episode. In 1983, the fatal wounding by the police of Levi Hart precipitated a march by Black citizens to the downtown court house and a police precinct. The Black community also raised questions regarding the police's failure to thoroughly investigate a string of murders of young Black women. Community organizations have often been formed to deal with police issues, among them the Community Justice Organization, Crisis, and Concerned Citizens Against Police Brutality. Boycotts and marches have been used to protest alleged police improprieties and other forms of discrimination against the Black community. The most memorable such event was Stop-Day, a citywide boycott called on 26 June 1963 by an ad hoc Black coalition to dramatize the plight of Black people in Boston. All Black citizens and sympathetic White citizens were asked to refrain from work, patronizing places of amusement, and using the mass transit system on the day selected for the boycott. Hubie Jones, community activist and university administrator, recalled that Stop-Day was controversial but extremely beneficial.

> We thought that there was needed a larger action to send a message straight across the city that Black folk were sick and tired about a range of things. Stop-Day stirred a lot of controversy in the Black community as well as in the city. There were major efforts to stop us from going ahead with Stop-Day. Some Black leaders decided to call a rally on the Boston Commons as a memorial to Medgar Evers on the day we had selected as Stop-Day. The then attorney general Ed Brooke got involved in it. Brooke called a meeting to discuss the issue. I got a call from someone saying, hey Hubie you've got to get down to St. Mark's Social Center because Ed Brooke is here and this place is jammed. There are a whole set of issues on the table. And the Stop issue is coming up at11:00, so you had better be here to speak to these issues. Stop succeeded in the sense there were three thousand people who came to the Carter Playground. We had a march into town. When we walked into the Boston Commons, that place erupted with a positive response. We claimed the attention of people's minds. We proved that people could be organized even when there was great dissension in the Black community when the thing got hot.[23]

The search for freedom, justice, and equality through protest in Boston in the 1960s was not unique. All across the Black Atlantic, Black citizens would be compelled to take up the strategy of protest during this transformative decade.

## The Politics of School Desegregation

The issue of public education has occupied a premier place in the protest agenda of the Black community in Boston. For many years Black citizens have been highly critical of the quality of the education Black students have received in the Boston Public School System. As early as 1958 Paul Parks, a professional engineer and member of a group called "Citizens for Boston Public Schools," had conducted a survey that documented in graphic terms the fact that Black youngsters were the victims of overt racial discrimination in the Boston Public Schools.

> My study showed that there was a lack of Black principals, a lack of permanent Black teachers, less money was being spent on predomi- nantly Black schools in this city than on White schools, our drop-out rates were higher because Black students weren't being taught, and they were using books and pencils and paper that had been used by other schools. They were tattered and torn but still sent down to the Black schools to be used by our kids.[24]

The impact of racism on the performance of Black youngsters was so grim that many Black parents began a feverish search for alter- natives to public education. Black parents complained that Black schools were overcrowded, obsolete, and dysfunctional. They found the school committee's solution to these problems—holding double sessions—completely unacceptable. One alternative solution was the identification of vacant seats in White schools; Black youngsters could be bused to these schools to occupy these seats through funds raised from private sources. This idea was the genesis of a private busing program founded in 1964, Operation Exodus. Within two years of its founding, Operation Exodus was busing 976 students a year at an annual cost of $65,000.[25] A parallel, and decidedly larger, busing program was launched in 1965 designed to transfer Black students from the central city to suburban school districts. This pro- gram was the Metropolitan Council for Educational Opportunity (METCO). The METCO program was born out of a voluntary agree- ment between Black parents and suburban school officials that fashioned a one-way busing scheme, from city to suburb. For many Black parents, METCO has become the educational program of choice. Jean McGuire, director of METCO, discussed the popularity of this program and its educational impact.

> There is an average five-year wait to get into our program. Most of the students on the waiting list are first grade or kindergarten. We now have 14,000 people on the waiting list. The most I ever replace are 250 seniors every year, about 7 percent of the senior class numbers in Boston. On average 75 to 79 percent of our kids go on to college. It's getting harder because colleges are more expensive, and the grants were limited and decreased under the Republican administration.[26]

The Boston Public School System is the only reasonable option for most Black parents. Consequently, strategies for educational improvement for Black students have focused mainly on intrasystem reform. The central target of the reform process has been school segregation. Widespread patterns of housing segregation have made school segregation a prominent feature of the Boston Public School System. An Advisory Committee on Racial Imbalance and Education appointed by the state education commissioner reported in 1965 that half of Boston's Black students (about 10,400) attended 28 schools that were at least 80 percent Black. The report identified 16 schools in the heart of the Black community that were over 90 percent Black.[27] Many Black parents blamed the maintenance of segregated schools and the adverse consequences of segregation on the educational achievements of Black youngsters on a host of policy decisions made by the Boston School Committee. They believed that these decisions made the school committee legally culpable since the decisions were in violation of the 1954 Supreme Court school desegregation ruling.

Black political protest in Boston has centered around the goal of eradicating segregation from the public school system. One early source of pressure for desegregation was the desire by Black elites to protect their neighborhoods from the movement into Boston of poor Blacks from the South. Using their influence on the education committee of the NAACP, Black elites initiated talks with members of the school committee regarding steps that needed to be taken to preserve and promote integrated education in the Boston Public School System. Initial talks between Paul Parks, a member of the NAACP Education Committee, and Louise Day Hicks, chair of the Boston School Committee, appeared promising. Hicks seemed to be sympathetic to the plight of Black students and amenable to working out a plan that would lead to forthright action on the issue of desegregation. But shortly after the meeting with Parks, Hicks changed her position, making it clear that she could not—for political reasons—carry the flag for desegregation on the school committee. Over the next twelve months, Hicks would become the symbol of White opposition to school desegregation in Boston. Paul Parks explained the reasons for this dramatic reversal by Hicks on the school desegregation issue.

> I asked her [Hicks] if she would meet with a group of Black parents at Freedom House. I wanted her to address the concerns of the Black parents in terms of their kids' education. So I went down to South Boston and picked her up and brought her over to Freedom House. On the trip back home she said "Paul this is absolutely awful. We have got to do something about this. There is no reason for Black youngsters to be suffering this way in our school system." So I am saying maybe we've made a hit here. The next day she called me and said "Can I talk with you." I said sure. She said "Paul I am sorry I can't help you. I was told by Superintendent Gillis [who was superintendent of schools] that if I came out and made any statement on this I would never win an election again." And that was the day she turned and began to be that image of racism that was demeaning to Black youngsters and their parents.[28]

Under the leadership of Louise Day Hicks, the Boston School Committee staked out an obstinate and highly visible position on school desegregation reform. Much of the committee's opposition to desegregation was politically driven. Hicks seized upon the desegregation issue as an avenue for raising her public visibility and expanding her political base in White ethnic communities. The political strategy was effective, eventually propelling Hicks to a seat on the city council, a seat in congress, and to the doorstep of the mayor's office.

The politics of school desegregation in Boston evolved over time into a confrontational dance between the Boston School Committee and Black political activists. On 4 June 1963 the education committee of the NAACP called for a public meeting with the school committee to discuss the status of Black students in the public school system. The meeting, held on 11 June drew a capacity audience. Ruth Batson, chair of the NAACP's Education Committee, made a passionate plea for members of the school committee to take affirmative steps to eliminate de facto segregation from the Boston Public School System. In response, the school committee flatly refused to acknowledge the legitimacy of the claim that de facto segregation existed in the Boston Public Schools. On this issue School Superintendent Frederick Gillis noted: "The Boston Public School districts are determined by school population in relation to building capacities, distances between homes and schools, and unusual traffic patterns. They aren't bound by ethnic or religious factors."²⁹ This became the official position of the Boston School Committee.

The intractable position taken by the school committee on the school desegregation issue ignited a storm of political opposition in the Black community. Formal Black resistance began to spread beyond the boundaries of the NAACP. One day after the confrontation with the school committee, on 18 June, two community leaders, Canon James Breeden, of St. James Episcopal Church and Noel Day, director of St. Marks Social Center, both affiliated with Massachusetts Citizens for Human Rights, called for a community boycott of schools, to protest de facto segregation in the public schools. Billed as Stay Out for Freedom, this protest drew the support of 8,260 students, including 3,000 Black students in attendance at 10 "freedom schools."³⁰ Intransigence by the school committee lead to a second school boycott on 26 February 1964 called "Freedom Stay Out." On this occasion, 20,571 pupils stayed out of school, with over 9,000 students in attendance at 57 freedom schools. A related mass march on city hall drew 1,800 participants. Among the march's special guests were James Bevels of the Southern Leadership Conference and Roy Wilkins national president of the NAACP.

Outside pressure on the school committee to change its position came from several sources: a report from the Massachusetts Advisory Committee on Racial Imbalance calling for the elimination of one-race schools, the passage of a Racial Imbalance Act by the Massachusetts legislature, the freezing of $52 million in state revenue for the Boston schools by the State Board of Education, and the cutting off of $7.5 million in federal funds for public education by the Department of Health, Education, and Welfare. Dr. Martin Luther King Jr. visited Boston to turn up the heat on the Boston School Committee; King staged a march from Roxbury to the Boston Commons that drew a crowd of fifteen thousand. Despite the pressure, the school committee refused to budge from its position that the public schools in Boston were not illegally segregated. Dissatisfied with the school committee's recalcitrance, the NAACP, in March 1972, filed a class action suit in federal court against the perpetuation of dual school systems in Boston. The Boston case was assigned to federal district judge W. Arthur Garrity. In June 1974

Judge Garrity ruled that Boston Public Schools were unconstitutionally segregated and ordered that a plan for desegregation incorporating the use of busing to achieve racial balance be implemented at the earliest possible time.

Reaction in the White community to Judge Garrity's decision was harsh. Whites in South Boston exhibited an intolerance to school desegregation not witnessed by the nation since the Little Rock riots of the 1950s. For months, crowds gathered outside South Boston High School to bombard buses transporting Black students from Roxbury to South Boston with rocks, sticks, fruit, and other objects. On the first day of desegregation, buses leaving the Gavin School and the L Street Annex were attacked by mobs of White protesters. When the melee settled, 18 buses were damaged and 9 Black students were injured by flying glass.[31] The attack on Black students at Hyde Park High School was ferocious; White resistance at this school included the stoning of buses and physical assaults against Black students in the hallways. Black students were not the only victims of racial violence. Andre Yvon Jean-Louise, a Haitian immigrant, was pulled out of his car and beaten by a mob in South Boston. Jean-Louise had entered South Boston in the afternoon to pick up his wife from the laundry. Theodore Landsmark, a Black lawyer with the Third World Clearing House, was trapped on the steps of city hall and assaulted with a flag pole by a group of antibusing activists returning from a downtown meeting with Louise Day Hicks. The situation grew increasingly dangerous as bullets were shot into the parked car of a Black family in Charlestown and nightriders peppered sniper fire into the homes of Blacks living at Columbia Point.[32] The perpetrators of these crimes found encouragement in the rhetoric of ROAR (Restore Our Alienated Rights), an antibusing group founded by Louise Day Hicks. Members of the Boston City Council also registered symbolic expressions of defiance. In Boston, White politics had taken on a vicious flavor. The refusal by Mayor White to take strong action to bring violence in the White community under control was especially disconcerting to Black leaders. Commenting critically on the mayor's behavior, NAACP president Thomas Atkins noted: "Political decisions were made not to clear the crowds away from South Boston High School." He also said, "Political decisions were made not to arrest people seen throwing rocks and bottles at children on buses. Political decisions were made to take a go-slow, take-it-easy approach at all costs."[33] As John Hillson has pointed out, "Such political decisions were made by Mayor Kevin White."[34]

The climate of racial violence that accompanied school desegregation in Boston reflected the abdication of responsibility by the entire White leadership structure of the city.

There was a gross lack of effective leadership in Boston at the time. You look at other cities that had problems with school desegregation, and in some instances there was violence. But at some point there developed a critical mass, where you had the leadership of the business community, of the electoral community, the religious community, coming together and saying look, this city is not going to fall apart because of this; we will get through this. That never happened in the city of Boston. Every single elected official that was White in office basically was opposed to it [school desegregation]. This is a strongly Catholic city. The predominant group at that time was Irish Catholic. The religious community did not come forward in any manner to allay some of the fears and anxieties of the population as a whole. It was just a gross lack of leadership; the ball was completely dropped. I think that was probably one of the darkest periods in the city's history. The absence of effective leadership meant that those who were narrow in their views and opinions were able to take center stage in many ways that under ordinary circumstances they would never have been able to do. So there was a total breakdown across the board.[35]

The business community appeared to be particularly guilty of allowing race relations to run out of control while it concentrated on its bottom line economic interests.

The day that hell broke lose in Roxbury around the issue of desegregation, I was meeting with a group called "The Vault." I don't believe the day I was meeting with them and telling them that hell was going to break lose out here they really cared. They were more interested in their investments in South Africa and other places in the world. So what if Roxbury blows up? That wasn't the source of major investment for them. As I said, they have promoted racism by inaction if nothing more.[36]

Violent clashes between Blacks and Whites in Boston over school desegregation were not fortuitous but grew out of a historical, cultural, and political context in which poor Blacks and working-class Whites were pitted against each other to assure that threats from below to the interest of the governing coalition would be minimized. The reality of the situation was that working-class Whites were also being disadvantaged in the Boston School System. They were made to believe that the busing of Black students into their schools was equivalent to giving up their world. As long as poor Blacks and working-class Whites looked at each other exclusively across the racial divide, members of the governing coalition could effectively avoid grappling with the critical issue of delivering quality education to all students enrolled in the Boston Public School System.

The struggle for school desegregation served as an immensely important unifying and organizing force in the Black community. Black leaders began the difficult task of preparing community residents to participate in the implementation of Judge Garrity's orders several months before the buses rolled out of Roxbury. Freedom House became the site of training sessions to teach volunteers how to participate in street patrols, handle violent confrontations, quiet the fears of students, and regulate the flow of communication. A united front was formed by major organizations such as SCLC, the Urban League, and the NAACP. The Lena Park Community Development Corporation and Roxbury Multiservice Center joined forces with Freedom House to form the Freedom House Coalition.[37] These organizations joined ranks with Black ministers and politicians to provide a protective shield around Black students under siege in the desegregation process.

Countermobilization in the Black community was expressed in the form of mass demonstrations. On 30 November 1974, fifteen thousand marchers, led by Coretta Scott King (widow of Dr. Martin Luther King Jr.), gathered on the steps of city hall to defend the busing process and send out an urgent call for racial peace. This march was called by a coalition of ministers, rabbis, and priests seeking a "strong, unified voice in Greater Boston for the peaceful implementation of desegregation."[38] Another march was organized on 14 December 1974 by State Senator Bill Owens, with the support of a group called the Emergency Committee. The Owens march was a more raucous affair, with members of the "Emergency Committee" clashing with the police over the right to veer from the official route down Massachusetts Avenue to march down Bolyston Street. In many respects, the Owens march was a turning point in the battle for school desegregation. This march effectively elevated the countermobilization activities of Black activists to national and international prominence; in doing so it substantially disrupted the political momentum of local antibusing forces.

The 1960s was a period of magnificent political learning and growth for Boston's Black community. Intensive involvement by Blacks in protest politics produced a heightened sense of political consciousness, valuable experience in political organizing, a realistic glimpse into the depth of racism in Boston, and an unvarnished commitment to enhanced collective power. These lessons would establish the foundation for the movement of the Black community into new and challenging dimensions of local politics.

## From Protest to Politics

The Boston experience clearly demonstrates the efficacy of protest as a political resource. This experience also illuminates the limitations of protest as an instrument of political incorporation. Protest strategies are organically episodic and situational; they do not lend themselves to the building of permanent organizational networks. James Q. Wilson has shown that political organizations must have a continuous supply of program material or they will wither and die.[39] Issue-based protest networks cannot usually fulfill the program material requirement and are therefore weak instruments for the mobilization of sustained power by minority groups. Blacks in Boston seeking to follow the path of the Irish and Italians into the inner circles of permanent power have embraced electoral politics as an alternative to discontinuous protest action. The transition from protest to electoral politics has been reinforced and stimulated by the growth of the Black population in recent decades to nearly one-fourth of the total population. This Black percentage, coupled with expanding Black political and racial consciousness produced by the Civil Rights movement, has substantially elevated the strategic position of Blacks as a potentially powerful force in the electoral process.

Black political leaders have attempted to solidify a base of power for Blacks in the electoral process by diluting the control of the regular Democratic organization over the political preferences and choices of Black voters. A significant step in this direction was made in 1960 with the election of Royal Bolling Sr. to the Massachusetts House of Representatives. Bolling ran for a House seat without the endorsement and support of the Taylor brothers or the citywide Democratic organization. He was able to win the election by capitalizing on the rapid expansion of the Black electorate in the Franklin Park area.[40] Bolling's victory demonstrated the viability of insurgency politics under circumstances of demographic and ideological change and the declining capacity on the part of the established party machinery to manipulate and control Black electoral behavior through material inducements.

The success of the Bolling campaign illuminated Black political potential. Developments in the civil rights arena, especially the virulence of White protest actions, made it clear that this potential could not be fully realized in the absence of an institutional structure to bind together the interests of Black politicians and hold them accountable to the broader community. The creation of such a structure began to take on realistic dimensions in 1971 with the organization of the Bostown Political Convention. Based on the theme of political independence, the Bostown Convention was designed to unify Black social, economic, and political interests under one permanent political organization, formulate an action agenda for the Black community, kick off a vigorous voter registration drive, provide a method for community endorsement of candidates, and create channels and institutional structures to facilitate grassroots citizen participation in the development and implementation of policies for the Black community. The accomplishments of the convention were impressive. A formal policy platform was adopted that incorporated the idea of an action agenda. Wide-ranging debate led to the endorsement of candidates and the construction of endorsement procedures.

The decision by the convention to send thirty-seven delegates from Boston to the 1972 National Black Political Convention in Gary was, in retrospect, pathbreaking. Involvement of Boston activists in the Gary Convention resulted in the founding of the Massachusetts Black Political Assembly. Delegates at the National Convention were encouraged to organize local affiliates or "assemblies" to promote the goals of programmatic unity and political independence. The Boston chapter of the Massachusetts Assembly took the Gary charge extremely seriously. Through planned systematic steps, the assembly movement became the pivotal foundation for the development and growth of independent Black politics in Boston.

> The assembly was an embryonic cadre involving grassroots workers, ecumenical leaders, progressive church members, and students. There were significant successes here in Boston made through the assembly structure. Black politicians who were not formal members of the assembly nevertheless benefited from its grassroots organizing strategies.[41]

The Black Political Assembly was a principal force behind the election of five Black politicians to the state legislature in 1972. Bill Owens, who was elected to the House of Representatives in 1972 and became the first Black member of the Massachusetts Senate in this century in 1974, attributes much of his political success to the Black Political Assembly.

> I was the first person in this area, and one of the first in the country, to be elected with the machinery of the National Black Political Assembly. Most of the other people did not enjoy the National Black Political Assembly's support. But many of their elections were influenced by the emergence of the National Black Political Assembly, which was the outgrowth of the 1972 Gary Convention. On a personal note, it was at the 1972 Gary Convention that I made a decision to run for state representative.[42]

Bill Owens emerged as a maverick politician whose political style and unconventional career moves created shock waves in the ranks of Black political forces. Owens made headlines when he intervened in a prison takeover by a Black group called the "Mau Mau." He was described by the rebellious Black prisoners as the only politician they could trust. Owens was able to free the prison hostages and provide the prison protesters the protection they were seeking. Owens rankled leaders of the Democratic Party by holding up the proceedings of the senate for three and one-half days in a successful effort to get a $30 million appropriation for the construction of a new campus for Roxbury Community College. Owens's conflict with the Democratic Party leadership became so severe that in 1982 he decided to leave the Democratic Party and run for the state senate as a Republican.

> I switched parties because I was in continuous fights with the Democrats. I had the feeling that the Democrats didn't give a damn about the Black population. My feeling was that if they were our friends we didn't need any enemies. So I might as well go to the enemy whoever they had determined our enemy was. And it was more of a statement and a reprimand to the Democrats than anything else. [43]

Bill Owens's decision to switch parties had a number of important ramifications. The decision was a setback to his career; he lost his race for the senate in 1982. His decision also created deep divisions in Black political circles. His chief Democratic opponent was the "Godfather" of Black Boston politics, Royal Bolling Sr. The Owens-Bolling contest illuminated ongoing tensions between the traditional Black elites and the young Black lions who cut their political teeth on the movement for political independence in the postprotest era. Owens attempted to make a dramatic comeback by running for the state senate in 1986 as an independent. He was defeated again by Bolling by approximately 1,300 votes. Running as a Democrat again in 1988, Owens defeated Bolling and regained a seat in the state senate. Owens was beaten again in 1992, this time by a newcomer, Black lawyer, and NAACP activist, Dianne Wilkerson. Owens attributed his defeat to the fact that 1992 was the year of the woman. "I think it would have been difficult to win that year for any male in a district where a significant female candidate was running against that person"[44] Dianne Wilkerson had a different perspective on the outcome of the election. "I attribute my success to the people who were frustrated with the incumbent I was running against. I believe they saw my campaign as a real opportunity for change. People saw me as someone who was going to work hard—who spent a long time working around the community—and was going to stand up and fight. In general, in 1992 I think people wanted change. I was part of that change."[45]

## The Black Political Task Force

Another important political institution with roots planted in the Bostown Convention and the National Black Political Assembly was the Black Political Task Force. Founded in 1978, the Black Political Task Force was established by Black activists as an organization to screen candidates for possible endorsement for public office. Over time the mission of the Black Political Task Force was broadened to encompass the coordination of the political interests of twenty-seven community organizations. In its hey-day, the Black Political Task Force became a political coalition with extensive mobilization capabilities and the political strength to make elected officials—Black and White—accountable for their decisions.

> The primary purpose of the organization [Black Political Task Force] was political empowerment and making elected officials accountable by organizing, screening and endorsing candidates. One of the things we needed to do was organize and sort out what we stood for. We had problems with that. Initially the task force was more progressive than it later turned out to be.[46]

The Black Political Task Force played the extremely important role of linking the policy actions of elected officials to the policy needs of the voters. Issues such as grassroots voter turnout and community voting strategies became the focus of considerable debate and action by the task force in its efforts to build and implement an effective political empowerment agenda for the Black community.

## Black Mayoral Politics

Black communities in big cities across the United States have attempted to expand their control over policy making by electing Black politicians to the mayor's office. Blacks in Boston view the mayor's office as a major political prize and have sought on several occasions to capture this office through electoral mobilization. The mayoral campaigns of Mel King in 1979 and 1983 were rooted in the earlier struggle to build a strong base for independent political action for the Black community. King was able to make a smooth and effective transition from protest to politics. He was one of the key organizers of the Bostown Convention and one of the founders of the Massachusetts Black Political Assembly and the Black Political Task Force. King is also credited with being the mastermind behind the 1977 election of John O'Bryant to the Boston School Committee.

King's 1979 campaign in the preliminary election was, in many respects, an extension of his many years of experience as a militant community activist. King deliberately positioned himself to the left of his opponents Kevin White, Joseph Timilty, and David Finnegan. King's campaign organization represented a coalition of Blacks, Latinos, and liberal Whites. The pivotal foundation of his campaign was a platform that stressed progressive issues: Black and Latino empowerment, neighborhood development, the redistribution of wealth, unemployment, ethnic cooperation, linked development, and the elimination of race and gender violence.

Mel King was able to mobilize an unprecedented number of progressive volunteers to work in his campaign. These individuals were attracted to King by his personality, his sense of integrity, his track record as a committed community activist, and the vision he projected of a new Boston sensitive to the needs of the poor. The message he delivered was so captivating that much of his platform was adopted by his opponents. King received strong opposition from the press. He was heavily criticized by the press for fomenting racism by emphasizing racial issues in his campaign. Boston newspapers also accused him of being a spoiler rather than a serious candidate for the mayor's office.[47]

The outcome of the election demonstrated that the press's spoiler label was off the mark. Although King did not make it into the final election, finishing third with 15 percent of the vote, he won the election in the Black community, receiving 65 percent of the Black vote. King's strong showing in the Black community was a dagger in the heart of the Kevin White machine, contradicting White's campaign boast that he would win the Black vote. With the Black electorate expanding, the White electorate diminishing, and Black voters responding to the messages delivered by the most militant Black politician in Boston, it became patently clear to White that he could not survive another contested primary election. Not only did the King campaign leave White's multiracial coalition in shambles, but it produced a new organization, the Boston Peoples Organization, to continue the process of community mobilization in the interim between elections. King's 1979 campaign was, in a real sense, a victory in defeat. It demonstrated that progressive Black politics was potentially an explosive force in the Boston political system—a force over which White no longer exercised control.

Kevin White's decision not to run for a fifth term as mayor guaranteed that the 1983 preliminary campaign would be a hard fought one among nearly equal competitors. Mel King ran a grassroots campaign sharply reminiscent of his 1979 effort. The second time around, he would organize a full rainbow coalition consisting of Blacks, Latinos, liberal Whites, feminists, and gays and lesbians. King drew on three decades of community activism to provide the City of Boston with an incomparable lesson in compassion and integrity.

> Mel King was a true bridge to the underclass. King, as a seasoned social worker and organizer, understood how to mobilize tens of thousands of people. No registration drive in the history of this state ever equaled what he accomplished. During his electoral campaign he secured the registration of  thousands of qualified voters. He should have been appointed to some substantial position just for this contribution to the service mission of the state. His campaign's rainbow theme and strategy transformed the politics of city hall. All Flynn did was copy it. Flynn attached his name to it. I see Mel King as a person who understood the change, knew how to convert it into a movement, who came extraordinarily close to becoming mayor, and the mayor still has a lot of symbolic import in Boston.[48]

King's preliminary campaign was brilliant enough to place a Black person in the final election for mayor for the first time in the history of Boston. In the preliminary election, King came in second with 47,800 votes or 29 percent. His chief opponent, Ray Flynn, received a mere 400 more votes than King. This time Blacks, Latinos, and Asians would not be torn by uncertainty; King received over 90 percent of the votes cast in minority neighborhoods. Support for King in minority neighborhoods remained strong despite the effort by the White press to depict Ray Flynn as a White progressive in the mold of Mel King.

> Mel King represented a threat to the racial hierarchy of this city. Mel King had a good chance of winning. The *Boston Globe* turned Ray Flynn into Mel King. Suddenly Ray Flynn was caring of all people like Mel King was—no difference between them. You had Flynn becoming a racial healer like King, and he was anything but a racial healer. He had helped to lead a boycott to shut down the schools to protest the busing. He didn't care about how many Black youth were being stoned or hurt, but rather "they are taking over our schools in our neighborhood." What you had then was the *Globe* cleaning up his record. And then the *Globe* perpetuates this. The *Globe* keeps talking about this racial healing. So if you talk about it long enough suddenly it's true.[49]

In the final election, Flynn beat King overwhelmingly, receiving over 80 percent of the White vote and a small percentage of the minority vote. King received 95 percent of the vote in minority neighborhoods and 20 percent of the White vote. Once again Boston demonstrated its inability to vote across color lines. But the King campaign again represented a victory in defeat. This King campaign established unequivocally that Blacks could be mobilized in local elections in significant numbers. The King campaign was also an important learning experience for the city of Boston. It gave to all Boston citizens an understanding of the status of the racial hierarchy in Boston and the endless possibilities for change that lay ahead if King's message of hope, compassion, and human fellowship was someday translated into a comprehensive public policy agenda.

Mel King's defeat in 1983 did not dissuade Bruce Bolling from embracing the strategy of Black mayoral politics a decade later. The resignation of Ray Flynn to accept an ambassadorship to the Vatican in 1991 left a vacuum in the mayor's office. Bruce Bolling stepped forward in 1993 to fill that vacuum. Bolling had not intended to run for the mayor's office, but the special election established to fill the mayor's position was too much of an opportunity for

Bolling to ignore. Bolling knew that the election would draw a mul-
ticandidate field, including interim mayor Thomas Menino. Bolling
calculated that if he developed a significant base of support in the
Black community and produced an impressive Black turnout, he
could get into the final race. His basic strategy was to run on his
track record as a twelve-year member of the city council, a record
that had moved link development policies, and other progressive
programs, through the city council. Bolling would also attempt to
take advantage of his reputation as a racial healer—someone who
understood that the fundamental issues of city government did not
differ dramatically from neighborhood to neighborhood. He would
stress in his campaign that the citizens of Boston had a great deal in
common, and would promise that—as mayor—he would work with
all citizens to improve the quality of life in the neighborhoods.

Bolling's campaign was controversial from its very inception. He
discovered, to his chagrin, that many people in the Black community—including a number of key Black leaders—did not share his
perception of the quality of his work in the council. The primary criticism was that he was too low-key and too willing to support legislation promoted by the downtown establishment.

> Bruce Bolling was not perceived to be a member of the Black commu-
> nity. Bruce Bolling was perceived to be Bruce Bolling. One of his
> downfalls was that he did not stand up to the city council in terms of
> the issues the Black community wanted him to stand up for. He never
> came back to find out what the community wanted. He thought he
> knew it all.[50]

Criticism of Bolling's candidacy reached a pivotal point when two
Black ministers publicized a letter they wrote to Bolling asking him
to drop out of the mayor's race so a stronger Black candidate could
be selected. The letter was written by Reverend Ray A. Hammond of
Bethel A.M.E. Church and Reverend Eugene F. Rivers III of the
Azusa Christian Community. Hammond and Rivers claimed that
they voiced the sentiments of many Black leaders who were disap-
pointed in Bolling's seeming inability to galvanize Black voters. The
letter from Hammond and Rivers represented the fallout from a
meeting of two hundred Black neighborhood leaders, elected officials, ministers, and other activists who had met earlier at Freedom
House to consider the adoption of a process that would lead to the
creation of a platform for the forthcoming election and the selection
of a candidate around whom the community could unify in the
mayor's race. A second meeting of the group, known as the Coalition

for Community Unity, after a protracted debate, decided to support Bolling's candidacy; Bolling obtained 89 percent of the vote, more than the 75 percent the coalition required for endorsement.[51] A crucial endorsement by State Senator Dianne Wilkerson was left up in the air. Wilkerson made it clear that she was hesitant to endorse Bolling because she believed he could not win and she was determined to be standing by a winner on election day. The decision by the coalition to endorse Bolling was not universally applauded.

> I was at the Coalition for Community Unity meeting where the endorsement for Bruce Bolling came up. Dianne Wilkerson's position in terms of who she supported was problematic. But the support for Bruce was also problematic because the support was on the basis of let's get a Black man elected mayor, and my line was that Clarence Thomas is Black, but I damn sure wouldn't vote for him as mayor of Boston. Bruce supported linkage, but he also comes out of a strong connection to the real estate industry. And then the police violence stuff, it took us a long time to get lukewarm support from him. He'd watch it and certainly come to the hearings, but in terms of being out-there, that's not Bruce's style. My argument in the coalition meeting was that what we needed was a political platform that reflected our interest as people of color and not a person of color whom you hoped would run some platform. That's old thinking. Identity politics is old thinking, especially in the nineties.[52]

The *Boston Globe* attempted to exploit the mounting division in the Black community by depicting Bruce Bolling as being out of step with the needs of the Black community and lacking the "passion" for public life required to be an effective mayor. Bolling objected strongly to this characterization of his candidacy.

> Passion for what? I saw myself as a change agent on the Boston City Council. I had a very lengthy record of accomplishment in terms of my record as a Boston City Councillor. And all were cutting edge issues. I had the passion to take on the mayor, to take on the status quo, to try to bring about change and be able to garner broad-based support to get a majority, to get these initiatives accomplished. To me, I showed compassion in ways that were positive.[53]

Although Bruce Bolling was sometimes accused of running a lackluster campaign, the charge was not justified. Bolling ran a strong, issue-oriented campaign in every part of the city. His campaign efforts in the Black community were especially strong. These efforts secured endorsements from over one hundred Black ministers. Despite the hard work of Bruce Bolling and his supporters, the campaign never caught fire in the Black community. This fact is revealed by the election turnout in key Black wards. Voter turnout in the city overall was 52 percent. In key Black wards the turnout was as follows: Ward 14 (Mattapan), 34 percent; Ward 12 (Roxbury), 44 percent; Ward 8 (Roxbury), 37 percent; Ward 9 ( Roxbury), 37 percent.[54] With these kind of turnout rates in the Black community, Bolling's campaign to get into the final election was doomed to failure. Bolling finished fifth in the preliminary contest.[55]

Bolling's vote in the mayor's race reflected two major problems for his campaign in the election. The first problem was that Bruce Bolling was not Mel King. Comparisons of Bolling with King were inevitable. Bolling simply did not have the charismatic personality or track record as a grassroots activist that King brought to the earlier contests. Black voters did not view Bolling's candidacy as a Mel King–type political crusade. Bruce Bolling did not have the power or the resources to reconstruct his image in the image of Mel King. Second, Bolling received only lukewarm support from prominent community organizations and political activists. This failure of support was submerged, in part, in hoary tensions between traditional Black elites and representatives of grassroots Black political interests. Dianne Wilkerson, the highest ranking Black elected official in Boston, refused to the very end to endorse Bolling's candidacy. On the eve of the preliminary election, Senator Wilkerson announced that she was committing the twenty-seven thousand votes over which she exercised influence to State Representative James Brett of Dorchester. When questioned about the possibility she may have been responsible for Bolling's defeat, Wilkerson replied: "Its not my job to galvanize a campaign for a candidate other than myself. You can't dump that in my lap."[56]

## Community Control: The Mandela Referendum

One important dimension of the campaign for Black power in the 1960s was the quest for community control. The theoretical perspective undergirding this political objective suggested that Blacks could change their subordinate position in American society by controlling their basic institutions and through community control reverse the flow of benefits produced by the broader political system. In Boston, the idea of community control moved beyond the realm of rhetorical discussion and wishful contemplation to the arena of political negotiation when a referendum proposal was placed on the election ballot in 1986 to separate most of the Black community from Boston and transform this territory into a free-standing district under Black control. The proposal was initiated by Andrew Jones, a writer for the *Boston Globe*, and Curtis Davis, a Boston architect. Called "Mandela" (after the heroic South African leader) the new district, running through Roxbury, Mattapan, and Dorchester, would encompass 90 percent of the Black community.[57] If approved by the voters, the proposal would transfer executive and legislative authority to a new governing structure created, managed, and controlled by residents in the stipulated geographic area.

The Mandela proposal was both an electoral and a protest strategy. It evolved out of persistent complaints by Blacks that the quality of services the Black community received was extremely poor. Mandela supporters believed that since the Black community was getting shortchanged in its receipt of services, it should be given the authority to control its own destiny by collecting its own taxes and spending the money raised by taxes according to its own desires, needs, and decisional processes.

It is not surprising that the proposal for Mandela created a political firestorm. The Flynn administration made it clear that it was unalterably opposed to the separation of the Black community from Boston. Flynn developed a master plan to defeat the proposal. That plan included strong attacks on the proposal in the media and the generation of strong countermobilization against the proposal within the Black community. The political campaign against the proposal in the Black community was led by Black ministers.

With opposition across the city building like a brush fire, the Mandela proposal had little chance of victory at the ballot box. The proposal was soundly defeated in every sector of the city, including the Black community. Several factors helped to assure that the proposal would be a losing proposition in Black wards. The campaign for Mandela never got off the ground in the Black community because Jones and Davis were political neophytes with no experience in community organizing. This problem was compounded by the fact that they had no basic constituency and were not connected to any existing community-based organization capable of creating a constituency for them.

> They [Jones and Davis] ran the line that you are either with us or you are with them. No respect was shown for organizations that had been around for a while struggling over this community control question to say OK let's see if we can work together. The GRNA [Greater Roxbury

Neighborhood Authority ] took the position that they agreed with the issue of community control, that was the core question here, but whether or not there had to be created something called "Mandela," or another way of quasi- autonomy, was still an open question. But Andrew, who was really the heart case on this one, wouldn't hear of it. No, it was Mandela or nothing.[58]

Jones and Davis were also unable to satisfactorily answer community concerns about how the district would survive if it cut itself off from the city of Boston. Black citizens wanted to know where the jobs were going to come from to support the district's economy, how local government would be run, how taxes would be collected, and who would be in control of general services, schools, and utilities. The supporters of Mandela were never able to provide the hard answers required to instill confidence in the proposal by rank and file Black voters. But even in defeat, many Mandela supporters remained convinced that a predominantly Black district was a brilliant idea whose time had come.

If we had our own community, we wouldn't have drugs coming in here. We could stop that cold. I wouldn't have kids telling me what caliber rifle bullet they want. What the hell do they know about rifles? The mayor conned them; they get these house Negroes right out front. The area [Mandela] wasn't all Black. They said we were too poor to control our community. You had Harvard Medical School. You had the University of Massachusetts. You had Northeastern University and the New England School of Fine Arts. All kind of things. Anytime you don't have to put in sidewalks, storm drains, electrical wiring, build schools, you are pretty rich aren't you. This is the "Common Wealth" and it is one of the oldest and richest parts of the country. It's a constant reeducation of who and what we are. There is a lot of leadership here to do what needs to be done to give us community control.[59]

It is clear that many citizens in the Black community did not share the dream of Mandela on the terms as they vaguely understood them when they cast their ballots.

## The Dissipation of Black Nationalism

Black political strategies in major American cities in the United States have usually incorporated a commitment to the concept of Black nationalism. The Black community in Boston has a strong nationalist tradition dating back at least to David Walker. Historically Boston has been the breeding ground of Black nationalists and Pan Africanists, among them W. E. B. Du Bois, William Monroe Trotter, Malcolm X, and Louis Farrakhan. The Civil Rights era of the 1960s witnessed the solid growth of Black nationalist activities in Boston, with branches of the Black Panther Party, The Republic of New Africa, and the Nation of Islam, among other groups, playing important and constructive roles in the development and articulation of the Black agenda. The strongest expression of Black nationalism came from the Boston United Front, a coalition of Black organizations formed in the wake of the assassination of Dr. Martin Luther King Jr. Through political bargaining and manipulation, the Boston United Front was able to secure a half-million-dollar grant from liberal White philanthropists to promote Black community development.

In the 1990s hardly a shadow of the Black nationalist impulse of the 1960s remains in Boston. Unlike Black nationalists in Chicago who functioned as a pivotal backbone of the Harold Washington campaign for mayor, Black nationalists in Boston maintained an arms-length distance from the campaigns for mayor of Mel King and Bruce Bolling. The Black United Front is now defunct, a casualty of internal wrangling and the demise of its major funding base. While the Nation of Islam remains an important force in Black community politics, its effectiveness has sometimes been diluted by the cozy relationship forged between its leaders and downtown administrations, especially the Flynn administration.

The strongest remaining remnant of the nationalist movement is the Community Information Center under the direction of Sadiki Kambon. A brief resurgence of interest in Black nationalist strategies erupted in the aftermath of the Million Man March led by Minister Louis Farrakhan of the Nation of Islam. The Community Information Center and the Nation of Islam joined forces to call a series of organizing meetings to address a range of community-based issues. Initially generating enthusiastic support, these efforts were, by the spring of 1996, in substantial disarray. As a viable political force and a program for liberation, Black nationalist strategies have had extreme difficulty surviving the system maintenance proclivities of the Boston political process.

# 6

---

# Resource Mobilization and
# Black Political Linkage

## Resources and Black Political Action

Black political incorporation and empowerment requires the development of an effective resource base. The specific combination of resources required for competitive and productive political action is highly dependent on the structural and behavioral character of the political system and the social, economic, and political status of the Black community within that system. Black incorporation and empowerment in local government in the United States requires the cultivation and effective application of at least the following resources.

1.  Numbers—Blacks must constitute a significant percentage of the population.

2.  Voting Strength—Blacks must be registered to vote in significant numbers and represent an important segment of the voting electorate.

3.  Leadership and Organization—Blacks must have committed leaders and strong, enduring organizational structures dedicated to community uplift.

4.  Unity and Cohesion—Blacks must manifest a willingness to work in harmony with each other for the promotion of the common good.

5.  Racial and Political Consciousness—Blacks must demonstrate a high level of racial and political consciousness and an unswerving commitment to political independence.

Blacks in a number of American cities have achieved substantial political incorporation and empowerment in these terms. Baltimore, Atlanta, New Orleans, Birmingham, and Detroit are outstanding examples of cities where Blacks have been able to hold on to top elected offices for several decades because of the ability of the Black community to use its political resources to extend its political influence citywide.[1] Thus far, the Black community in Boston has achieved, at best, a weak form of political incorporation and empowerment because of the difficulty it has experienced in developing and applying a stable network of politically viable resources. In this respect Boston remains a second tier city with plenty of room for growth and development (see figure 6.1). Clearly, the desire to move up the hierarchy of power is prevalent throughout the Boston Black community. The critical challenge the community faces is finding the keys to translating desire and hope into effective political action. For the Irish in Boston the secret was found in the conversion of their buildup in numbers into dominant power and control in the electoral arena. Through effective political leadership and organization and a high sense of group interests, the Irish were able to move into strategic positions in the city bureaucracy and, eventually, the broader economy.

The endurance of racism as a factor in the political system has made the barriers to incorporation and empowerment much higher for the Black community than they were for the Irish. But external obstacles are only one aspect of the political puzzle. The Black community in Boston has been required to grapple with a myriad of internal issues impacting on its capacity to mobilize for collective political action. Many of these issues relate to the capacity of the community to develop and utilize the irreducible minimum level of effective political resources required for entree and influence in the wider political system. This chapter examines the dilemmas encountered by the Boston Black community in its efforts to develop, maintain, and take advantage of a potent base of effective political resources.

## Demographic and Voting Patterns

If numbers are an important political resource, the Black community in Boston appears to be in a strategically favorable position to rapidly climb the ladder of political success. As we noted in chapter 2, since World War II Boston has become a racial mosaic.[2] The most

## Figure 6.1. Index of Political Incorporation

| | BLACK MAJORITY POPULATION | STRONG BLACK REGISTRATION & VOTING | STRONG BLACK LEADERSHIP & ORGANIZATION | BLACK MAYOR | BLACK COUNCIL MAJORITY | STRONG BLACK CONTROL OVER CITY POLICY |
|---|---|---|---|---|---|---|
| BALTIMORE | YES | YES | YES | YES | YES | YES |
| ATLANTA | YES | YES | YES | YES | YES | YES |
| NEW ORLEANS | YES | YES | NO | YES | YES | YES |
| BIRMINGHAM | YES | YES | YES | YES | YES | YES |
| DETROIT | YES | YES | YES | YES | YES | YES |
| BOSTON | NO | NO | NO | NO | NO | NO |

Source: Data Collected from City Hall, Baltimore, MD; City Hall, Atlanta, GA; City Hall, New Orleans, LA; City Hall, Detroit, MI; City Hall, Boston, MA

salient dimension of demographic change in the postwar years has been the decline of the White population from 95 to 59 percent since 1950 and the rise of the Black population from 5 percent to 23.8 percent across this same period. Currently, the total minority population in Boston, including Asians and Latinos, is over 40 percent. These numbers represent enormous political potential for the Black community. In Boston, the gulf between Black political potential and Black political power is quite wide. An important mitigating factor is the high social diversity of the Black population. The demographic development of the Black community over the past four decades has drawn from separate immigrant streams. In the 1950s and 1960s, the bulk of the Black population migrating into Boston came from other parts of the United States, especially the South. This movement was significantly curtailed in the 1970s; it was eclipsed by the migration into Boston of Blacks from the West Indies.[3] Recent decades have seen the heavy influx of Cape Verdeans, Haitians, Ethiopians, Jamaicans, and Nigerians, giving to the Black community a highly international and heterogeneous flavor.

While diversity has strengthened the cultural base of the Black community, it has also been an effusive source of intraracial disharmony and conflict. African Americans and West Indians have frequently not seen eye to eye on a variety of policy issues. Blacks have been geographically separated along nationality lines, with African Americans primarily concentrated in Roxbury and Dorchester, and Cape Verdeans, West Indians and Africans living on the outer periphery in Mattapan, Rosalindale, and Jamaica Plain. These social and geographic divisions in the Black community have made it extraordinarily difficult for Black politicians to build programs of operational unity among broad segments of the Black population. Foreign-born Blacks have been especially difficult to mobilize because they do not psychologically or culturally relate to domestic political issues, do not respond to electoral appeals, and often do not qualify to vote. Overcoming these problems sometimes requires the development of separate campaign organizations and strategies for each nationality group in the Black community.

Conflicts between African Americans and Latinos have further diluted the political strength of the Black community. Residential dispersion by Latinos has kept the two communities socially and politically divided. A number of Latino leaders that had functioned as liaisons and boundary negotiators between the two groups were persuaded by David Dinkins to leave Boston and come to work in his mayoral administration in New York.[4] The upshot has been that no institutional ways have been forged to create a common political agenda or bind together the social, economic, and political interests of the African American and Latino communities.[5] To the contrary, Blacks and Latinos have often been in competition with each other for public and private funds available for community development. Rivalry between Black and Latino CDCs over issues of turf and funding has been particularly fierce. The failure to build cooperative alliances with Latinos has restricted the possible leverage parameters of Black political power and left Blacks to fend for themselves while Latinos searched for ways to broaden their resource bases by infiltrating positions within the ranks of the regular Democratic Party organization. Black-Latino division and conflict have been greatly accelerated by the incredibly rapid growth of the Latino population and the effort on the part of the Menino administration to give symbolic representation to Latinos by replacing elected Black school committee members with appointed Latino school committee members. Thus, internal divisions in the minority community, magnified by the use of divide and conquer tactics by downtown administrations, has substantially diluted the power potential of the Black community in the political process.

One area where that power dilution shows up most graphically is at the ballot box. Blacks are not newcomers to the electoral process in Boston. As early as 1901 Blacks were using their votes to choose between Republican and Democratic candidates they believed to be most supportive of their interests.[6] Despite the active involvement and participation of many Blacks in public elections, the overall participation rate of Blacks in elections has tended to fall below that of the city as a whole. For example, in the 1993 preliminary race, with a prominent Black candidate on the ballot, the average registration for Blacks in key Black wards was 57.75 percent, while the average registration in key White wards was 71.57 percent (see figure 4.1). As we noted in chapter 5, Black turnout in this election in key Black wards was substantially below the city turnout rate of 52 percent (see figure 6.2).[7]

These statistics suggest a pattern of demobilization in the Black community (see figure 6.3) . Lurking beneath these numbers is a high level of cynicism: many Blacks have a low sense of political efficacy, low trust in government, and low regard for the options available to them regarding choices of candidates.

Blacks have turned out to vote when they believed they had outstanding candidates to vote for like David Nelson, Tom Atkins, and Mel

Figure 6.2. Comparison of Black and White Voter Turnout
in Boston by Ward, 1993

| Black Ward Turnout | White Ward Turnout |
|---|---|
| Ward 14 ( Mattapan ) 34% | Ward 1 ( East Boston )    63% |
| Ward 12 ( Roxbury )  44% | Ward 2 ( Charlestown )   69% |
| Ward 9 ( Roxbury )    37% | Ward 6 ( South Boston ) 80% |
| Ward 8 ( Roxbury )    37% | Ward 7 ( South Boston ) 74% |
|  | Ward 16 ( Dorchester )   71% |
|  | Ward 18 ( Hyde Park / Roslindale ) 65% |
|  | Ward 20 ( West Roxbury / Roslindale ) 79% |

Source: Adapted from data included in Hubert E. Jones, "The State of Black Boston:
A Snapshot," in Joseph R. Barresi and Joseph S. Slavet (eds.), *A Special Report:
Boston's Update '94: A New Agenda for a New Century* (Boston: The John W.
McCormack Institute of Public Affairs, University of Massachusetts Boston, 1994)

King. It is also my experience that in order to get currency from the
Black community you have to get currency from the White community. Once Blacks see that White folks are embracing your candidacy
and believing you have a chance, it turns on the Black political structure.[8]

Cynicism alone cannot fully explain patterns of relatively lower registration and turnout in the Black community. The upsurge of immigration from the West Indies, Caribbean, and Africa has increased
the percentage of Black voters who are unqualified to vote and have
little interest in Boston city politics. At an earlier time, the Irish
solved this problem by meeting Irish immigrants at the boat and
leading them to registration offices. Black immigrants are not met
by political runners; even if they were the legal requirements for
voting would not permit their immediate registration. Legal
processes for voting currently in force in Boston are, in fact, so cum-
bersome that the barriers these processes present for low-income
minority voters can only be overcome by the expenditure of vast
amounts of money and the mounting of extensive "get out the vote
campaigns."[9] Even these efforts do not reach many potential minority voters whose economic situations are so dire they do not have the
time, the energy, or the interest to participate actively in the electoral process.

**Figure 6.3. Comparison of General City Election Voter Turnout in Boston, 1983 and 1987**

|  | 1983 | 1987 |
|---|---|---|
| **District Three** | | |
| *Dorchester | 75% | 41.8% |
| **District Four** | | |
| *Mattapan | 68.4% | 31.8% |
| Codman Square | 69.1% | 29.8% |
| Franklin Field | 71.5% | 35.5% |
| **District Seven** | | |
| *Roxbury | 67.6% | 34.8% |

*Black Voting District

Source: City of Boston Election Department Annual Report 1981 and Worksheets for 1983, 1985, 1987, and 1989.

Black political participation is also stifled by the absence of comprehensive, stable organizations to mobilize Black voters on a consistent, predictable basis. Blacks in Boston have failed to construct a citywide organization dedicated to voter registration and turnout. As a consequence, the process of voter registration and mobilization has had to start from the ground up each election season, with separate campaign organizations pursuing isolative political strategies. In the absence of a communitywide political structure, routine service demands go unattended, and the capacity on the part of the Black community to fully apply its potential power in the political process is seriously impaired.

> We need to go back to the old Chicago and New York ward-boss system to make people accountable. We need to have people responsible in the voting wards so that you will know who is registered and who is not registered, who votes and who does not vote, so you can identify and extract your concerns. When you elect people to positions, they must be held accountable for getting things done, whether its having your trees planted, your sidewalks repaired, whether its street lighting, summer jobs, pools in the neighborhoods, or recreational areas restored. That's political power. That's what its all about.[10]

The implications of relatively low Black political participation in Boston are immensely important. Black political linkage requires both the ability to elect Black candidates to office and hold them accountable for their actions and to influence the election and policy choices of nonBlacks. Neither of these goals can be obtained without strong Black political participation. In this regard we should note that participation is an absolute requirement for turning political potential into political power. James Jennings has pointed out the commanding importance of the Black community in Boston as a potential force in Boston politics. Jennings reported that between 76,600 and 86,00 Blacks were eligible to vote in Boston in 1984; this figure represented 25 to 30 percent of all eligible registered voters in the city.[11] With nearly one-third of the eligible vote in its hands, the Black community is strategically positioned to play a critical role in city elections. But with the Black community typically registering only half of its potential voting strength, and turning out less than 40 percent of its registered electorate, much of its potential power has been grossly diluted. The difference between the votes the Black community is eligible to cast and the vote it actually delivers in campaigns is one measure of the extent of its political underdevelopment; it is also a gauge of its distance from the center of decision making, where the fate of the citizens of the entire city is determined.

## Civil Rights Institutional Leadership

Black political linkage is also intimately connected to the institutional base of the Black community. Traditionally, civil rights organizations in American cities provide the political leverage needed to assure that Black political interests will be strategically and substantively represented in all phases and organized sectors of municipal decision making. In Boston, the work of the two major civil rights organizations—the NAACP and the Urban League—has deviated from this traditional role. The Boston branch of the NAACP has aspired over the past two decades to play a leading role in the articulation and implementation of a progressive social, economic, and political agenda for the Black community. This objective has become an illusion with no basis in reality The internal operational environment of the Boston branch of the NAACP has been so fraught with turmoil that it has been virtually impossible for this organization to satisfy the demands of serious and productive civil rights advocacy.

The downward slide of the Boston branch of the NAACP began in the 1980s under the administration of branch president Louis Elisa. An aggressive and outspoken community activist, Elisa was asked to step down as president in the wake of charges of financial mismanagement and failure to remit payments for membership dues to the national office. Apparently, the move against Elisa was orchestrated by members who were upset by his attacks against individuals and organizations that were the source of large contributions to the Boston branch. There was considerable concern that if Elisa continued his broadsides against these forces, contributions might dry up and the Boston branch forced to close its doors. Elisa was replaced by Jackie Robinson, a former Boston branch president, whose essential mission was to remove the ethical stain surrounding the organization's operation and to place it back in good standing with the national office. Robinson's second term was rocked by scandal when newspaper reports accused him of using his professional consulting services to solicit minority contracts for minority businesses that were actually owned by nonminorities. The adverse publicity surrounding this scandal had a deleterious impact on the NAACP's membership. Many people withdrew from the Boston branch because they no longer had confidence in its leadership.

A lot of people began to lose respect for the NAACP. Not that they had much anyway because they had not been effective since the Civil

Rights movement was over and a lot of people had started moving into more professional positions. A lot of people didn't feel the NAACP was keeping up with the times. They were losing a lot of members anyway. But when that scandal broke it brought more negative feelings towards the NAACP.[12]

The mounting turmoil in Boston forced the national office of the NAACP to step in and place the Boston branch in receivership. This action meant that the oldest branch of the NAACP was in serious danger of losing its charter.

Evidence of the organizational chaos reigning in Boston can be found in the fact that the Boston branch remained in receivership for four years, from 1991 to 1995. The national organization finally relinquished control of the Boston branch upon the election of Leonard Alkins as the new local president in December 1995. Noted for his unimpeachable integrity, Alkins began the arduous task of rebuilding an organization whose membership had slipped from 5,000 to 600.[13] Alkins viewed the challenges that lay before him with optimism and hope.

> The effectiveness of the NAACP in Boston is not as strong as what it has been but it's increasing each day now that we have reorganized and rejuvenated the Boston branch to address the issues and involve the community. As a civil rights organization, the NAACP has always been identified with the Black church, it has always been identified with youth, and it has always been identified with inclusion of the people into the process of addressing the issues. I would say at this moment, we are 50 percent back to the plateau where we were. We have rejuvenated our youth movement. We have rejuvenated our involvement with Black churches. Our membership is building rapidly because we have reactivated the committees and included the people in the decision making. And it's now an organization of we as opposed to I.[14]

The near collapse of the NAACP as an organized political force has broad implications for racial politics in Boston. A significant void in the mobilization capacity of the Black community has been left by the internal problems experienced by the NAACP. Historically, the NAACP has played a highly important role as an institutional link between the Black community and governmental decision making processes in major American cities. The NAACP assumed this responsibility in the 1960s and 1970s in Boston, especially in the context of the fight for school desegregation, and, as a consequence, rose to the center of organized Black political action. The political disengagement of the NAACP for nearly a decade because of internal strife has reduced the effective resource base of the Black community at a time when the community's social and economic needs have escalated because of cutbacks in government funding for urban social programs, increased unemployment, and the hardening of White racial attitudes on issues such as welfare and affirmative action.

In the past the NAACP in Boston has served as a valuable training ground for Black leadership; momentum in this area has been lost as a new generation of leaders has turned to other sources for hope and inspiration. The priority presently being given by the Alkins administration to youth outreach is a reflection of the recognition by the Boston branch that certain critical components of its leadership development responsibilities have diminished and need to be recaptured very quickly. In view of the fact that political incorporation requires both internal and external linkage, the disruption in the 1990s of the NAACP's role as a major instrument for community representation and leadership development has had a critical impact on both the maintenance capacity of the broader political system and the empowerment capacity of the Black community.

Although not saddled with the kind of internal problems experienced by the NAACP, the Boston Urban League has also substantially withdrawn from the process of community representation and mobilization. Under the current president, Joan Benjamin, the League has focused its attention centrally on job training and economic development. Its job training approach has promoted an "efficacy" model that is heavily motivational and nonpolitical. "I've tried to get them [the staff of the Urban League] to explain to me what efficacy is all about. The best that I can get is that it's a feel good thing where people say you can do it, you can do it, you can do it. They believe that the main thing that keeps us from succeeding is that we don't feel good about ourselves."[15]

The League is given high marks for its programs targeted at family and youth development. Its Community Mobilization and Education Project has provided extensive support for youth services agencies in Roxbury.[16]Missing from the League's mobilization strategies are the militant confrontational tactics used by Mel King in the 1960s to place this agency in the forefront of Boston's civil rights struggle. This strategic orientation is apparently incompatible with the League's efforts to secure large donations from the corporate sector. Relying on advice from its predominantly White executive board, the League has taken deliberate steps to transform itself from a civil rights organization with clear political objectives, to a community development organization removed from the process of political conflict and community representation. On this score one respondent closely associated with the Urban League observed: "That group [the Boston Urban League] occupies itself with jobs and training. It plays a low-key role in the political affairs of the Black community. The League does not organize meetings to discuss issues concerning the community such as police brutality."[17]

The political atrophy of the Urban League coupled with the political paralysis of the NAACP has left the civil rights flanks of the Black community almost totally unprotected. Without key organizations such as the NAACP and the Urban League leading a frontal assault against the institutional bases of White dominance and control, the concept of political linkage for the Black community becomes a magnificent ideal that is extraordinarily difficult to realize in the practical world of Boston politics.

## The Nonprofit Sector

Over the years the Boston Black community, like Black communities in other major American cities, has relied on nonprofit organizations to deliver important services in key areas such as education, recreation, economic development, health, housing, employment, and youth development. Private nonprofit organizations serve as extensions of formal governmental institutions in the Black community. They function to fill in the service gaps left by government bureaucracies whose structures are often not best suited to deliver high-quality services to specialized constituencies. In the Black community, private nonprofit agencies serve as alternative sources of service delivery; in this capacity they play important linkage roles both in the administration of important program services and the mobilization of community influence within the formal structures of local government.

The service delivery capacity of nonprofit agencies in Boston has, in recent years, been severely restricted by problems associated with their internal operation. Respondents in this study identified the three main nonprofit agencies in the Black community as the Lena Park Community Development Corporation, the Roxbury Multiservice Center, and Freedom House. In the 1990s all three of these organizations have experienced leadership crises. Each of these organizations has found it difficult to find suitable replacements for retiring executive directors, making it necessary for the executive boards of the organizations to step in and take up the responsibilities of day-to-day management. Their executive search efforts have been hindered by the shift in Black leadership talent from the community sector to the corporate sector. One impact of the implementation of affirmative action policies by corporate America has been the siphoning off of highly trained Black leaders from central roles in community organizations into well-paid executive and middle-management positions. The pool of talented and committed Black leaders who are willing to run nonprofit organizations, usually at considerable personal sacrifice, has grown extremely thin, creating a growing leadership crisis.

Leadership problems experienced by nonprofit organizations have been compounded by a serious financial crisis. Many nonprofits find it impossible to balance their budgets because of funding cutbacks by city, state, and federal agencies. While the number of organizations seeking funds has proliferated, the amount of money available for community service programming has declined drastically. The consequence has been predictable: too many organizations chasing too few dollars. The Lena Park Community Development Corporation, the Roxbury Multiservice Center, and Freedom House are all teetering on the borders of financial collapse because of the scaling down of public funding.[18]

> Government financial retrenchment is a major problem for our nonprofit organizations. You haven't seen a championing of expanding government at the local, state, and federal levels. If anything there has been an erosion of government. That's a very real issue, especially when agencies may be getting 60 to 70 percent of their resources in terms of federal and state grants.[19]

Community nonprofit agencies are feeling the pinch of private-sector cutbacks as well. Because of declining profits, a number of private corporations have severely cut back their philanthropic endeavors. In the face of these fiscal exigencies, many nonprofit organizations in Boston have had to contemplate some form of merger to maintain operational viability. "There is no question we need the services these organizations produce. But when you get a number of organizations that have been doing similar kinds of things, maybe you need to look at it differently now. How do you get the biggest bang for the buck? Maybe some of them need to merge."[20]

The financial problems of nonprofit agencies have left them vulnerable to political manipulation. During the Kevin White years, enormous pressure was placed on nonprofit organizations to work on the mayor's reelection team as a precondition for maintaining their city funding allocations. Demands from the Menino adminis- tration have not been equally brazen; but Menino has kept nonprofit organizations on a short leash by severely restricting the flow of dol- lars going into the budgets of these agencies to do community work.[21]

The nonprofit agencies that have remained most politically inde- pendent and viable are those with private endowments or other means of reliable private support. One such agency is the United Southend Settlement House. This agency, one of the oldest social service organizations in America, has been highly successful in its efforts to secure private investments for its job training services at its Harriet Tubman House and other community service ventures. Youth Enrichment Services (YES) has had a similar experience. YES answered the call for outdoor youth programs when the city of Boston cut off all youth services programs except for afterschool activities at public libraries. Demands for political reciprocity inspired administrators of this agency to rely exclusively on private sources of funding. Health centers such as the Roxbury Comprehensive Health Center, Whittier Health Center, the Harvard Street Health Center, and the Mattapan Community Health Center have been able to remain relatively independent of political control. They have been able to maintain their operational viability and political independence by attracting into their ranks young professionals who see their positions as avenues to success in a variety of medical fields, such as hospital administration. These agencies have been the source of considerable pressure for medical reform on issues such as third-party payments, increased funding for research on infant mortality, and the involvement of teaching hospitals in the delivery of community services.[22] A comprehensive system of health regulation has helped to assure that the fiscal via- bility of these agencies would not fall below acceptable levels.

## Black Church Leadership

For many citizens of Boston, Black church leadership has been an enigma. Throughout most of its history, the Black church in Boston has been a crucial resource in the mobilization of political power for the Black community. The Black church remains the Black commu- nity's most organized, socially cohesive institution. It exercises a claim on the money, minds, and loyalty of Black citizens unmatched by any other institutional force. Despite its transcendent influence, the Black church in Boston has failed to serve as an effective vehicle for consolidating the social, economic. and political resources of the Black community and promoting the realization of community objectives. In many American cities, the Black church has been a unifying force, pulling together a variety of civic interests in the common pursuit of community-wide policy interests. One of the most critical areas of community disempowerment in Boston is the prevailing disconnection between the Black church and community-based organizations and leaders.

> There is little political interaction in Boston between the Black church and other social institutions, especially social agencies. There is a disconnect between these forces. You will not find many ministers on the boards of social agencies in this town. You will not find many political leaders playing major leadership roles in Black churches here to the extent you would find it in Atlanta, Philadelphia, or New York. There is a gap. I can't explain the phenomenon because you don't find it like this anywhere else that I know of in the country in a city of this size.[23]

Much of the blame for the operational distance existing between the Black church and community-based organizations is attributed to the leadership deficiencies of Black ministers. The charge is frequently heard that Black ministers in Boston are incapable of playing effective community roles because most of them reside in the suburbs rather than the inner city. Black ministers who reside in the suburbs, it is contended, do not take up the cause of civic leadership because they have no vested interest in the problems of the city. Black ministers—even ministers who do not live in the suburbs—have argued strongly against the logical import of this claim. One of the strongest critics of the charge is Reverend Eugene Rivers III of the Azusa Christian Community in North Dorchester.

> If one consistently applies that [suburban residency] as criteria by which to validate or invalidate one's political leadership, that would be a criticism worthy of serious consideration. But since, if one applies that criteria, one would invalidate a whole series of people who make significant contributions to the city, I am not sure its not simply a cheap shot. Now, the charge, quite aside from its polemical import, nevertheless raises a valid question. Is one asserting in making the charge that no one can make a significant contribution without subscribing to some territorially based criteria for legitimacy? I live in

this city; I live in this neighborhood. It is not clear to me that if you live in the city that makes you more committed and a more effective activist than if you don't live in the city. Now, all things being equal, however, the activists who live in the neighborhoods where they organize are, in more cases than not, more likely to be effective than political activists who commute. So I too recognize the limitations of a commuter leadership model where the leadership commutes in to lead the masses. That's perhaps not the most effective way to approach it, although I think one would need a more integrated set of criteria by which to evaluate the legitimacy, hanging your hat on the fact that if a person is a suburbanite, while polemically an interesting point, that is not necessarily the most substantive point, if that is the only standing criticism that one deploys to evaluate somebody.[24]

Critics of Black ministers have also accused them of playing buffering roles for the downtown political establishment. Some respondents in this study spoke harshly of the role played by ministers in the struggle over the retention of the elected school committee. They recalled in vivid terms the reactionary role played by Black ministers in preventing State Senator Bill Owens from successfully negotiating a compromise to keep the elected school committee structure from being abolished.

Bill Owens was on the floor, and his last-minute efforts to save the bill failed because these ministers went down to the statehouse to block that bill. That angered me. They [Black ministers] are so out of touch it's a shame. And the really ironic part of it was that none of these guys lived in the city. Not one. So this issue of an appointed committee wasn't going to affect their kids. They were being Uncle Toms for whatever reason. These guys were standing there on the statehouse steps with their arms folded like they had done something. They would never admit that what they did was wrong. They would never admit they undermined the Black community's interests. I felt like punching them out. The only thing that kept me from doing it was the fact that I was a Christian.[25]

Black ministers active in city politics reject the charge that they have been buffers for the downtown establishment. Reverend Eugene Rivers III questioned the logical construction of the charge.

A buffer against what? That's an accusation, not a logical argument. One needs to unpackage that. If that's just a convoluted way of saying the preachers have been Toms for the man against the Black activists and progressive forces of the Black community, then we'd have to examine the evidence because that's an assertion minus either argumentation or evidence. In my judgment the charge to be sustained would require a logical argument, then examples, then a demonstration that the examples constitute tangible evidence.[26]

Rivers contends that in reality Black ministers function less as buffers than as a pragmatic alternative to activists who have no rational political agenda.

> The activists are organized more around what they are against than what they are for. They call the ministers running dog opportunists who have sold the Black community down the river. We ask them, "Well brothers, what is your alternative agenda?" And there is nothing there except freedom for Black people, which is like waiting for the mothership. The activists do not understand that on occasion war is a five-dimensional chess game which is not won or lost in zero sum conflict. I might win one knight or rook, but that's not the end of the game. There are at least ten or fifteen additional moves to be made.[27]

From Rivers's perspective, a candid appraisal of the Black political experience in Boston would show that ministers have been on the cutting edge of many struggles designed to protect and promote the interests of the Black community.

> Black ministers could have been a buffer if they wanted to play the typical client-buffer-Tom role in exchange for nothing. They could have been the ones who functioned as a buffer to do an end run around the activists. That was not the case here. When Ray Flynn attacked [Black school superintendent] Lois Harrison-Jones, we [Black ministers] threatened to picket Flynn's home in South Boston and attacked Flynn more vigorously than anyone had attacked him in this town.[28]

Although the ministers and activists were able to forge a workable coalition to defend the position of Lois Harrison-Jones, the coalition fell apart over the issue of the structure of the school committee. Many ministers disagreed with the activist position that the elected committee structure should be preserved. On this issue Reverend Rivers noted:

> We [Black ministers] saw the elected school committee as nothing more than a political soup kitchen for individuals who should have gotten real jobs and in most cases know very little about education. Just because you run for an office dosen't mean you're qualified to serve if that job description requires that you have some technical command of the relevant issues in education. I don't make an argument for democracy, ipso facto, in some primitive way when the conse-

quence may be that this is not the kind of issue that should be determined electorally, since the requisite skills to perform the functions are not guaranteed by the electoral process. There is no logic in that for me. If I want to establish a system of accountability, it is more logical for me to have one person to blame than thirteen. There was an openended debate around these matters. This was no back door subterfuge, in the dark of night, smoked-filled room deal. People said up front this is our position. If you believe in democracy you believe in democracy win or lose. So we had democracy, and they lost.[29]

The fallout from the school committee controversy still reverberates strongly in the Black community and remains a source of tension and division between Black ministers and Black activists.

It should be noted that all Black ministers in Boston have not been politically active or the targets of accusations that they have functioned as political buffers. Many members of the Black Ministerial Alliance take pride in the fact that they have maintained their distance from the political programs and strategies of the downtown establishment. A number of politically active ministers have taken strong steps to reestablish the Black church as an instrument for positive community uplift and advancement. The Ten Point Coalition, founded in 1992 by Reverend Ray Hammond and Reverend Eugene Rivers III, is the premier church organization devoted to the regeneration of the Black church's activist mission in the service of Black community development. Composed of an organizational base of forty-two churches, the Ten Point Coalition is an outgrowth of organizing work among drug dealers and street gangs by the Azusa Christian Community led by Reverend Rivers in the four corners section of North Dorchester. Rivers took the lead in organizing this Black church coalition in the aftermath of a gang-related stabbing at a funeral at Morning Star Baptist Church in 1992.[30] Rivers's goal was to establish a network of Black churches to work at the street level with at-risk Black youth in economically depressed neighborhoods. Church workers would concentrate their efforts on crime prevention and control. The basic idea was to use the financial and leadership resources of the Black church to intervene in the lives of Black youth and provide them with alternative models for self-development. On the basis of his wide-ranging discussions with Black youth, particularly drug pushers in the four corners area, Rivers authored a ten-point program for Black Christian education and intervention. Churches were asked to adopt, in part or in total, the following proposals:

1.  To establish four or five church cluster-collaborations that sponsor "Adopt a Gang" programs to organize and evangilize youth in gangs. Inner-city churches would serve as drop-in centers providing sanctuary for troubled youth.

2.  To commission missionaries to serve as advocates for Black and Latino juveniles in courts. Such missionaries would work closely with probation officers, law enforcement officials, and youth street workers to assist at-risk youth and their families.

3.  To commission youth evangelists to do street-level, one-on-one evangelism with youth involved in drug trafficking. These evangelists would also work to prepare these youth for participation in the economic life of the nation.

4.  To establish accountable community-based economic development projects that go beyond "market and state" visions of revenue generation. Such economic development initiatives would include community land trusts, micro-enterprise projects, worker cooperatives, community-finance institutions, consumer cooperatives, and democratically-run community development corporations.

5.  To establish links between suburban and downtown churches and frontline ministries to provide spiritual, human resource and material support.

6.  To initiate and support neighborhood crime-watch programs within local church neighborhoods.

7.  To establish working relationships between local churches and community-based health centers to provide pastoral counseling for families during times of crisis.

8.  To convene a working summit meeting for Christian, Black, and Latino men in order to discuss the development of Christian brotherhoods that would provide rational alternatives to violent gang life.

9.  To establish rape crisis drop-in centers and services for battered women in churches. Counseling programs would be established for abusive men, particularly teenagers and young adults.

10. To develop an aggressive Black and Latino history curriculum, with an additional focus on the struggles of women and

the poor. Such a curriculum would be taught in the churches as a means of helping youth to understand that the God of history has been and remains active in the lives of all people.[31]

Rivers's Ten Point plan represents a challenging undertaking. His championing of this cause has brought him both notoriety and considerable personal influence. The capacity of the Ten Point Coalition to make a significant dent in the incidence of street violence and drug use in the Black community has yet to be determined. What is certain is that the Ten Point Coalition has not produced a comprehensive church network. Rivers's aggressive style has attracted some ministers into the ranks of the coalition and repelled others. The community of Black ministers in Boston is highly fragmented. A common view of the Ten Point Coalition is that its ultimate objective is to fill the power vacuum emanating from an existing weak church base in the Black community. Many are curious to see whether the politics of self-aggrandizement will supersede the objective of community uplift in the organization's programmatic agenda.

The progressive face of the Black church is still an unfinished product. Black citizens are continuing to receive mixed signals from church-based leaders, leaving them in a quandary regarding the extent to which they can trust such leaders to negotiate in their interests in highly sensitive sectors of the policy-making process.

## Black Educational Leadership

The educational arena represents another important source of leadership for the Black community in Boston. In the wake of the demise of the elected school committee, much of the responsibility for representing the interests of the Black community in the educational process has fallen on the shoulders of the Black Educators Alliance of Massachusetts (BEAME). BEAME is an organization of Black teachers and administrators concerned with issues of educational equity for Black children and Black professional educators. It has had an important hand in the hiring of two Black superintendents and the implementation of desegregation reforms. In recent years BEAME has engaged in an ongoing battle with the Boston Teachers Union over seniority rights. This issue relates to the effort on the part of the Boston Teachers Union to protect the jobs of White

teachers in a school system with an overwhelming minority population. BEAME has objected strenuously to the use of Black teacher
professional dues to fight for White teacher seniority rights.

Citywide Parent Councils have also had a measurable impact on
the distribution of educational benefits in the Black community.
The Citywide Parent Council structure emerged in 1974 out of the
school desegregation implementation process. Judge W. Arthur
Garrity ordered the establishment of councils in every school as a
way of getting parents talking and interacting across racial lines.
Over time the councils were given the authority to operate as advocacy groups for children in the school system. In this role they participated in the evaluation of teachers and principals and in the
creation and designing of courses and the selection of teaching
materials. In the Black community, parent councils have assumed
important political roles. They have contributed to the introduction
of a multicultural curriculum in the school system so that Black
children can gain a sense of their historical contributions and developmental potential. In 1988 they took the school committee to court
to block the closing of schools in the Black community without public hearings. A protest campaign in 1996 led by the parent councils
successfully blocked the closing of the famous Wheatley School in
the Black community. Victimized by the school committee's power of
the purse, the Citywide Parent Council downtown headquarters
saw its staff reduced from twenty-eight in 1986 to six in 1996.
Despite its limited staff, this office, under the guidance of its director, Hattie McGinnis, remains an important resource for grassroots
citizen mobilization.

Many parents continue to seek alternatives to the Boston Public
School System. METCO remains an important option for parents
who can afford to send their children to suburban schools. After
forty years, METCO's involvement in a system of one-way busing
remains a controversial issue. This program is often accused of
siphoning off the best Black minds from the Boston school system
and delivering them to surrounding school systems. Jean McGuire,
director of METCO, declared this allegation to be a myth.

> They say we recruit the cream of the crop. Nobody ever asks that
> about the private schools, about forty thousand students. Are they the
> cream of the crop? To me all students are the cream of their parents'
> crop. I guest there is such a thing as chocolate cream. But it's very
> interesting. In Boston they say we siphon off. What does that mean?
> What do you know about a student in kindergarten? Ninety-nine per-
> cent of my students come in kindergarten and first grade. As soon as

they get to the suburbs, they put them in special education. I have to fight to keep our kids from being tracked to the bottom and put in special ed. classes saying they need speech therapy. So out there you're all 766, special needs. Then in Boston you're the cream. Both statements come from racist beliefs and thinking.[32]

For many Black parents the key issue is Black control over the institutions that educate their children. Their concern about programs like METCO resides in the fact that when Black children are bused to the suburbs, any semblance of Black control disappears. This fact has profound implications both for the values instilled in the children by the educational process and for the leadership resources and directions of the Black community in the decades ahead.

One possible solution to the community control question is independent schools. The Paige Academy represents an important step in the direction of Black community control. Founded in 1978 by its director, Angela Paige Cook, the Paige Academy is the only African-centered independent school in New England. The academy is a nonprofit private school that operates independently from the Boston Public School System. Its financing comes from tuition, grants, donations, and special contracts. The curriculum of the academy is based on the seven principles of Kawanzaa developed by Dr. Maulana Karenga of California State University, Long Beach. Paige Academy demonstrates that independent Black schools can serve as valuable educational resources. This school prepares students to compete academically with students in public and other private schools, while simultaneously giving them a positive sense of personal and racial identification. Students coming from this kind of background are often well suited to play important roles in the ongoing process of community development and institution building.

## Black Middle-Class Leadership

Black communities in the United States seeking to achieve political incorporation have relied heavily on middle-class leadership. In particular, well-trained Black professionals have brought to the task of community mobilization a rich variety of communication, management, and motivational skills. Boston's Black middle class began to make major leadership waves in the 1940s. This decade witnessed the consolidation of Black community power in the hands of prestigious Black families with deep roots in the culture and history of Boston. Freedom House became the institutional base of this leadership class. The geographic home of this group was the Washington Park section of Roxbury, where large homes and manicured lawns set group members apart from poorer areas of the Black community. The early Black middle class was instrumental in the founding and management of the community's most venerable institutions, including the Urban League, the NAACP, Freedom House, Roxbury Community College, Roxbury Multiservice Center, and Lena Park Community Center. The power and authority of the early middle class began to wane in the face of mass mobilization during the civil rights era and the shift in funding bases of nonprofit organizations in the 1980s. The legitimacy of this class as a leadership force also began to dissipate under the weight of class tension spawned by the expansion of low-income families into middle-class neighborhoods.

Boston began to experience a serious Black middle-class leadership crisis in the 1970s. This fact is curious since the crisis coincided with the massive influx into Boston of Black college students from across the United States to take advantage of new educational and employment opportunities produced by the movement for civil rights. Indeed, since the early 1970s, Boston has been a virtual Mecca for the Black professional class. The crisis emerged from the reluctance of the new Black middle class to embrace the community leadership responsibilities abandoned by the old. Living and working largely in the suburbs, new Black professionals have not, by and large, maintained operational and emotional attachments to inner-city Black neighborhoods. To the extent that they connect to the central city Black community, that connection is social not political. The consequence is that the Black community in Boston has suffered immensely from the failure to harness the talent and the resources of one of the most well educated contingents of Black professionals in America.

> We have Black folk in Boston strategically placed all over this town. This is not the seventies. A whole corps of African American talent has come out of the undergraduate schools, out of the graduate schools, out of the professional schools. It is a shame that this network is not being used to build the boards of these social institutions that are falling apart. What are we doing to get these people on boards, to get them connected? Absolutely nothing. The disconnect in the African American community here is incredible.[33]

The disengagement of Black professionals from inner-city leadership has been a product of both preference and classic patterns of social distance. Many Black professionals have preferred to give their time, talent, and energy to the suburban communities where they live and work. Suburban schools have been a magnet for Black middle-class families, motivating Black professionals to play highly significant roles in suburban school politics and administration. Their primary connection to the Black community is to the Black church and through the money they give to Black causes such as the NAACP and the United Negro College Fund. As relative newcomers, they have also found themselves socially and politically ostracized by a Boston Black community that is very inhospitable to outsiders.

> The Boston Black community is quite parochial and insular. I came to Boston forty years ago to go to graduate school. To a lot of old timers I am still an outsider. I wasn't born and bred in Boston. I have always taken it upon myself to be involved in community affairs. But if I didn't make myself available, no one would come to me and say "how are you helping to move the African American community forward?" Nobody would come to my doorstep and say, "Wait a minute, what's going on here? Why aren't you involved?" [34]

Black professionals moving into Boston from other cities often find networks of social relations among native Black Bostonians impossible to penetrate.

> I get people who call me up and say, "I've been here two years and I can't get into this town. Nobody is helping me to connect to the social and political life of this community. If I were in any other city, somebody would be telling me you've got to go to the NAACP banquet this year. That's required. You've got to go to the Urban League dinner or to this church's awards program. Nobody is pressing tickets on me. This is unreal. What is this place?" And I knew as I sat there talking to these people giving them advice, within a year they would be gone, particularly if they were professional women. They were never going to get connected in a serious way here. [35]

Professor Martin Kilson of Harvard University believes in the years ahead the upscale, entrepreneurial class in the Black community will become the dominant Black political class. His belief is predicated on the notion that Black constituencies have become more disparate and therefore more susceptible to being influenced by a new sophisticated, highly-trained Black leadership class without baseline community roots.[36] This argument suggests that the management and technical skills of this new political class will enable its member to "dovetail the several constituencies of Black leadership."[37] Many of these new Black politicians, Kilson contends, will be Black Republicans loyal to the Black community and endowed with remarkable political savvy. Kilson believes that this group of Black professionals will rise up to create a Black agenda that will unify the Black community under one political tent, even as the community becomes more socially diverse and physically dispersed.[38] A possible prototype of this kind of new Black leader is Suffolk County District Attorney Ralph Martin, an important player in Boston Republican politics and an individual who is being touted as possibly a strong contender for the mayor's office in future elections.[39]

Just how large and how influential the Black upscale, entrepreneurial class will become in the future is an open question. What can be said at the moment is that members of this class have not come forward to fill the huge vacuum left by the departure of the old guard. The longer this vacuum remains unfilled, the more difficult it will be for a new political class, whatever its makeup, to summon the collective will of the community to engage in cohesive political action. The absence of effective professional leadership constitutes one of the greatest barriers the Black community faces in its efforts to penetrate the highest circles of power in the Boston political system.

## Black Political Dilemmas

The numerical representation of Blacks in Boston has substantially increased their importance as a political force in city politics. By the ordinary rules of ethnic succession, Blacks in Boston should be strategically poised to take control of the party structure, the mayor's office, the city council, and the city bureaucracy. Racial transition in these areas would, in turn, create a wealth of economic enhancements for Blacks in the private sector and markedly improve benefits for the Black community in the service delivery process. But the hard reality is that Blacks in Boston do not exercise political power sufficient to realize these objectives. How can the disjuncture between Black potential and Black accomplishment be explained?

Any meaningful explanation must take note of the political dilemmas faced by the Black community in Boston. We have touched on some of these dilemmas in previous sections of this study; a full understanding requires that we amplify our previous analysis and go beyond that analysis to illuminate a welter of internal problems impacting on Black mobilization, incorporation, and empowerment. First it should be noted that Black numerical resources have not been politically strong enough to enable Blacks to undermine White control and escape the consequences of dominant White power in the racial and governmental hierarchy. Thus while Black numerical representation has sharply increased, the power of governance has remained firmly in the hands of a corporate-dominated governing coalition that has shielded Irish and Italian control of city government from substantial Black incursion. The neighborhood-based, fragmented character of the Boston political system has prevented the Black community from forging multiethnic alliances of the kind required to place a significant number of Black leaders into influential positions within the dominant governing coalition. Blacks and Whites in Boston continue to see the political process in zero sum terms. White liberals willing to embrace and promote a Black agenda constitute an insignificant, and often invisible, force. Black-Latino alliances have faltered because of differing perceptions of group interests and appropriate strategies. Blacks in Boston have literally been compelled to carry their political agendas alone. For the Black community in Boston, isolative political engagement has been an ineffective road for the pursuit of the goals of group advancement, empowerment, and incorporation.

In the Boston context, the resource of numbers is also negated by the balkanization of the Black community along residential, ethnic, ideological, and class lines. Under circumstances of extensive internal diversity, the goal of collective struggle becomes extraordinarily difficult to achieve and sustain. At the moment the organizational machinery required to pull disparate Black constituencies together for cohesive political action is virtually nonexistent. The Mel King campaigns demonstrated that well-organized grassroots efforts could produce appreciable results. The dismantling of the King campaign apparatus left a vacuum in grassroots organizational work that has not been filled. No candidate or issue has surfaced since King to ignite the political passion of the Black masses. The central tendency has been toward parochialism and passivity. In recent years Mel King has talked about building a "Rainbow Party" to satisfy the need for sustained grassroots mobilization and political education. Thus far, the critical building blocks of this structure have not been constructed.

It is clear that a fundamental missing ingredient in the resource base of the Black community in Boston is a well-developed organizational network to mobilize the collective power of the Black electorate and lobby for Black interests within formal and informal institutional channels of civic governance. The absence of this network accounts in large measure for the unidirectional character of the policy process on issues of supreme importance to the welfare of the Black community. These decisional patterns are reinforced and compounded by the withering away of civil rights leadership institutions and the systematic erosion of the political influence and service delivery capacity of the nonprofit institutional sector. The implications of these patterns for Black empowerment and incorporation are transparent. An infinitely weakened organizational infrastructure gravely limits the ability of the Black community to participate in the formulation of policy, challenge public policies adverse to its interests, and hold officials accountable for actions they take that are injurious to the social and economic progress of the community.

A pattern of internal conflict among Black organizations and leaders is a source of additional political dilemmas for the Black community. This pattern is most prominently displayed in the ongoing conflict between ministers and activists around an array of public issues. The pattern is also evident in the unwillingness of Black elected officials, leaders of nonprofit agencies, and leaders of civil rights institutions to form a united front to create and promote a common Black agenda. The 1960s were marked by the establishment of functional alliances among major community groups to plot common strategies and implement a community-wide agenda. In the 1990s large fissures developed in the political relations of important community groups. The dominant pattern was that of operational independence and parochialism, with each group developing its own programmatic agenda and flying off separately under its own motive force. This pattern prevented the emergence of a movement center, stifled the growth of oppositional leadership, and halted the momentum sparked by the Civil Rights movement toward political development and incorporation. "We are fragmented in the Black community in a variety of ways, within religious institutions, within electoral officials, within the business community, within the social community, with lot of not for profit agencies having a horrific time in terms of coming to grips with going forward."[40] Some observers find it extremely ironic that dis-unity in the Black political community has reached a crescendo at precisely the time when Blacks have accumulated the potential resources to become a major force in Boston politics.

> The thing that saddens me the most is that the opportunities are greater than they have ever been and our ability to seize the time to take advantage of our newfound strength in terms of numbers and the will to bring about change seems to have dissipated to a horrifically low level. We are on the threshold of literally taking this city over in a very positive way, not just for Blacks and people of color, but for everybody, and our eyes have kind of glazed over. We can't extricate ourselves from the mire and the muck to engage in any concentrated efforts to organize, to mobilize our resources, and to become the new era of leadership. That is totally on us. That is not an outside phenom-enon. It is the fault of our collective abilities to come to grips with our potential, and it rests on everybody within the community.[41]

We should not be surprised that a highly competitive political process exists within the Black community. The routine operation of the political system produces a variety of opportunity structures within racial and ethnic communities that generate internal conflict and competition. Social agencies in the Black community often com-pete with each other for dollars available in municipal budgets for social programming. Personality conflicts emanating from the fund-ing process can create tensions between agencies that last for decades. In Boston the key issue is not competition or bruised egos, but the absence of an organized process to promote operational unity, order, and collective political engagement. Black political incorporation and empowerment require effective communication across a range of institutional structures. Meetings between Black elected officials and Black ministers, for example, do not occur auto-matically, but require fluid communication flow and careful, highly diplomatic, coordination. The development of strategic plans by leadership coalitions capable of garnering widespread community support requires the construction of internal linkage systems, bind-ing together the interest of an eclectic crew of politically activated forces.

The fundamental objective is not only to devise an organizational process to unify diverse community interests, but also to create a permanent citywide intracommunity coalition that is able to sustain gains already achieved and move the phenomenon of political incor-poration to higher levels. Given its history of conscientious, courageous, and productive political development, these goals should be well within the rational grasp of Boston's Black community. But we should not discount the impact of the external political environment on the internal politics of the Black community. The pressure to keep the Black community in Boston underdeveloped and politically subordinate will be extremely intense in the decades ahead. This fact makes it extraordinarily important that the Black community maximize its capacity for unified, conscientious, and courageous struggle and, concomitantly, maintains an unswerving commitment to freedom, justice, and political independence. As one respondent in Boston poignantly observed: "Black citizens in this city must understand that when all the resources within the Black community are connected and activated, Blacks can win and make a difference."[42]

# Black Politics in Liverpool

Part Three

Black Parties in Europe

# 7

## Liverpool: Local Governance and Black Political Empowerment

### Formal Structure and City Governance

The legal position and character of Liverpool City Government in the governing process of Britain is markedly different from the legal position and character of Boston City Government in the governing process of the United States. Liverpool City Government reflects the impact of Britain's unitary structure of government on local decision making, a structure that is at sharp variance with the institutional norms that determine the character and scope of local government in the United States. The power and authority of local governments in the United States are derived fundamentally from the constitutional powers reserved to the states; local governments are creatures of states and can exercise no powers beyond those granted by the states. Under the British unitary system, local governments are the creatures of the central government and have no authority to pursue policies that contravene central government mandates. In Britain, acts of Parliament establish the powers of local government, often spelling out in detail what local authorities are obligated to do as well as the legal limits of their powers and responsibilities.[1]

Local government occupies a central place in the governing process in Britain. The requirements of effective and rational social management and service delivery have dictated that local authorities be given a broad range of responsibilities by the central government. Structural reform acts passed in 1888 and 1894 ignited a process of local consolidation that resulted in the abolition of separate boards for services such as education, health, and social welfare and the concomitant centralization of these functions into the opera-

165

tional procedures of general purpose governments known as local authorities. Today, most critical services at the local level are administered by local authorities, including provisions for health, education, welfare, housing and recreation, and environmental protection. Local government in Britain is big government; one-third of all government expenditures in Britain are administered by local authorities. The cost of local government is an issue of great importance in British politics; it has often motivated central government officials to freely exercise their power to monitor the fiscal policies and priorities of local governments and to transfer administrative responsibilities to independent units when such action suggested that the central government could obtain better value for investments made in the provision of local services.

The principal administrative instrument of local government in Liverpool is the city council. Both legislative and executive responsibilities are lodged in the city council. The City of Liverpool has no independent chief executive. In 1973 the statutory office of Lord Mayor was abolished. Since 1973 the chair of the council has assumed the responsibilities previously vested in the Lord Mayor. Beyond the role of chairing council sessions, the responsibilities and duties of the council chair are purely ceremonial. The only remaining official power retained by the council chair is the right to cast a deciding vote on the rare occasions when votes for and against measures before the council are tied. In contrast to the mayor of Boston, the chair of the Liverpool City Council cannot initiate budgets, appoint members of the city bureaucracy, or veto measures passed by the council. In the absence of an independent executive, the local authority in Liverpool is the city council.

Liverpool City Council is a massive and complex legislative and administrative agency. Since the abolishment of county councils by conservative officials in major metropolitan areas in the 1980s, the Liverpool City Council has functioned alone in Merseyside as a comprehensive district council. Electoral districts for the council are divided into thirty-three wards; three councillors are elected from each ward, establishing a total body of elected councillors of ninety-nine members (an assembly nearly as large as the United States Senate). Liverpool city councillors must run for reelection every four years. Councillors retire in rotation. Council elections are held every year for four consecutive years. The fifth year is a fallow year, a year when no member is up for election. During the next election season, the process of rotation starts over again. The heart of council operation rests in a series of main committees and subcommittees.

Council business is conducted on a five-week cycle. Each council committee is required to meet at least once within the five-week period. At the end of five weeks the entire council will meet to ratify or reject committee and subcommittee recommendations.

Structural reform completed in 1988 reduced the number of main committees in half and slightly increased the number of subcommittees (see figure 7.1). Party representation on main committees is apportioned according to the percentage of seats held by each party in the council. All committees do not command the same degree of influence or enjoy equal levels of funding. Clearly, the most powerful committee of the council is the Finance and Strategy Committee. Much of its power derives from its control over the resources of the council, especially the budget.

> He who controls the purse strings controls everything. The Finance and Strategy Committee is in a powerful position to determine what monies will be spent. Anything that requires the expenditure of money must go through that committee. The Finance and Strategy Committee is the committee of the council that controls the budget. If they are not happy with your proposal, it will get nowhere.[2]

Another key committee is the Education Committee. This committee is the only statutory committee of the city council, its legal position established under central government regulations requiring the maintenance of education committees by all local authorities. One clear indication of the importance of the Education Committee in the Liverpool City Council is the size of its budget. In 1990, the net expenditure of the Liverpool City Council was 386 million pounds. Of that amount, the budget for the Education Committee was £178 million, far and away the largest for any committee of the council. The next closest competitor was the Housing Committee. However, under council rules, the Housing Committee operated under a separate account and was required to raise its own funds from rents and other income sources rather than tapping into the appropriations of the general budget. Funding for other departments included the following: Finance and Strategy, £68 million; Social Services, £55 million; Community Service and Neighborhood Development, £26 million; and Legal Land and Transportation, £24 million.[3]

The Personnel and Equal Opportunities Committee also plays an important role in the council's operation. This committee has responsibility for the management and recruitment of the council's thirty-two thousand-person work force. It is the sole employing com-

**Figure 7.1. Liverpool City Council Committee Structure**

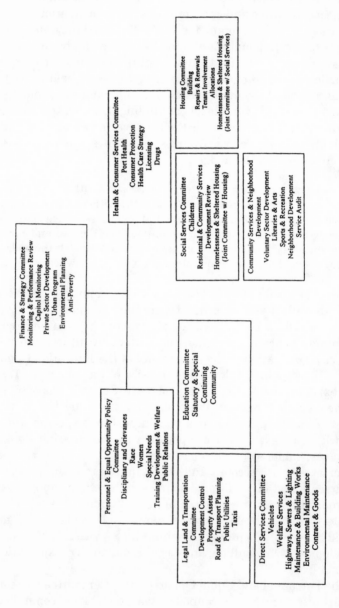

Source: Adapted from data distributed by the Liverpool City Council, 1989.

mittee of the council and deals with all matters that relate to the rates of pay and conditions of service of all council employees. The committee also recommends changes in the council's structure, monitors the efficient utilization of manpower resources, and implements the council's equal opportunities policies in all areas.[4]

Liverpool City Council has extensive investments in public housing. These investments have elevated the position of the Housing Committee to one of great importance in the council hierarchy. Responsibilities of the Housing Committee include the management and maintenance of all residential properties owned by the council and the execution of the council's statutory powers to lend money for mortgages and home improvement.[5]

Although the work of the main committees is more visible and contentious, the most valuable work of the council is often done in subcommittees:

> In a main committee you probably get 30 members plus advisory members, plus the press and the public. Subcommittees have only a half dozen members, so the atmosphere is more relaxed. At the subcommittee level you get a lot of debate because you don't tend to get press attention focused on its activities. The work of the subcommittee is challenged in the main committee only where there is political mileage to be made. If a position is taken in a subcommittee which the opposition is totally opposed to, yes it will get raised in the main committee, and there will be a bit of a debate, but it will be a political debate. People will be scoring points off each other politically, so you don't get an intelligent debate in terms of discussing the merits of the particular issues involved. It becomes a bit of a slugging match, whilst in the subcommittee it is very serious and intelligent discussion that you tend to get.[6]

The heart and soul of local government in Liverpool is the elected member. Elected councillors are expected to be the eyes and ears of the citizenry at-large; their presence in local government provides assurance that the people's democratic rights will be preserved.[7] Efficiency and sound management of local government requires that elected members turn over the day-to-day administration of government affairs to council officers. Under British rules, officers serve at the pleasure of the council and are bound by professional standards of conduct to carry out its mandates. They are expected to ride above the political fray; both their views and their behavior must be nonpartisan and nonpolitical. Council officers sit in on meetings of committees and subcommittees; they are quite free to bring their own ideas to the table and are expected to answer questions as objectively and authoritatively as possible. They must not involve themselves in political decision making; this is the exclusive prerogative of the elected member. Once a council decision is made, council officers are expected to implement that decision completely and without objections.

Chief officers serve as heads of major city departments. Upon appointment to their posts by the council, chief officers have the right to hire deputies and other staff members. Residing at the top of the administrative hierarchy is the chief executive. The principal responsibilities of the chief executive are to coordinate the work of chief officers and their staffs and to represent the city's interests in wider public circles. The success of the council's work depends heavily on informal communication between elected members and council officers. In the real world of local governance, the rituals of communication and cooperation are difficult to maintain. One of the growing trends in Liverpool City Government is the recruitment of highly trained, aggressive council officers who are assuming broader responsibilities in the implementation of the council's political agenda. We should note in this regard that the role of the chief executive has grown in the wake of the council's increasing involvement in initiatives created and funded by the central government.

> There is a task force for Liverpool from central government. They allocate money for socially desirable activities, housing rehabilitation, landscaping, the roads. You get an area where you are going to channel a lot of money, building houses, improving roads, building sports centres. The chief executive would have a key role in organizing the input of the departments of the council. The city has increasingly decided to spend money that way. The chief executive increasingly plays a role in helping to develop and implement the strategy.[8]

Concerned about the expanding role of council officers in the governing process, some councillors have attempted to dilute the influence of officers by blocking their reports to committees and preventing their ideas from influencing the council agenda. On this issue one council officer noted:

> I think it's a dangerous phenomenon, but there are ways in which individual members, depending on who they are and how they want to behave, will put you under pressure not to put a report up or tell you that what you want to raise is not appropriate. By virtue of the fact that you are employed by the council, they're putting you under pressure and threatening to make your life hell. This kind of pressure can clearly influence you to conform with what they're saying.[9]

The council leader is another major player in council deliberations. The position of council leader has no basis in law but derives its authority from the fact that the person who occupies this position has been designated as the leader of the majority party. The council leader has the capacity to wield a great deal of personal power. With support from the majority party, and in the absence of a central policy making unit within the council, the council leader is in a position to forge working coalitions to iron out or resolve major problems. Council leaders often pyramid their power by serving as chair of the Finance and Strategy Committee. In lieu of this kind of formal leadership role, some leaders have opted to devise other strategies for influencing the council's legislative agenda. Thus in the late 1980s, Labour Party leader Keva Coombes declined to serve as chair of Finance and Strategy but expanded his powers by demanding that all reports by council officers be reviewed by him before being submitted to council committees and subcommittees.

In the 1990s the tug of war between political leaders and officers has continued to escalate as the power of chief officers to hire their staffs has been curtailed by demands by councillors that such appointments receive the scrutiny and approval of the council.

> In the past there was a clearer distinction in the role and function of
> an officer and the elected member. Now, over the past six or seven
> years, those roles have gotten blurred. People aren't supposed to be
> appointed because of political views or affiliations. Yet we are now
> sometimes asked to send applications together with the indication of
> who will be appointed to the chair and deputy chair of the Personnel
> Committee before we can offer the appointment. I can tell you times
> when appointments were changed from the legitimate procedure to
> appoint politicians solely on the grounds of political affiliation and
> friendship.[10]

Council leaders have felt obligated to reduce the autonomous decision making authority of department officers to prevent officers from crossing too far over the line of political management and control as well as to maintain credibility in the eyes of their party members who wish to use the council to significantly increase their stock of patronage and other valuable political resources. In the words of John Hamilton, former Labour leader of the council, "[T]he first responsibility of a council leader is to take care of the needs and desires of his own group."[11]

Discussions of local government in Britain often overlook the important role played by the district auditor. The central government has set up district auditor offices in every major metropolitan area. These offices serve as quangos, or independent governmental units. The parameters of their jurisdiction and responsibilities are set forth by central government statutes. The primary responsibility of the district auditor is to investigate the expenditure policies and practices of local government to make sure those policies and practices are in compliance with existing laws. The activities of the district auditor include the examination of council minutes and financial records. From time to time the district auditor will conduct exercises to see if local citizens are getting value for money from the local authority. These exercises often involve comparative analyses of the fiscal policies of authorities across the country to make sure that policies pursued in the local jurisdiction are in line with those being implemented elsewhere. In recent years the district auditor has played an immensely important role in the regulation of fiscal policies and practices embraced by the Liverpool City Council.

> The district auditor has become a much more important element in the local government world. They play a fairly important interventionist role. They watch what we do and will often request information from the authority and scrutinize that information. They will fire warning shots across our brow every so often, particularly in the run up to the budget making process. They offer unsolicited advice. The city treasurer has to have a lot of contact with that machinery. Our policies in Liverpool are probably more scrutinized than in other places by that machinery because of what has happened here.[12]

## The Policy Environment

Like Boston City Government, Liverpool City Government does not exist in splendid isolation but functions within the context of a broader social, economic, and political environment. One significant difference in the environments of Boston and Liverpool is the comparatively minor role played by business in the policy making process in Liverpool. This policy role of business in Liverpool is explained, in part, by the small number of locally based major companies operating in Liverpool. As we noted in chapter 2, many businesses in Liverpool exist as branches of companies with their central headquarters located in other parts of Europe as well as the United States. For the most part, business leaders in Liverpool have not consolidated their political resources to maximize their impact on the policies of the local authority. Movement in this direction has been undercut by the countervailing power exercised by organized labor. In this regard it is worth noting that Liverpool is fundamentally a working-class city; the mobilization of the working class for political purposes has meant that the power wielded by organized labor has been more extensive and potent than in any other British city. To the extent that business interests are organized, they are organized through a Chamber of Commerce dominated by two companies: Little Woods (and the John Moores Family) and the Royal Insurance Company, both Liverpool-based economic conglomerates.

Economic crisis has deeply affected the political culture and environment of Liverpool. Several factors have made economic crisis a compelling challenge for Liverpool. First, the decline of the port has resulted in the loss of jobs, job training and development opportunities, competitive wages, and corporate and industrial activities tied to shipping and related dock work. Economic crisis in Liverpool has also been fueled by a drastic loss in population. The decline in the number of young people in the city has been exceptionally severe, with many young people choosing to move to the suburbs or to more attractive locales farther south. The upshot has been the concentration in Liverpool of older, high-cost citizens with a wide variety of special needs and few resources to pay in taxes to support expanded governmental social spending in their behalf.

> The authority has very serious financial problems. Because of the loss of its young professional income base, it is compelled to spend lots of money on social services and school reorganization. To meet these needs it has had to set a very high community charge and to borrow money from Swiss and Japanese banks at exorbitant interest rates. It has also indulged in a severe budget-cutting exercise. Every department has suffered cuts in its spending programs, which were already reduced. So we are barely limping along.[13]

Liverpool's economic crisis has been greatly exacerbated by cuts in grant support by the central government. In this regard one city council officer noted that between 1978 and 1990 the level of central government subsidy for Liverpool dropped from 66 percent in 1978 ("When I first came to Liverpool") to one-third by 1990.[14] Cuts in grant support have mirrored the population decline Liverpool has experienced over the past two decades. But population decline does not tell the entire story. Under Conservative administrations in the 1970s and 1980s, the central government sought to solve its own budget problems by reducing public spending by local authorities.

Liverpool became a special target because of its reputation as an outpost for the "Looney Left" and "Militant" elements of the Labour Party. An alliance of the intellectual Right and the popular press resulted in a virulent attack by conservative forces on "radical" local authorities; this attack became the keynote of the third election victory by Margaret Thatcher as prime minister in 1978.

Over the past two decades Liverpool has found itself under siege from the central government. Key elements of the attack have included not only measures to reduce central government grant support, but efforts to circumscribe the scope of the city council's administrative authority. The power of the council to manage and expand its public housing programs has been restricted by the central government's decision to place housing responsibilities and funds in independent agencies called "housing authorities." Other aspects of local government were placed in the hands of task forces and development corporations, all funded directly by the central government. Central government has also approved policies that allow local school systems to opt out of city educational programs (this is called "local management of schools") and to subject the provision of a wide variety of local services to competitive tendering (a process that allows private firms to compete with government service units for contracts to perform services in behalf of the local authority). In response to these changes, city officials have had to develop ingenious schemes to keep the control of education policies and service responsibilities within the firm grip of the local authority.

> We have not awarded a contract yet outside the local authority. Everything is still in the hands of the politicians. The buildings cleaning contract, which had to go to tender, was won by the direct services organization. It is a matter of great concern to us that some of the private companies that put themselves forward are interested in profits in ways the city is not. They are business organizations. When you give contracts outside the local authority, councillors lose day-to-day control. The city's own departments are a part of local government. They are a part of the democratic process. And local councillors still have control.[15]

## Party Politics

Liverpool's political environment has been marked by interparty competition. Boston-style machine politics has not become rooted in

Liverpool's political culture. One-party dominance in Boston has been superseded in Liverpool by fierce competition between major political parties. Before the 1960s the basic motif of the electoral process was competition for the hearts and minds of voters by the Conservative Party and the Labour Party. Electoral conflict tended to reflect sectarian conflict between Protestants and Catholics, with the Conservatives receiving strong political support from Protestants, and Labour being dubbed the "Catholic Party." The decade of the 1960s marked the beginning of a radical shift in party alliances in Liverpool. The Conservative Party lost its base of power in the city as a consequence of the ethnic integration of neighborhoods and the decline of religion as a factor in city politics. Religious divisions in political life began to disappear in the wake of decisions by the city council to eliminate urban slums and reassign residents in council housing according to need rather than ethnic affiliation. Under the weight of these decisions, the coincidence between religion and public service disappeared. The delivery of public service along religious lines had been the bedrock of Conservative Party politics. The breaking up of ethnic neighborhoods meant that the geography of public service no longer matched the geography of residence.

Into the breach left by the growing inability of Conservatives to campaign for votes on the basis of religion stepped a group of new, dynamic political actors, the Liberal Democrats. During the early 1970s, the Liberals began to campaign for the votes of working-class Protestants and Catholics on the basis of community politics. The key element of Liberal strategy was a promise of improved consumer services, such as refuse collection, housing repair, street lighting, and improved pedestrian crossings.[16] Although Liberal activists were not seasoned politicians, they turned out to be effective campaigners. In the 1973 council elections, they pulled off a minor miracle by taking seats from both Labour and Conservatives and assumed formal control of the council.

The Liberal Party victory in 1973 began a decade of political stalemate in which none of the three major parties held majority control of the council. For most of this period the Liberal Party assumed administrative control with support from the Conservative Party. Michael Parkinson has called this period of Liverpool city government the "lost decade."[17] During this era many pressing problems went unattended as the Liberals found themselves incapable of fashioning a coherent urban agenda and the Labour Party continued to feel the wrath of the voters because of a disastrous slum clearance program in the 1960s that saddled the city with enormous debt. The absence of firm control and clear direction undermined the professional performance of the city bureaucracy, substituting political expedience for rational, cost efficient, bureaucratic decision making.

Liberal leadership meant the abandoning of Labour's policy of new home construction in favor of an extensive housing rehabilitation program involving cooperative arrangements between city government and the private sector.[18] Complementing this approach was a commitment to holding down tax rates while promoting a major rise in council house rents. These policies were pursued with political intent. Liberal policies were designed to maximize the party's appeal to the skilled working-class and lower middle-class voters who served as the foundation of the party's rise to a position of prominence and power in Liverpool politics. These policies were implemented, however, at the expense of inner-city voters whose houses were allowed to deteriorate, who were blocked from moving into new houses, and who were required to finance continued spending by the council through the payment of higher rents.

A backlash against Liberal policies citywide in the 1983 municipal elections resulted in the return of Labour control of city council. Although the new leader of the council, John Hamilton, was a pragmatic political moderate, the policy agenda of the Labour Party in the council was dominated by a radical left wing faction of the party known as the "Militant Tendency." Militant politicians embraced a hard Troskyist position on the class struggle that left no room for distinctions among members of the working class on the basis of race. The influence of Militant within the ranks of the Labour Party emanated from the fact that during its ten-year hiatus from majority control, the Labour Party had become too bureaucratized and highly fossilized. Moderate leaders of the party had lost contact with the electorate. Militant politicians were able to exploit the vacuum in Labour leadership because they were young, charismatic, articulate, determined, and represented the most organized focal point for socialist ideas in the Labour Party in Liverpool.[19] As the most cohesive and organized segment of the Labour coalition, Militant politicians were able to work their way onto party committees and into powerful posts within the local authority.

The Militant Tendency used its power in the city council to embark on a campaign of "urban socialism" that gave priority to extensive home construction in seventeen areas and a major expansion of the council's work force. Cuts in revenue to local authorities proposed by Prime Minister Margaret Thatcher threatened to wreck Militant's housing program and undermine the fiscal viability of the local economy. Militant politicians in Liverpool opposed Thatcher's urban economic policies with great passion. Escalating conflict with the central government over a range of issues, including the setting of the city's tax rate, culminated in the surcharging and expulsion of forty-seven councillors en mass from the Liverpool City Council in 1986.

Most of the councillors removed from office were a part of the Militant Labour faction. This action constituted a blow to the power of the Militant Tendency from which it could not recover. Power in the Liverpool Labour Party shifted from the Militant Tendency to the Progressive Caucus, a group of moderate left councillors who were strongly opposed to Militant's ideology and policy orientation. The selection of Harry Rimmer as council leader to replace John Hamilton (one of the forty-seven expelled councillors) provided a strong signal that the power shift in the Labour group had been consummated. Deputy council leader under Hamilton, Rimmer was prominently associated with the Progressive Caucus. After six months, Rimmer resigned as council leader in protest against the unwillingness by the central government to reexamine the tax rate approved for Liverpool. Rimmer was replaced as leader in 1987 by Keva Coombes. A left wing councillor not affiliated with any major faction, Coombes attempted to steer a middle course between the Progressive Caucus and Militant Tendency politicians, seventeen of whom remained in the council. Coombes gradually lost the support of the Progressive Caucus in the wake of allegations that he was stacking his administration with friends and supporters. Moving to strengthen his relations with the far Left, Coombes supported the decision by Militant not to implement the poll tax (or community charge) imposed by the central government. His defiant position lead to his dismissal from the council, along with that of sixteen additional members of the Militant faction. Supporters of the Progressive Caucus were highly critical in their assessments of Coombes's tenure as council leader. "Coombes's approach was too fractured and unsystematic. He did not plan strategically. He did not bring people together. He was a one-man band. Now that he is gone we will probably see a more democratic style of policy making emerging in the council."[20]

The responsibility of promoting greater democracy in the council was placed, once again, in the hands of Harry Rimmer. Under Rimmer the Progressive Caucus took firm control of the council's

178 BLACK ATLANTIC POLITICS

most important posts, including chair of the Finance and Strategy Committee and chair of the Education Committee. The power of the Progressive Caucus was moderated by the fact that municipal elections in 1990 and 1994 resulted in hung councils, preventing Labour or the Liberals from compiling solid working majorities. Rimmer was replaced as council leader in 1996 by Frank Prendergast. During Prendergast's tenure, the balance of power in the council between Labour and the Liberals remained razor thin.[21] The expressed desire on the part of the Progressive Caucus to provide "more rational approaches to policy,"[22] must confront the hard reality that the Labour Party cannot do almost anything in Liverpool without the deference, compliance, and support of the experts in pavement politics: the Liberal Democrats.

## Black Political Linkage: The Nonissue of Race

Structural ingredients of Liverpool City Government and their concomitant political milieu present formidable challenges to political actors seeking to promote Black linkage, representation, incorporation, and empowerment. In many respects, barriers to Black advancement in Liverpool are higher and more resistant to change than those faced by Blacks in Boston. The Black community in Liverpool, like the Black community in Boston, has been compelled to grapple with the issue of political linkage. The ability on the part of Blacks in Liverpool to make and carry out decisions through the instruments of local government has been rendered exceptionally difficult by British attitudes that deny the existence of race as a factor in the distribution of public goods. In the United States, racial practices such as neighborhood and school segregation have often been not only officially sanctioned but also implemented by the institutions of the state. Britain does not have a history of de jure segregation and discrimination. The absence of legal support for racial practices in Britain has produced an important paradox: while overt prejudice is expressed and practiced, it is rarely officially acknowledged. British laws and institutions have tended to accept without dispute the notion that race is not a special problem to be addressed through assertive government action but is merely a form of general deprivation that can be ameliorated through efforts designed to improve social and economic conditions for all citizens in society.

At the local level, efforts to marginalize the issue of race have become the pivotal touchstone of British local policy.[23] In the absence of national mandates, a pattern of ideological color-blindness has emerged that accepts the proposition that local authorities are not required to move beyond general purpose programs in their efforts to eradicate problems faced by Blacks in the inner city. Assumptions undergirding this color-blind approach reinforce notions that Black groups have no role to play in the policy making process and therefore need not be engaged as partners or actors in that process.

Issues centering on race have been extraordinarily difficult to engage in Liverpool because of the generalized belief that race policies in Britain are designed to tackle unique problems experienced by immigrants rather than problems that may be applicable to a nonimmigrant Black community. Blacks in Liverpool are victimized by the assumption that they are regular scousers who speak with a Liverpool accent and do not face social and cultural problems distinct from those of the working-class population as a whole. Liverpool's chief education officer expressed a deeply held view when he told a group of community activists in 1978 that he "did not believe the system was any more rigged against blacks than against the Liverpool Irish, Welsh or Scots."[24] In a letter to activists written before the meeting, he averred the opinion "to allege racial discrimination is to incite discord."[25] The chief education officer's dismissal of race as a factor in the policy process stands in stark relief to the conclusion of the Gifford Report that social and economic conditions in Liverpool's Black neighborhoods were uniquely horrific.[26] In effect, what the Gifford Report did was to expose governmental intransigence on race issues that had served as a critical roadblock to Black political advancement over many decades. Commenting on this issue, one respondent noted: "No one is seriously addressing the question of equality, service distribution, and access. People don't want to be called racists; their way of avoiding that is to deny that race is an issue."[27]

Under the weight of ideological color-blindness, the Black community in Liverpool has not only been victimized by policies of racial neglect, but also the rational rules of bureaucratic behavior. In Liverpool City Government, the routines of service delivery make it exceedingly difficult to deal with the issue of race. The geography of delivery is an issue that is rarely discussed by the captains of the city bureaucracy.[28] Following the rational rules of bureaucracy, which are supposedly racially neutral and therefore color-blind, these service delivery procedures do not discriminate in relation to geographic location. They do discriminate negatively and constitute a form of passive discrimination by ignoring the special history and the extraordinary needs of the Black community. Seemingly paralyzed by the rational rules of bureaucracy, government professionals in Liverpool have no machinery in the normal delivery process for giving preference to racially oppressed communities. Victimized by bureaucratic intransigence and inertia, Blacks often find that the only way they can obtain better service delivery is to leave the Black community and move (if they can) to nonBlack communities where the quality and quantity of services are significantly higher.

### Liberal Politics and Black Political Linkage

Effective Black linkage to the city council in Liverpool has been an extraordinarily difficult objective to achieve. One critical obstacle to the realization of this goal has been a commitment by the council to a strategy of nondecision making. For many years all of the major parties failed to acknowledge the deteriorating economic plight of the Black community and to embrace vigorous programs of positive action and equal opportunity. From the early 1960s to the 1980s, Liverpool councillors refused to seriously engage the issue of race or to execute policies that would incorporate the interests of the Black community into the decision making processes of the city council.

The Liberal Party's pursuit of its political goals precluded the serious adoption of innovative programs to address the critical problems of employment, crime, education, and health in the inner city. Liberal administrations did not give strong consideration to the development of a comprehensive program to promote and achieve social and economic reform for the Black community despite an abundance of evidence—much of it presented by an activist group called the "Liverpool Black Organization"—that Blacks were suffering in unconventional ways under the heels of the prevailing racial hierarchy. Concessions the Liberals did make on racial matters were, for the most part, weak and unproductive.

A departure in the party's usual behavior of ignoring racial issues was made in 1980 when the Liberal-dominated Finance and Strategy Committee placed race officially on the council agenda for the first time by adopting an equal opportunity policy for the committee. Under pressure from several community groups, including the Liverpool Black Organization (LBO), the Merseyside Anti-

Racialist Alliance (MARA), and the Merseyside Community Relations Council (MCRC), the full council voted to adopt an equal opportunity policy and set up a consulting group on race called the "Race Relations liaison committee."[29] At first blush, the establishment of the Liaison Committee appeared to be a major breakthrough. The committee was composed of twelve elected officials and twelve representatives of community organizations. Invitations to sit in on the committee's meetings were extended to representatives of all the major service organizations, as well as four nonvoting members from the Joint Shop Stewards Committee. Blacks viewed the committee as the first opportunity for the Black community to establish formal linkage with the policy making structures of the council. This perception was reinforced by procedures that called for the committee to report to the Finance and Strategy Committee at least once during each council cycle. In recognition of their growing sense of empowerment, Black representatives on the committee organized themselves into a group called the "Black Caucus." Members of the Black Caucus quickly discovered that their mere presence on the liaison committee did not guarantee substantial influence into the decision making process. They found that the work of the committee was greatly hindered by the refusal of the council to assign senior officers to the liaison committee. Their confidence in the ultimate value of the committee was significantly shaken when their recommendations for the setting up of a working party on racial harassment on council estates, a training scheme for housing managers, racial monitoring in employment, and a housing shelter scheme for the Black elderly were all rejected.[30]

Conflict across party lines also posed a serious threat to the work of the committee. Labour Party leaders strenuously opposed a proposal sponsored by Liberal council leader Trevor Jones requesting that members of the liaison committee examine ways of making the employment of Blacks in the council's work force commensurate with the percentage of Blacks living in the council's recruitment area. The fight against Jones's proposal was led by Militant leader Derek Hatton. Arguing against the implementation of equal opportunities policies in the council, Hatton contended that such policies would exacerbate racism by showing favoritism to Blacks and ignite a strong backlash by far right groups.[31] Hatton made it clear that Militant believed that working-class unity could only be preserved if the council refrained from endorsing or implementing race-specific programs or reputational schemes.

In the final analysis, the Race Relations Liaison Committee had only a minor impact on council policy. Members of the Black Caucus found the challenge of effectively penetrating the key domains of policy-making power and authority in the council overwhelming. Patterns of policy intransigence on race matters could not be substantially altered. To its deep regret what the caucus found was not only opposition from the elected members but also great reluctance by leaders of the organized city bureaucracy to seriously entertain the possibility of changing their policy approaches to embrace actions designed to promote the achievement of equal opportunity for the Black community.

## Militant Politics and the Black Community: The Sampson Bond Affair

The 1983 municipal elections represented not just a victory for the Labour Party but also a spectacular ascendance into power of the Militant Tendency. Under the new organization of the council, Derek Hatton became deputy leader and chair of the Race Relations Liaison Committee. Although John Hamilton was selected as the council leader, much of the power in the council devolved into the hands of Hatton and his Militant colleagues. The rapid shift in power in the council was signaled by the filling of council posts with Militant supporters, the recruitment of a new local security force (sometimes referred to as "Hatton's army"), the cutting off or reduction of funds going to community groups viewed as Militant opponents, and the freezing of vacant posts for community organizations that refused to toe the Militant line.[32]

The most audacious power move made by Militant was the appointment of Sampson Bond, a Black building surveyor from London, as the principal adviser to the council for race relations. For a number of months, members of the Black Caucus had urged the council to set up a network of race advisory units in key city departments. As a part of this recommendation, the clear need for the appointment of a principal race adviser with broad coordinating responsibilities emerged. The Black Caucus anticipated that the individual appointed to this post would be someone from the local Black community with broad experience in race relations work and community organizing. Leaders of the Militant Tendency, while embracing the concept of a principal race adviser, decided to bypass local Black community leaders and to recruit a Black Militant supporter from London to fill this key post. Derek Hatton traveled to

London to personally interview Bond for the post and arrange for his travel to Liverpool to talk with members of the local search committee. During the meeting Hatton, who chaired the session, insisted that Bond be shortlisted despite reservations about his qualifications expressed by members of the committee representing the Black Caucus. Although Bond's interview was clearly the weakest of the six candidates on the shortlist, Hatton pushed a recommendation for Bond through the committee, insisting that what was needed in the post was not a seasoned political activist (Bond had no community organizing experience) but someone who was willing to implement race policies according to the socialist principles of the Labour Party. The vote on the committee in support of Bond was 6 to 4, with all 6 Labour councillors voting for Bond and 3 members of the Black Caucus, and 1 Liberal councillor casting dissenting votes. Christine Duala, an observer at the meeting representing the NALGO labour union, recalled the heavyhanded tactics used by Hatton to engineer the Bond recommendation.

> Derek Hatton said, "I know what I am looking for," and the meeting went downhill from there. He said, "I am looking for someone with new blood, fresh ideas. I think Sam Bond is the one for me." We said, "wait a minute. What qualities does he have? His application shows he has not been involved in any major Black struggles." He was supposed to be a member of Brent [London] NALGO. This NALGO has a strong workers' movement, yet our sources in London say he hasn't shown his face there. All these questions kept coming up, and Hatton said "No, no, no. I am looking for fresh blood. I think he's the best candidate for the job. That's all I am saying. You shall have your say in a minute." And he just went around the table, and all six of these Labour representatives went around the table, one after the other, saying that Sampson Bond was the best person for the job.[33]

Outraged by the recommendation in Bond's favor, the three Black Caucus representatives stormed out of the meeting. They were followed by Christine Duala, who vowed to recommend to her union that all council activities be boycotted until the recommendation of Sampson Bond to become the principal race relations adviser was reversed. News of the Bond recommendation swept across the Black community; the reaction of Blacks to the recommendation was almost unanimously hostile.

> Derek Hatton said this is a Black man; he'll do you. This made people angry because Sam Bond had no background in community relations or social relations. It was an appointment that devalued the struggle

in Liverpool. Simply because he was Black we were supposed to be satisfied. We wanted more than that.We wanted someone who knew what the problems were.[34]

The overriding perception of the Bond recommendation in the Black community was that Bond was a political hack who was being brought in to serve as principal race relations adviser not because of his professional competence and experience but because he was a loyal, faithful, and mindless supporter of the Militant Tendency.

> They brought in this guy from London, a building surveyor, to do this job, who also turned out to be a Militant supporter and concurred with the views and beliefs of the Militant Tendency. Although he was going to take on the job of principal race relations adviser, he just didn't believe that Black people were an issue. It seemed to us that that was a bit off the wall. We said no can do and thought that they would automatically rescind it and start the process again. But they were so entrenched on this position that they thought it's only the Black people from Liverpool—we are the local authority. We will beat them down until they accept.[35]

Militant leaders quickly learned that the Black community was not willing to passively accept the Bond appointment. When Derek Hatton arrived at his office a day after the search committee vote, he was greeted by a noisy picket demonstration led by NALGO and members of the Black Caucus. This protest escalated to the level of face-to-face confrontation when representatives of the picketing groups staged a sit-in in Hatton's council office. The sit-in ended when Hatton agreed to sign a document that promised to overturn the commitment to Bond and readvertise the post of principal race relations adviser. Hatton wasted no time reneging on his promise. Attending the District Labour Party Conference the next day, Militant politicians from Liverpool charged that Hatton had been held hostage by members of the Black Caucus and only signed the promise to readvertise under duress. Hatton and his supporters made it clear that they had no intention of backing away from the Bond appointment. Under the firm control of the Militant faction, the District Labour Party voted overwhelmingly to support the recommendation that Sampson Bond be appointed as the principal race relations adviser to the Liverpool City Council.

In the wake of the District Labour Party's actions, relations between Militant and the Liverpool Black community descended into open warfare. Militant leaders used the pages of the *Militant* newspaper and council documents to denounce members of the

Black Caucus as violent, criminal, alien, and self-interested.[36] Black Militant supporters from London were recruited into Liverpool to set up a new group, called the "Merseyside Action Group" (MAG), to challenge the power and influence of the Black Caucus in the Black community. MAG made little headway in the implementation of its action agenda. Indeed, once Bond was formally appointed, it became difficult for him and his Militant supporters to find an audience in the Black community. One member of the Black Caucus remembered the following episode from an effort by Bond to take his case to the Black community at a large public meeting.

> Leaders of MAG came to Granby and paid twelve persons £100 each to serve as body guards for Bond and escort him into the meeting. A van pulls up and twelve guys get out, six on each side, and Bond is walking in the middle. When he walked into the sports center, his minders told the people to sit down you're listening now. The people said no. He was coming in like a dictator. People started throwing chairs. They ran outside and tried to turn the van over. No one was interested in listening to what this traitor had to say.[37]

In defense of community interests, members of the Black Caucus devised a host of fightback strategies. A great deal of attention was focused on building networks of support among trade unions, the clergy, and neighborhood organizations. The caucus systematically published responses to Militant charges in the *Liverpool Echo* and the *Black Linx*. Mass marches and rallies were organized to push for the removal of Bond from his post. As a final step, the caucus held a meeting with national Labour leader Neil Kinnock to voice its concerns about Militant's race policy agenda. At the conclusion of the meeting, Kinnock expressed reservations about the propriety, efficacy, and legitimacy of Militant strategies, tactics, and policies. After he returned home, Kinnock received a sharply worded letter from Derek Hatton criticizing him for meeting with the Black Caucus, "the enemies of the Labour movement."[38] This attack gave additional credibility to feelings in national Labour circles that Militant politics in Liverpool was raging out of control.

Long after the decline of Militant power in the city council, a highly charged debate continued regarding the impact of Militant's brand of urban socialism on the welfare of Black citizens in Liverpool. In a retrospective analysis of local authority policies during the Militant years, Militant leaders Peter Taaffe and Tony Mulhearn claimed that the council's urban policies had an extremely positive residual impact on social and economic conditions in the Black community. Among the achievements cited were the following:

1.  Expenditure of 48 million pounds on housing—more than any other local authority's housing budget.
2.  Rehousing 1,730 families.
3.  Building of 178 dwellings.
4.  Carrying out large-scale improvements of 1,782 dwellings.
5.  Demolition of 2,100 empty slums.
6.  Carrying out of major landscape work.
7.  Rebuilding of 150 shops.[39]

Missing from Militant's litany of achievements were a number of positive action programs proposed by the Black Caucus that were rejected out of hand. One respondent sharply criticized Militant's approach to Black community programming.

Militant's claims of doing great things for the Black community are absolute and total rubbish. Militant's philosophy is such that to put any kind of efforts of financial resources into tackling the issue of racism would be always divisive of the working-class struggle. The classic example was their refusal to build the housing program for the Black elderly. In the 1980s a survey was done, and one of the things that came out was that none of the Black elderly were going into elderly accommodations. A proposal was put forth to build a home for the Black elderly. The 75 percent was actually obtained from central government. Plans had begun to move for construction of this, and the Militants literally stopped it. If that working-class elderly happened to include Black people, that's fine. But the idea of doing something only for the Black community was politically unacceptable.[40]

The Sampson Bond affair came to an inglorious end with the destruction of Militant's power base in the council in the aftermath of the mass ejection of Militants from the council in 1986. One of the top items on the agenda of the Progressive Caucus upon seizing power was the termination of Bond's contract. Seeing the handwriting on the wall, Bond resigned, married a woman from the South, and returned home to resume his career as a building surveyor.

Obstacles to Black Political Empowerment

The trench warfare waged between Black leaders and the Militant Tendency was emblematic of deeper problems encountered by the Black community in Liverpool in its continuing struggle for social, economic, and political advancement. Black leaders in Liverpool have been compelled to confront the fact that obstacles to Black empowerment are pervasive, institutionalized, and extremely difficult to surmount. The size of the Black community in Liverpool represents a considerable political liability that Black leaders have had to bear. Constituting only approximately 8 percent of the population, Blacks in Liverpool are marginalized in the electoral process because of their inability to register a decisive impact in most local elections. In this area Boston's Black community enjoys a substantial political advantage over Liverpool's Black community. At approximately 24 percent, Boston's Black community has the potential of playing a key balance-of-power role in citywide elections and as a central controlling force in selected district elections. While Boston's Black population is spread out across a number of wards, the Black population in Liverpool is concentrated in the Granby Ward and (to a smaller degree) in the Abercromby Ward. For Blacks in Liverpool, this means that Blacks have a realistic chance of influencing the election of six of ninety-nine councillors in the Liverpool City Council. This is an important statistic since the policy-making behavior of councillors is heavily constituency driven. Thus, one reason many councillors do not view targeted programs for the Black community as high priority issues is that there is no substantial concentration of Black residents in their wards. Liverpool is a highly segregated city, a fact that is vividly revealed in the racial makeup of council districts. Under these circumstances, many councillors view support for Black programs as a political liability since they will not gain Black votes for such support and run the realistic danger of stirring up a political backlash from their White constituents.

Black electoral influence is further reduced by a pattern of relatively low Black registration and turnout in Black wards. Although election participation data is not systematically preserved in Liverpool (one has to go to the polls and visibly eyeball the data before it is discarded), knowledgeable informants suggest that in most elections less than 20 percent of the eligible Black population turns out to the polls. A survey conducted in 1990 in a five-block area in the heart of Toxteth by the author and Sam Semoff, an

American living in Liverpool, found that while 69 percent of Black respondents indicated they were registered to vote, only 41 percent indicated they had turned out to vote in the last election (see figure 7.2).

Low Black electoral participation reflects in great measure strong Black community disaffection from the Labour Party. The simple truth is there is no Labour Party in the Black community. Very few Blacks identify themselves as Labour Party members or activists (see figure 7.2 ). This fact was bought home in dramatic fashion at a meeting of the Labour Black Sections movement held in Liverpool in 1990 and attended by the author. Almost all of the delegates at this meeting were from out of town. Only five Blacks from Liverpool (out of a total of over sixty people) considered this meeting important or interesting enough to attend. Many Blacks in Liverpool express open hostility to the Labour Party, an attitude that served as the seedbed for a serious independent political movement in the Black community in 1986. Strong anti-Labour Party feelings flow, in part, from the reluctance of the Labour Party to seriously embrace a Black agenda.

> We thought at one time Labour would be the key. Labour said they would support us once they got in office. We discovered that they were not taking us seriously. We were especially angry that Liverpool-born Blacks were not made a part of the decision making process.[41]

Fallout from the Sampson Bond affair also drove a deep wedge between the Labour Party and the Black community.

> The Militants acted so badly they lost the Black vote. They were thick. They were nut cases. I didn't know that one could be so stupid in life. This was not Militant. This was Labour. This was socialism. They really believed that people were comrades together. But some of the worst racism is at the working-class level.[42]

A number of respondents suggested that the Labour Party did very little to recruit Blacks as active members or get them out to the polls. Blacks did not systematically receive notices of party meetings. Applications for membership by potential Black candidates were sometimes held up and not processed until the election deadline had passed. Some of these problems stemmed from willful action; others were the by-product of weak organization.

> The Labour Party as an organization is not very active in Toxteth. Local attendance at Granby ward meetings is small. Blacks are not

**Figure 7.2. Results of Political Participation Survey in Liverpool**

N = 157, 69% Black, 31% White

|  | Blacks | Whites | All |
|---|---|---|---|
| Registered to vote |  |  |  |
| Yes | 69% | 92% | 76% |
| No | 31 | 8 | 24 |
|  |  |  |  |
| Turnout last election |  |  |  |
| Yes | 41% | 47% | 43% |
| No | 30 | 45 | 34 |
| N/A | 29 | 8 | 23 |
|  |  |  |  |
| Party Membership |  |  |  |
| Yes | 3% | 8% | 4 |
| No | 80 | 90 | 83 |
| N/A | 17 | 2 | 13 |
|  |  |  |  |
| Vote for a Party |  |  |  |
| Yes | 52% | 67% | 57% |
| No | 10 | 18 | 13 |
| N/A | 38 | 15 | 30 |
|  |  |  |  |
| Which party |  |  |  |
| Labor | 47% | 55% | 50% |
| Liberal | 2 | 6 | 3 |
| Green | 0 | 4 | 1 |
| Independent | 3 | 0 | 2 |
| Conservative | 0 | 2 | 1 |
| N/A | 48 | 33 | 43 |
|  |  |  |  |
| Factors that influenced vote |  |  |  |
| No other choice | 33% | 37% | 34% |
| Unemployment | 24 | 25 | 24 |
| Removing Thatcher | 1 | 18 | 8 |
| General Improvements | 19 | 6 | 15 |
| Drugs | 7 | 20 | 11 |
| Housing | 13 | 18 | 15 |
|  |  |  |  |
| Organization Membership |  |  |  |
| Yes | 30% | 24% | 28% |
| No | 66 | 76 | 69 |
| N/A | 4 | 0 | 3 |

Source: Liverpool Community Survey, 1990

the only ones who have given up on the party; Whites are absent in large numbers as well. The lack of involvement in Labour politics has become a large national problem. Participation by Blacks in Granby has been particularly weak because of historical Black exclusion from the political system, coupled with discrimination and isolation. Because of these historical issues—which have become institutional-ized in the political system—Blacks have developed the feeling that the Labour Party is not relevant.[43]

The price Blacks have had to pay for their isolation from the main structures of the Labour Party has been steep. It has meant that the Black community has been robbed of a key mobilization vehicle; it has also meant that the Black community has been excluded from important party policy-making committees, including committees that select candidates to run for public office.

Low Black electoral participation is also indicative of the isola-tion of the Black community from the trade union movement. Trade unions constitute a critical source of support for the Labour Party in Liverpool. Not only do unions contribute huge sums of money to electoral campaigns, but they also serve as vital instruments for the mobilization of opinion and votes in elections. The trade union movement in Liverpool has been largely a White movement; Blacks have been almost totally shut out of positions of power and influence in that movement. NALGO is the only major union active in Liverpool with an officially sanctioned Black Section component. Trade unions in Liverpool have operated as closed shops, filling job vacancies with friends and family members, locking outsiders like Blacks out of the process. It should also be noted that union atten-tion tends to be focused on the employed, with wage and workplace issues rising to the top of the political agenda. Since Blacks are heavily unemployed, they are automatically left out of the main-stream of union concerns and involvement. Racism inside of the union movement has effectively thwarted all efforts by the Black community to use trade unions as levers of political power. Unions have done almost nothing to build enduring structures for Black electoral mobilization. For Blacks in Liverpool, unions have often been part of the problem rather than part of the solution. As one respondent observed: "Dealing with racism is not in the interest of unions. This is how 80 percent of the members feel."[44]

Low Black numerical participation in elections coupled with the isolation of Blacks from the electoral machinery have virtually assured that Blacks would receive only token representation in the city council. Blacks were totally shut out of seats on the city council until 1987, when Judy Nelson and Liz Drysdale won seats on the council. Actually, only Liz Drysdale qualified as a Black representative. Judy Nelson was an avowed supporter of the Militant Tendency elected from Anfield, an overwhelmingly White ward. Throughout her service on the council she never identified with Black causes and cultivated no contacts with the Black community. Liz Drysdale was one of three Progressive Labour supporters elected from the Granby ward in 1987 (the other two were Gideon Ben-Tovim and Phillip Hughes). Bringing to the council a long history of community activism, including membership in the Black Caucus, Drysdale's election raised the hope that for the first time a Black councillor would provide entree into key areas of decision making on the council. Drysdale served on the council for four years, compiling an outstanding legislative record but receiving mixed reviews of her performance from her Black constituents, many of whom wanted her to be more active and assertive on race equality issues. Drysdale declined to run for reelection in 1991 and was replaced on the council by another Black community activist, Petrona Lashley. Lashley's low-profile demeanor did not engender for her a high level of confidence and support in the Black community. She was, however, very effective in forging political ties with Labour Party leaders; indeed she was so effective that by 1994 she had been elevated to the distinguished post of Deputy Lord Mayor and was scheduled to become the Lord Mayor during the next election cycle. Her political career was dealt a fatal blow, however, by the publication of an article in the *Liverpool Echo* in August 1994 that revealed that she had a record of three convictions for prostitution dating back to 1973.[45] This revelation cut the grounds from under Lashley's political position in the Labour Party. Wishing to cut their losses and close the door on the scandal, which made national headlines, party leaders from London insisted that Lashley be de-selected as a council candidate at the next election. Although there was wide speculation that Black community activist Carleton Benjamin would be selected to replace Lashley, her seat went to a White politician, Alan Dean, after Benjamin decided not to put his hat in the ring. Thus by 1995 the Granby Ward was operating again without a Black councillor to represent its interest. This situation placed great pressure on Gideon Ben-Tovim, longtime White community activist and Senior Lecturer in Sociology at the University of Liverpool, to step up his advocacy of race equality issues in behalf of his Black constituents in the Granby Ward. The election of Stephanie Watson, a Black woman from the Abercromby ward, to the city council, also helped to fill some of the vacuum left by the disappearance of formal Black representation on the city council for the Granby Ward. However, Watson's decision to leave the council in 1998 to pursue professional and political opportunities outside of Liverpool once again left the Black community without racial representation on the city council.

## Black Political Dilemmas

The Atlantic waters that separate Liverpool from Boston have not prevented parallel systems of hierarchical power and control from taking root. Political dilemmas faced by Blacks in Liverpool both emulate, and in some instances surpass, those faced by Blacks in Boston. Like Blacks in Boston, Blacks in Liverpool are compelled to operate in a political environment that does not easily lend itself to minority political incorporation. Historically, the Black community in Liverpool has faced a mobilization of bias that has firmly locked Blacks out of key decision making arenas in local governance and politics. As we have seen, one central aspect of this system of bias has been the existence of British attitudes that question the legitimacy of claims by Blacks that they should be recognized as important players in the political process. The idea that race is not a legitimate factor that should be taken into account in the distribution of public goods has meant that the doors of government have been shut in the face of Blacks at every level. Routine processes and procedures of local government have been based on the assumption that Blacks will be the objects of public policy but not major participants in the policy process. This has meant, in turn, that the structural orientation of the policy process has been almost entirely unidirectional. Efforts to incorporate Blacks into the governing process often generate strong passion and political conflict because they are viewed by the White majority as extralegal, aberrant, and extreme.

In contrast to Boston, where key decision-making authority is lodged in the hands of a strong chief executive (the mayor), the pivotal locus of decision-making authority in Liverpool resides in the city council. Structural characteristics of the local authority have reinforced the prevailing mobilization of bias and served to guarantee the marginalization of Black interests in the policy process. Thus, many of the city council's most important decisions are made by committees and subcommittees that are virtually invisible to most Black citizens. Individuals and organizations wishing to pro-

mote Black incorporation are disadvantaged by the fact that decision-making authority in the council is divided into plural committee centers that operate with a great deal of autonomy. By the time
issues reach the level of open public debate in the general council,
the fundamental elements of choice in the policy process have
already been decided. Having little direct input into the council's
committee system, Blacks find themselves operating at the back
end rather than the front end of the policy process.

   Political incorporation in Liverpool places a premium on the ability to manipulate the internal policy structures of city council. Much
of the decision-making authority of the council rests not only in communication links between the elected members but also in the
sophisticated transactional interactions that take place between the
elected members and council officers. Trade unions have also
become incorporated into this process. Over the years trade unions
have established immensely important functional links with both
elected members and officers. In Liverpool, the power of trade
unions is an extension of the power of the council. Trade union members often serve formally as advisers and consultants on council
committees and subcommittees. Operating through formal and
informal channels, trade unions are able to exercise control over
council employment policies by preserving the internal trawl and
freely exercising nominating rights. In addition, the existence of the
Joint Shop Stewards Committee as a functional component of the
council means that almost nothing occurs within the council's committee structure that does not come to the attention of trade unions
and is not subject to their intervention. The results have been that
union interests have been addressed systematically and compre-
hensively by the council. In contrast, the Liverpool City Council has
tended to address the needs of the Black community through ad hoc,
functionally isolated programming arrangements. This method of
isolative, piecemeal allocation of programming resources has fallen
short of the kind of decision making process that is needed to find
long-term remedies to vexing community problems.

   Disjointed, unsystematic devices for financing and implementing
community programs are inherently incapable of achieving the kind
of structural change and redistribution of benefits needed to make
adjustments in the policy impact of Black political activity. To the
contrary, they provide potent ammunition to public officials who
wish to give the illusion that the requirements of progressive social
programming are in place, while continuing to construct barriers to
the achievement of systematic changes that will provide real power

and long-term benefits to the Black community. Indeed, it was in recognition of the crucial need to establish internal structures to promote systematic program development for the Black community that the Black Caucus persistently called for the establishment of a central race unit and race advisers in the major departments. It should be noted in this regard that the absence of an independent chief executive in Liverpool has deprived the Black community of access points beyond the council to push for a more systematic and productive race policy agenda. Control over many aspects of the council's action agenda and service delivery processes by the central government has moved the Black community in Liverpool several steps lower in the chain of political command. It should be noted that in areas where the council has had the ability to use its discretionary powers to promote Black policy interests, the character of the prevailing political culture and representational structure of Liverpool City Government have made it extremely reluctant to do so. The primary strategic approach of the local authority has been to marginalize Black interests by denying the relevance of racial issues to the ongoing policy concerns of Liverpool City Government.

Effective program targeting for the Black community has also been undermined by the absence of a strong Black base in the electoral arena. Because of their limited numbers, heavy concentration, and high nonvoting rate, Blacks do not function as major electoral constituents for the established political parties. Unlike Blacks in Boston, Blacks in Liverpool cannot play a key balance-of-power role in local politics. This fact has encouraged politicians running outside the Granby and Abercromby wards to view the Black vote as nonessential. Even if the Black vote citywide was consistently larger, it would be difficult for White politicians to justify substantial program targeting for Blacks in view of the economic problems experienced by the White working class in Liverpool. On this issue one respondent observed:

> Liverpool is a big, White, racist city in an era of declining resources when the working class is suffering severe economic deprivation. When the local authority is losing cash, the last thing a place like this will do is think of the needs of the Black community. In this city you have a racist White working class and a lack of resources. The combination has meant that the Black community has been excluded from the mainstream. Liverpool, more than any other city, doesn't understand how to address the problem of race and Blacks. In other cities the Black community may not do much better, but there is a language

to deal with discrimination. In Liverpool, Blacks are such an invisible group that to even get a dialogue going is very difficult.[46]

For the reasons considered above, race remained off the agenda of the local authority throughout the 1960s and 1970s. However, the outbreak of major rioting in the Black community in the 1980s would change the political calculus of city government in ways never anticipated by key power players in Liverpool governance and politics.

# 8

## The Toxteth Riots and the Race Policy Agenda

### The Politics of Race

The view of Britain as a country with a peerless record of social integration and minority group absorption was thoroughly shattered in the 1980s by the outbreak of widespread civil disorder in major British cities. Few incidents of mass rebellion in the history of Britain matched the ferocity of the social and political uprisings in Bristol, Brixton, and Liverpool in the early 1980s. These events would have a profound impact on the structures and processes of governance at the local level. In Liverpool the strenuous efforts on the part of elected officials to keep race issues off the public agenda had to give way to the implementation of a policy agenda that gave special recognition and credence to the uniquely horrific conditions faced by the city's oppressed Black community.

It is important to note that the urban riots in Britain in the 1980s were not wholly independent events but the logical and natural consequence of ideological and policy shifts in which the issue of race emerged as the central focus of political conflict and controversy. In Britain, the politics of race is rooted in the post–World War II movement into Britain of Black workers from the West Indies. Although the 1948 Nationality Act extended British citizenship to all subjects of the crown throughout the empire, Britain had long considered itself a White nation, providing authentic national identity and membership only to those who could trace their lineage to the blood of the "bulldog breed" that had built the country over many centuries. Black immigration into Britain was considered special and troublesome; it introduced into the social milieu people of a different color who brought with them an alleged alien culture.[1] A major escalation in the flow of Black immigrants into Britain in the 1940s was broadly viewed as an ominous threat to British heritage, culture, and the "British way of life." This perception of Black immigration was clearly illuminated in debates in the 1950s around the question of whether or not the 1948 Nationality Act should be revised as a means of controlling the flow of Black immigrants into Britain. Major themes in these debates emphasized the impact of Black immigration on the racial character of the British population and the social costs involved in allowing Black immigrants to consume precious employment, housing, and health resources needed to satisfy the demands of native British citizens.

Dialogue on the issue of race began to take on the tone of a major crisis in the wake of the Nottingham and Notting Hill riots of 1958. Although both riots principally involved attacks on Blacks by Whites, these incidents signaled to the nation the growing potential for racial strife in British cities.[2] Opponents of Black immigration interpreted these events as proof that unrestricted Black settlement would undermine the rule of law and subject British society to the nefarious influence of alien cultures. Increasingly, Black communities were being characterized as problem areas where crime, vice, and other antisocial activities flourished. Black immigrants were alleged to constitute a foreign wedge whose attachment to alien practices and values was so strong that their effective integration into British society represented a challenge beyond the grasp of traditional social agencies and institutions. Confined by racially discriminatory practices to areas of high-density/ low-income housing, Black immigrants to Britain were routinely compared to the residents of "dark ghettoes" in the United States, whose alienation from mainstream culture threatened to undermine the stability of public order.

By the end of the 1950s the question of the future of Black immigration began to dominate the policy agendas of British governmental institutions and political parties. A highly visible pattern of racial politics began to reach full fruition with the passage of the Commonwealth Immigrants Act in 1962. This act sought to control Black immigration into Britain by requiring that Commonwealth citizens and United Kingdom citizens holding passports not issued in Britain or through the British High Commission obtain employment vouchers as a condition of immigration to Britain. Although the act spoke in broad terms about Commonwealth immigration as a whole, the primary emphasis was on control of immigration from Black countries and territories within the British Empire.[3]

Leadership in the passage of the act came from the Conservative Party, its initiatives in this area fueled by the demands of working-class British citizens that their interests be protected from competition by the influx of Black workers from the Commonwealth.[4] The Labour Party, while initially expressing opposition to racially motivated immigration controls, eventually shifted its political posture and strongly endorsed the movement for Black exclusion. The shift was triggered, in part, by the success of the campaign for parliament by Conservative candidate Peter Griffiths in 1964 in Smethwick. Griffiths's campaign deliberately sought to provoke a racial backlash against Black immigration by relying heavily on the slogan "If you want a nigger for your neighbor, vote Labour." The message of the Smethwick election was too stark and explosive for Labour political strategists to ignore. After 1964 Labour politicians began to strongly embrace the notion that Black immigration control was essential to the maintenance of effective race relations in Britain.

The new thinking by Labour leaders on the issues of race and immigration found dramatic expression in the passage, under Labour guidance, of the second Commonwealth Immigrants Act in 1968. This act sought to adjust entrance into Britain of massive numbers of Asians uprooted by political developments from their homes in East Africa. Carefully worded provisions of this act allowed immigrants from Ireland, Australia, Canada, and other White countries to enter Britain without restrictions, while bringing Blacks and Asians under strict enforcement provisions of immigration laws. The explosive racial climate in Britain in 1968 was amplified by the red hot rhetoric of Conservative MP Enoch Powell. In a series of speeches, Powell warned of an impending social disaster in Britain if major changes were not made in British immigration policies.

> As I look ahead I am filled with foreboding. Like the Roman, I seem to see the River Tiber "foaming with much blood." The tragic and intractable phenomenon which we watch with horror on the other side of the Atlantic, but which there is interwoven with the history and existence of the States itself, is coming upon us here by our own volition and our own neglect.[5]

To prevent this doomsday scenario from becoming a reality, Powell proposed the imposition of tighter immigration controls coupled with the repatriation of Blacks and Asians to their homelands.

Enoch Powell's "Rivers of Blood" speeches opened the floodgates to the unvarnished practice of racial politics in Britain. Conservatives, taking power in Parliament in 1970, responded to Powell's challenge by passing the 1971 Immigration Act. In a sweeping move, this legislation eliminated the right of nonpatrials (citizens with passports not issued in Britain) to settle in Britain without work permits. The effective result of this change in the immigration laws was to reduce the status of Black and Asian Commonwealth immigrants to that of aliens.[6] This redefinition of the status of Black and Asian immigrants affected the quality of their existence in Britain in a multiplicity of ways. Blacks and Asians found themselves subjected to increased verbal and physical assault. Growing racial tensions were reinforced by the emergence of the National Front in British electoral politics. Adopting a platform that broadcast extreme hostility to the presence of Blacks and Asians in Britain, the National Front made significant progress toward becoming the fourth major party in Britain by polling 16 percent of the vote in a parliamentary by-election in West Bromich.

The rise to prominence and respectability of right wing groups like the National Front symbolized the redefinition of Black citizens in Britain as the enemy within. In particular, the growing concentration of Black youth in the inner cities was viewed as a major danger to the maintenance of peace and order in Britain's largest metropolitan areas.[7] The issue of Black youth and crime became a special focus of political controversy. Liberal and conservative forces began to associate street crimes with the alleged criminal inclinations of Black youth. Black communities were identified as criminal areas, and Black youth were viewed as naturally violent elements in society whose antisocial behavior represented an extraordinary threat to the preservation of public order in British cities.

Primary responsibility for confronting the "breakdown" in law and order in Black communities was placed in the hands of urban police. Relying on hard policing methods undergirded by the reluctance by courts and politicians to control their actions in the face of threats emanating from Black communities, urban police established major beachheads in inner-city communities as armies of occupation. Hard policing tactics involved the liberal use of 'sus' laws to arrest individuals on suspicion of loitering with intent to commit an arrestable offense. Criminal procedures associated with 'sus' arrests made this device particularly offensive to Black citizens. Under the 'sus' laws no victim was required, no witness necessary other than two police officers, suspects could only be tried in magistrate's court (without the right to trial by jury), and the defendants were required to prove that they were not guilty of acting suspiciously when arrested. Police harassment under "sus" laws became fertile ground for the harvesting of anti-police attitudes in the Black community. Repeal of 'sus' laws in 1981 did not significantly affect Black attitudes toward the police. Many Black citizens observed that after 1981, 'sus' procedures were replaced by strenuous stop and search tactics that produced roughly the same results.

Hard policing methods in Black communities have also included saturation policing. In this regard, squads of special duty police are assembled to stage a raid against troublesome groups or business establishments operating in high crime areas. Black citizens complain that these raids have been disproportionately targeted at the Black community and invariably involved wholesale violations of citizen rights. Complaints of police abuse are not limited to situations involving collective action. In the book *Policing Against Black People*, the Institute of Race Relations in London has compiled case studies of hundreds of instances where individual Black citizens have accused the police of forced entry into their homes without search warrants, obtaining confessions through force, strip searches and sexual humiliation in police custody, and the fabrication and planting of evidence.[8]

Fighting what they considered to be a system of police oppression, Black youth engaged in a series of violent clashes with the police in the 1970s. In June 1973, Black youth clashed violently with the police in Brockwell Park, South London. Two years later, Black youth in Chapeltown, Leeds, rose up in opposition to the continuing use of 'sus' tactics by the police. In 1976 full-scale rioting by Black youth at the Notting Hill Carnival injured 500, including 150 that needed hospital treatment. A major precipitating element in this conflict was the presence at the carnival of 1,600 police massed to prevent pickpocketing and other "crimes." Open warfare between Black youth and the police was repeated at the carnival in 1977. In the same year, marches by the National Front in the Ladywood area of Birmingham and the Lewisham area of London produced another round of violent clashes between Black youth and the police. The violent disruptions in Black communities in Britain in the 1970s represented the opening acts in a searing drama that would, in the 1980s, engulf major British cities, including Liverpool, in urban unrest of cataclysmic proportions.

Revolt in Liverpool: The 1981 Toxteth Riots

The new decade in Britain would begin on a tumultuous note with the outbreak of major rioting in Bristol in April 1980. In this incident Blacks living in the St. Paul section of Bristol rose up in reaction to a raid staged by thirty police officers against a popular neighborhood cafe called the "Black and White" in search of illegal drugs and liquor. The resulting unrest, involving over 2,000 rioters and 600 police, destroyed 20 buildings, injured 50 police ( 27 seriously), produced a loss of £150,000 from looting, and led to the arrest of 134 individuals on charges ranging from assault to arson.[9] One year after the Bistol riots, widespread rioting in the Brixton section of London erupted. Again the critical flash point was relations between the Black community and the police. Tensions between the Black community and the police emerged in the backdrop of a police operation called "Swamp 81." This operation involved the saturation of Brixton with 112 plain clothes policemen in search of muggers, robbers, and other criminals. At the conclusion of the operation, 943 people had been stopped and 118 had been arrested.[10] Viewing Swamp 81 as a form of police harassment, Blacks in Brixton rose up in rebellion, transforming a minor incident between a Black youth and a constable into a full-scale riot.

Waxing and waning over three days, the Brixton riots became the most destructive civil disruption in British history. In total, 450 people were injured, including 150 police officers. Property damage was extensive: 156 buildings were damaged, 28 by fire. Widespread looting virtually cleaned out major businesses in the shopping district. An official inquiry into the Brixton riots by Lord Scarman concluded that both appalling social conditions and friction between Black youth and the police contributed to the disruption.[11] The report recommended social and economic intervention by the central government and adoption of community policing strategies by urban police to prevent the outbreak in the future of major riots on British soil.

Preventive measures could not be instituted fast enough to contain the epidemic of urban unrest in Britain. Social and economic conditions in Liverpool made the city a ready target for urban revolt. The arena of police-community relations was a uniquely potent source of hardship and aggravation for Liverpool's Black community. Liverpool police had gained a nationwide reputation for hard policing. Saturation raids against Black establishments, the liberal use of 'sus' laws to execute arrests, and the concentration of police resources on the task of maintaining twenty four-hour mobile patrols in Toxteth gave an ominous impression to citizens that the entire Black community was under attack. Police leaders attempted to justify hard policing strategies by citing statistics intended to demonstrate that a disproportionate amount of crime in the city occurred in the Black community. The underlying implication was that Blacks were naturally violent and that public peace virtually demanded that the police do everything possible to keep these violent impulses under control. In truth, the police had a difficult time separating the issue of race from the issue of crime.

Conflict between the police and the Black community in Liverpool is not new. The Falkner riots in 1972 centered on violent clashes between Black youth and the police. Similarly, in 1975 Black youth in Toxteth responded violently to the relentless use of hard policing tactics, including around-the-clock surveillance of Granby by street patrols. Complaints of police abuse in the 1970s were so numerous, it became necessary for the Merseyside Community Relations Council ( MCRC ) to organize a special committee to monitor ongoing relations between the police and neighborhood youth. Even these efforts offered no guarantee that the gulf between community life and police perceptions and behavior would be effectively breached. In 1980 relations between the community and the police had reached such a low point that the MCRC severed relations with the police on the grounds that the police were reluctant to admit that racist attitudes existed on the force, and the police liaison scheme established to promote community police cooperation had little impact and no value.

The Toxteth riots of 1981 were unique events in Liverpool's history. They were distinguished by their size, intensity, ferocity, and endurance. Riding on a wave of inevitability, these events were, literally, disasters waiting to happen. At the bottom of the events was an attitude of absolute intolerance by the Black community for the rough and inhuman treatment Blacks received at the hands of the police.

> People said that they had had enough because of the treatment that had gone on over the months. People were being stopped and searched in the streets for nothing. You couldn't sit anywhere. Like where I use to live there was a dairy. In the dairy there was a doorway. We used to sit in the doorway, and the police would come up the side of the dairy and ask what we were doing there and tell us to move because we were loitering. We couldn't go out at night. If you had a plastic bag, or any kind of bag, it was opened. If you were a man you were always getting stopped. People had just had enough.[12]

The key precipitating event was the attempted arrest in Granby of a Black youth suspected of stealing a motor bike on Friday, 3 July 1981. Tempers reached the boiling point among Blacks witnessing this event. Responding to the pleas for help by the young Black man that had been arrested, Black witnesses began raining down a torrent of bricks, concrete, and other objects on the fenders and hood of the arresting police unit. In the following hours violence in the Black community escalated. Throughout the evening, Black youth pounded police vehicles moving in and out of Toxteth with bricks and concrete.

Episodes of violence receded during the daylight hours of 4 July but picked up steam around 10:00 P.M. after a contingent of fifty youth sealed off Parliament and Grove Streets with a physical barricade.[13] By this time the unrest had taken on a multiracial character with nonBlack youth joining with Black youth to attack approaching police vehicles.

> It started off small, and as people heard about it it got worse and worse. And the group got bigger. It was not just one group; it was numerous groups. People were coming from outside Liverpool 8 into the area. Black, White, Chinese—it was everybody. They were coming from the Dingle, Smithdown Road, Wavertree Road, Hale Road. A lot of people just came to see what was going on. And when the shops began to be looted, they joined in.[14]

Officers seeking to dismantle the barricade across Parliament and Grove Streets were pelted with sticks, bricks, stones, and other weapons. Police commanders ordered the deployment of basic British military formations involving the construction of parallel lines behind standard police shields. Like warriors in the field, police officers beat their shields, shouted out challenges to their adversaries, and made regular baton charges into the ranks of the protesters. The response they received from the swelling tide of rioters was so intense, the police had no choice but to pull back and regroup. One respondent explained the ferocity of the people's response:

> People had got to the point where they felt they had no territory, where they felt their rights, liberties, and personal freedoms were impinged upon so much that they actually confronted it and said excuse me I have a right to stand on this street. A great deal of the fighting that took place was around certain areas and so-called territory. People gained control of a significant proportion of their own environment, for whatever period of time, and kept the police out of that. That was the high point. All sorts of people were involved in the looting on Lodge Lane and that sort of business, but the bulk of the people that were involved in it were not involved in that end but in

direct confrontation on Upper Parliament Street. The object of that confrontation was to force the police back out of the area and to claim a stake, and to claim a territorial right to say that we live here, we demand that we get something better for we live here. In this case issues like fair economic conditions and employment were there, but on that day it was more you get out, we've had enough of this.[15]

By 2:00 A.M. on 5 July, another barricade across Upper Parliament Street had been built. The police immediately sent in reinforcements to reopen this street. At the same time, units of the Merseyside County Fire Brigade were sent in to put out fires being produced by burning vehicles set ablaze by the rioters. Both police squads and fire brigade units were forced to retire because of attacks from rioting youth.[16] At this point police casualties were mounting; safety forces were losing total control of the riot area. In the face of these realities, two strategic moves were made by police commanders. First, a firm boundary was established to prevent the riots from moving north out of Toxteth to the downtown shopping district. Second, urgent calls for assistance were made to police departments in Greater Manchester, Cheshire, and Lancashire.

As the morning wore on, the intensity of the attack on police by rioting youth significantly escalated. Police found themselves having to fend off attacks from petrol bombs as well as bricks and stones. Cars stolen from an automobile showroom by rioters were driven toward police lines before being abandoned by their drivers at the last minute. By 6:00 A.M. reports of widespread looting of shops on Upper Parliament Street were being received by the police. A tally of casualties performed by the police showed that during the evening forty-six officers had been treated at the Royal Teaching Hospital.

Although the center of conflict on the evening of 5 July remained the Upper Parliament Street area, significant violence also erupted in the Lodge Lane area, where hundreds of youth fought with police, and a number of shops were looted and vandalized. The ranks of the police force were growing thin, despite reinforcements from Manchester, Cheshire, and Lancashire. A number of premier buildings in the Upper Parliament–Princess Road area were burned down or seriously damaged by fire, including the Racquets Club, Westminster National Bank, and the Rialto Furnishing Store. By 12:30 A.M. the police were in full retreat, moving backwards down Upper Parliament Street to within one hundred yards of the Anglican Cathedral. With the backs of the police forces against the wall, a highly controversial decision was made by Chief Constable

Kenneth Oxford to use CS gas (a potent form of tear gas) to disperse rioters and open a wedge so that the police could take control of Upper Parliament Street and spread their forces to recapture Lodge Lane. The use of CS gas against rioters in Liverpool was controversial for several reasons. First, this represented the first time CS gas had been used in mainland Britain to quell disorder. Second, Oxford decided to use the gas without first getting the required permission from central government, although Home Minister William Whitelaw later gave post hoc approval, saying it was the correct thing to do under the circumstances. Third, the use of this gas defied warnings from the U.S. manufacturer, Smith and Wesson, that the gas cartridges were intended to penetrate windows, doors, and toughened glass and were not to be fired at crowds.[17] Fourth, a number of the cartridges fired were fired directly at people and automobiles. This behavior left four people wounded, two of them seriously, including Phil Robins, a football player for Southport FC who suffered wounds in the chest and back.[18] Fifth, Liverpool police were criticized for using a virtual arsenal of weapons: CS gas launchers, eighteen rounds of one and one half canisters, seven rounds of one and one half Ferret cartridges, thirty four rounds of bore Ferret cartridges, and fifteen grenades.[19]

By 7 July most of the violent action in Liverpool had disappeared. The situation of relative calm was short-lived. On 26 July a new cycle of rioting commenced. During this period officers patrolling the area outside the Caribbean Center on Upper Parliament Street were stoned. Barricades were again erected across Upper Parliament Street. To confront this challenge, police commanders adopted a new strategy: officers would be given the authority to use their police cars as battering rams. This strategy resulted in several tragedies. One youth, Paul Conroy, was rammed against a wall, producing severe back injuries. Another youth, David Moore, who was physically handicapped, could not move fast enough to get out of the way of a speeding police vehicle seeking to move people out of the street and against the nearest wall. Moore was killed by a police van; interestingly, this van disappeared from police custody a few days after his death.[20] By 30 July the pattern of violence endemic in the second riot cycle had run its course. For a number of weeks beyond this date incidents of sporadic antipolice violence continued to crop up in the city and the suburbs. Liverpool police were also not inactive. Long after the riots were over, the police were enmeshed in a vigorous campaign to identify and prosecute rioters and confiscate stolen property.

It got to the point that after the riots they were walking on buses and taking people down to the police station to see if they were involved. You would get your house searched. They would give stupid excuses like they were searching for electrical goods. They had no idea you had electrical goods. I had been bought a tape by my mum for my birthday. They came in my house without a search warrant searching for electrical goods and wanted to know where the tape came from. Did I have a receipt? How much did it cost, and when did I get it? And what was it for? And I know the same thing happened to many people. They claimed they were searching around for electrical goods.[21]

The Toxteth riots of 1981 would leave deep and indelible foot-prints in the political soil of Liverpool. Because many of the most basic issues remained unresolved, another cycle of major violence would be visited on the city in 1985.

## Political Reaction

The eruption of major rioting in Liverpool ricocheted throughout the city's political communities. For the Black community the riots had the effect of substantially expanding its existing resource base. One manifestation of this expansion was the founding of the Liverpool 8 Defence Committee. The committee grew out of a com-munity meeting held at Stanley House (a venerable meeting site) after two days of rioting to explore community responses to the pre-vailing crisis. Strong support was voiced at the meeting for the idea of establishing a community defence committee. The primary agenda of the committee would be several-fold: to help defend com-munity residents who were victims of police oppression and open to racism in the courts; to collect statements of witnesses of police bru-tality; to arrange legal help, including the securing of lawyers and bail money; to coordinate information about the fate of people in cus-tody; to arrange transportation to and from Risley Prison; and to col-lect statements from witnesses of racist attacks.[22] Membership in the Defence Committee was open to all members of the community. Headquartered in the basement of the Charles Wootton Center for Further Education, the Defence Committee quickly became a thorn in the side of the police. Members of the Defence Committee were actively involved in documenting allegations of police brutality through the compilation of photographic and other evidence. The political agenda of the Defence Committee rapidly expanded to include sharp verbal attacks against the police. Chief Constable

Kenneth Oxford, the individual the Defence Committee blamed principally for the sorry state of police-community relations in the city, was a primary target of the organization's public attacks. Members of the Defence Committee described Oxford as a "police chief on the rampage." On 15 August 1981 the Defence Committee helped to organize and lead a massive march of over ten thousand people designed to place unvarnished pressure on Oxford to resign and to promote democratic control of the police.[23] Indeed, a vibrant and vociferous "Oxford Out" campaign swiftly became the center-piece of the Defence Committee's evolving political strategies. On the legal side, the interventionist efforts by the Defence Committee established the critical foundation for the development of two community institutions: the Liverpool 8 Law Centre and the Immigration Advice Unit. Both the Law Centre and the Advice Unit would become important elements in the ongoing service delivery network crystallizing in the aftermath of the riots in the Black community.

The Merseyside Community Relations Council (MCRC) also served as an important element of this network. MCRC attempted to play a key brokering role between the community and the police authority. This task was made extremely difficult because of the inclination of MCRC officials to place the blame for the conflict squarely on the shoulders of the Liverpool Police.

> It cannot be stressed too strongly that the single most immediate cause of the riots is the deep anger and resentment felt by young people against the police. No social and economic responses will have a significant impact on the situation unless local youngsters can see and feel a change in the way in which they are treated by the police on the streets.[24]

MCRC leaders were clearly irritated by the fact that their previous efforts one year earlier to establish a dialogue between the police and the community through the maintenance of an active liaison committee had been flatly rejected on numerous occasions by police officials. They believed that the police authority's attitude was a big mistake—one for which it was paying dearly. Playing the role of both peacemaker and diplomat, Wally Brown, chair of the MCRC, attempted to break new ground in the negotiations with the police authority by soliciting the active and constructive intervention of the city council. In a passionate speech before the council, Brown appealed to councillors to set aside their partisan differences and do what was required to address issues of police governance and neighborhood development in Liverpool 8.[25] Brown's leadership in the midst of the city's worst social crisis elevated the MCRC to the pinnacle of power, influence, and respectability in the Black community.

The riots also produced enhanced political consciousness and electoral activism in the Black community. Accompanying this enhanced consciousness and activism was a major split in electoral interests and loyalties in the Black community. One faction, led by Liz Drysdale and Gideon Ben-Tovim, gravitated toward close engagement with the leadership and institutions of the Labour Party, while another faction, led by Shaun Deckon and Delroy Burris, moved in the direction of political independence.

The spontaneity and ferocity of the riots caught the Liverpool City Council unprepared to provide an effective response. In the early aftermath of the riots, the Liberals and Labour spent a great deal of time blaming each other for the riots. At one point partisan debate became so intense and personal that Lord Mayor Cyril Carr admonished Liberal and Labour leaders that they were "fighting like alleycats."[26] Proposals in the council to establish an appeals fund to promote recovery in Toxteth, provide compensation for the victims of riots, transform Lodge Lane into a shopping district, and hold a reception for members of the emergency services were all voted down. The only issue the council could agree on was the conducting of a survey of Toxteth residents to obtain their opinions regarding the basic needs of the area. During round two, councillors focused their attention on alleged outside agitators who supposedly invaded Liverpool 8 to stir up trouble. Liberal leader Trevor Jones accused these "troublemakers" of making selected properties in the city political targets. The council also seriously entertained the possibility of cutting funds to community agencies such as the Charles Wootton Center and South Liverpool Personnel (an employment center) because of their close affiliation with aggressive political organizations such as the Liverpool 8 Defence Committee.

The most visceral city reaction came from the office of Chief Constable Kenneth Oxford. Strongly defending the actions of the police, including the use of CS gas, Oxford blamed the riots on a crowd of Black hooligans "hell bent on stirring up trouble. . . . This was a concentrated premeditated attack of behaviour by a small hooligan element. My message to them is that they cannot win. I will not allow no-go areas."[27] Members of the Black community strongly objected to Oxford's characterization of the conflict as a Black riot, pointing out an obvious fact from scenes of the riots broadcast on television: many participants in all aspects of the riots were White. In a long report to the commission investigating the Brixton riots headed by Lord Scarman, Oxford stuck by his interpretation; this report addressed the long history of violence in Liverpool and analyzed the special problems police encountered dealing with the natural proclivities toward violence allegedly possessed by many of the residents of Liverpool 8.[28]

Oxford's analysis deepened the level of conflict existing between the Merseyside Police Authority and the County Police Committee headed by Granby County Councillor Margaret Simey. A strong advocate of public control of the police, Simey castigated the behavior of the police in Liverpool 8 and suggested that if she lived in Liverpool 8, given the incidence of deprivation and police harassment there, she would riot too. Simey cast doubt on police descriptions of enforcement strategies and tactics in the Black community: "The police say one thing, the people say another. It's time we listened to the people."[29] Elaborating on her personal views and experiences with the Liverpool police Simey told the author:

> I came from Scotland, and we're passionate there about education. The trouble with the police force from start to finish is they are recruited from Liverpool. And Liverpool is a city of major ignorance. Therefore your police are ignorant. And if you choose your police from Liverpool, there is the tradition of the Irish bully boys. You choose your police from a society that is blind ignorant about race and is brought up—use your fist in an argument, don't talk, fight. And when you put those types in charge, you're bound to have disaster. All along they couldn't accept that a woman was in the chair. That wasn't right according to the way they had been brought up. Women are in the kitchen making tea, and here I was in the chair. And I was too old. See they all retire at fifty-five. What was this old woman doing there? And I represented Granby. Well that was a criminal community. I was standing up for criminals, so right from the start there was no hope at all. We tried so hard.[30]

A working party set up by the Police Committee eventually wrote a report censuring Chief Constable Oxford and the entire Merseyside Police Force for their handling of the Toxteth riots.

Under tremendous pressure, Oxford attempted to extend an olive branch to the Police Committee and the Black community. One major concession was the substitution of street patrols for van patrols in the Black community. Oxford attempted to break the log jam on dialogue by inviting a wide variety of community groups to meet with him to discuss possible solutions to community problems, including the activation of a permanent liaison committee. The success of the meeting was marred by the refusal of members of the Liverpool 8 Defence Committee and MCRC to attend. When Oxford left the meeting, he was surrounded by a large picketing force composed mainly of members of the Defence Committee.

Fallout from the riots at the level of central government was also quite severe. Most of the initial reaction from central government officials was very negative. Prime Minister Margaret Thatcher denounced the riots in Liverpool as acts of lawlessness that would not be tolerated or rewarded. Home Secretary Whitelaw gave a report to Parliament that deplored the violence and praised the actions of Chief Constable Kenneth Oxford and safety forces in Liverpool. Conservative MP Teddy Taylor called for the use of water cannons: "[W]e can't allow the police to become Aunt Sally—where they are called in only to have petrol bombs and bricks thrown at them. One day a policeman is going to get burnt."[31] Conservative MP John Stokes suggested that a great part of the blame for the riots lay with the vociferous immigration lobby who sought "excuses all the time for the excessives of blacks."[32] Over time, cooler heads prevailed. Prime Minister Thatcher and Home Secretary Whitelaw made visits to Liverpool and promised to mobilize resources from the central government and the private sector to rebuild riot-torn areas and address the multitudinous needs of the inner city. The most dramatic response was the designation of Environmental Minister Michael Heseltine as "Minister of Merseyside." Heseltme conducted an extensive tour of the city and decided that what it needed most was economic development. To realize this goal, Heseltine took several immediate steps. First he appointed a task force of twenty four entrepreneurs to advise him on new economic initiatives. Second, he met with an assortment of community groups to discuss his plans for Liverpool. Third, he announced the creation of the Merseyside Development Corporation to spearhead the rehabilitation of the Albert Dock. Fourth, he proposed the issuing of a major grant by central government to underwrite the staging of an International Flower Festival in Liverpool. Heseltine's principal objective was to bring on line high-profile projects that would jump start Liverpool's sagging economy. He theorized that with the economy on the rebound, citizens in the inner city would have no reason to riot.

## Positive Action and the Race Policy Agenda

The outbreak of full-scale rioting in Toxteth represented a defining era in the evolution of the public policy process in Liverpool. Arguments against the conceptualization of public policy in racial terms were compelled to give way to more realistic appraisals. The smoke cascading across the city from Liverpool 8 made it painfully clear that something was terribly wrong with a political system that drove its citizens to such depths of fury and emotion. Liverpool 8 was speaking out in agonizing terms in voices no politician could afford to ignore. Poverty and police brutality in the Black community were no longer Liverpool's hidden secret; the overwhelming burdens this community had to bear were now center stage and open to examination by social critics around the world.

For those who cared enough to listen before the riots, social and economic deprivation in Liverpool 8 was no new revelation. Members of the Black Caucus had commented endlessly on this theme. In their official duties as members of the Race Relations Liaison Committee, members of the Black Caucus collectively and meticulously set forth a reform agenda. Among the key items in this agenda were the adoption by the council of a comprehensive equal opportunity agenda; overhaul of employment procedures and staff training, ethnic monitoring and the setting of equality targets; positive action employment training schemes, access to further education courses; Black business development; improved police complaints procedures; review of policies in education, housing, and health, and the establishment of race advisory units. The failure of council policies in these critical areas was chronicled in detail in a series of research reports by the Merseyside Area Profile Group.[33] A companion study issued by the Commission for Racial Equality documented wholesale council discrimination in the allocation of housing provisions for Black citizens.[34] As a follow-up to the study the CRE issued a nondiscrimination notice to the Liverpool City Council, an action that prohibited the council from engaging in further unlawful acts in the area of housing allocations. The recommendation by the Scarman Report on the Brixton riots that local authorities adopt "positive action" policies to advance the social and economic agenda of minority citizens placed additional pressure on Liverpool officials to acknowledge the special needs of Blacks and bring to the public domain appropriate remedies.[35] Before completing his report, Lord Scarman visited Liverpool and declared that the social and economic conditions of Blacks in Liverpool were worse than those of Blacks in Brixton. Lord Gifford's inquiry into race relations in Liverpool 8, *Loosen the Shackles,* echoed and amplified the Scarman Report's conclusions. Gifford declared Liverpool 8 to be the most oppressed community in Britain. He challenged the council to take steps to remove the yoke of oppression from the necks of Blacks by establishing a central race unit and a race relations committee operating under the umbrella of the Finance and Strategy Committee and chaired by the council leader.[36]

Liverpool City Council turned a pivotal corner on the issue of race policy when it agreed to the appointment of Sampson Bond as the Principal Race Relations Adviser. Bond's position was intended to be the first of several race adviser appointments, the others being assigned to departments. Opposition to Bond's appointment by the Black community and trade unions rendered the staffing of additional appointments a virtual impossibility. The transfer of power in the council from the Militant Tendency to the Progressive Caucus raised the prospect that Liverpool would follow the lead of London, Birmingham, and Woverhampton in incorporating race issues into the active policy agenda. Three councillors from the Granby Ward, Gideon Ben-Tovim, Phil Hughes, and Liz Drysdale, stood out as prominent members of the moderate Progressive Caucus. It should be noted that Drysdale and Ben-Tovim successfully climbed the hierarchy of power in the council. Drysdale became the deputy chair of the Personnel Committee and the chair of the Race Subcommittee. Ben-Tovim became chair of the Special Needs Subcommittee and chair of the powerful Education Committee. These developments provided an opening wedge for the initiation of several modest positive action programs. Almost without notice, a Black social work unit was set up in the Social Services Department. This unit was established in recognition of the need to train Black social workers to deliver social services to the Black community. Participants in the social work scheme were sent away to training courses. As they became qualified they were put into the ranks of the regular district team of social workers, and their places in the Black unit were filled with other Black recruits. The program for Black social workers was followed by similar programs for Chinese and Vietnamese. As the process of race policy implementation progressed, additional modest ethnic units were established in the library and arts units of the council.

The most dramatic breakthrough occurred in the establishment of race units in several main departments. After almost five years of political struggle, race units were set up in education, housing, and career services. The unit in housing was created in direct response to the notice of discrimination issued to the Liverpool City Council by the CRE. This unit would have the responsibility of supervising the process of housing allocation to assure that the pattern of racial discrimination documented by the CRE investigation did not continue to deprive Black citizens of equal housing opportunities. The unit in education began to function in 1991 with the appointment of Dave Clay, longtime community activist and administrator with the MCRC, as assistant director of race equality in the Department of Education. This unit operates with a staff of seven including Clay, three area liaison officers, an assistant education officer, and two administrative staff. Since its founding, the unit has intervened in the educational process in behalf of Black children and their parents in a number of highly important ways. One area of intense concern has been the exclusion of Black children from school (mainly through the denial of their applications for admission) in disproportionate numbers. To address this concern, a monitoring process has been established to determine the number of Black students excluded and assess the causes and consequences of such exclusion. Parents seeking assistance in the school admissions process have been given a wide range of help by the unit's staff. An antiracist code of practice has been published and circulated to inform school officials of proper procedures for dealing with racial incidents in school.

Responding to the special social and academic needs of Black students, the race unit in education has assisted in the recruitment of a Black psychologist into the school system and promoted the systemwide development of a Black Studies curriculum. A special problem that has come to the unit's doorstep is the plight of potential Black teachers in Liverpool that have routinely been denied teaching certificates because their training has been received overseas. This overseas designation appears to be principally reserved for teachers coming from Black countries as distinguished from White foreign teachers whose certificates from European universities are readily accepted. In all of these endeavors, the unit has moved far beyond its formal charge to function as both a service and advocacy agent for its Black clients. Dave Clay observed in this regard:

> Despite us having no advocacy role within our remit, the reality is that 80 percent of our work is advocacy work. Black parents come here either because they did not get grants or did not get their choice of schools, or they wanted to protest the way their children were being treated. What started to happen, because there had never really been such a unit, parents started to come to us rather than going to admis-

sions. So we started taking on an advocacy role, although in the eyes of some we were compromising our position. But since no one in the authority came to us and actually said, you cannot do this or should not continue to do this, we continued to do it and represent parents on that level.[37]

Positive action in Liverpool has taken other forms. In 1988 the council approved a proposal by Merseyside Skills Training LTD (MST)—a private agency— to train six hundred Black workers for the council across all departments. A special project sponsored in the council by Liz Drysdale, the MST training scheme represented the council's response to the frequently voiced criticism that Blacks constituted less than 2 percent of the council's work force of over thirty thousand. The first phase of this program would last for three years and would be funded by the council at a cost of more than £1 million a year. Trainees would be employed by the council and gain experience in council offices. They would be expected to attend a local college one day a week to work toward acquiring academic qualifications. Training exercises would provide practice in interviewing techniques and instructions on how to fill out forms.[38]

The MST program was considered by the council to be a major commitment to positive action. If successful it would go a long way toward helping the council reach its goal of 10 percent Black representation in its work force. Black employment prospects were also bolstered by the council's decision to abolish the internal trawl (filling job vacancies by internal advertising) and end nomination rights for unions. These actions were intended to break the pattern of control by trade unions over city jobs and create opportunities for minorities to effectively compete for positions in the city council. The process of minority inclusion also involved the publication of job vacancies in the council in the *Liverpool Star*, a free newspaper. It also entailed a major overhaul of recruitment procedures. Departments filling vacancies were required to fill out forms after a decision had been made; the form was to be sent to the Office of Personnel and Management. A statistical analysis of this data would be performed each quarter and forwarded to the Personnel Committee and the Race Subcommittee. If these units believed that the actions of departments were questionable, they could request departments to submit detailed reports explaining prevailing discrepancies.

Positive action initiatives included council funding in support of the activities of community groups out of funds created by Section 11 of the 1966 Local Government Act. Priority attention was given by the council to the need by Black students for access to further education opportunities. This emphasis led to the establishment of an access program at Sandown College; also, funding for further education programs at the Charles Wootton Centre frozen by the Militants was released. The council provided increased support for other groups, including the South Liverpool Personnel, ethnic cultural centres, Liverpool Black Sisters, the Methodist Youth Centre, Liverpool 8 Law Centre, Mary Secole House, MCRC, Charles Wootton I Tech, and the Women's Technology Scheme. Urban grant arrangements facilitated the establishment of new community programming efforts such as World Promotions, the Immigrant Advice Unit, and the Equal Opportunities Initiative (EOI). World Promotions was the primary organizing force behind the staging of the annual Caribbean Carnival. EOI was a community research unit providing comprehensive reports on social and economic problems affecting minorities living in Liverpool 8.[39] Positive action measures implemented by the council were complemented by efforts to persuade private employers doing business with the council to incorporate equal opportunity initiatives into their contract compliance agreements.

Thus, the race policy agenda of the city council created both the prospect and the expectation that progressive equal opportunity initiatives in both public and private arenas would move Liverpool's Black community substantially down the road to political power, incorporation, and social and economic equality.

## Symbols and Politics: The Limits of Political Linkage

Despite the development of a significant race policy agenda in Liverpool, the linkage process in city government remains a key area of political constraint for the Black community. Like Blacks in Boston, Blacks in Liverpool have not penetrated pivotal arenas of decision making and power. For the Black community the positive action agenda has delivered more symbolic reassurance than substantive goods.[40] The institutionalization of structural mechanisms to manage and implement race policies has not fundamentally changed the social values, political orientation, and policy preferences of Liverpool City Government. This fact raises serious questions regarding the strategic impact of race units in the policy making process. In the case of Liverpool, the redistributive impact of race units has been greatly undermined by the absence of councilwide coordination. Lord Gifford acknowledged the need for such coordination in his call for a strategic or central race unit.[41] Leaders of the council have flatly refused to take Gifford's advice seriously. In the intervening years since Sampson Bond's departure, no steps have been taken by the council to either appoint a successor to Bond or to set up a central race unit. Opposition by Councillor Liz Drysdale to the establishment of a central race unit provides one possible explanation for the failure of the council to establish this objective as a major priority. One senior officer of the council who had a long-standing relationship with Drysdale saw her position on this issue and a range of other Black-related issues as obstructionist:

> I think I would put a significant amount of responsibility onto the member of the council who is chair of the Race Subcommittee, Councillor Drysdale, and the rest on the lack of commitment and ability of other members of the council to counter her ability to block and to influence. She has expressed her views to me on a variety of issues, including the central race unit. She said to me that she couldn't see the point of having a central race unit. In her view she was hoping to see Black people employed wherever in the council. That argument has some strength to it. Where it falls short is, you can say o.k. employment in the council is one aspect. But employment in the council, no matter how much she and others might be committed to it, won't happen overnight. It isn't a thing where you click your fingers and say, "we'll employ Black people." I think it would be fair to say, and expected, that she would promote the struggle of Black people and work within the council and I think now, in my opinion, she is working heavily against it. I regret saying that. I've had to fight with her and other people in the city to promote things for the Black community that she has done her best to thwart.[42]

Fundamental responsibility for both promoting and implementing race policy initiatives has been left to the directors of race policy units. Procedural and structural arrangements in the council have prevented them from acquiring the power and space they need to move forward an effective race agenda. Decisions regarding policy recommendations coming from the separate departments are made by the department's senior management team. Directors of departmental race units are not a part of this team. Procedures and structures of the council make it almost impossible to circumvent the authority of this team from the outside. Reports from race unit directors must go through senior assistant directors, members of the management team, and finally the director. If the director approves, the report goes to the chair of the conference committee of the Race Subcommittee, then the chair of the Race Subcommittee, and finally to the chair of the Main Committee. Reports from race unit directors can be killed at any stage in this process. During the time she was on the council, Liz Drysdale often frustrated the policy efforts of race unit directors by refusing to call meetings of the Race Subcommittee. Thus, despite their good intentions, race unit directors have been compelled to operate as ambassadors without portfolio. Often their most useful roles are those of buffers for the council with external council constituents rather than advocates for policies that would fundamentally alter the council's policy relations with minority citizens.

> In terms of real change, race equality units in the council have accomplished very little. One of the problems of putting race equality units into a White institution that has been historically racist is that institution only wants equality units that actually manage in a way that keeps the institution supported. And I think the workers who are there as individuals, there's a real battle. If you haven't gone in there with some strong knowledge of what the needs of the Black community are, then you will be easily undermined and swayed into what they want. I know there are good people in those units working hard, but it's not going to affect the services provided. Basically, race equality units don't provide leadership for the Black community because the job of these units is to look after the interest of the council. So I can't see anyone would realistically think that they were there to achieve change for Black communities.[43]

The buffering role of race equality units can be vividly seen in the work of race liaison personnel in the Education Department. These individuals have played valuable roles as bridges between the council and educational officials in schools that have used central government laws to opt out of the Liverpool School System. In some instances the operational framework of race equality units has been so awkwardly and vaguely laid out and the resources committed to them so limited that it is difficult to determine what useful role they are intended to play beyond their importance as symbolic gestures. On this issue one worker in the Career Services Department observed:

> This equality unit was set up without any thought. This unit has been functioning for eighteen months and there were three posts designated for one unit. That in itself tells me that the whole issue of the equality unit initiative was not taken seriously because if it would

have been staffed properly, it would have been staffed fully. There would have been a policy development officer, a case worker, an unemployed specialist worker. There would have been an employer liaison officer. We were set up as a piecemeal office. We have told management the unit has not been thought out. The Career Service has never dealt with the issue of race and gender. We must constantly remind our managers, who do not want to discuss the race issue no less than take it up, that when you're dealing with the city council you're dealing with a racist institution.[44]

Some of the positive action programs adopted by the council have had a far more limited impact than anticipated. For example, the MST job-training scheme has not radically altered the representation of Blacks in the city's work force. One key reason for this is that the program has operated as a training agency not an employment agency. As the following respondent explains, British laws permit the development of race-exclusive training programs but prohibit the use of race-exclusive criteria in the hiring process.

When we consider people for jobs, we must consider them on the basis of equality of opportunity. We cannot say to Merseyside Skills trainees that we will give you preferential treatment because if we did we would actually be offending the law because all of their trainees are Black, and we would be discriminating in favor of Black people. If we said to the citizens of Liverpool there are one hundred positive action trainees, and we are going to fill one hundred posts from those positive action trainees, what we will be doing will be taking one hundred Black people on and disfranchising all the White people coming through schools getting qualifications and who are hoping to get a job with the city council and trying to build a career. There is a danger there would be a reaction from other sectors of the community.[45]

The reality has been that a number of individuals have completed the MST training program without securing city jobs because of the absence of vacancies or because they were deemed less suitable for available positions than other applicants. "I think initially the idea of MST was to achieve good quality training for the Black community and offer opportunities for jobs. Unfortunately the politics of the council didn't work to insure those workers, after training, had jobs. Many of them after one year were put back on the dole."[46] The delivery capacity of the MST program has been further complicated by the transfer of operational control of council training from MST to central units of the council.

The implementation of the positive action agenda of the city council has also fallen short in other areas. Liverpool City Council has refused to install monitoring procedures that would provide accurate data on the ethnic make-up of its work force and the ethnic impact of its service delivery policies in housing, education, health, and other areas. Monitoring responsibilities have been left almost completely to the Personnel and Management Department, whose data collection activities have sometimes fallen far below desirable levels of efficiency and accuracy.

All of the application forms for city council jobs have a monitoring sheet. But I do not believe at all that the city council is in fact monitoring. That was proven to myself and another colleague just over eighteen months ago when we actually sat with a Joint Shop Stewards Committee of the trade union movement when a gentleman from the boilermakers union actually stood up when we were discussing the whole issue of monitoring and said the city council has files upon files of monitoring forms that are unused. So no one is monitoring. The city council could not tell you at present how many Black people work within the work force and how many don't, how many Black people are applying for jobs on an annual basis, and how many aren't. And if they did, I would call them liars because I don't believe they're monitoring.[47]

There is also evidence that the internal trawl has not completely disappeared.

The internal trawl is supposed to have been abolished, but we learned six months after it was supposed to have been abolished that one trade union was still having access to certain posts within the council. Black people are not on the inside to see what's happening, so we can only take their word.[48]

Without question, trade unions continue to exercise great influence on the council's job circulation and recruitment policies. Thus NALGO vetoed the publication of council vacancies in the *Liverpool Echo* rather than the *Liverpool Star* because the *Echo*, unlike the *Star*, was distributed beyond the boundaries of the city and would generate competition for Liverpool jobs from professional government workers living in the jurisdictions of other local authorities. Blacks continue to complain that they do not receive copies of the *Star* on a regular basis.

Liverpool 8 has never gotten this free newspaper. If we weren't getting the free paper, we weren't getting the supplement where all the jobs were. We had to fight with the council for three months. We were saying to the city council on the basis that these newspaper people have not given Black people the right to apply for jobs in this city for three months. Will you not stop giving them? Because the city council was pouring thousands into this paper, and there they were discriminating against us. Don't give it. Break the contract.[49]

Liverpool officials blame problems with the circulation of the *Liverpool Star* on unreliable paper carriers and the high crime rate in Toxteth, which means that "people are not happy going there pushing things through doors."[50]

Weak Black political linkage in Liverpool, in many respects, mirrors the problems encountered by Blacks in Boston. Like the Boston City Council, the Liverpool City Council has failed to incorporate independent Black political organizations into the policy making process. Here it should be noted that the Race Relations Liaison Committee was disbanded by the council in 1985. Since that time no independent Black organization has played a productive consultative role in the policy-making process. This fact is key to the analysis of Black linkage politics in Liverpool. Ben-Tovim, Gabriel, Law and Stredder have suggested that statutory and semistatutory committees comprised of community representatives have the best opportunity to engage in consultative exercises involving serious dialogue and responsible action on race policy issues.[51] No such community consultative committees have been engaged by Liverpool City Council since the demise of the Race Relations Liaison Committee. Groups from the Black community that have been co-opted on council committees have lacked statutory authority, been subjected to ad hoc procedural arrangements, restricted to subcommittees, and maintained a dependent clientage relationship to the council because of their heavy reliance on council grant support.[52]

The result has been the marginalization of Black interests in the city decision-making process. Blacks have not been able to mobilize sufficient independent power to compel the council to maintain race equality as an item at the top of its action agenda.

As groups have become more dependent on council funding, the focus on pressure on the council has not continued. This has left a big gap. It's almost as if no one really cares any more. A head of steam has been building up in the council to do something about Black problems. Now we need more external pressure to make the council act.[53]

In the absence of mobilized community pressure, there exists no broad institutional framework for the channeling of Black demands into the council's policy-making process. Blacks have not been able to depend on anticipatory reaction in council decision making because race relations legal mandates are so permissive in Britain that local officials have broad discretion in determining what issues they will and will not recognize, legitimize, and support.[54] This fact has permitted the council to engage in nondecision making in a number of policy areas germane to the social and economic well-being and progress of Black citizens. Except in times of crisis, Black-related economic, educational, and housing issues rise only to the level of symbolic manipulation rather than sustained policy development and resolution.

> The city council is now cosmetically improving a lot of the housing space. I've got a cousin in a housing estate. She's getting a porch on the front of her house, a garden made smaller, a new central heating system, and windows. And I thought to myself, "Why aren't they getting new fittings for the back kitchen? Why aren't they getting showers? Instead of doing up the outside and making them prissy, why don't they change the inside of the houses?" They're looking like slums.[55]

In the face of the council's expansion of its positive action agenda, the menace of racial terrorism for Blacks caught in the council's housing system continues unabated.

> The city is saying Black people can move wherever they want to in this city. That is absolutely not true, and they know it. Our housing policies have got to change. Black people have got to be able to move about this city just like they can move anywhere else. If Black people go out there and are racially terrorized, it's got to be White people that are evicted and asked to move—not put it on Black people to move back to Liverpool 8. Because that's what's happened. All the pressure has been put on the Blacks to come back. And because other Black people see them low because they've been terrorized, they welcome them back to Liverpool 8. You've got to come back. You'd be a fool if you didn't come back.[56]

Racial power sharing in Liverpool has been more myth than fact, even in the wake of the formal institutionalization of an expansive positive action agenda. Equal opportunity reforms, while cosmetically intriguing, have failed to challenge the institutional foundation of hierarchical racial structures that have served as the pivotal touchstone of Black subordination and White dominance in this important city in the Black Atlantic.

## The Politics of Urban Regeneration

Strategies of urban regeneration forge a crucial bridge of analytical linkage between Boston and Liverpool. In the post–World War II era, both cities have searched diligently for formulas to halt the unremitting spiral of social and economic decline. While Boston's regeneration strategies have been reliant on local initiatives, the regeneration process in Liverpool has been driven heavily by the policy priorities of the central government. Under Labour leadership in the 1970s, the centerpiece of national regeneration strategies in Britain were inner-city partnerships. Seeking to link the central government with local authorities and community groups in cooperative organizational networks, the primary objective of inner-city partnerships was to use public-sector resources to stimulate effective regeneration policy programming at the local level. Although the principal funding for the partnerships was to come from central government, local governments were expected to play a leading role in the search for effective solutions to urban problems. This approach reflected Labour's profound belief that the undermining of city economies by private-sector disinvestment could only be controlled through the actions of public-sector institutions, especially those operating at the local level. The emphasis on community involvement made it clear that a central objective of the inner-city partnership program would be the transformation of social and economic conditions in central city neighborhoods experiencing severe economic problems. Through rational planning involving direct community participation, strong efforts would be made to regenerate the economies of inner cities by halting the dispersal of jobs and other human resources from these areas.[57]

Both the goals and the structure of urban regeneration were radically altered by the Conservatives when they took office in 1979. Margaret Thatcher was swept into office on the back of promises to reduce the national debt by cutting back on public spending, taxation, and employment. The Conservative manifesto also promised to minimize government intervention and to decentralize the administration of a range of governmental programs to local authorities. Impressed with the performance of public-private partnerships in the United States, Thatcher's solution to the regeneration conundrum was to shift the emphasis of central government policy from public-sector expenditure to private investment. Unable to control extraordinary spending costs at the national level, Thatcher strongly embraced the strategy of imposing cut-backs on local spending as the most rational and effective means of keeping public spending in check. In place of the public-sector programs financed by Labour, the Conservative Party proposed a series of wealth-generating schemes fueled by the strategic and intensive involvement of the private sector in the urban regeneration process. In keeping with this approach, the inner-city partnership program inherited from Labour was radically altered by the Conservatives. Local participation in the program was reduced to the point that the word *partnership* hardly seemed appropriate; private interests were allowed to take over many local projects almost completely. By 1986 urban regeneration grants were being administered that totally bypassed local authorities and provided direct funding to private institutions to implement local development programs. Under Conservative management, the strategic focus of urban regeneration efforts shifted from social welfare and employment to a concentration on physical construction and rehabilitation.[58]

Local planning and authority were undermined by the creation of enterprise zones that sought to promote private business investment by setting aside strategic parts of cities where inducements such as tax exemptions, capital allowances on commercial and industrial buildings, and the relaxation of occupational and safety regulations might spur the establishment of productive business enterprises. Private development was also given substantial support at the expense of local control through the Simplified Planning Zone System. This system allows private developers to begin projects in certain defined areas without obtaining permission to operate from local planning departments.[59]

Margaret Thatcher's emphasis on private leadership in the regeneration process has served as the pivotal foundation of urban strategies advanced by her successors Conservative leader John Major and Labour leader Tony Blair. As prime minister, Major continued to promote the substitution of private investment for public initiative in the urban development process. Tony Blair's urban policies have been surprisingly conservative, embracing both a private property enhancement focus on policy leadership issues and a Clintonlike "welfare to work" posture on issues dealing with personal responsibility and government support for family maintenance. In this atmosphere of conservative social disengagement,

Black political linkage and incorporation have been extraordinarily difficult objectives to achieve. Following the dictates of central government policies, policy-making institutions have continued to push Black needs and interests to the bottom of the public agenda. Many key actors in the local regeneration process operate in arenas removed from Black input and control. Central government officials are elusive, invisible, and unknown; local government officials can foreswear responsibility because they are neither the initiators nor the executioners of key policy objectives. Pressure to engage equal opportunity issues does not rise from below; legal mandates from above are so weak, vague, and permissive that they often send messages of avoidance rather than messages of affirmation and persistence. Regeneration in this context almost invariably means property-led initiatives that bypass Black community leaders and institutions in their efforts to maximize profits for elites from economic ventures sheltered from public scrutiny.

The wealth production, private investment model of urban regeneration was first introduced into Liverpool by the Merseyside Community Development Corporation (MDC) in 1981 on the heels of the Toxteth riots. Central government's actions in bringing the development corporation concept to Liverpool had the effect (fully intended) of taking responsibility for the redevelopment of 865 acres of dockland area out of the hands of local authorities and into the hands of a single-minded agency that would perform required tasks rapidly and create an attractive environment for private-sector investment.[60] The MDC would function as an independent quango beyond the effective control of local authorities. In pursuing its objectives, the MDC could ignore existing plans for the dockland area developed by local authorities. The MDC quickly emerged as a premier power source in the local regeneration process. It usurped the role of local authorities in many facets of the tourist industry by transforming the Albert Dock into a commercial and shopping area, restoring the waterfront, establishing maritime and Atlantic Slave Trade museums, hosting an International Garden Festival, and sponsoring a Tall Ships race.[61] Black citizens were eager to note, however, that very few of the resources generated by MDC flowed in the direction of the Black community. In 1981 MDC agreed to give a Black group, Third World Promotions, funds to stage the first Liverpool Caribbean Festival. When difficulties arose with the execution of this event, the corporation rejected all subsequent requests for funds from this group. Blacks were especially disturbed that the

Black community received no benefits from the International Garden Festival and the renovation of the Albert Dock.

> Institutions like MDC actually came about because of the riots here in Toxteth. They received millions of pounds because young unemployed Black males and females came out on the street and in the uprising showed they were disgruntled with the rate of change that was taking place in this city. That came about because it was supposed to help us. Going down on the site of the Albert Dock, there was not one Black working on the working side of it. There were no Black contractors. There are very few Black people now who visit there because of the informal immigration which we call the fee to get in. If you look at the Maritime Museum and the Liverpool Museum, our particular contributions to this city have been obliterated, just washed over, just as it was done in the Beatles sense.[62]

Clearly, the MDC was not a government entity designed to accommodate Black community demands for linkage and power. No Black person served on the corporation's board; efforts to involve Black organizations in a consultative capacity never produced meaningful results.[63]

Blacks were also not the targets of the Merseyside Task Force, another central government agency. Task forces were set up by the central government in several cities to promote regeneration in the areas of housing, the environment, traffic flow, and neighborhood development. Initially, the Merseyside Task Force was designed to function as an urban partnership between the city council, the chamber of commerce, and community groups. However, the Liverpool partnership fell apart in 1982, leaving in its place a one-to-one relationship between the city government and the task force. As the relationship evolved, the task force became principally a conduit for central government funds; it flatly rejected the notion that it was obligated to take up supervisory and monitoring responsibilities as well.

> We do not have the right to tell the authorities what their policies should be. In terms of race relations, we have to stand back and say that is the council's decision. We are not guardians of that legislation. It's a national act which is, in its implementation, a responsibility of the local authority. We were concerned that for a long period what appeared to us to be the worst housing problems in the city were not being addressed. We made that concern clear. But we don't have any formal role in telling the local authority how they should run their housing management, their housing allocation program.[64]

The laissez faire attitude of central government administrators encouraged the council to promote a racially discriminatory housing program that bypassed the Black community in favor of housing improvements for estates on the edge of the city. "The city council's judgment was that that was where the housing conditions were worse."[65] The task force bowed to the council's refusal to disperse Blacks to housing estates outside the segregated confines of Toxteth. "The objective was to keep the community together as long as they wanted to stay together."[66] Task force officials also believed that while they had the obligation to fund council education programs, they had no power to demand that the council pursue quality education objectives. "We were not the primary government agency to deal with this issue. The things we can do are at the margin of the problem not at the heart of the problem."[67]

The failure on the part of the Merseyside Task Force to engage equal opportunity objectives or to emphasize programs targeted for Liverpool 8 encouraged Black leaders to call for the establishment of a task force in the Granby Toxteth area. The original request for a task force in Liverpool 8 was made in 1981; it was rejected. Eight years later (August 1989), a task force was finally set up in the Granby Toxteth area. Although neither managed or controlled by Blacks, the Granby Toxteth Task Force set forth a progressive agenda focused principally on promoting Black economic development.

> The task force's activities are economically based. They've been established to tackle the economic ills of the inner city, working on the principle that if you tackle the economic ills and introduce a wage culture and reduce unemployment, then a lot of the endemic problems of housing, poverty, and so on will be answered by this sort of approach. So we focus in on support for enterprise and to try and find ways of improving the quality and quantity of training schemes. Therefore looking to improve the skill base among unemployed people, we are looking to create jobs by improving the local business base and to improve self sufficiency initiatives in the business area.[68]

In the area of education, the task force started CHOICE (Children of the Inner Cities Education Program) and REACH OUT. The Purpose of CHOICE was to encourage inner-city students to finish their high school programs and go on to college. REACH OUT was designed to help students with special domestic situations to pursue studies in higher education by studying part-time at home using university materials. By June 1996, the survival of the Granby

Toxteth Task Force was in jeopardy; faced with serious budget deficits, the central government had given the task force a six-month deadline to close down. Across its life history, its track record of accomplishment was marred by the fact that it never established a viable consultative relationship with Black organizations.

Disadvantages to Liverpool 8 citizens derived from the gradual closing down of the task force in the Granby Toxteth area were deepened by the programmatic disconnection of the Toxteth area from the most ambitious regeneration program in the history of Liverpool, City Challenge. City Challenge was introduced into the lexicon of urban development programming by the central government in 1991. This program involved a competition between local authorities for annual grants of £7.5 million over a five-year period. The structural design of City Challenge differed from those of previous urban programs because it did not involve management and control by any single entity and encouraged the creation of "robust, effective partnerships between national and local government agencies, and between the public, private and voluntary sectors—partnerships that will create consensus, deliver effective programme management and achieve strategic goals."[69] Liverpool was the recipient of one of the first City Challenge grants. In a strategic move, the city council decided to bypass inner city communities and to focus its City Challenge efforts on downtown and outer-fringe development (see figure 8.1). This decision was in keeping with two major components of council decision making in the post-Militant era: (1) to shore up city relations with the central government by emphasizing cooperation rather than conflict; and (2) to transform Liverpool into a city that would be a strong market for tourism.[70] Leaders of the city council were insistent that City Challenge go into an area of the city that had great development potential. Consequently, it directed City Challenge money to the center city and to the fringe of the city—areas that would produce attractive shopping centers, museums, amusement parks, and other enterprises that would stimulate growth by pulling tourists away from London, Birmingham, Manchester, Edinburgh, Glasgow, and other major cities.

The primary emphasis of City Challenge was flagship projects, not minor programs designed to stimulate development in inner-city neighborhoods. In the eyes of city council leaders, this emphasis made it axiomatic that Toxteth would be left out of City Challenge. "We tried to get money from City Challenge, and we weren't eligible. And I think it was a deliberate decision to leave this area out. Because when I looked at the development plan put out by the coun-

Figure 8.1. Urban Redevelopment Areas in Liverpool

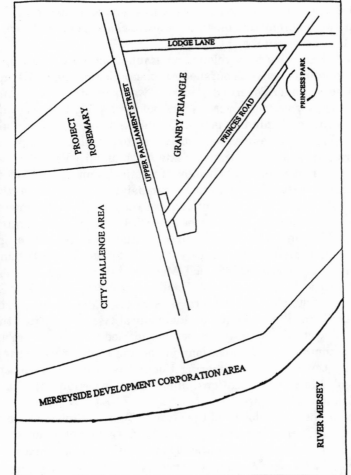

LODGE LANE

PROJECT ROSEMARY

UPPER PARLIAMENT STREET

GRANBY TRIANGLE

PRINCES ROAD

PRINCESS PARK

CITY CHALLENGE AREA

MERSEYSIDE DEVELOPMENT CORPORATION AREA

RIVER MERSEY

Source: Adapted from data included in the Final Report, Granby Toxteth Community Project

cil in its early stages, I looked at this map with different things marked out for different areas, and it was just blank for Granby."[71] Toxteth political leaders asked to be included in City Challenge. The best they could get from city officials was the suggestion that Toxteth could possibly be the beneficiary of spillover resources generated by City Challenge projects. This response made it clear that City Challenge's idea of partnership, as interpreted in Liverpool, did not include the promotion of social, economic, and political linkage for the Black community.

As an alternative to development grants from City Challenge, Black community activists pursued European Community (EC) program funding under Poverty 3. Poverty 3 was operative as a funding vehicle in Liverpool for several years before Black groups became acutely aware of its funding potential. Once that possibility became salient, planning resources were mobilized to establish a Black-led regeneration vehicle, the Granby Toxteth Community Project. Over a three-year period, the Granby Toxteth Community Project mounted an extremely ambitious campaign to regenerate the Granby Triangle, an area running between Upper Parliament, Princess Road, and Lodge Lane (see figure 8.1). The project operated with a staff of nine, including the director, Audrey Young. The original steering committee for Poverty 3 was established in 1989 and consisted of Liverpool City Council, Merseyside Task Force, Granby Toxteth Task Force, Liverpool Health Authority, University of Liverpool, Council for Voluntary Services, Merseyside Race Equality Council, and Churches Ecumenical Assembly. After the Granby Toxteth Community Project was formed in 1991, a number of Black community organizations joined the steering committee, including the Afro-Asian Steering Committee, the Federation of Liverpool Black Organizations, and the Consortium of Black Organizations (see figure 8.2).

Much of the methodology of the Granby Toxteth Project was driven by the EC's concern with documenting the extent of poverty and devising strategies for systematically eradicating poverty in declining areas in Europe. Among the specific objectives of the project were the following:

1. To highlight the effects of poverty and racism in the Granby Toxteth Community and the impact of poverty on the daily lives of individuals.

2. To ensure the active participation of the Granby Toxteth Community in the development of policies aimed at the alleviation of poverty and racism.

**Figure 8.2. Granby Toxteth Community Project Organizational Structure**

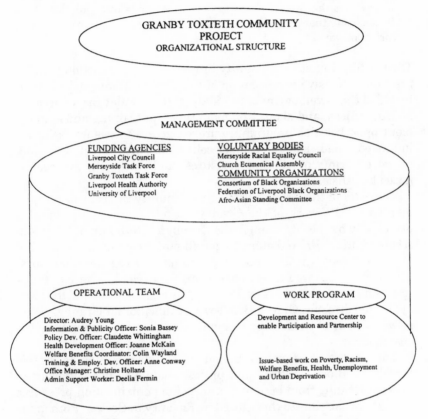

Source: Adapted from data included in the Final Report, Granby Toxteth Community Project.

3.  To ensure the active participation of partner agencies and other organizations in the attack on poverty and racism.

4.  To build up community resources for attacking poverty and racism.[72]

A central principle undergirding the strategic approach of the project was multidimensionality. Audrey Young, the director of the project, explained this feature of the organization's work.

In Eurospeak this means that poverty is multifaceted in terms of its cause, symptoms and characteristics. Individuals are in poverty, the area is in poverty, and deprivation is widespread throughout the locality. So therefore the work of the project will operate at a range of levels because of the multifaceted dimension to the issue. It also means that the project needs to develop a range of actions which demonstrate that the issues are complex and must be addressed in a variety of ways.[73]

The Granby Toxteth Community Project set forth an action plan for the comprehensive regeneration of the Granby Triangle. This plan included the development of the Rialto Site/Berkeley Street area for houses, offices, and shops; the mounting of a training and employment opportunities program, improved access to leisure facilities; improved road safety; refuse collection and street cleaning; improved crime prevention measures; and more effective coordinated health care.

The work of the Granby Toxteth Community Project was complemented by the work of the Granby Toxteth Partnership. Funded principally by the city council, the Granby Toxteth Partnership represented a coordinated effort to get all major community groups in Toxteth involved in community planning and regeneration work. The partnership would serve as the principal conduit for city funds to community groups. Alex Bennett, former head of MCRC, was appointed director. Gideon Ben-Tovim, councillor for Granby, would serve as chair of the Liaison Committee to the partnership from the city council.

The existence of research and administration teams staffed largely by Black activists and professionals was not sufficient to prevent Granby from becoming a target of gentrification pressures remarkably similar to those faced by Roxbury in Boston. Both areas represent prime development real estate. In fact, Granby stands in almost the same geographic proximity to downtown Liverpool as Roxbury stands to downtown Boston. Both communities are approximately one and one half miles south of the downtown business district. While pressure on Roxbury has come from the spillover of development from downtown business interests, pressure on Granby has come largely from the activities of private housing associations. A preponderance of responsibility for inner-city housing development and redevelopment in Granby has shifted to housing associations in the wake of policies by the central government that have ceased to allocate money for housing development to the Liverpool City Council and directed funds instead to private housing associations, such as Merseyside Improved Housing, Liverpool Housing Trust, Cooperative Development Services, and the Steve Biko Housing Association. Housing associations have become major players in the regeneration process in Liverpool. Some of them represent vast organizational networks that stretch across the country and possess incredible financial resources. Unlike the leaders of local authorities, the leaders of housing associations are almost completely shielded from public oversight and control because they are private administrators who do not have to stand before the voters in elections. The only Black housing association, Steve Biko, has attempted to develop an alternative housing agenda that stresses community participation and neighborhood development. Filling in the vacuum left by the council, Steve Biko provided thirty flats in a sheltered housing scheme for the elderly worth £1.5 million and ten one-bedroom bungalows worth one half million pounds.[74]

The neighborhood development approach of Steve Biko has been the exception, not the rule. Recognizing the potential value of property in Granby, housing associations have attempted to buy up property in Granby to pave the way for the construction of homes for the urban gentry. In pursuit of this strategy, the leaders of housing associations set off an acrimonious dispute by sending homeowners in Granby letters that proposed to buy up homes in the area that would later be demolished to promote redevelopment. "People were up in arms. A lot of people bought houses here years ago. Property here is very cheap, and we pay a lot of mortgages. A lot of people bought their homes as pensioners prior to their independence, not wanting to go on welfare. When this letter was put in everybody's door, people flipped their lid."[75] Community groups took their case to the council only to find that informal agreements had already been made by councillors to allow housing associations to demolish homes in Granby. "Councillors told them they could do what they wanted in Granby if they didn't get strong opposition."[76] City councillors deny that they have conspired with housing associations to demolish neighborhoods in Granby.

> What the council is doing is not in any sense trying to break up the community, but to try to find some decent housing for those who are there. Most of the housing in the Granby Triangle is not owned by the council but is owned by housing associations or private landlords. Estate action has been a project we have put forward in partnership with the government to use government money to improve the lot of council stock in Granby. And there I think the situation is that the local people have had their housing improved; they've been able to stay in their housing, and there's been no attempt to disperse them. These are council tenants, and there's quite a bit of improvement that's gone on in much of the area. Since the council doesn't own any

of the property in the Granby Triangle, it's very much the responsibility of housing associations, and they're bringing in the money from the Housing Corporation, which the government funds. So although the council has a planning role, we're very much not a big financial player. What we've got now is an agreement with housing associations to get rid of half of the bad property in the area and to replace it with new buildings in the area, and in the other half not to get rid of them totally but to rehabilitate the area. Housing associations have wanted to demolish and rebuild because it would be cheaper for them and a better deal to start afresh.[77]

A better deal for whom? Demolition would possibly produce severe psychological fallout, provoking many Granby citizens to grieve for a lost home. Further, many of the homes slated for demolition represented lifetime investments that could not be replaced by programs offering rent subsidies. The arguments for demolition were not very convincing when juxtaposed against the massive racial and class transfer of choice property that would accompany the regeneration of Toxteth based on principles of wealth production rather than principles of community uplift and neighborhood preservation.

Another source of pressure on the Black community in Granby is the Rosemary project. This project involved the construction of middle class housing and a women's hospital in the middle of Granby. Project Rosemary originated as an idea by the dean of the Anglican Cathedral. It started out as a modest effort to construct residences to house the staff of the cathedral in an area near Grove Street. The area was in decline; recently a housing estate had been knocked down and a school building closed and abandoned. The dean sought to redevelop the area by expanding the church housing program and establishing additional housing sites for students at the University of Liverpool. In its third phase, the project took on massive proportions with the building of the Women's Hospital.

Project Rosemary has been the object of major controversy. Activists in the Black community have held numerous meetings protesting the project because of its location in the middle of Granby and because the dean of the Anglican Cathedral did not consult with community residents until the project was well under way. Black activists also observed that the project was of little value to the residents of the surrounding community: the costs of the houses that were constructed were far beyond the financial means of community residents; the Women's Hospital served mainly a White middle-class clientele; few Black workers participated in the hospital's construction; and almost no Black people held meaningful positions on the hospital's staff. Black activists also found it ironic that while Blacks could not find money to support significant projects in the Black community, the Anglican Church encountered little difficulty raising money for the Rosemary project through public housing grants and other public as well as private sources.

Project Rosemary appears to be only the beginning of major gentrification efforts in Liverpool 8. Liverpool leaders have been proud to promote the city's new image as a "city of learning." The critical essence of that image is the enlargement of the physical plants of the two major inner-city universities, the University of Liverpool and John Moores University, both of whom are geographically located adjacent to Granby. The University of Liverpool has substantially penetrated the outer perimeters of Granby through its residence hall building initiative in the central city. This program is the university's response to the dilemma posed by the fact that while its campus is almost entirely located in the central city, its residence halls have been located more than five miles away, near Smithdown Road and Greenbank Road. Since a city of learning requires a physically united university community, the University of Liverpool is living up to its obligations in the regeneration process by relocating and expanding its halls of residence in the center city. Faced with the kind of physical dilemma earmarking the relationship between Northeastern University and the Black community in Boston, the University of Liverpool has forged ahead with plans to buy land in Granby to accommodate its need for additional student housing in close geographic proximity to its central city campus. The increasing expansion of the physical plant of John Moores University will undoubtedly mean that its contributions to the implementation of the "city-of-learning" initiative will come at the expense of Granby citizens who wish to retain their investments in private property in the area.

As in Boston, the Black community in Liverpool faces important dilemmas in the urban regeneration process. These dilemmas illuminate and magnify the problem of weak Black linkage and incorporation in the political process. Also as in Boston, the future of the Black community in Liverpool is intimately tied to its capacity to mount strategies and mobilize resources capable of penetrating the power nexus of the larger political system.

# 9

## Liverpool: Political Strategies and Political Empowerment

### The Politics of Protest

Structural dimensions of the racial hierarchy and institutional environment operative in Liverpool have stimulated and nurtured a variety of Black political responses. Black resistance to racial oppression, in the form of organized protests, has been a prominent and persistent ingredient in the medley of strategies adopted and implemented by the Black community in Liverpool in its ongoing efforts to advance Black interests through political empowerment.[1] It is important to underscore the fact that racial discrimination in Liverpool, as in Boston, has not gone unchallenged. Blacks in Liverpool have compiled a legacy of protest that dates back several centuries. The first Black citizens of Liverpool were runaway slaves who challenged the system of racism locally, nationally, and internationally.[2] This tradition of Black resistance was reflected in the raging battles fought by Black seamen against Whites who sought to kidnap them in Liverpool and transport them across the ocean to serve as slaves in America. Law and Henfrey describe one such incident taking place in 1857: "A fight broke out on deck between the Black seamen and White officers. At the magistrate's hearing on shore the next day, the courtroom and the local press were openly sympathetic to the black seamen who were freed as a result."[3]

Many Blacks in Britain were involved in the international movement to abolish slavery. As early as 1780, Olandah Equiana, an Ibo from Nigeria, mounted strong protest campaigns against the slave trade, becoming in the process England's first Black political leader.[4] In 1783 he denounced in emotional terms the mass murder

237

of 132 Black slaves thrown into the sea from the Liverpool slaver *Zong*.[5] Equiana's autobiography, published in 1789, became a central force in the campaign to rouse public opinion against the slave trade in Britain. Blacks in Britain were drawn into the abolitionist campaign by visits from American Black abolitionists such as William Wells Brown and Frederick Douglass.[6] Edward Blyden, an articulate spokesman for the cause of African nationalism, published material on Africa in Liverpool and met with business and community leaders in Liverpool on a regular basis.[7] Commitment by Blacks in Liverpool to the politics of protest was deepened by memories of the anti-Black riots of 1919 that witnessed brutal assaults on Black men, including veteran Black seamen, by White workers angry because of Black competition for jobs and developing relations between Black men and local White women.[8] White mobs reaching the strength of ten thousand, looted and set fire to Black homes, chased a Black seaman named Charles Wootton to his death into the Mersey River, and made a bon fire on Beaufort Street of furniture and bedding dragged from Black residences.[9] Succeeding generations of Blacks in Liverpool would profit from the profound lesson delivered by the 1919 riots: that Black safety, security, and advancement would depend heavily on the willingness and capacity of the Black community to engage in militant, collective struggle.[10]

Black protest began to take on a formal organizational presence in Liverpool in the 1930s. The Liverpool Association for the Welfare of Coloured People was founded in 1937. This group was patterned after the League of Coloured People established in London under the leadership of Dr. Harold Moody in the early 1930s.[11] During the 1930s the League of Coloured People established itself as a militant voice on behalf of the rights of Black people, sponsoring conferences and lectures on race issues and presenting the case for social legislation to promote Black advancement before parliament, local authorities, and other public bodies.[12] The Association for the Welfare of Coloured People began to enthusiastically embrace a similar program of community activism in Liverpool.

Black protest activities increased in the 1940s as Black workers arriving from the West Indies found that they were excluded because of their color from entering dance halls and other places of amusement. To confront these problems, a Liverpool branch of the League of Coloured People was established. A local organization called the "International Race Relations Committee" was also founded to challenge customs that prevented Black people from patronizing a range of public establishments in Liverpool. One

member of this group recalled some of its most emotionally stimulating experiences.

> We split ourselves into groups of two. They had ballrooms in Liverpool
> that did not accept Blacks. One was the Rialto, one was the Grafton,
> and one was Reeces. I and my colleague went to the Rialto. We had
> White girlfriends, and we sent them in beforehand. When we came to
> the door, we were told, "We don't allow coloureds in here." I said, "I am
> going in—here's my money." I said, "take note—I am not crashing, I
> am paying. The only way you can stop me from going in is send for the
> police." But he said, "The girls won't dance with you." I said, "Won't
> they? Let's put it to the test." After a tremendous discussion, they let
> us in. We went in, picked out our girlfriends, had a dance, and so on.
> The fact that they let us in didn't mean the doors were open for
> Blacks. But we did this on a regular basis.[13]

The campaign of the International Race Relations Committee to
break down race discrimination was given a substantial boost by the
case of a Black soldier who was fined one farthing by a judge (less
than a penny ) when he refused to leave the Grafton Rooms dance
club after being denied entrance dressed in his uniform.

> The judge was extremely critical of the Grafton Rooms which had
> refused to allow the Black soldier to enter. He said here we have the
> Grafton Rooms that was refusing to admit, not only the individual,
> but Her Majesty's uniform into its establishment, a uniform worn by
> an individual who was, at that moment, actually fighting in order
> that that establishment could be kept open.[14]

This decision was broadly publicized in the media and interpreted
by Blacks as a major victory. The mood of victory and accomplishment in the Black community was also elevated by the case of
cricket player Learie Constantine who won a lawsuit against the
Imperial Hotel in London when the hotel refused to rent him a room
because of his race.

Black community activism in the 1940s was stimulated considerably by the establishment of Stanley House in 1946. Although
founded by Whites and controlled by a council composed mainly of
Whites, Stanley House was located in the Black community and
served a predominantly Black clientele.[15] With an active membership in 1954 of 285, Stanley House emerged as the largest Black
association in Liverpool.[16]

Black participation in race riots in 1948 precipitated the founding
of the Colonial Defence Committee to raise funds for Black defen-

dants, secure legal defense for Blacks charged with criminal offenses, and promote better race relations in Liverpool.[17] This group dissolved after several years. It was replaced by the Colonial People's Defence Association (CPDA), a group committed to a broad racial empowerment agenda. Under the CPDA, the politics of racial uplift emerged full-blown in Liverpool. Functioning with an all-Black leadership, CPDA committed itself unswervingly to the goals of racial unity and the abolition of all forms of social discrimination. In support of these objectives, it adopted a rich variety of interventionist strategies, including lobbying city hall for Black employment, the application of pressure on trade unions to persuade them to become involved in the fight for local antidiscriminatory legislation, the provision of legal defense for Black defendants, legal advice and employment assistance for new arrivals, organizational networking through participation in conferences across Britain, and the sponsorship of local public meetings.[18]

The Merseyside West Indian Association (MWIA) was founded in 1951 as a separate political caucus focusing on the special interests of West Indians. As a political action group, it championed the causes of West Indian workers who alleged that they had been victims of racial discrimination in employment.[19] The MWIA launched a vigorous protest with the Home Office in London against the closing of the Colonial Office in Liverpool. Police issues also found their way on MWIA's political agenda. It protested loudly when a West Indian charged that his home had been searched by the police without a warrant.[20] Although not as broadly based or activist oriented as the CPDA, the MWIA was nonetheless an important instrument of political opposition in the Black community.

Large-scale race riots in Nottingham and Notting Hill in London in 1958 signaled the opening of a new chapter of race relations in Britain. Whites were becoming angry and violent as larger numbers of Black faces began to appear on the streets, in schools, and in work places. Blacks interpreted the 1962 Commonwealth Immigrants Bill and its provisions designed to reduce Black immigration to Britain as the low point in British race relations. A number of organizations sprang up to lead the fight against new threats to Black civil and human rights. In Birmingham the Coordinating Committee Against Racial Discrimination was founded (CCARD); this group led marches through the streets to protest the immigration bill.[21] The Conference of Afro-Asian-Caribbean Organizations (CAACO) was established in London. This group campaigned vigorously against the immigration bill and in support of Black rights in the United States.[22]

Visits to Britain by Dr. Martin Luther King Jr. and Malcolm X led to the founding of two significant umbrella race relations organizations. The Campaign Against Racial Discrimination (CARD) was inspired by a trip to Britain by Dr. King in connection with his visit to Norway in December 1964 to accept the Nobel Prize. It involved the organizational merger of a variety of Asian and Afro-Caribbean groups. Political ferment in the Black nationalist community centered around the activities of the Racial Action Adjustment Society (RAAS), a radical group formed in the wake of a visit by Malcolm X to London in February 1965.

Blacks in Liverpool were not untouched by these events. The growth of Black activism nationally and internationally was reflected in the changing political perspective of Blacks in Liverpool. Blacks born in Liverpool were especially in tune with the American component of the nationalist movement of the 1960s. American Black troops stationed in Liverpool during World War II forged strong relations between Blacks in America and Blacks in Liverpool. These Black Americans were actively involved in Stanley House; many of them found brides in Liverpool and took them back to America. During the 1960s, Blacks in Liverpool closely identified with Black American music, Black American fashions, and Black American politics. The actions of prominent Black Americans such as Dr. Martin Luther King Jr., Malcolm X, Huey Newton, Bobby Seal, and Angela Davis were closely watched and imitated by Blacks in Liverpool. Major marches for Angela Davis were held in Liverpool to support her struggles with the American legal system. A Liverpool group, the Young Panthers, sprang up for a short period to articulate the philosophy of the most radical sectors of the Black nationalist movement. Events in other parts of the world, such as the Sharpville Massacre in South Africa, also inspired mass marches and organizational efforts among Blacks in Liverpool.

The 1970s witnessed the growth in Liverpool of virulent White racist activity by fringe groups such as the National Front. To confront this threat, White liberals joined hands with Black radicals to form the Merseyside Anti-Racialist Alliance (MARA). Founded in 1978, MARA became an important vehicle for the launching of antiracist initiatives in Liverpool. The idea of a broad-based, antiracist alliance in Liverpool grew out of a workshop on racialism at the Mersyside Left Forum held at the University of Liverpool in March 1978. The organization was formally launched at a meeting held at the Caribbean Center in April 1978, attended by approximately 150 individuals.[23]

During its most active phase, MARA pursued a political agenda focused on educational and police issues, the dissemination of information through newspaper articles and radio programs, the mounting of campaigns against the passage of discriminatory immigration legislation and the deportation of Black families to South Africa, and strong opposition against the efforts of the National Front to establish a base of political power in Merseyside. As a part of its countermobilization against the National Front, MARA drew up a joint statement to be issued by major party candidates against the participation of National Front candidates in three public elections in Merseyside. It also joined the Anti-Nazi League in a counter demonstration against a National Front rally in New Brighton and served as the main sponsor of a concert, Rock Against Racism, attended by five thousand persons in September 1978 in Walton Park. Lacking a significant resource base, MARA eventually collapsed, folding its membership and organizational initiatives into the structure and agenda of the Merseyside Community Relations Council.[24]

The 1970s also marked the emergence of autonomous protest organizations led by Liverpool-born Blacks. Racial antagonism arising from the marginalization of the Black community was brought to a boil when an article appeared in the *Listener* magazine that repeated the description by the police of the local Black community as being composed of half-castes, many of whom were the products of "liaisons between black seamen and white prostitutes in Liverpool 8, the red-light district." The *Listener* article was based on a documentary broadcast over BBC about the Merseyside Police Force. Blacks in Liverpool were infuriated by the article. With the help of MARA, they staged a massive protest march to BBC Merseyside, demanding both an apology and a formal investigation by Liverpool's chief constable. Political consciousness stirred by the *Listener* march led to the formation in 1979 of the Liverpool Black Organization. Out of this formation emerged a set of new, dynamic Black political leaders. Eventually, persons associated with the Liverpool Black Organization would begin to channel their political energies through other organizations, including the Merseyside Community Relations Council, the Race Relations Liaison Committee, the Black Caucus, the Liverpool 8 Defence Committee, the Liverpool 8 Law Centre, and the Immigrant Advice Unit.

Black protest campaigns have given the Black movement in Liverpool a unique personality. A mosaic of organizations and personalities has moved in and out of the political process. The Black movement in Liverpool has, in the main, been discontinuous and focused on the resolution of specific rather than general social and economic issues. Its contributions to the ongoing progress of the Black community have been important. The upsurge of riots in the 1980s and the mobilization efforts of the Liverpool 8 Defence Committee created a high sense of political consciousness in the Black community and a keen awareness of its power potentials. At the same time, the virulent racism of the political establishment, as manifested by the Sampson Bond affair, made it clear to some sectors of the Black leadership corps that authentic Black political empowerment required that protest strategies be supplemented by major strides toward the development of an effective base of organized Black political action in the electoral arena.

## The Struggle for Independent Black Politics

Across the Black Atlantic frequent calls have been made for the pursuit by Blacks of a politics of independence. These calls reflect the desire by Black leaders and the Black masses to establish autonomous bases of power that are not subject to manipulation and control by dominant White-led political forces. In the United States one important expression of the quest for political independence was the work of the National Black Independent Political Party (NBIPP) in the 1980s. Although national and international in its political orientation, this movement had little impact on the contours of electoral politics in Boston, with the goal of Black empowerment in that city being pursued by Mel King and other prominent Black politicians principally within the confines of the Democratic Party. The main thrust of Black politics in Britain at the national level has been toward the creation of satellite Black sections within the overarching structure of the Labour Party. Black political activists in Liverpool have, on occasion, deviated from this pattern by vigorously promoting strategies of electoral independence.

The Black independence movement in Liverpool has direct links to the conflict between the Labour Party and the Black community generated by the Sampson Bond affair. Efforts by Black leaders and organizations to persuade city councillors to abandon their support for Bond as principal race relations adviser, left deep scars of division between the Black community and the Labour Party. Blacks deeply resented the heavy-handed tactics used by Militant leaders to impose Bond on the Black community without its consent. Feeling betrayed by the Labour Party and alienated from the established political process, many Blacks turned to independent politics as an avenue of community protest and racial uplift. Commenting on the growing disillusionment by Blacks with the Labour Party, one Black activist noted:

> We were disgruntled with what the Labour Party had done to us over the years. They had years of blanket support of every Black person around here. They had a free ticket. The Liberals and Conservatives wouldn't bother to canvass the area. It was a safe seat. And with this seat they had done absolutely nothing for us. We sat down and agreed that Labour's bad behavior in the Bond episode was the last straw; we had to take control of our own affairs.[25]

To spearhead the Black independent politics movement, a new organization was created, the Federation of Liverpool Black Organizations (FLBO). The FLBO represented the consolidation of leadership forces active in various phases of the Black empowerment movement. Although its formal structure gave it the veneer of a mass-based organization (with an active membership of 365 persons), the primary political work of the FLBO was focused on influencing the policy preferences and behavior of existing community organizations and public bureaucracies. Recognizing the limitations of its own policy resources, the FLBO infiltrated existing organizations and institutions in an effort to stimulate rigorous enforcement of Black community objectives.

> If we found the Tate Gallery wasn't employing Black people, we asked the CRC, "What are you doing about that?" If we found the Liverpool Health Authority was going to employ workers to look over the primary needs of Black people, we were going to see who was on the selection committee, how long the post was for, what was the brief that would be given to that particular worker, how much power would we have to influence the Health Authority's recommendations and subcommittees? We tried to use our brief as a bang-on-the-door kind of approach to let them know that look we're watching you and we want to know things are getting done in accordance.[26]

Interorganizational lobbying represented only one facet of FLBO's operational agenda. In many respects, its most significant influence lay in the electoral arena. In 1987, it secured its place in the history books by becoming the first Black organization in Britain to run independent candidates for seats on a local council. Seeds for the independent electoral movement in 1987 were planted one year earlier when Delroy Burris, a local Black community activist, mounted a personal campaign for the city council. Although Burris's campaign generated little electoral support (about three hundred votes), his efforts inspired the leaders of FLBO to call a series of community meetings to consider the possibility of putting forth Black candidates for the council capable of galvanizing broad-based community mobilization. The result of these meetings was an agreement that at least two candidates would run for the council in 1987 under the banner of the FLBO. Within the FLBO a groundswell of support surfaced for Maria O'Reilly as one of the independent candidates for the council. O'Reilly was a longtime community activist and public administrator who had played a key role in the work of the Liverpool 8 Defence Committee, the Black Caucus, the Merseyside Community Relations Council, and the Liverpool 8 Law Center. O'Reilly opted not to accept the nomination for the council. Through protracted internal consultation and debate, members of FLBO agreed upon the names of two persons to stand for election to the council in their behalf: Delroy Burris and Shaun Deckon. Burris was a sentimental favorite because of his previous heroic efforts as a lone wolf candidate for the council in 1986. Deckon was a community activist and a recent graduate of the University of Liverpool who had established a strong community base through World Promotions, the community institution that had taken principal responsibility for the organization and management of the annual Caribbean carnival.

Initially, the spirits of FLBO leaders were raised by the fact that the three council seats in the Granby Ward were wide open because of the dismissal of Granby councillors from the council as a part of the government's actions against the forty seven councillors who had been removed and surcharged because of their failure to set a community rate. The political calculus became more problematic with the endorsement by the Labour Party of Black activist Liz Drysdale and White liberals Gideon Ben-Tovim and Phillip Hughes as council candidates from the Granby Ward. Drysdale had originally been a part of the Black forces that had developed and promoted the independent strategy. She broke ranks with this group when approached by the Labour Party to run on the party's ticket. To demonstrate that she had legitimate community support and represented a viable alternative to the independent candidates,

Drysdale solicited, and received, the endorsement of a local Black women's organization, the Liverpool Black Sisters.

The 1987 campaign for the city council in the Granby Ward was an extremely controversial one. Posters and graffiti crafted by the supporters of the independent candidates accused Liz Drysdale of being a traitor and a sellout. Drysdale countered convincingly that she was allied with the Progressive Labour Caucus, not Militant, and had an enviable track record as a community activist, having served as a member of the Black Caucus and having been actively involved in the campaign against Sampson Bond. Drysdale, in fact, ran on a strong antiracist platform. She argued that she believed she could more effectively promote Black community interests by running on the Labour ticket than as an independent with no structural base of institutional political support. On election day, Drysdale led the voting in the Granby Ward, receiving over 70 percent of the Black vote. From the very beginning the Black independent candidates found themselves running against a number of critical obstacles. One major obstacle was the energetic and forceful campaign run by the Labour Party in the Granby Ward in support of its candidates. Labour Party leaders viewed the campaigns of Black independents as serious threats to both local and national party interests. The strategic tactics used by the Labour Party demonstrated in impressive fashion its capacity to crush the opposition in one of its most strategically significant wards. Commenting on the role of the Labour Party in the election, Shaun Deckon, a candidate in the race for the FLBO, observed:

> When we went to the elections, a lot of people thought we were going to win. We knew we were not going to beat the Labour machine. They realized that we were a threat, and they realized that if every Black community in Britain began to take on board this kind of support, boy, we would have a lot of trouble getting back into Parliament, so we've got to crush them. They went about crushing us systematically by spreading lies, typical racial stereotype lies, one's a ponce, one's a mugger, one has a criminal record, the whole gambit of lies that the average White person would feel threatened by."Oh my God I didn't know they were like that." So they spread a lot of lies about us. They also tried to stop funding for various organizations who were actively involved in our campaign.[27]

The Black independent candidates attempted to conduct high-pitched emotional campaigns similar to those run successfully by local Black politicians in the United States. Their efforts produced an elevated sense of political consciousness but did not substantially increase Black registration and turnout. Their campaigns did not enjoy a greater degree of success, in part, because they were led by amateurs going against a wealthy and powerful party organization. Weaknesses of the campaigns' appeals were also attributable to the fact that the campaigns of both candidates remained in a perpetual state of disarray.

> Many people who didn't vote for them would have supported the independents if they could have been more organized and addressed the issues more competently. The persons who ran as independents were espousing their personal views. If you are going to stand on a platform and say you are running in behalf of Black people, you have to say it in an ideological and practical sense. That element has to be attached to an organization. There was no organization. It was two individuals standing on the independent ticket speaking their minds. As far as organization, it was not apparent.[28]

Mobilization efforts by the Black independents were also undercut by political tradition and party loyalty. Campaign activists found that despite the political and moral transgressions of the Labour Party in the Black community, many Black citizens, especially the Black elderly, could not bring themselves to vote for candidates who were not endorsed by the Labour Party. "A lot of the elders didn't want to change. They had come to the country and voted Labour from day one. Even me dad told me that he was going to vote Labour or not vote at all."[29]

The results of the election represented a major defeat at the ballot box for the independent politics campaign. Despite the expenditure of considerable time and effort, the independent ticket could only muster 10 percent of the vote. Given the margin of difference in the election and the dominance of the Labour Party in the Granby Ward, it is doubtful if either of the independent candidates would have won a seat on the council even if all three of the Labour candidates had been White. The numerical electoral advantages of the Labour Party in the Granby Ward were simply too great for the independents to prevail. The independent campaign was not, however, a fruitless effort. A number of grassroots activists involved in the campaign gained invaluable organizing experience and keen insight into important power dimensions of the political process. The campaign stimulated high political consciousness and facilitated programmatic networking across organizational lines. Most critically, the campaign vividly illuminated the continuing social and economic problems of the Black community and placed pressure on the city council to target the Granby Ward for special services and resources. Shaun Deckon pointed out the residual impact of the campaign on the service delivery process in the Black community.

> The main thing we wanted to do was to show Black people they could organize for themselves and get things done. We did get things done. We got the whole area cleaned up at one stage. This area that you see now is a cleaned up area. This pit that we got outside is a cleaned up area. There were cars parked all over the place, graffiti all over the walls, rubbish all over the place. The council would not come and clean the area. It was us that forced them to come every day and clean the area. We got them to put up the bins. They hadn't done anything before. Our campaign made it clear that they were going to have to do something to maintain that hold on the Black vote.[30]

After the election the leaders of the FLBO remained steadfast in their conviction that the independent strategy was a rational and effective avenue for Black empowerment. They viewed the election results not as a source of remorse, but as an important sign that key segments of the Black community were committed to change.

> Time and time again the Labour Party had let us down. We had to show them that we were prepared to make an organizational stance, a political stance that would disrupt them. If other Black communities in Britain took our lead, we'd actually have some bargaining power with the Labour Party, so that when their members got in they would not just sit back as they had been doing previously. They'd have to start doing something in Black areas, pushing through policies that made sure we got race relations subcommittees set up that actually convened on a regular basis and that directors of various social service agencies were challenged on their racism. I welcomed that we had 10 percent of the vote which showed me there were people looking for change, people who voted for change. Because people will shout about things in any kind of situation, but when it comes to the vote many people won't bother with it. But it showed me that 10 percent of the people who voted put our name on the card; they actually wanted some change. That was beside the people who were unregistered to vote. If, at the height of that election around the Sam Bond issue, we would have had registered voters, we would have put in a very serious challenge to the Labour Party.[31]

In raising the issue of political independence, Black leaders in Liverpool highlighted an issue that has poignant implications for the future course of strategic action in Black communities on both sides of the Atlantic. In the United States, the goal of political independence has not been reached, even in circumstances where Blacks occupy formal control of the bulk of the public offices and constitute the primary constituents of the dominant party organization. Perhaps in Britain the results, over time, will be dramatically different.

## Contested Territory: The Politics of Black Education

Black community leaders in Liverpool, as in Boston, clearly recognize that the condition of Black political underdevelopment is deeply embedded in the functions of educational processes and institutions. The British educational system has historically robbed Black people of the cultural resources and technical skills they need to establish bases of influence in the economic system and the political order. Many Black children in Liverpool do not receive a rudimentary form of education in the public schools. Their culture and special needs are ignored, they are the objects of racial harassment, and they are denied the personal attention required to motivate them to realize their higher possibilities. One parent talked in highly emotional, but searing, terms about the endless failures of the educational process in Liverpool.

> The problems of Black people in this city begin with education. They begin with the kind of system of education that we have. It is overtly racist in the sense of teacher attitudes, the kind of curriculum, the kind of ethos, the assumptions that are made about the intelligence of Black children. It's deeply ingrained in the attitude of the teachers and in the curriculum. For instance, my son is fourteen this year. If it had been left to the establishment to teach him as a young Black child his relevance in society, he wouldn't have any. He's completely ignored. My son was writing poetry at nine, yet he's in remedial class for English. If you look at the remedial classes, you will find that they mostly contain Black children, even today. You look at the children that are sent to special schools, children needing special care, psycho problems, the majority of those children are Black children. They are held back continually by attitudes and assumptions. The kind of curriculum that would benefit our children in terms of their natural feelings of equality and identity, basic decency, are ignored. They are mistreated in every subject. Their English history contains no aspect of their part in history, why they are here, what was the motivating force behind it. There's no geography. My son was told not long ago that the West Indies was near the African coast. There is no acknowl-

edgment of a Black consciousness, a Black identity, the need for a Black person to be recognized as a person in this society in the schools. They teach European languages, and they give no credence to Caribbean languages. In history, geography, social studies they give no credence to the, fact that racism exists, that sexism exists. The important relevant issues for Black children are ignored. In this environment the child becomes depressed, he gets the feeling he is being ignored, he's being picked on, he's given no room for improvement. He's given no idea he can improve.[32]

Jonathan Kozol's charges of savage inequalities against the Boston Public Schools appear to apply with equal force to the Liverpool Public Schools. In Liverpool the failings of the school system are reflected in the character of Black political socialization and mobilization. Inequalities in the education process have produced high Black school drop-out rates, leaving many Black teenagers unqualified to pursue higher education degrees. Many who manage to get high school credentials cannot meet the tough A-level British requirements for admission into institutions of higher learning. The results have been that for many years, very few Blacks in Liverpool have received college and university degrees. Most of the precious few that get into and survive the higher education system have moved to more cosmopolitan cities, such as London and Manchester. Lacking an alternative source of economic mobility for its citizens in the business sector, the Black community has had to pursue its political objectives without the benefit of middle-class leadership. The Liverpool situation is qualitatively different from the situation in Boston where middle-class leaders are present in abundance but are underutilized. This difference has undergirded the disparity in approaches to the politics of education pursued by Black communities in the two cities.

As we have seen, the principal approach to Black educational politics in Boston has been the eradication of social barriers to Black progress through a political campaign to promote school desegregation. In Liverpool, the principal issue has been access to higher education to increase Black competitiveness in the professional marketplace and build a viable middle-class leadership base.

The political call for access was first made in 1974 when community leaders lobbied the city council to establish an institution to address issues of educational and occupational mobility in the Black community. The council responded by allocating twenty thousand pounds to establish an Adult Education Center in the heart of the Black community with offices in the Rialto Building. Operating with

a limited staff, the Adult Education Center offered a basic preparatory program that included math, study skills, life and social skills,
bookkeeping, typing, computer studies, economics, government, and
commerce. A unique feature of the program was an emphasis on
Black Studies. Black Studies was introduced to overcome the
absence of Black courses in the high school curriculum and to provide a cultural dimension to the learning process that would encourage students to acquire a high degree of racial consciousness and
inspire them to make an unflagging commitment to the goal of community development.

The Adult Education Center moved into larger quarters at
248–50 Upper Parliament Street in 1978. Center leaders changed
the name of the program to the Charles Wootton Centre for Further
Education in honor of the Black sailor who was chased into the
Mersey River and killed by a rampaging mob during the anti-Black
riots of 1919. A grant of £28,500 by the Merseyside Task Force eventually allowed the centre to purchase outright the site of the relocation. The centre remains housed on these premises.

As the clientele base of the Charles Wootton Centre increased,
the curriculum of the centre expanded to include a medical secre-
taries course and a basic education teacher training course. The cen-
tre also spearheaded the development of an Access to Higher
Education Program located at Sandown College on Grove Street.
Designed to answer, in part, the Black community's push for entree
into the system of higher education, the Grove Street Access
Program represented a tripartite venture among the Charles
Wootton Centre, Sandown College, and the Liverpool Educational
Authority.

From the very beginning the development work of the Charles
Wootton Centre has been steeped in controversy. Questions have
continuously been raised regarding the wisdom of the council providing public funds to promote alternative educational experiences
for members of the Black community. These questions sprang from
the refusal of many city leaders to accept the proposition that Blacks
were uniquely deprived of developmental experiences in the educational process and therefore entitled to funds specifically set aside
for their social and economic improvement. Gradually, concerns
were also raised that the Charles Wootton Centre was crossing the
line between education and politics. These concerns reached a
crescendo in the aftermath of the 1981 riots because the centre
allowed its basement to become the headquarters of the Liverpool 8
Defence Committee. The political connection between the centre

and the Defence Committee gained the centre a widespread reputation within the downtown establishment as a staging area, or "riot house" for Black revolutionaries. Charles Wootton's involvement in postriot activities led the existing Liberal administration in city council to cut off funding to the centre. The rationale given by Liberal leaders for the action was a major decline in the city of Urban Aid and Section 11 funding, the alleged role of centre leaders as "riot engineers," and the alleged decision by the centre to teach Black Studies as a form of "racist studies." Council funding for the centre remained suspended for twelve months. During this period the centre was almost compelled to close its doors. The centre was able to limp along because of small donations from trade unions, churches, and community organizations. In 1982 talks between Charles Wootton officials and council leaders commenced. The council agreed to resume funding the centre under the stipulation that three members of the council be added to the centre's Management Committee, and the council be given monitoring authority over the centre's curriculum.

The aura of crisis in the centre's relationship to the council significantly escalated with the ascendance of the Militant Tendency to power in the council in 1983. Centre officials were confronted with a major dilemma by council leader demands that all discussions of the centre's budget be routed through the office of Sampson Bond. Centre officials believed they could not morally or politically accept these demands because they conferred unwarranted legitimacy on Sampson Bond. The dilemma for the centre deepened with the demand by Militant leaders that budget requests by the centre be submitted on a monthly basis. On this subject Charles Wootton Centre Director Chief Ben Agwuna recalled:

> When this problem started the Militants did not suspend our grant. The money was in there. Every month we had to apply to the city council for money to pay the rents, lights and so on. We had to justify our budget from month to month. The management team of the centre started panicking. We had to rush through our charitable status so that if the centre went bankrupt, the Management Committee would be protected from liability. It was only because the staff stood fast that the centre remained open.[33]

Throughout the Militant era, the Charles Wootton Centre operated in a state of siege. During this period the centre was able to secure just enough money from Manpower Services to keep its doors open. The centre was compelled to institute emergency measures, including the laying off of staff and the reduction of key remaining staff to part-time hours. The centre had to contend with efforts by other city colleges to steal its staff by offering staff members higher wages and full-time appointments.

The fiscal problems of the centre did not end with the removal of Militants from power in the city council. While members of the Progressive Caucus were more receptive to the requests by the centre for funding, the centre remained underfunded. The funds the centre received from the council did not keep pace with its expanding clientele base and the broadening of its catchment area. Initially, leaders of the centre were optimistic that the election of three new progressive councillors from the Granby Ward would significantly increase council sensitivity and responsiveness to the centre's request for increased operating funding. This optimism was transformed into high hopes by the appointment of Councillor Gideon Ben-Tovim of the Granby Ward as chair of the Education Committee. But high hopes turned into disappointment when it became clear that Councillor Ben-Tovim was disinclined to yield liberally to the centre's requests for increased funding because he believed its budget projections were unrealistic. Assessing the operational status of the centre in 1996 Ben-Tovim observed:

> The Charles Wootton Centre is going strong; it is still looking for resources. They've developed a good teaching staff the last few years, but I think one of their problems is that they are carrying too much staff for the number of students they have. They've inherited a lot of staff from a number of programs in the past. These people are well known in the community, but for the number of students, they've got problems justifying their funding to the funding agencies.[34]

The fiscal situation of the Charles Wootton Centre has been complicated by the refusal of the council to restore seventy thousand pounds removed from the operating budget of the centre in reaction to a judgment won by the centre against the council in a public inquiry set up by the secretary of state for the environment in 1986. Annual appropriations to the centre stemming from this case have been a major bone of contention in the lobbying efforts of Chief Ben Agwuna before the council in behalf of the centre. Fiscal stability for the centre has also been undermined by the funding procedures of the European Social Fund (ESF), a major source of supplementary support for centre programs. Efforts by the centre to secure ESF funds have been stifled by matching fund requirements. Appeals by the centre to the council for matching fund appropriations have been routinely turned down, rendering the centre ineligible for a considerable portion of potential ESF funding. The ESF allocations the centre has received have been given under arrangements that require the centre to borrow money from private sources upfront, with accompanying bank charges and interests, and to wait up to twelve months for reimbursement of its expenditures. These arrangements have created serious cash flow problems for the centre; it has contributed in a major way to the pattern of deficit spending that has marked the centre's fiscal status in recent years (see figure 9.1 ).

Competition from other educational programs has tended to stifle programmatic development at the Charles Wootton Centre. Funds that could be potentially claimed by Charles Wootton have been redirected by the council to fund the Elimu Program, an after school project that targets Blacks in Liverpool 8 for tutoring in the areas of math, English, and Black Studies. Additional educational programming funds have been directed toward the maintenance of the Access to Further Education program on Grove Street as a part of the academic curriculum of Liverpool Community College. In recent years, the community college has become one of the greatest threats to the long term survival of the Charles Wootton Centre. The appointment of educator and community activist Wally Brown as principal of the community college has raised the possibility that the entire academic program of the Charles Wootton Centre will become absorbed into the ambitious programmatic agenda of the community college. Wally Brown articulated the goals of the community college in the following terms:

My ambition is to eventually have the best college in the country. I want to build the best college in Europe as a community college. Liverpool is an economically deprived city for everybody. When there is economic deprivation the people who seem to be the least powerful don't even get on the first rung, and in this city Black people seem to be the least powerful. So first of all I have to develop an organization which is quality, which is strong, which can match what takes place across the country, which can deliver qualifications and a standard of education which can match what takes place across the country, and in buildings which are equal. On top of that I have to ensure that access to the institution is open to everybody. It is in theory, but in practice the college fails the Black community very badly. Black students don't use the college the way that they should because traditionally the college is seen as a White establishment. So I have to build a place that not only stresses equality but is also accessible. I have to bring in more Black staff. I have to try to bring in structures that

**Figure 9.1. Budget Report, Charles Wootton College, 1993**

| | 1993 £ | 1992 £ |
|---|---|---|
| **Operating Income** | | |
| Liverpool City Council (& FEFC) | 319,600 | 310,900 |
| European Social Fund (ESF) | 168,510 | 24,358 |
| Granby Toxteth Task Force | 13,613 | 2,200 |
| Merseyside TEC Ltd | 19,784 | 23,085 |
| Donations | 3,250 | - |
| Other Income | 17,177 | 15,060 |
| | **541,934** | **375,603** |
| **Operating Costs** | **508,353** | **364,915** |
| **Administrative Expenses** | **94,995** | **65,674** |
| **Deficit** | **61,614** | **54,986** |

**Balance Sheet (at 31st March 1993)**

| | 1993 £ | 1992 £ |
|---|---|---|
| **FIXED ASSETS** | | |
| Tangible Assets | 106,070 | 58,006 |
| **CURRENT ASSETS** | | |
| Debtors | 26,922 | 48,263 |
| Cash at bank | 2,465 | 61 |
| Cash in hand | - | 81 |
| | 29,387 | 48,405 |
| **CREDITORS** | | |
| Amounts falling due within one year | 66,501 | 32,628 |
| NET CURRENT (LIABILITIES) / ASSETS | (37,114) | 15,777 |
| TOTAL ASSETS LESS CURRENT LIABILITIES | 68,956 | 73,783 |
| NET ASSETS | 68,956 | 73,783 |
| **RESERVES** | | |
| Revaluation reserve | 57,299 | - |
| Reserve Fund | 11,657 | 73,783 |
| | 68,956 | 73,783 |

Source: Charles Wootton College Special Twentieth Anniversary Report. Permission Granted.

make sure that racism is dealt with, that Black students will feel comfortable working in the college community. Black people must have access to the entire budget. They must have access to everything, all the high tech equipment, all the resources, and feel free to go in any building. I want to develop a strategy so that I'll be able to say you go there you'll be o.k. Because I've put a structure in there to make sure it's o.k. And if it's not o.k. I'll know about it within ten minutes, and I'll be able to deal with it. I can't do that at the moment. So when I say the best college in the country, it's taking account of all the issues so that Black people will be able to fight for their qualifications alongside everybody else on a fair, level playing field.[35]

The capacity of the Charles Wootton Centre to compete with Liverpool Community College for minority further education students in the future is structurally limited by the fact that the centre is dependent on council funding, while the college has become financially independent of the council and receives funding directly from the central government.

Despite its perpetual funding problems and the growth of competitive institutions, the Charles Wootton Centre has been able to maintain its role as a key community-based educational institution. Indicative of its continuing importance was its formal designation as a "college" in 1992. Enrollment in the college has continued to increase; all of its courses are oversubscribed. This fact provides poignant testimony to the pressing need for a greater supply of educational resources in the Black community. The curriculum of the college has continued to expand. The college introduced its own Access to Further Education Program in 1991. Since that time over five hundred students have enrolled in the program. In 1992 the college instituted the Pre-Higher Education Entry Program (Pre-HEEP). This program is specifically targeted to meet the needs of Black students by allowing them to satisfy the A-level requirements of the British higher educational system in an environment immensely conducive to their success. Commenting on this facet of the college's work, Chief Agwuna noted:

> We have very flexible arrangements here. The A-level work that they do here is more than enough to get them into the university system. What we are doing is preparing them for A-level examinations. We provide for them a more relaxed and flexible environment. They can study here rather than going to a very alien environment. One of the problems we found with adult learners is that their confidence has been destroyed. Even if they get to the university, their confidence is shaken again. We have people asking, "How did you get to the university? Did you get to the university through the back door?" We want to demonstrate that most of them can do A-level work so that when they get to the university if someone asks how they got there, they can say, "I did as you did. I got an A-level." So their confidence will be there.[36]

Justification for the continuation and expansion of the college's work lies in the remarkable academic achievements of its students. In its 1994 annual report, the college could proudly proclaim that 57 percent of the students enrolled in its Pre-HEEP Program in the 1992 through 1993 academic year had been placed in universities and other higher education institutions. Students enrolled in the medical secretaries course during this period achieved a 100 percent success rate on professional examinations (eleven out of eleven students), with 67 percent gaining distinction. One student gained admission to London University Medical School. The 1994 annual report contains pictures and biographical information of former students that had received B.A. and M.A. degrees from colleges and universities. One student, Mark Christian, has received a Ph.D. in sociology from the University of Sheffield. A pioneering Liverpool-based institution, the Charles Wootton College has made enormous contributions to the struggle to broaden educational opportunities for Black citizens. The success of its efforts has established the foundation for the creation of a new middle class leadership corps to fight the battle for Black political empowerment.

## Gentrification and Neighborhood Politics: The Strategy of Countermobilization

Urban redevelopment schemes in major cities in the United States and Britain have been the source of strong political reaction by organized neighborhood groups. In the Uptown neighborhood of Chicago, plans for urban renewal in the area called for massive physical reconstruction, including the demolition of thousands of private dwellings. These plans generated fiery protests from neighborhood groups such as the United People and Voice of the Poor. On the heels of a militant anti-urban renewal campaign, gentrification plans for Uptown were scaled back significantly. Across the Atlantic a more modest campaign was being waged in the Sharrow neighborhood of Sheffield to modify plans for urban redevelopment that would destroy private housing and build a three-ring limited-access highway system that would isolate the neighborhood from the downtown core. The campaign was led by the Sharrow Action Group (SAG) in the 1970s and the Broom Hall Tenants Association (BTA) in the 1980s. Organized political action by neighborhood groups saved thousands of units of housing in Sheffield from demolition during the height of that city's program of urban redevelopment.[37]

Liverpool has not escaped the political impact of neighborhood resistance to urban redevelopment schemes. As we have seen in chapter 8, redevelopment plans in the Black community in Liverpool have been driven by the economic ambitions of housing associations. Plans by associations to demolish housing units in Liverpool 8 have precipitated strong protest efforts by grassroots activists operating under the banner of the Granby Residents Association. One of the first organizing tasks pursued by the association was the refutation of arguments put forth by leaders of the housing associations as justification for the demolition of property in Liverpool 8.

> They were saying that the reason why some of the housing had to come down was there was flooding underneath. So straightaway the Granby Residents Association wrote the water board and said, "What is this about flooding?" The water board wrote back and said, "It is not true. There is no flooding in the area at all," and that in fact we had one of the best foundations in the city, and that all of the pipes had been replaced only three years before. Then they were saying that the properties were in such bad repair they would have to come down structurally, and we said how can it be, the area had improvement grants twenty years ago. Every house has at least a twenty-year loan, and some people have put more money in than that. We got people to do free surveys for us to confirm that most of the property in the area was sound.[38]

The next strategic move of the association was to get the council involved. Leaders of the association initially found most councillors unreceptive to their pleas for help. Members of the council took the position that since housing associations received their mandates for action from the central government, councillors were powerless to prevent them from imposing their will on neighborhood residents. Association leaders were ultimately able to break down substantial council intransigence by accusing councillors of abdicating their responsibilities and selling out to the housing associations. Strong arguments were also marshaled by association leaders that the council was promoting poverty in Liverpool 8 by pushing people out of their residences, most of which were debt free, into expensive housing under the control of private housing associations.

> With these arguments, we were able to finally get the support of left wing Labour councillors. Many Liberal Democrats also supported us. We considered it a major victory when the council said it would take the lead in making changes in the area. This decision put the housing associations behind the scenes, and they started behaving themselves.[39]

Leaders of the Granby Residents Association took the position that the Granby Toxteth Triangle should be designated a renewal area. This designation would mean that every house in the area would have to be inspected. Only those houses declared by inspectors as unfit would be demolished. The intended effect of this strategy was to prevent housing associations from tearing down entire blocks under circumstances where some, but not all, of the houses were judged to be unfit. In their fight to stave off gentrification in Liverpool 8, members of the Granby Residents Association have labored under a number of disadvantages. First, support for their campaign by neighborhood residents has been far from unanimous. Indeed, some residents have championed the demolition campaign. These individuals argue that unless the social class status of the community changes, the value of their property will decline, leaving them financially worse off rather than better off. The split in opinion among neighborhood residents has made it difficult for the residents association to recruit institutional allies to its cause. "We were shocked when the Liverpool 8 Law Centre refused to help. They said they couldn't take sides because some people wanted to move and others did not."[40] Second, the residents association has not effectively linked the campaign against gentrification to the economic fortunes of community residents. Thus, many residents do not perceive the connection between the anti-demolition movement and the future quest for jobs, business development, and economic security for Black citizens within the framework of the larger municipal corporation. Third, the Granby Residents Association has not become strategically incorporated into the decision-making networks of key community coalitions such as the Granby Toxteth Partnership. We now know from the deep, abiding, and compelling experience of freedom fighters in the Black Atlantic that collective struggle and coalition building are essential components of transcendent and effective movements for Black empowerment and incorporation in the African Diaspora.

Organizational unity and cooperation are two of the most serious and difficult issues facing the Black community in Liverpool in the waning years of the twentieth century. The compelling need for continuing countermobilization against the omnipresent and ominous threat of urban gentrification represents an area of social and economic concern that poses a critical test of the Black community's capacity to implement its strategic objectives and forge a stable base of effective power in Liverpool's political system.

# 10

## Linkage Politics and
## Political Resources

### Resource Dilemmas: Numbers and Diversity

Black political incorporation and empowerment in city politics turns decisively on the capacity of the Black community to develop and effectively leverage political resources. The issue of resource development and leverage for Blacks in Liverpool is very important because of the city's exceptional history of racial exclusion and discrimination. No other group has been compelled to mobilize in the political system from a lower and more restrictive resource baseline than Blacks.

Our examination of Black politics in Boston has underscored the importance of numbers as a political resource. In Liverpool, where Blacks are less than 9 percent of the city's population, Black political incorporation and empowerment are deeply circumscribed by the absence of a strong numerical resource base in the Black community. The absence of significant Black numbers means that the interests of the Black community can easily be marginalized and ignored. In this regard, Blacks in Liverpool are locked in a strategically different position in the political system from Blacks in Boston where the potential Black vote is nearly one-quarter of the overall city vote. Black numbers give the Black community in Boston potential access to key positions in the governmental process, although, as we have seen, the distance between potential and reality remains quite large in the Boston case.[1] For Blacks in Liverpool, prospects for "potential access" are severely undercut by the absence of significant Black representation in the electorate. Access depends in large measure on the ability of a politically active group to bargain for attention on the basis of its strategic importance in the electoral

261

process. Blacks in Liverpool do not have such bargaining capabilities. Their weak numerical electoral base not only gravely circumscribes their ability to decide the fate of White politicians, but it provides them with little control over the outcome of elections involving Black politicians. Black politicians such as Liz Drysdale must depend upon strong support in the White community if they are to have a realistic chance of winning elections, even those run in Liverpool 8 where potential Black political influence is most significant. This syndrome of dependence limits Black access to the policy-making process and constitutes a major barrier to the building of independent bases of power in the Black community.

The political disadvantages that ensue from a weak numerical base are compounded in the case of the Black community in Liverpool by extensive social and cultural diversity. The issue of diversity is more complicated in Liverpool than in Boston. As we noted in chapter 2, in the United States the term *Black* is used to refer to individuals of African and African Caribbean heritage; in Britain *Black* is used to refer to all nonWhite minorities, including a host of individuals from the South Asian subcontinent. The issue of who is Black and who is not has become a highly controversial one. Application of the term to refer to all nonWhites has not been universally accepted. Some Asians have rejected this term, arguing that the broad use of the term *Black* robs Asians of their separate identities and diminishes the histories of oppression and resistance by Asian people in the United Kingdom.[2]

Identity issues emerging from the terrain of national and religious loyalties have produced a high degree of political fragmentation and conflict in the Black community. Nationality issues became salient in the 1960s with the formation of organizations such as the Jamaican Merseyside Association and the Merseyside West Indian Council to promote the common objectives of citizens of West Indian background. What began as minor impulses toward separate ethnic development became a prodigious source of political conflict in the 1970s with the decision by the city council to begin funding the construction of nationality- and religious-based cultural centres in the Black community. Opening its doors in 1977, the Caribbean Centre was the first of such centres to be funded and erected by the council. This centre was the product of strong lobbying efforts by African Caribbeans who argued that their social, economic, and cultural needs were being ignored despite their major presence in the city as tax payers and voters. Similar arguments posed by other groups led to the establishment of the Pakistani Centre, the Hindu Centre, the

Sikh Centre, and the Chinese Centre. Liverpool-born Blacks have sharply criticized the development of these nationality and religious centres because the council has not recognized their special needs by establishing a cultural centre that celebrates and promotes their ethnic heritage. Having no centre of their own, Liverpool-born Blacks have tended to congregate at the Methodist Youth Centre, a nonprofit agency initially supported by the Methodist church and later funded principally by the city council. Confined to subordinate roles in the operation of the Methodist Youth Centre, Liverpool-born Blacks have continued to press the issue of the need for a centre that specifically promotes their cultural identity and is operated under their primary control. The need for a separate facility for Liverpool-born Blacks has been magnified by tensions surrounding the rules that govern the operation of centres by other ethnic groups. Railing against the informal policy of the Caribbean Centre to offer permanent membership only to individuals born in the Caribbean, Liverpool-born Blacks, in the summer of 1981, staged a sit-in at the centre designed to broaden its constituency base and dramatize their claims for a separate centre of their own. This sit-in represented one of the key precipitating events leading to the outbreak of full-scale rioting in the Black community in the summer of 1981.

From the perspective of the city council, the funding of ethnic centres has been an effective strategy for keeping the Black community divided and politically demobilized. A great deal of the potential political strength of the Black community has been diluted by the focus of individual ethnic communities in the Black community on the parochial programmatic agendas of their individual cultural centres. These agendas have been mainly social not political. The centres serve principally as gathering places for religious, cultural, and recreational programs. At the Caribbean Centre the playing of dominoes is a central preoccupation. The Hindu Centre is housed in a building that was a former church; it caters principally to individuals of Indian heritage who belong to the Hindu faith. In addition to its overt religious mission, the centre seeks to appeal to young people who are losing touch with their culture and to provide a central place where the Hindu community can build bridges to other communities.

Political issues rarely engage the time and attention of cultural centre leaders. They do not view themselves as citywide political activists but as guardians of the social, religious, and cultural interests of their centres' members and their immediate families. Thus, unity and cohesion in the Black community have suffered from the pronounced tendency of subgroups in the Black community to view their interests in specific rather than communitywide terms. The upshot has been a badly fragmented process of interest articulation characterized by the lobbying of separate community groups, organized around cultural centres, for group-specific rather than collective benefits. This process has produced both intragroup and intergroup divisions. In the Somali community, two distinct factions have emerged to compete for separate group benefits, including separate cultural centres. Considerable tension has also developed between elements of the Somali community and elements of the British-born Black community. Blaming the attitude of British-born Blacks for the decline in constructive relations between Somalis and British-born Blacks, one ethnic Somali respondent observed.

> Black-born British should help us, especially the Law Centre. But you never see any Somalis get a job through the Law Centre or anywhere. We stay in the Black community because we know we won't be accepted in the White community. But we never expected that the Black community would call us "niggers" because we are the same color. We want the Blacks to show us the way, but they won't bother. And I don't know why. There have been no efforts to work these things out; no one has bothered. Our Somali community is poor, and we could use their help.[3]

Conflicts between British-born Blacks and Asians are also serious. Asians criticize British-born Blacks for their alleged lack of ambition and industry and governmental dependency. British-born Blacks in turn accuse Asians of being selfish, ruthless, and irretrievably tied to the social, economic, and cultural institutions of the dominant society. These contrasting perceptions reveal in graphic terms why unity and cohesion in the political process by the Black community has been an extremely elusive objective.

### Institutional Leadership: The Merseyside Community Relations Council

Black political incorporation and empowerment require the application of community organizational power to overcome obstacles to effective Black political linkage. In Britain, community relations councils (CRCs) have become the key institutional instruments for the forging of operational links between Black organizations and local government. CRCs find their legal authority in the second Race

Relations Act passed in 1968. Local CRCs operate under the authority of the Commission for Racial Equality (CRE) (originally designated as the Community Relations Commission) established by the 1968 act. They are charged with the formal responsibility of coordinating work in local areas designed to promote equal opportunities for minorities and eliminate institutionalized practices of racial discrimination. Principal funding for local CRCs comes from the CRE and local authorities. In the absence of other avenues for linkage, CRCs have become the chief mechanisms for forging financial and political ties between Black community organizations and policy making authorities. On this subject Brian Jacobs notes:

> The CRCs in particular provided a channel into which demands could be directed and through which Black leaders could liaise with politicians and government officials. The degrees to which Black groups were eager to work through such channels was indicative of the importance of the CRCs in bringing organisations together within a relatively ordered formal setting.[4]

An important consequence of the interventionist role played by CRCs is the moderation of independent politics in the Black community. As government-funded agencies, CRCs often serve as mediating forces between Black organizations and the institutions of local government. CRCs in many British cities control access to government funding by community organizations. This arrangement has sharply reduced the boundaries of political action for these groups. On the basis of cost-benefit projections, Black community organizations have often been willing to sacrifice autonomous political development for the benefits to be derived from the stable and productive relations they have established with governmental bodies through the intervention of CRCs. Jacobs contends that cooperation by Black organizations in this process of interest accommodation is the rule rather than the exception. He concludes that Blacks in Britain may be successful on some occasions of modifying public policy, "but this has been achieved through a compromise between Blacks and policy-makers largely based upon the adaptation of Black organizations to prevailing administrative and political practices."[5] To put the matter more precisely, Black community organizations in Britain have often been forced to choose between independence and accommodation, autonomy, and co-optation. The political dilemmas these choices evoke grow directly out of the fact that the pivotal keys to critical governmental resources are often held by CRCs committed to the processes and values of "clientage politics."

The Merseyside Community Relations Council (MCRC) has sometimes marched to a different drummer. Established in 1969, MCRC became, in the 1980s, the center of the Black movement for social, economic, and political equality. During the 1980s MCRC developed a national reputation of being the most action-oriented, community-centered CRC in the country. The development of its activist orientation coincided with the transfer of leadership control of the organization from leaders of the Asian community to leaders of the Liverpool-born Black community. Between 1969 and 1980, members of the Liverpool-born Black community had maintained considerable distance from the MCRC because they viewed it as an instrument for promoting exclusively the policy agenda of the immigrant community. This perception, while inaccurate in some respects, was not totally without merit. The first chairs of the MCRC, Dean Patley and Safir Uddin, were Asian leaders that presided over conservative administrations heavily committed to the advancement of immigrant interests. The policy orientation of the MCRC did not dramatically change until the election of Wally Brown as chair in 1980 and Dorothy Kuyu as executive director shortly thereafter. Both Brown and Kuyu were well-known political activists in the Liverpool-born Black community.

Brown had gained his political spurs as president of the Liverpool Black Organization. As chair of the MCRC he established a commanding presence as the city's most visible and influential Black community activist. Brown's most notable political contribution was the formation of the Black Caucus as an umbrella organization involving the integration of the work of the most prominent organizations in the Black community engaged in the struggle for racial equality and community advancement. This new mechanism, operating under the guidance of the MCRC, brought focus and direction to Black political activities and established a critical basis for coordinated strategic planning and policy influence. With regard to his contributions to the process of organizational cooperation, Wally Brown observed:

> I was able to bring together a Black caucus of all the community organizations. I was able to bring them into one forum. At that time we were battling with the local authority to get them to set up an equal opportunity committee and a race advisory group for the city council. That was one achievement. But in achieving that, we had to have a mechanism to feed into that. And that mechanism was the Black Caucus. I think in bringing these people under my leadership, that was a major achievement because they had different points of view.

And to be able to go into the race advisory meetings with a common purpose and be able to hold that line was an achievement. Many groups in Britain go into advisory situations, and they go with what's in their heads. There is no strategy; they argue against each other. Council meetings go very fast. If you are not organized, you don't have a chance. We were able to caucus people and develop strategies. There were people who didn't agree with our line, but we were still able to maintain unity within the caucus. That was a major achievement.[6]

The forging of a unified coalition of Black organizations under the umbrella of the MCRC represented a significant breakthrough in Black politics in Liverpool. A number of organizations that had well-developed policy agendas decided to abandon their autonomous programs and fold into the MCRC coalition, among them the Merseyside Anti-Racialist Alliance (MARA) and World Promotions. Eventually, virtually all of the major Black community organizations, including those representing immigrant groups, would become affiliate members of the Black Caucus. This development created one of the most powerful and effective minority group alliances in the history of Liverpool (see figure 10.1).

Under the leadership of Wally Brown, the MCRC established an impressive track record of community involvement and leadership. The organization played a role in the formation and work of the Race Relations Liaison Committee, the Black Caucus, and the Liverpool 8 Defence Committee. Its research department served as a valuable resource for the Black Caucus in its efforts to compile appropriate documents to validate the need for equal opportunity policies in the city council. The MCRC served as a critical strategic arm of the campaign to remove Sampson Bond from the position of principal race relations adviser to the city council. It was highly instrumental in changing the focus of community relations with the police from endless debates and fruitless attempts to establish liaison committees, to a communitywide boycott of police-initiated meetings until the police department agreed to fundamentally change its enforcement tactics in Liverpool 8.

The direction of the MCRC under Wally Brown was not universally applauded. Members of the Afro-Asian-Caribbean Standing Committee pulled out of the MCRC coalition because of growing concerns that the interests of immigrant communities were being neglected and new policy objectives adopted without careful analysis and debate. Liberal Democratic leaders of the Liverpool City Council were so concerned about the "radical" activities of the

Figure 10.1. Liverpool Black Caucus Coalition

> **Liverpool City Council**

> **Merseyside Community Relations Council**

> ### Black Caucus Coalition
>
> Afro-Asian-Caribbean Standing Committee
> Black Workers Association
> Charles Wootton Centre
> Elimu-Wa-Nane Multiracial Adult Education
> Hindu Cultural Organization
> Liverpool 8 Defence Committee
> Liverpool 8 Law Centre
> Liverpool Black Organizations
> Merseyside African Council
> Merseyside Anti-Racialist Alliance
> Merseyside Bangladesh Association
> Merseyside Bengali Association
> Merseyside Caribbean Council
> Merseyside Chinese Community Services
> Merseyside Somali Community Association
> Pakistan Association
> Princes Park Methodist Youth Club
> South Liverpool Personnel Limited
> World Promotions

Source: Adapted from data included in the Liverpool Black Caucus, *The Racial Politics of Militant in Liverpool* (Liverpool and London: Merseyside Area Profile Group and Runnymede Trust, 1986), and Gideon Ben-Tovim, John Gabriel, Ian Law, and Kathleen Stredder, *The Local Politics of Race* (London: Macmillan Education LTD, 1986).

MCRC that they cut off funding for several positions in the organization's staff.

Leadership is an important element in the process of Black incorporation and empowerment. The leadership corps of the Black community in Liverpool suffered a major blow in 1983 with the decision by Wally Brown to leave Liverpool and take up a professional post in Manchester. Formal leadership of the MCRC devolved into the hands of White members of the management committee. In the wake of these events, the Black organizational coalition that had been pulled together under the umbrella of the MCRC began to fall apart. Although the MCRC played an important interventionist role in the Toxteth riots of 1986, it could not summon the collective support of Black organizations of the kind that had been so crucial to its presence as a pivotal political force in the early 1980s. By this time, most Black community organizations had reverted to a process of separate development. Perceiving the MCRC as a weak source of issue development, community mobilization, program initiative, and funding, these organizations began a search for alternative avenues for keeping their key organizational programs alive.

The most telling blow to the MCRC was delivered in 1992 when the CRE announced plans to cut off funds to the MCRC and close down its offices. This decision was made in the wake of evaluation reports that showed that the MCRC was no longer providing value for money. These reports suggested that the agency was not being well managed, with a number of complaints from the staff about mismanagement filtering up to the CRE in London. The agency was also charged with being overburdened with bureaucratic constraints that prevented it from properly handling its large case load. The reports suggested that the agency no longer enjoyed the support of community organizations and could therefore not provide effective leadership on a range of race policy issues.

Black activists protested the decision to close the MCRC. They demanded that its remaining budget of £200,000 be held in reserve and redistributed to community organizations. Eventually, the CRE did share part of the residual funds with Black organizations. The bulk of the funds, however, were given to the Liverpool City Council to establish a new race relations organization, the Merseyside Race Equality Council. In contrast to the old organization, the new organization would not focus principally on race issues in Liverpool 8 but would seek to address race equality issues throughout the Merseyside area. Clearly, the new organization would not be given the political leverage enjoyed by the old organization to build a cohesive coalition of Black organizational interests and power. The burning reality is that since the mid-1980s, the MCRC has dropped off the political map as an empowerment resource for the Black community.

## The Nonprofit Sector

Although extensive, the service delivery activities of the Liverpool City Council have been far from all-encompassing. A host of Black community needs have escaped the networks of policy development and execution that operate as official arms of the council in the service delivery process in the Black community. Over the years a number of community-based, nonprofit groups have sprang forward to fill in the gap between community needs and the programmatic outputs of the city council. As in the case of Boston, nonprofit organizations in Liverpool function as important alternative sources of service delivery. While these organizations have shown a wide variation in structure, program objectives, and operational styles, their political orientations and activities have shared a mutual constraint: substantial dependence on the city council for financial support. In Liverpool, nonprofit organizations have not been mere neutral extensions of the council's policy role in the Black community. They have served as major buffering institutions, brokering the policy interests of the Black community and stifling the growth of independent Black policy objectives and Black political mobilization. Nonprofits unwilling to live up to buffering expectations or incapable of keeping their constituents within the orbit of the council's policy parameters, have suffered financial adversities that have profoundly threatened their operational viability.

A key nonprofit agency in the Black community caught up in the web of council politics is the Liverpool 8 Law Centre. This agency grew out of the plight of Black defendants arrested during the 1981 Toxteth riots. Many Black youth charged with riot crimes found themselves totally without legal defense. To address this problem, a group of community volunteers was formed to give Black defendants advice, monitor their cases, and recruit barristers from London to handle their cases. This volunteer group became involved in 376 cases. The depth, scope, and intensity of the work suggested the need to establish a formal law centre to provide the kind of comprehensive and coordinated approach to legal services required to give Black defendants the legal protection they desired and deserved.

The decision to established the law centre precipitated the next step: a serious search for funds. In this process a decision was made in the early planning stages not to seek funding for the centre from the city council.

> Experience had shown that when you receive money for something like a law centre from the city council, you are faced with a dilemma because a lot of law centres are involved in taking the local authority to court. We did not want to get trapped in a legal box and limit the scope of our activities. We also realized that the council would be reluctant to give us money because authorities do not like to pay someone to prosecute them.[7]

The eschewing of council support meant that the founders of the law centre had to turn to private sources for support. The principal private entity to step up to the plate was the Catholic church. The Archbishop of Liverpool agreed that a law centre was needed and engineered substantial church support.

Leaders of the law centre found that the financial support the centre received from the church and other private sources was not enough to stave off financial crisis. As a last resort, the law centre was compelled to petition the council for both capital improvement and operating funds. "Our private money was only short-term seed money. We couldn't go on like that forever. We had to approach the city council for money or close our doors."[8] True to earlier predictions, council support for the centre drastically limited the scope of its capacity to function as a legal advocacy and defense group for the Black community. Although the law centre continued to monitor complaints of police brutality and other allegations of civil rights infractions, it clearly recognized the need to toe a pragmatic line on issues involving Black community conflict with the city council because of the omnipresent threat of the reduction or elimination of council funding.

The Immigrant Advice Unit—a nonprofit agency housed in the Liverpool 8 Law Centre Building—has also had to grapple with political and administrative restrictions emanating from dependence on council funding. The Advice Unit was established in 1989 to reduce the burgeoning case load of the law centre and to mobilize professional expertise to deal with the mounting problems encountered by minority immigrants in Liverpool. These problems stemmed in large measure from the many changes in immigration laws occurring in the wake of White fears that the strong influx of minority immigrants into Britain in the 1980s would radically alter the "British way of life." Funded mainly by the Liverpool City Council, the Advice Unit has had to adjust its work to pressures form the council to protect the City of Liverpool from the prospect of a massive relocation of minority immigrants into the city. Because the city council holds the purse strings, it is able to define, and limit, the arena of the Advice Unit's legitimate operational authority. Not only does this situation restrict the nature and character of the services that can be realistically provided by the Advice Unit, but it also magnifies its role as an organizational buffer, moving the process of client interaction and political advocacy into "safe" areas that are principally defined, constructed, and maintained by the council.

Another nonprofit group, the Liverpool Black Sisters, was founded in the early 1970s as a social service agency committed to providing support for Black women and their families. The basic agenda of the Black Sisters centered around childcare, economic, and school issues. A strenuous effort was made to address the employment needs of Black women by putting together training packages that would generate support for skills development programs that would increase the qualifications for Black women in a number of business and service areas. Utilizing the case work approach, the Black Sisters organization operated drop-in centres for Black women victimized by domestic violence. It also joined forces with the Immigrant Advice Unit and the law centre to deal with the legal status of immigrants threatened with deportation. The Black Sisters organization attempted to forge operational alliances with other groups, sending members to networking meetings outside of Liverpool and joining the Black Caucus coalition formed by the Merseyside Community Relations Council. Much of its political outreach work was blunted by low levels of political consciousness among Liverpool Black women, chauvinist attitudes among Liverpool men, and dependence on financial support from the Liverpool City Council.[9] Like other Black nonprofit organizations, the Liverpool Black Sisters organization found itself cross-pressured between council demands and citizen needs. The organization believed that its top priority was to make sure its resource base did not fall below the level required for operational viability. Pragmatically, this meant the striking of compromises with the council to assure the uninterrupted flow of the funds required for organizational survival.

A number of nonprofit Black community organizations have concentrated on the service rather than the political side of their roles to avoid the prospect of endangering their funding base. One such organization is Mary Secole House. The primary agenda of this agency is to assist its clients to deal with stress-related mental problems stemming from domestic conflicts and social pressures induced by ongoing practices of institutional racism. The agency was named in honor of a Black nurse who entered the Crimean War in 1855 and saved thousands of soldiers infected with cholera, dysentery, jaundice, and many other severe ailments. The idea for the house was initially developed by the Black Sisters in the early 1980s. Mary Secole House began as a drop-in centre for community residents suffering from stress and mental illness. In 1989 the agency received a grant of £181,000 under the Urban Program to fund capital construction. The grant was to be administered by the city council. Under the terms of the grant, the council would pay 25 percent of the initial capital costs. The council allocated another £100,000 annually for four years to pay for operating costs. These funding allocations represented the products of a titanic struggle with the council over the issue of funding a health treatment centre catering to a predominantly Black clientele.

> A lot of work went into getting money for the house. The powers that be didn't feel there was a need for yet another drop-in centre when there were so many other drop-in centres in the community. What they failed to realize at the time was that very few were using those resources because they couldn't identify with the facilities being provided. The idea was to have not another drop-in centre but to have one specifically geared towards addressing issues that produced stress in Black people in a racist society.[10]

The strategic approach adopted by the Mary Secole House included an outreach program involving visits to hospitals and private homes. As a separate component of the service program, an advocacy unit was established to empower clients to represent their own interests in their interactions with outside providers, such as the Health Authority and the Social Services Department.

The realistic scope of the house's work was constrained by its funding sources. During the 1992 through 1993 budget cycle, Urban Programme funding for Mary Secole House was terminated, leaving the agency heavily dependent on funding from the city council to keep its doors open. The expiration of Urban Programme funds coincided with plans to expand the agency's operating hours to evenings and weekends. Like other nonprofit Black agencies, Mary Secole House found itself trapped on the horns of a dilemma: it was compelled to bow to the council's will in the setting of the health programming agenda or risk the possibility of having its pivotal funding base evaporate. Speaking to this dilemma, one member of the agency's Management Committee noted:

> Unfortunately our hands are tied. That's the way things are. On certain issues, we cannot challenge the local authority. Some of our workers are paid by them. So we have to be very careful of what political issues are campaigned about and challenged. I feel very angry and frustrated sometimes about the whole set-up. Because once again we are being subjected to the White man's terms and conditions. Sometimes we feel like tokens going out in the community administering or looking at policies. You get to the point on the ladder where you can't progress any further.[11]

South Liverpool Personnel (SLP) has played a very active role in the establishment of functional linkages between the Black community and the private sector. Much of its activism has remained embedded in the internal environment of private networks; it has strategically avoided pushing into external public arenas where crucial decisions are made about budgets and system-level policy initiatives. SLP was set up as an advice and employment agency in 1972. It received its initial funding from the Urban Programme and the Commission for Racial Equality. Urban Programme funds for the agency were terminated in 1992. Since that time it has been funded mainly by the city council. Throughout its history, SLP has functioned primarily as a job placement center. Maintaining a large client roster, SLP has sought to match job seekers with potential employers. In doing so it has had the awesome task of convincing potential employers that they should recruit, interview, and hire low-income, unskilled Black workers. The agency provides unemployed Black workers training opportunities and arranges consultations with key agencies, such as Career Services, the Department of Education, and the Manpower Services Commission. For potential employers it offers a ten-point list of guidelines to assist them in making good hiring decisions. The agency's recent financial history has been characterized by a ceaseless struggle with the council over its budget and program agenda. In 1989 the agency's staff was cut to two when the council authorized appropriations for two staff positions and proceeded to block SLP from advertising for the positions. A second request for permission to advertise yielded a response that the positions had been "frozen." In effect, SLP's plans to enlarge its staff to better serve the needs of its clients were the victims of nondecision making. This action had the effect of not only denying the agency adequate staff but also limiting its administrative options to only those that the council found acceptable. SLP was denied the opportunity to play an increased advocacy role in behalf of its Black clients; at best it could operate as a political buffer, serving the needs of the council to deliver symbolic benefits, while holding in check the boundaries of the political order on the pivotal questions of minority recruitment, training, and hiring.

The Women's Technology Scheme (WTS) is an example of a non-profit agency that has continued to grow and prosper. It has managed to disentangle itself from the political web of the city council by vigorously pursuing European Social Funds (ESF). The agency is supported by a fifty-fifty split appropriation between the Liverpool City Council and ESF. In 1990, the agency was able to change the ESF funding cycle from one year to three years, giving it greater flexibility to engage in long-range planning. The key to the success of WTS has been the high quality of its leadership and programs. Under the capable guidance and leadership of Black administrator Clair Dove, WTS has sought to provide opportunities for minority women to hold responsible jobs by training them in technical fields such as electronic engineering and computer analysis.

> We were looking at women who had underachieved at school, who had left school with few, if any, qualifications and women who were either unemployed or underemployed, so they would be doing jobs that were quite low-level positions, female stereotype positions. We wanted particularly to encourage Black women to apply onto the scheme. We also wanted the staff to reflect the Black community here in Liverpool. So we wanted it to be a positive action scheme. We were aware that Black women suffered from the effects of racism in the society as a whole. They also have been subjected to sexism not only by White males, with their racism, but White females with their racism, and Black men with their sexism. And so Black women have been at the lower end of the scale. If you wish to look at how oppression fits, you have to look at Black women who, in the main, have suffered from extremes all around. You have to address that in a particular way.[12]

Because the scheme was Black-led and emphasized positive action, it was compelled to fight for credibility in the broader society. It was able to do so by offering high-quality training programs, recruiting a very competent staff, and creating an environment that was conducive to exceptional student achievement. The success of the program is verified by the achievement of its graduates. The scheme has been successful in placing women in positions that were totally unavailable to them before their enrollment in the program. Of equal importance has been the political success the program has enjoyed. Because of the high quality and credibility of its efforts, the scheme has generated across-the-board political support. The city council has often held WTS up as a model community program worthy of continuing public support. Clair Dove has built around her a prestigious and diverse management team whose political influence cuts across a range of public and private arenas. The history of WTS demonstrates that Black nonprofit organizations can be successful if effectively managed and politically integrated into the structures of community and governmental power.

On the other side of the coin, it should be acknowledged that the political process contains a number of deadly pitfalls for nonprofit organizations that are not politically well connected. As examples we can point to the organizational demise of several nonprofit organizations during the 1990s. Changes in the funding base for community organizations produced by the termination of the Urban Programme have led to the defunding of community agencies such as World Promotions and the Charles Wootton Technology Centre (or Charles Wootton I-Tech). Like WTS, the I-Tech Centre specialized in electronic and computer technology training. Its courses were certified as preparatory courses for the achievement of national qualifications in several technical fields. As a part of the recruitment process, it offered clients from sixteen to eighteen payments up to £57 plus a subsidy of part of their travel expenses; clients over eighteen were given £75 plus part of their travel expenses. Cutbacks in funding by the council forced the I-Tech Centre and World Promotions to close their doors. Their political flanks were so open, the closing down of these important community organizations generated no protest action by Black political leaders and grassroots citizens.

Plans by the council to terminate the Educational Opportunities Initiative in Liverpool 8 (EOI) did not receive an equally passive reception in the Black community. EOI was a community research project set up by the council to assess the need for adult educational programs in Liverpool 8. Headed by Black sociologist Ruby Dixon, EOI produced a number of hard-hitting studies documenting the need for increased investment in adult education programs in the Black community. The original intent of the council was to make EOI a drop-in centre for adult learners. This proposal was dropped after leaders of the Charles Wootton College complained that such a project would undermine the college's long-standing adult education courses. It was finally agreed that EOI would concentrate on conducting surveys in Liverpool 8 that would produce a series of special reports on educational needs in the Black community. Apparently, leaders of the council became uncomfortable with the explicit, critical nature of the resulting reports. EOI was running on a three-year funding cycle. During the second year of the cycle, Ruby Dixon was notified that the Liverpool 8 project would be terminated and her office moved to the north end of the city. Ruby Dixon fought the move, arguing that such a move would destroy her credibility in Liverpool 8. Her objections caught the attention of Dave Clay, who intervened to temporarily halt the closing of the office in Liverpool 8. Clay's action did not represent a long-term solution. Eventually, EOI was closed permanently on the premise that the council could not "afford" to keep such a project alive.

The fiscal and political collapse of the Toxteth Activities Group (TAG) has pushed the crisis of nonprofit organizations in Liverpool's Black community to new levels. TAG was founded in 1981 by members of the clergy and local residents in the wake of the Toxteth riots. Its primary objective was to provide quality training services to citizens in the Toxteth community. The agency began as a small voluntary organization concerned with providing camping activities for children and social events for senior citizens. From this inauspicious beginning, TAG evolved into one of the premier nonprofit agencies in Liverpool. TAG's program agenda included computer training, job search counseling, welfare rights counseling, business advisory services, employment training, and home visits for senior citizens. As its resource base grew, TAG was able to purchase and manage its own sports and leisure center. A pickup service with its own vans allowed the agency to serve meals to senior citizens at two satellite venues. Hundreds of meals were also prepared and delivered directly to senior citizens and the disabled who were not physically strong enough to travel to the satellite centers. A furniture workshop provided training in furniture manufacture and repair. This program contracted out its services to external organizations and sold its products to the public. Revenues from the program were recycled into the budget to provide funding for other agency programs.

By 1986 TAG had been designated a national training scheme, making the organization eligible for central government funding through the Merseyside Training and Enterprise Council (MTEC). Through its community outreach activities, TAG became a central vehicle for linking community needs to the policy objectives and resources of local and central government.

TAG's positive contributions and vast network of resources were not sufficient to maintain the organization's presence as a viable nonprofit community institution. TAG's viability was based centrally on its capacity to generate revenue from government sources. Its financial base began to collapse in the wake of the decision by the central government in the late 1960s to shift the emphasis of the Urban Programme from community action initiatives to corporate-driven redevelopment schemes. In the case of TAG this meant the systematic defunding of the agency by its main funding source, the Merseyside Training and Enterprise Council (MTEC). Efforts were made by TAG leaders to secure funds from the city council to replace the funds withdrawn by MTEC. The response they received was extremely disappointing.

> We applied to the city council for help. The problem with city council grants is that they are usually one-off payments where you get a lump sum for one year but no continuing funding. The council is under great pressure because the more the country's economy goes into decline the more people are knocking on the door asking the council for money. Two or three years ago we may have had 50 applicants going to the funding bodies, whereas now you have 250 applicants, the need is so great. And they all want a bigger piece of the cake, but there are now more pieces to share.[13]

Unable to raise bail out money from alternative sources, TAG had no choice but to close its doors in 1992. The offices and programs of TAG were converted into a private company, the Liverpool Training and Management Consultants. Relying on a totally private funding base, the new company is striving for self-sufficiency by expanding its capacity to compete in the commercial world and access new potential commercial markets.

The collapse of TAG is indicative of a larger pattern of governmental policy making that has had a devastating impact on the operational viability of nonprofit community organizations in Liverpool. Commenting on this pattern, Carleton Benjamin, chief executive of TAG, noted:

> In recent years there has been a systematic stripping away of funds from Black organizations. These policies are being implemented by agencies like METC, like Liverpool City Council, like City Challenge, and other government agencies which have supposedly been set up to help the economic and community development of an area like Granby Toxteth but are now systematically cutting funding on a peri-

odic basis. The problem has a broad base. Liverpool City Council has suffered in the past years through central government funding cuts. That effect has been catastrophic in terms of our agencies because once powerful White agencies get cut, then automatically they will cut the Black agencies. Because Black agencies run on a shoe string, they do not have the means or the capacity to find additional sources of funding for themselves. Inevitably, they must close down first and foremost before they can even think about trying to reorganize, regroup, or redevelop the project or agency.[14]

The ability on the part of government agencies to selectively defund nonprofit Black community organizations, and the dependence of these organizations on such funding, has severely limited the utility of nonprofit organizations as sources of political strength for the Black community in Liverpool. For these organizations, the policy process has been clearly unidirectional. Clinging to life through a capricious process of selective resource allocation, these organizations have been pushed to the margins of the political system. Lacking permanent fiscal support, they facilitate political control of Black social policy making by external governmental institutions, while insulating their Black constituents from important arenas of public decision making. The structuring of the role of Black nonprofit organizations as political buffers represents a key factor in the shaping and limiting of Black community choice in the governmental process. In the absence of an independent funding base for community organizations, the goal of effective linkage will remain an elusive objective for Liverpool's Black community.

## Internal Conflict and Political Development

Blacks in Liverpool confront the challenging task of building an effective organizational alliance capable of mobilizing the collective power of the Black community in the political system. As we have seen in the case of Boston, the building of such an alliance is extraordinarily difficult under circumstances of widespread social diversity, institutional erosion, and the absence of an independent funding base for social development. In recent years the organizational infrastructure of the Black community in Liverpool has been highly fragmented. Divisive tendencies stimulated by nationality and ethnic group differences have been reinforced by a culture of suspicion and distrust that has prevented Black community leaders and organizations from joining forces to fight for a common race agenda.

Black groups in Liverpool tend to concentrate on their differences rather than the thing they have in common, challenging the system. The issues do not center on confronting the White power structure but break down to Liverpool-born Blacks against immigrants, the West Indian community versus the African community, the African community versus the Asian community. Rivalries between groups in the Black community have been intense, parochial, and destructive. It is easier to organize around buildings than it is to collectively confront the power structure.[15]

The character of Black political leadership has been a formidable stumbling block to Black political unity and mobilization.

The problem of mistrust among Blacks in Liverpool is buried deep in the community's history. A bunch of cowboys came to the forefront of Black organizations and tried to rip them off to satisfy their own purposes. A lot of the community saw that and distanced themselves from that sort of action or behavior. We are trying to break that historical sort of barrier and tell people that we do need to come together because there is strength in unity.[16]

The pattern of disunity among Black leaders and organizations was temporarily broken by the formation of the Black Caucus by the Meresyside Community Relations Council (MCRC) under the leadership of Wally Brown. When Brown left for a post in Manchester, the glue that held the Black Caucus together quickly evaporated. Black organizations pulled away from MCRC to pursue their separate agendas, a process that was accelerated by changes in the funding process for community organizations. What had been a consolidated effort to obtain communitywide benefits from government authorities became an arena of intense competition. The rule of thumb became separate development. Few efforts were made to devise collective strategies to overcome the hostility and intransigence of government funding agencies. Even in instances where program agendas were compatible, the scramble for maintenance resources set Black political organizations in Liverpool on an invariable collision course.

Poignant efforts to intervene in this environment of political conflict and competition were made by the Consortium of Black Organizations (CBO). During the early years of the 1990s, this association functioned as a coordinating unit for the program initiatives of over forty community organizations. The primary objective of CBO was to rationalize and consolidate the efforts on the part of community organizations to lobby public and private agencies for funds. Although CBO did not replicate the role of the MCRC as a political action coordinating unit, it did establish a solid reputation, especially in the private arena, as a skilled contract mediator in behalf of Black organizations. As an organization, CBO was not able to maintain sufficient internal unity to sustain its liaison role in the political process. Its credibility and internal cohesion began to slip after it failed in its efforts to secure funds from the Granby Toxteth Task Force to hire a permanent program coordinator to manage the day-to-day affairs of the organization. Negotiations for the funding of the coordinator's position were protracted, lasting more than nine months. To prevent the work of CBO from piling up, an interim coordinator was recruited to work for no salary. After nine months, negotiations with the Granby Toxteth Task Force collapsed. With no prospects for permanent placement with CBO, the interim coordinator left her position to secure regular employment. The loss of the coordinator's position delivered a serious blow to the credibility of CBO as a catalyst for Black organizational development. Gradually, member organizations began to pull out of the organization and return to their positions of autonomous programming and separate development (see figure 10.2).

The cost of autonomous programming and separate development for Black organizations in Liverpool has been incredibly high. As in Boston, these patterns have produced a decentralized, unfocused

**Figure 10.2. Dominant Patterns of Interest Articulation in Liverpool's Black Community**

Source: Adapted from Liverpool Black Caucus, *The Racial Politics of Militant in Liverpool* (Liverpool and London: Merseyside Area Profile Group and Runnymede Trust, 1986), and Gideon Ben-Tovim, John Gabriel, Ian Law, and Kathleen Stredder, *The Local Politics of Race* (London: Macmillan Education LTD, 1986).

process of Black interest articulation. Serious commitments to coordinated strategic planning and collective struggle have been abandoned. Clearly missing from the political armor of the Black community in Liverpool is a citywide coalition that is able to sustain gains already achieved and establish the groundwork for forward movement toward substantive incorporation and empowerment. Until such a coalition is institutionalized, the unvarnished capacity on the part of the city council and the party system to deflect Black policy proposals away from pivotal centers of decision making will remain a salient characteristic of local politics in Liverpool.

# PART FOUR

# Comparative Racial Politics

# 11

## Boston and Liverpool: The Comparative Context of Black Politics

### Black Political Incorporation

Following in the pioneering footsteps of Ira Katznelson, this study has examined political linkage between city governments and Black communities in Boston and Liverpool.[1] The concept of political linkage is one that seeks to illuminate the extent to which racial minorities are able, over time, to promote political incorporation and empowerment by increasing their ability to effectively influence the making of governmental decisions affecting their well-being in society. In liberal democracies such as the United States and Britain, linkage in the policy process is an important prerequisite for political empowerment. Research on minority politics shows that all groups do not have equal access to the institutional structures and resources that produce the empowerment benefits necessary for political incorporation.[2] According to Katznelson and Weir, groups in society may be: (a) incorporated fully and equally and may possess the capacity to affect the contours of policy change; bb) incorporated fully and equally but have relatively little influence on the political system; (c) incorporated in a partial and structurally subordinate way but possess the capacity to influence policy outcomes at some moments; or (d) structurally subordinate and without resources to affect what the state does.[3] Black communities in Boston and Liverpool have faced obstacles to their political development that have made it extraordinarily difficult for them, as a collective force, to move beyond category (d) on the Katznelson and Weir incorporation scale.

The similarity of the obstacles to incorporation faced by Black communities in these Atlantic world cities is striking. Data from this study suggest that parallels of this kind are not fortuitous. A key underlying assumption of the concept of Black Atlantic politics is that racially hierarchical political systems tend to produce parallel policy outcomes for Black communities despite vast differences in the formal structures, political histories, and policy environments of the host societies. In this regard the concept of Black Atlantic politics is no mere metaphor for the practice of politics by Blacks in geographically separate parts of the Atlantic world. The deeper meaning it conveys is one that illuminates the existence of a hierarchical system of racial subordination that produces major obstacles to Black policy linkage in the electoral arena, in health, in housing, in education, in police governance and control, and in other key areas of decision making. This study of Boston and Liverpool confirms that differences in governing structures, social values and outlooks, and political history do not substantially modify the policy outcomes produced by hierarchical racial systems. Obstacles to Black political linkage remain high throughout the Black Atlantic, even in countries in the Caribbean operating under formal Black control. Black citizens in Caribbean countries such as the Bahamas, Jamaica, and Barbados suffer under the weight of indirect rule. Critical Black community linkage functions are undermined by the limited scope of democratic institutional processes and control over the domestic economy exercised by foreign banks, the International Monetary Fund, and other White-dominated instruments of capitalist power. White majority political environments such as Boston and Liverpool provide a plethora of opportunities for direct rule by White-led political regimes. These patterns of direct rule produce remarkably similar dilemmas of political empowerment for local Black communities; they also provoke the fashioning of political strategies by Black leaders and their supporters that are remarkably similar in content, orientation, and impact.

Blacks in Boston and Liverpool share a common legacy of struggle against racial oppression. Both Boston and Liverpool are Irish port cities with long histories of racial discrimination. Staunch opposition to school desegregation by White citizens and institutions in Boston has given that city the reputation of being one of the most overtly racist cities in North America. Liverpool is widely known for its opposition to housing integration and the use of hard policing methods in Liverpool 8. Blacks in both cities have suffered severe economic deprivation. Avoidance of "good practices" in the realm of equal opportunities has been the sine qua non of social policy development in both cities. The city bureaucracies of both cities reflect a high degree of Black underrepresentation. Discrimination in this area has had a devastating impact in Liverpool where the city council is the largest employer, and the formal and informal adherence to union nominating rights and the internal trawl has severely restricted the turnover of city jobs along racial lines.

Boston and Liverpool have maintained distinct approaches to the accommodation of Black demands. Boston's tradition of machine politics institutionalized a system of exchange relations that provided patronage benefits and modest policy innovations to the Black community as compensation for its Democratic political loyalties. In Liverpool, the issue of race was grafted onto a political culture that refused to recognize race as a legitimate category of policy demand. In terms of broad policy outcomes, the salience or nonsalience of race in these cities does not appear to be a major factor in the process of benefit allocation. Differences in the style of group accommodation have not been profound enough to affect the scope and rate of Black political incorporation. Practices of institutional racism are widespread in both societies, and they impact on the political incorporation of Blacks in much the same way. Blacks in both cities remain largely shut out of corporate and business enterprise. Protests over the teaching and learning processes in the public schools in both cities have not markedly improved the educational performance of Black children. Black youth in both cities remain heavily unemployed and are becoming deeply alienated from the culture and politics of the broader society. Job search programs have faltered on the terrain of youth interactions with street-level bureaucrats that give them early arrest records and bad reputations.

The parallels we find in policy outcomes in both cities are the product of a racial hierarchy that insulates Black communities from centers of power where autonomous, systemwide, "big" decisions are made. In White-dominated cities such as Boston and Liverpool, the impact of the racially biased hierarchy is immediate and catastrophic. Policies that promote White privilege and Black subordination are accepted as part of the natural routines of government. Thus in Liverpool official complicity in the bias allocation of council housing was never acknowledged until the CRE conducted a comprehensive study and issued a cease and desist notice. In Boston, years of complaints by welfare mothers were greeted with a police raid on the welfare office rather than a bureaucratic response designed to produce policy reform. On vital policy issues, the workings of the racial hierarchy tend to make the visible invisible. As

Michael Parenti notes, issues relating to the grievances of the powerless are transformed into nonissues by those whose interests are
given preferential recognition and treatment in the political
process.[4] Blacks in Boston and Liverpool have had their interests
systematically organized out of the policy process by the norms, procedures, and behavior of dominant White governing coalitions.
Nondecision making and the marginalization of Black input into the
policy process are issues that have no solid geographic boundaries in
the Black Atlantic. Even in the most democratic societies in the
Western world, the reach of racial democracy stops firmly at the
water's edge.

## Governmental Structures and Policy Outcomes

An examination of the formal structures of city government has
been central to our analysis of Black politics in Boston and
Liverpool. This focus is in keeping with Katznelson's contention
that the examination of structural factors must be the starting point
of comparative racial research.[5] Our analysis has illuminated major
differences in the structure of government in Boston and Liverpool.
Boston City Government is a strong mayor form of government that
centralizes decision making authority in the mayor's office. Liverpool City Government has no formal chief executive. The chair of the
council, or Lord Mayor, has no formal executive powers. The principal powers of government in Liverpool are lodged in the city council.
Compared to the Liverpool City Council, the Boston City Council is
small. Liverpool has ninety nine councillors, and Boston has thirteen. Unlike the Liverpool City Council, the legal authority of the
Boston City Council is confined mainly to legislative matters.

The differences in governmental structural arrangements in the
two cities have immensely important implications for Black politics.
Boston's structural arrangements make the mayor's office a prime
target of Black political action. The mayor of Boston has extensive
policy-making authority. Boston mayors exercise phenomenal control over the budget-making process in city government. Not only
does the mayor initiate the budget and establish its base line, but he
controls access to state and federal funds, as well as access to services from city departments. Boston mayors have also been adept at
maintaining good relations with the media, labor, business, and the
leaders of suburban governments. The mayor's extensive formal
powers are backed up by the electoral power and financial resources

of the local party system. The relationship between the mayor's office and the Black community has been almost entirely unidirectional The maintenance of this relationship over multiple administrations has been a formidable barrier to effective Black linkage in the governing process. A highly decentralized ward-based process under Mayor Curley and Mayor Haynes prevented the Black community from entering into the policy distribution network. Demands from the Black community were blocked by the buffering roles played by Bal and Shag Taylor. The primary rewards went to the Irish community via the Irish organizational network that ran all the way to the top of the party system. Blacks were kept at bay by patronage benefits that modestly satisfied the desires of individual Black politicians but did nothing to promote the social and economic interests of the Black community as a whole.

Both Mayor Haynes and Mayor Collins became urban renewal specialists who rewarded Black support at the polls with federally funded programs that destroyed Black neighborhoods. Kevin White provided symbolic reassurance to the Black community but little else. His Little City Hall Program became a convenient mechanism for distributing patronage benefits to Blacks that would keep the Black community quiescent and disconnected from the structures of power in city hall. White's personal political machine provided little room for the accumulation of major Black social and economic benefits. The intent of the evolving relationship between the mayor and the Black community was to demobilize Black organizations and keep the Black electorate under the paternalistic control of city hall. Under White, Blacks were mainly the beneficiaries of symbolic benefits in the form of the appointment of Blacks to high-level positions in his cabinet; these Black appointees were expected to serve as effective buffers between the mayor and his Black constituents. The fundamental structure of the relationship between the Black community and city hall remained impervious to change under Mayor Flynn and Mayor Menino. Flynn's brand of urban populism did not deviate from the firmly established pattern of Black dependency. Menino has used his relationship with Black ministers to take back power from the Black community by exercising his political clout to maintain an appointed rather than an elected school committee.

Executive-centered leadership in Boston has been a graveyard for effective Black political linkage. The reason for this is not very complicated: Blacks do not have the electoral strength to impact significantly on the mayor's programmatic agenda. Turnout in mayoral elections in the Black community tends to be far below the community's electoral potential. The Black vote is also not independent; it can be captured by the Democratic Party without the expenditure of major political resources. Clearly missing in the Black community is a communitywide network for organizing the Black vote and maximizing its impact in the political process. Since mayoral candidates are not strategically dependent on the Black vote, they can ignore Black policy interests without fear of retribution. We can only wonder how different this situation would be if Mel King had succeeded in his mayoral crusade. It is important to note in this regard that one of the objectives of the King campaign was to establish a rainbow coalition to organize and mobilize minority political power in the electoral process.

The structural design of Liverpool City Government has pushed the center of gravity of local decision making toward the city council. Pivotal policy making authority is decentralized into council committees. Because of its control over the budget, the Finance and Strategy Committee is the most powerful committee of the council. Council structural arrangements pose immense difficulties for Blacks seeking to promote Black community linkage. One major problem rests in the fact that council committees are able to operate fairly autonomously. In Liverpool, there is no independent chief executive to nudge council committees in a particular policy direction. Committees are relatively free to establish their own policy agendas. Until the early 1980s the politics of race in Liverpool meant that Black issues never penetrated the agenda of council committees. Adopting the British model of color-blind decision making, the unique position of the Black community in the social order was never recognized, legitimized, or embraced by even the most community-oriented council committee, the Education Committee. As former council leader John Hamilton observed:

> No one saw Black problems as a problem. This is still an attitude of mind on the part of many Labour Party people. "Just integrate with us and you're all right." The only problem they saw was the integration of the Catholic and non-Catholic. Black issues came much later. They did come along, they began to develop bit by bit.[6]

The Liberal Democratic Party finally gave recognition to the race issue with the passage in the early 1980s of its Equal Opportunities Policy Statement and the appointment of the Race Relations Liaison Committee. These concessions proved to be no match for the ability of council members to ignore race issues, bury them in committee, or pass them on to members of the professional staff as inconsequential matters to be studied out of existence. Important proposals for race policy reform introduced by the Race Relations Liaison Committee died excruciating deaths. Clearly the council was interested in delivering symbolic reassurance not substantive goods. The Liaison Committee was in a poor position to fight for its proposals because it was a nonstatutory committee that served at the pleasure of the council.

When the Militant Tendency took control of the council, all consideration of positive action initiatives was brought to a halt. To assure that no such initiatives would become a part of the council's agenda, Militants imported a Black administrator from London, Sampson Bond, to quash such initiatives in their formative stages. Bond made a strong effort to separate the Black Caucus of the Liaison Committee from its constituency base. The objective was to break the back of the Black community by rendering it leaderless and hopeless. The strategy almost succeeded. The Black community was tremendously disadvantaged in this struggle because it had no foothold in the party structure or the city bureaucracy. Its resource base was extremely low. The Black community had no representation in the city council. The leadership of the trade unions was racially exclusive, sometimes hostile, and deeply racist. The Liverpool 8 Defence Committee was politically isolated, the Merseyside Anti-Racialist Alliance was on the verge of collapse, and the Charles Wootton Centre was fighting for economic survival. No community-wide organization existed to mobilize Black votes in elections. Given the Black community's limited numbers, it is doubtful that a high mobilization campaign would have detracted the Militants from their anti-Black community agenda.

The establishment of race units in education and housing by the Progressive Labour Caucus raised expectations that the council would embrace a comprehensive race policy agenda. These expectations were dashed when it became clear that these units would not have ready access to the central policy making institutions of the council. The decentralized structure of the council prevented the race units from developing a race policy network in the council. What was obviously needed was a central race unit—one of the key recommendations of the Gifford Report—to coordinate the work of all race policy programs councilwide. Given the politics of the council, no proposal for such a unit could possibly get off the ground.

The existing race units proved to be no answer to the linkage needs of the Black community. After several years it became clear that their scope of operational authority was too limited. They could operate in the seams where no services were provided but could not develop wide policy streams where new and innovative solutions to pressing Black problems could be created and implemented. Many of their proposals for structural reform and community outreach became buried in bureaucratic minutia or were killed under the weight of rules governing the relationship of subordinates and managers in the prevailing administrative hierarchy. In the absence of autonomous decision making power, race units assumed the role of buffers, providing the illusion of representation without wielding the power associated with policy implementation.

The collapse of the Merseyside Community Relations Council (MCRC) meant that the lines of political interaction between the race units in the council and policy-producing agencies in the Black community were totally and irretrievably severed. These units were compelled to operate in splendid isolation from their constituency base. Under these circumstances, they had no choice but to look inward for support from powerful political and administrative units in the council. The erosion of their community base was accompanied by a decline in commitment to struggle around major policy initiatives. Programs like the MST training scheme would become difficult—if not impossible—to move through the council. With no Blacks in the council and few White council allies, political support for such endeavors simply would not be available. With increasing council reluctance to embrace and implement race policy initiatives, Black community organizations would have no choice but to turn to the task forces, or to the European Social Fund, for critical financial support.

The policy environment of the Boston City Council is also extremely perilous for the Black community. Blacks in Boston face a conservative city council that has shown little interest in embracing a program of affirmative action for the Black community. Affirmative action goal setting and targeting are virtually nonexistent in the Boston City council. No equivalent of the race units established by the Liverpool City Council have been set up, or even seriously entertained, by the Boston City council. Initiatives to monitor hiring policies in the line departments have been weak and ineffective; these measures have mainly been warmly embraced and promoted by Black councillors. The promotion of substantive racial linkage has been principally left in the hands of Black city councillors. Men of great integrity and commitment, they have worked diligently— often without fanfare—to fashion a coherent race policy agenda. The fundamental dilemma they have had to confront is the task of selling their agenda to their White colleagues. Their numerical representation in the council weighs heavily against their success. Given the conservative ideological bent of their council colleagues, Black city councillors have often found it impossible to secure majority support in the council behind their legislative initiatives.

The Boston City Council also operates through a committee system. Maintaining—at best—a distant relationship to this system, the Black community is left out of the central core of policy making in the council. In contrast to the pattern in Liverpool, Blacks in Boston are never invited to serve as co-opted members of council committees. Black attendance at council meetings is erratic and discontinuous. The most useful sources of inside information on council business are the offices of the two Black councillors. This process is both burdensome to the councillors and unreliable for Black citizens seeking serious input into council affairs. Black councillors Charles Yancey and Gareth Saunders have made genuine efforts to maintain close relations with Black community organizations and to pass important race policy legislation in the council. Their efforts have been limited by resistance by a majority of the council to race policy initiatives and the omnipresent threat of a mayoral veto of any legislation that appears to fall beyond the boundaries of the prevailing race policy consensus.

Black representation and influence in major city departments is weak. This is a very important structural issue since many council initiatives, including budget proposals, originate in departments. Blacks also have little authoritative representation in high policy circles of the party system. The system of voting for council positions gives the Black community little political influence in council elections except in elections in the two predominantly Black districts. Low Black turnout and voting rates militate against the exercise by Blacks of a balance-of-power role in most elections. Deep social divisions in the Black community further undermine the use of the ballot by Blacks as a political weapon in the legislative process. The decline in civil rights leadership has deprived the Black community of a political force that might circumvent the obstacles inherent in the legislative process and move the Black community directly to the core arenas of policy making. Unlike business groups, Black interest groups do not operate as strategic dependents in the policy process. They are therefore routinely denied the special entree that goes to business interests that are wealthy and well connected.

In Boston and Liverpool, Blacks have been compelled to operate in the margins of the policy-making process. Functioning from a low resource base and confronted with a wide variety of institutional obstacles, Blacks in these cities have been unable to establish the kind of administrative, legislative, and political linkages required for strong political incorporation. Although the institutions, structures, and procedures of racial domination in the two cities have been different, the policy outcomes for the Black community reinforce the notion that broad patterns of racial domination exist throughout the Black Atlantic and pose formidable dilemmas for the achievement of enduring Black political incorporation and empowerment.

## Urban Regeneration

Evaluations of the political influence of Black communities in the Black Atlantic cannot be analytically separated from processes of urban regeneration. Black communities throughout the Black Atlantic are increasingly being exposed to schemes of corporate capitalism to expand its financial base by undermining the physical and fiscal viability of those communities under the guise of urban regeneration. Boston's Black community is a classic example of a community that has had to endure monumental disruption and dislocation because of corporate-centered regeneration schemes. Urban renewal policies under Mayor Collins dictated the demolition of the South End to facilitate the expansion of downtown redevelopment. This project alone displaced thousands of Black families. Boston's urban bulldozer has continued to move south, cutting deep into Roxbury and pushing Blacks down the Southwest Corridor into Mattapan, Jamaica Plain, and Roslindale. Because of its close proximity to downtown, Roxbury has become a primary target of urban regeneration schemes. Corporate-centered regeneration in Boston has had the effect of shrinking the Black land base and driving up the value of property and the price of rents to the point that many Blacks can no longer afford to live in the central city. The political repercussions of these developments have been astronomical. In the service of corporate-led regeneration, important institutions have been destroyed, such as churches, schools, parks, and playgrounds. Political alliances forged over many decades have broken down. The natural boundaries of neighborhoods have shifted in ways that undermine the cohesive integration of social groups into functional political networks. Class conflicts have developed as members of the Black middle class have come forward to capitalize on projects to construct new facilities intended to serve as anchors for the physical reconstruction of large portions of the Black community.

Regeneration in Liverpool has moved along remarkably parallel lines. Although regeneration initiatives are driven more by central government incentives in Liverpool than in Boston, both processes emphasize private-sector leadership and investment. In Liverpool central government-funded quangoes have been established to guide and direct redevelopment activities in the Black community. These government entities have joined forces with private housing associations to promote housing demolition in the Black community. Like the Boston Black community, the Liverpool Black community is located on prime real estate close to the downtown core shopping district. The Black community in Liverpool is caught in a web between grassroots efforts to fight regeneration and pressure from private interests to give up its land and move out of the way of urban "progress."

Corporate-led regeneration in Liverpool has produced significant political costs for the Black community. Political resources that could be mobilized to fight city hall have been siphoned off into internal conflicts over issues of land distribution and neighborhood preservation. These conflicts have been sources of deep division in the Black community as issues such as the value and impact of land contracts offered by housing associations are vigorously debated. If achieved, the gentrification of the Black community will break up potential voting blocks, spreading Black political resources across several voting districts. An immediate impact of this result would be the permanent loss of Black representation in the city council for the Granby Ward.

Black incorporation requires a stable base of political support for the Black community. Internal conflicts associated with regeneration contradict the notion of stability and weaken the capacity of the Black community to negotiate in its own interest in the political process.

## Policy Leadership: The Dilemma of Racial Buffering

Since the days of the African slave trade, Blacks in the United States and Britain have depended upon Black leaders to point the way to freedom and progress. Black communities in Boston and Liverpool have been compelled to grapple with the problem of the absence of a strong middle class leadership base to create and implement a forceful Black agenda. In Boston, many potential middle class Black leaders have been drawn into corporate America by high-salary and fringe benefit inducements. This segment of the Black community has become highly suburbanized and politically disconnected form the Black community's organizational base. In Liverpool, the issue has not centered on corporate co-optation but the paucity of college-trained professionals who are willing to stay in Liverpool and make a commitment to political activism.

Black communities in Boston and Liverpool have also had to struggle with the power of White institutions to use Black leaders as buffers in the political process. The mediating role of racial buffers has often had the impact—intended or unintended—of depressing the capacity of the Black community to pursue forms of autonomous or independent politics.

In Boston, mayoral administrations have depended on Black buffers to run their ward organizations in Black neighborhoods and deliver the Black vote for endorsed party candidates in elections. Mayoral administrations connected to the Black community through buffers can avoid negotiating policy linkages to the Black community because they are able to gain Black electoral support without making commitments to the Black community beyond the distribution of material benefits to a small number of cooperating Black politicians. Independent Black politics only begins to flower when the mediating roles of political buffers are moderated or over-turned by the power of Black political activists committed to a politics of grassroots political empowerment and effective Black community policy linkage.

High-level Black mayoral appointments represent an important potential source of linkage by the Black community in Boston City Government. As political symbols, these appointments signify the evolution of the Black community to a position of preeminence and influence in the political process. The symbolic import of these appointments often does not conform with the realities of racial politics since Black mayoral appointees are often compelled to be racial buffers for city administrations rather than Black intermediaries who provide vital links to a multitude of key city decision making agencies. The political potential of these appointments is quite large. If Black political appointees were able to chart an independent course, they could relieve city councillors of some of their responsibility for operating as linkage facilitators in local government. The dilemma the Black community faces is that individuals who would be willing to take on this vital interventionist role would probably not qualify (from the mayor's perspective) for appointment, and, if appointed, would be removed, like Doris Bunte, because they were deemed not to be loyal members of the mayor's team.

The buffering roles played by some Black ministers in Boston has generated considerable controversy. Many ministers appear to have gone out of their way to strike cozy, interdependent relationships with city administrations. Their willingness to play leading roles in issue campaigns endorsed by city hall has raised serious questions regarding the sincerity and depth of their commitment to the development and implementation of a Black agenda. These issues have important implications for Black political incorporation. Ideally, Black ministers should be role models of authentic, community-oriented leadership. Community suspicions that they are pursuing personal agendas in their political roles can have a detrimental impact on the use of Black churches as training grounds for future Black leaders. These suspicions also become fertile ground for the growth of political division and disunity around policy issues of vital importance to the welfare of the entire Black community.

Racial buffering issues in Liverpool have surfaced at the level of organizational political activity. The political legacy of the Merseyside Community Relations Council (MCRC) illustrates the contributions toward effective linkages that can be made when a community organization is deeply committed to a race equality mediating agenda. Despite its existence as an official governmental coordinating unit, MCRC was willing to place its funding base at great risk in pursuit of policy objectives it believed to be essential to the Black community's long-term progress. Black nonprofit organizations in Liverpool have not had the political space or resources to duplicate the quasi-independent political posture exhibited by MCRC. Their dependence on governmental funding—especially from the city council—has compelled them to sharply limit their advocacy roles in the service of Black community causes. On all but extremely rare occasions, the activities of nonprofit Black organizations in Liverpool do not challenge the legitimacy or primacy of dominant White forces in the prevailing political order. For this reason, they represent a weak ingredient in the political resource base of the Black community. The quality of their contributions to Black community incorporation could possibly be significantly increased if they were able to cultivate a permanent funding source committed to community advancement and disconnected from the fiscal institutions of government. Nonprofit organizations can be important training grounds for effective Black political leadership. They can also be useful sources of policy innovation. The service needs provided by the Toxteth Activities Group (TAG) in its heyday not only closed an important skills training gap but also illuminated the kind of self-development the Black community could undertake if it matched its innate ingenuity with hard work and commitment. Nonprofit organizations can play vital intermediary roles in the elevation of the Black community to the takeoff stage of development. If they are to play these roles, they must develop independent sources of funding, come to the political table with good ideas, and display the kind of leadership integrity required to galvanize community support and unify community interests around common objectives and common political strategies.

### Black Political Behavior: The Impact of Community Conflict

It is axiomatic that unity and cohesion are important ingredients in the process of political incorporation. Conflict and disunity have been rife in the Black communities of Boston and Liverpool. Diversity issues run to the heart of this state of affairs. In Boston, the fault lines of conflict have moved along class and ethnic lines. The economic mobility and geographic dispersion of the Black middle class have created divisions in the social fabric of the Black community. Middle class Blacks are accused of abandoning their inner-city brothers and sisters in their pursuit of the American dream in suburbia. Important community institutions have experienced difficulty attracting Black professionals as board members and career officers. As federal programs eliminate entitlement programs for inner-city residents, the gap between the affluent and the poor grows increasingly wider. Low-income communities are left to fend for themselves against an escalating tidal wave of conservative White political opposition. Cutback policies introduced by Boston City Government have stimulated a fierce competition for funds by nonprofit organizations. Often sharing overlapping service responsibilities, these organizations have been reluctant to draw up a common programmatic agenda. A critical failing in Boston has been the unwillingness of Black professionals trained in social and organizational planning to step in and draw up a master plan for social service provision in the Black community.

Ethnic diversity has also been a source of conflict in Boston's Black community. Leaders of immigrant groups in the Black community often express strong concern that the needs of these groups are not reflected in the policy programs of prominent African American–led social service and civil rights institutions. Conflicts around social and economic issues have translated themselves into deep political divisions, with immigrants refusing to support African American leadership on a range of political issues, including the election of candidates for public office.

Ideological differences have also driven wedges between various segments of the Black community. Black ministers have constituted the most conservative force in the Black community. Their positions on public issues have been challenged by Black elected officials and moderate leaders of Black community organizations. The nationalist component of Black opinion has largely disappeared. This fact reflects the dissipation of protest politics in the Black community. Clearly the primary line of ideological division is between Black elected officials and Black ministers who appear increasingly to be moving onto a political island by themselves.

Black conflict in Liverpool appears to issue mainly from competition for government grants. Unity in the Black community has suffered badly from the decline of coordinating institutions such as the Merseyside Community Relations Council (MCRC). Liverpool's Black community, like Boston's, is disadvantaged by the absence of a master plan for collectively processing organizational needs and citizen demands. Separate development by Black community organizations breeds suspicion, inefficiency, and political incapacity. Conflict at the organizational level negates both group and personal development, creating a vacuum of leadership and power that reinforces the special advantages that accrue to White power elites by virtue of their relatively unchallenged monopoly over the key institutions of decision making in local government.

Ethnic divisions in Liverpool's Black community are another important source of social and political division. On basic public issues, Liverpool-born Blacks and Asians appear to be worlds apart. A widely held view in the Liverpool-born Black community is that development in that community has been held back by the special attention that has been given to the concerns of Asian immigrants. Liverpool-born Blacks believe that they are the most oppressed segment of the Black community, their position stemming from the callous neglect of their needs by local government because they are "natives" not immigrants and because of their mixed racial heritage evolving from the extensive interracial marriage pattern existing in Liverpool. The upsurge of Black political activities in the 1980s reflected the determination by Liverpool-born Blacks to move to the forefront of Black struggle. Asians have been reluctant to join them in that struggle. They have preferred to engage in separate development, believing that their best interests lay in integrating into the larger social order rather than joining hands with Liverpool-born Blacks as an outside dissident force. Asian efforts to step forward to provide communitywide leadership have typically yielded poor results. Many Liverpool-born Blacks attribute the decline and eventual collapse of the MCRC to the takeover of the organization by a conservative Asian leadership element with few political skills and no political base in the broader Black community. The continuing existence of separate national and religious cultural centres, and the endless complaints by Liverpool-born Blacks that they have no authentic centre to call their own, provides a clear symbolic representation of the kind of racial and ethnic divisions that have come to shape the social and political life of the Black community in Liverpool.

The impact of intracommunal conflict in Boston and Liverpool has been to drive Black communities in these cities away from the centers of local power and decision making. Black linkage cannot be realized under conditions where the Black community brings into the political process a medley of separate agendas. Hierarchical racial systems have within them an abundance of instruments for killing minority empowerment efforts that do not reflect a consensus of opinion and a unity of political engagement. Bidirectional decision making flows from the exercise of collective power. A division of power strengthens the capacity of dominant elements in the policy-making process to engage in nondecision making while delivering reassurance to subordinate insurgents. Collective mobilization reflects both cognitive liberation and group solidarity. In the absence of such resources, Black community groups in Boston and Liverpool can expect that their quest for empowerment will not yield appreciable positive results.

## Strategies of Political Incorporation

Throughout the hundreds of hours the author spent discussing politics with citizens in Boston and Liverpool, one inquiry tended to reign above all others: the way forward. Our respondents offered a rich variety of answers to this question The consensus of opinion was that Black political leaders and their supporters must carefully analyze the content of past struggles and replicate some of the ingredients of those struggles. Boston and Liverpool have rich and illuminating histories of Black political protests. Today such protests have largely disappeared from the political landscape. The transition from protest to politics in some Black Atlantic world cities has neither been smooth or overwhelmingly effective. Blacks in Boston and Liverpool do not have the resources required to produce the electoral results Blacks have achieved in Cleveland, Birmingham, Detroit, Baltimore, and Atlanta. For the moment, the way forward for Blacks in Boston and Liverpool appears to rest outside the electoral process. This may not continue to be the case for Blacks in Boston. Black electoral potential in Boston is growing by leaps and bounds. Mel King's heroic political campaign in 1983 gave Blacks in Boston a glimpse of the positive results that can emanate from high minority mobilization. Continuing White outmigration to the suburbs and the ongoing dethroning of Irish power may well be a prelude to a Black takeover of the Democratic Party and city hall in Boston. But this will not occur automatically. Black leaders must effectively deal with a welter of internal problems that promote ethnic, racial, and class divisions and keep Blacks away from the polls in massive numbers.

Although some respondents in Liverpool speculated about the possibility of Black takeover of the Labour Party, such talk, at this time, is sheer fantasy. Given the weak representation of Blacks in the party's membership, there is no reason to believe they will muster sufficient political strength in the near future to stage a political coup and seize the reins of the party. At best Blacks in Liverpool can look forward to a liberalization of the party's position on race policy issues under a new, more progressive White-led party regime.

The way forward for Black communities in both cities appears to rest in their ability to mobilize resources in the political system in their own behalf. Black leaders in Boston and Liverpool must increase their ability to inspire Blacks in their cities to work in the public arena to realize common objectives. Voting practices in the Black community in this regard are not encouraging. Blacks in both cities regularly vote at less than half strength. If Black incorporation and empowerment are to be achieved, there can be no substitute for community mobilization. An urgent need in Boston and Liverpool is the development of community-wide instruments to mobilize Black interests in public protest efforts and in the electoral process. These instruments—regardless of their concrete organizational forms—must take responsibility for planning, recruitment, and formal participation. An affiliated research team must provide assessments of gains and losses and offer recommendations for future strategic action.

The organizational infrastructure of the Black community must be rebuilt or reinforced. Operational decline of pivotal institutional organizations such as the NAACP and the MCRC is deeply troubling. These organizations must function to bring together under one umbrella the interests of all community organizations seeking to promote a race equality agenda. The fiscal collapse of nonprofit organizations cannot be allowed to continue. Sources of independent funding for such organizations must be found so their political work is not compromised by their revenue streams. On this subject Ray Quarless of the Steve Biko Housing Association in Liverpool observed:

> Problems arise for our nonprofit organizations because you are always under the constraints of the funding body to a certain extent. Problems arise because your funding is always of a short-term nature, and you have a constant headache every one year, every two years, or every three years of trying to find your money and where it's going to come from next. I've seen organizations come and go simply because of the lack of initiative in being able to secure funding for subsequent years. I don't know how that can be addressed, but it will have to be addressed because there are organizations that have established themselves, and Black people cannot afford to lose these agencies. They have become part and parcel of the Black way of life. It is important, and it is necessary that we are able to develop a financial strategy which collectively brings in the money, not for one organization but for all the organizations, and that all the organizations are not subjected to the possibility of making redundancies, the possibility of trimming down the service they provide, the possibility at the end of the day of going into extinction. That cannot be allowed.[7]

Strong, committed, independent, well-financed nonprofit organizations must continue because the service needs of the Black community are mounting. Cities in the United States and Europe are becoming the homes of high-cost Black citizens whose human needs are not being fully satisfied by the public sector. Black communities cannot afford to farm the problems of their citizens out to other communities. They must find a way to give their citizens the benefits that they need through their own unimpeachable resource networks.

The climb toward political incorporation and empowerment appears to be longer and steeper for Blacks in Liverpool than for Blacks in Boston. Blacks in Liverpool do not have the psychological advantage of operating in a national context of Black success in local elections. The low Black numerical representation of Blacks in Liverpool constitutes an important resource encumberance that cannot be quickly or easily overcome. Further, the virtual absence of a middle-class leadership base in Liverpool means that the process of Black infiltration of central power structures such as the city council, city bureaucracy, trade unions, and political parties will represent a more challenging obstacle for Blacks in Liverpool than Blacks in Boston. The Black protest movement in Boston has been more focused and organized, creating a higher degree of racial and political consciousness among grassroots Black citizens in Boston than can be found among grassroots Black citizens in Liverpool. These differences in developmental potential do not measurably alter the fact that the building blocks of Black political progress in both cities are fundamentally the same: the fashioning of an internal Black community coalition committed to the goal of challenging the prevailing racial hierarchy and implementing a progressive race policy agenda.

Internal divisions in the Black communities of Boston and Liverpool must be laid to rest. The culture of competition must be replaced by the culture of unity. Conflicts over funding and policy agendas are antithetical to the achievement of the primordial goals of incorporation and empowerment. The issue of Black unity is imbued with implications that extend far beyond the borders of Boston and Liverpool. Lessons we have learned from Boston and Liverpool have authentic and deep meaning for Black people struggling for freedom, justice, and equality across the African Diaspora. Too much energy has been expended, and too many lives have been lost in the effort to bring Africans in the Black Atlantic to the doorstep of liberation to have important political opportunities shattered because of internal disagreements. The early Africans who traveled around the world in search of freedom did so to provide the infrastructure for communities that could radiate the African spirits of peace, fellowship, harmony, consciousness, and prosperity. The search for community is no less a challenge to Africans in the Diaspora today than it was in the time of the noble and wise individuals who laid the foundation for the social, economic, political, and cultural construction of the Black Atlantic.

# Notes

Chapter 1. The Black Atlantic: Race and Local Politics

1. Joseph E. Harris, "The Dynamics of the Global African American Diaspora," in Alusine Jalloh and Stephen E. Maizlish (eds.), *The African Diaspora* (College Station, Texas: Texas A&M University Press, 1996), p. 8.

2. Ibid., p. 9.

3. Ibid.

4. Ivan Van Sertima, *They Came Before Columbus* (New York: Random House, 1976).

5. Molefi K. Asante and Mark Mattson, *Historical and Cultural Atlas of African Americans* (New York: Macmillan Publising Company, 1992), pp. 16–17.

6. Paul Gilroy, *The Black Atlantic: Modernity and Double Consciousness* (Cambridge, Massachusetts: Harvard University Press, 1993), pp. 15–19.

7. Ibid., p. 15.

8. Ibid., pp. 17–19.

9. Ibid., p. 17.

10. Benjamin Quarles, *Black Abolitionists* (London: Oxford University Press, 1969), pp. 136–37.

11. Kenneth M. Stampp, *The Peculiar Institution: Slavery in the Ante-Bellum South* (New York: Vintage Books, 1956), pp. 141-191.

12.A. Leon Higginbotham Jr., *In the Matter of Color* (Oxford: Oxford University Press, 1978), p. 28.

13. Ibid., pp. 50–51.

14. Audrey Smedley, *Race in North America* (Boulder, Colorado: Westview Press, 1993), pp. 52–53.

15. Joel Kovel, *White Racism: A Psychohistory* (New York: Vintage Books, 1970), pp. 18–19.

16. John Hope Franklin and Alfred Moss Jr. *From Slavery to Freedom; A History of African Americans* (New York: McGraw-Hill, Inc., 1994), seventh edition, pp. 259–63.

17. Florestan Fernandes, "Beyond Poverty: The Negro and the Mulatto in Brazil," in Jorge I. Dominguez (ed.), *Race and Ethnicity in Latin America* (New York: Garland Publishing, Inc., 1994), p. 124.

18. Ibid., p. 130.

19. For a detailed analysis of race in Venezuela, see Withrop R. Wright, *Café Con Leche: Race, Class, and National Image in Venezuela* (Austin, Texas: University of Texas Press, 1990).

20. George Priestley, "Post-Invasion Panama: Urban Crisis and Social Protests," in Charles Green (ed.), *Globalization and Survival in the Black Diaspora* (Albany: State University of New York Press, 1997), pp. 101–103.

21. Ibid.

22. Anthony Desales Affigne, Manual Avalos and Gerald Alfred, "Race and Politics in the Americas," paper prepared for the Annual Meeting of the American Political Science Association, New York, August 1994.

23. John D. Kasarda, "Urban Change and Minority Opportunities," in Paul Peterson (ed.), *The New Urban Reality* (Washington, D.C.: The Brookings Institution, 1985), pp. 33–67.

24. Alphonso Pinkney, *Black Americans* (Englewood Cliffs, New Jersey: Prentice Hall, 1993), fourth edition, pp. 71–77.

25. Stephen Small, "Racism, Black People and the City," in Charles Green (ed.), op. cit. p. 362.

26. Colin Brown, "'Same Difference': The Persistence of Racial Disadvantage in the British Employment Market," in Peter Braham, Ali Rattansi, and Richard Skellington (eds.), *Racism and Anti-Racism: Inequalities, Opportunities and Policies* (London: Sage Publications, LTD., 1992), p. 59.

27. A. Sivanandan, *A Different Hunger: Writings on Black Resistance* (London: Pluto Press, 1987), p. 34.

28. Mack H. Jones, "A Frame of Reference for Black Politics," in Lenneal J. Henderson Jr. (ed.), *Black Political Life in the United States: A Fist as the Pendulum* (San Francisco: Chandler Publishing Company, 1972), pp. 8–9.

29. Richard A. Keiser, *Subordination or Empowerment? African-American Leadership and the Struggle for Urban Political Power* (Oxford: Oxford University Press, 1996), p. 5.

30. Ibid., pp. 5–6.

31. Ibid., pp. 5-9.

32. Doug McAdam, *Political Process and the Development of Black Insurgency, 1930–1970* (Chicago: University of Chicago Press, 1982), pp. 36–55.

33. Vincent Harding, *There Is A River* (San Diego: Harcourt Brace and Company, 1981).

34. Ira Katznelson, *Black Men, White Cities* (Chicago: The University of Chicago Press, 1976), Phoenix edition.

35. Hanes Walton Jr., *Invisible Politics: Black Political Behavior* (Albany: State University of New York Press, 1985), p. xx.

36. Ibid., pp. 1–19.

37. John Solomos, *Race and Racism in Contemporary Britain* (London: Macmillan Education LTD, 1987), p. 6.

38. Ibid., p. 10.

39. Dianne M. Pinderhughes, *Race and Ethnicity in Chicago Politics: A Re-examination of Pluralist Theory* (Urbana: University of Illinois Press, 1987), p. 38.

40. Michael Parenti, "Power and Pluralism: A View from the Bottom," in Alan Shank (ed.), *Political Power and the Urban Crisis* (Boston: Holbrook Press, Inc., 1973), second edition, pp. 243–44.

41. Michael Parenti, *Power and the Powerless* (New York: St. Martin's Press, 1978), p. 27.

42. Robert Dahl, *Who Governs?* (New Haven, Connecticut: Yale University Press, 1962).

43. Ibid., pp. 115–40.

44. For a critique of Dahl's theory of anticipatory reaction, see Michael Parenti, "Power and Pluralism: A View from the Bottom," op. cit., pp. 244–45.

45. Robert Dahl, op. cit., pp. 169–183.

46. Marguerite Ross Barnett, "A Theoretical Perspective and American Racial Public Policy," in Marguerite Ross Barnett and James Hefner (eds.), *Public Policy for the Black Community: Strategies and Perspectives* (New York: Alfred Publishing Company, Inc., 1976), pp. 20–22.

47. Penn Kimball, *The Disconnected*, (New York: Columbia University Press, 1972).

48. Michael Parenti, "Power and Pluralism: A View from the Bottom," op. cit., pp. 255–59.

49. The concept of nondecision making is developed in Peter Bachrach and Morton S. Baratz, "Two Faces of Power," in Harlan Hahn and Charles Levine (eds.), *Readings in Urban Politics: Past, Present and Future* (New York: Longman Press, 1994) second edition, pp. 149–58.

50. Michael Parenti, "Power and Pluralism: A View from the Bottom," op. cit., p. 258.

51. On the issue of mobilization of bias in the political system, see E. E. Schattschneider, *The Semi-Sovereign People* (New York: Holt, Rinehart and Winston, 1960), pp. 30–36.

52. Ibid., p. 35.

53. Ibid.

54. Rufus P. Browing, Dale Rogers Marshall, and David H. Tabb, *Protest Is Not Enough* (Berkeley: University of California Press, 1984), pp. 6–10.

55. Rufus P. Browning, Dale Rogers Marshall, and David H. Tabb, "Taken In or Just Taken? Political Incorporation of African Americans in Cities, paper prepared for the Annual Meeting of the American Political Science Association, Washington, D.C., August 1997, p. 1.

56. Rufus P. Browning, Dale Rogers Marshall, and David H. Tabb, "Can People of Color Achieve Power in City Government? The Setting and the Issues," in Rufus P. Browning, Dale Rogers Marshall, and David H. Tabb (eds.), *Racial Politics in American Cities* (White Plains, New York: Longman Publishers, 1997), second edition, p. 9.

57. Rufus P. Browning, Dale Rogers Marshall, and David H. Tabb, "Minority Mobilization in Ten Cities: Failures and Successes," in Rufus P. Browning, Dale Rogers Marshall, and David H. Tabb (eds.), *Racial Politics in American Cities*, second edition, op. cit., p. 25.

58. Kwame Ture and Charles V. Hamilton, *Black Power: The Politics of Liberation* (New York: Vintage Books, 1992), pp. 54–84.

59. Rufus P. Browning, Dale Rogers Marshall, and David H. Tabb, "Minority Mobilization in Ten Cities: Failures and Successes," in Rufus P. Browning, Dale Rogers Marshall, and David H. Tabb, *Racial Politics in American Cities*, second edition, op. cit., p. 27.

60. Raphael J. Sonenshein, "Post Incorporation Politics in Los Angeles," ibid, pp 53–59.

61. Raphael J. Sonenshein, "The Prospects for Multiracial Coalitions: Lessons from America's Three Largest Cities, ibid, pp. 266–73.

62. For a discussion of Black-Latino coalitions in the 1989 mayoral campaign of David Dinkins in New York, see John Hull Mollenkopf, *A Phoenix in the Ashes* (Princeton: Princeton University Press, 1992), pp. 178–93;

Latino support for Harold Washington in Chicago in 1983 and 1987 are discussed in William Grimshaw, *Bitter Fruit* (Chicago: The University of Chicago Press, 1992), p. 193.

63. Terri Sewell, *Black Political Participation in Britain* (London: Lawrence and Wishart, 1993), p. 83.

64. See Clarence N. Stone, *Regime Politics: Governing Atlanta, 1946–1988.* (Lawrence: University Press of Kansas, 1996), pp. 3–15.

65. Penn Kimball, op. cit.

66. Barbara Ferman, *Challenging the Growth Machine* (Lawrence: University Press of Kansas, 1996), pp. 3–15

67. Ibid., pp. 11–15.

68. Georgia Persons, "Black Mayoralities and the New Black Politics: From Insurgency to Racial Reconciliation," in Georgia A. Persons (ed.), *Dilemmas of Black Politics* (New York: Harper-Collins Publishers, 1993), p. 44.

69. Lucius J. Barker and Mack H. Jones, *African Americans and the American Political System* (Englewood Cliffs, New Jersey: Prentice Hall, 1994), third edition, p. 84.

70. Terri Sewell, op. cit., p. 18.

71. On the accomplishments of Black mayors, see Peter Eisinger, "Black Mayors and the Politics of Racial Economic Advancement," in Harlan Hahn and Charles H. Levine, op. cit., pp. 249–60.

72. Lucius J. Barker and Mack Jones, op. cit., pp. 25–59.

73. William E. Nelson Jr. and Philip J. Meranto, *Electing Black Mayors: Political Action in the Black Community* (Columbus: The Ohio State University Press, 1977).

74. Ibid, pp. 362–63.

75. Georgia A. Persons, op. cit., p. 40.

76. Ibid., pp. 60–63.

77. Dennis Judd and Todd Swanstrom, *City Politics: Private Power and Public Policy* (New York: Harper-Collins Publishers, 1994), p. 120.

78. The concept of strategic dependency is developed in Clarence N. Stone, "Systemic Power in Community Decision Making: A Restatement of Stratification Theory," in Harlan Hahn and Charles H. Levine (eds.), op. cit., pp. 159–79.

79. The classic case is Atlanta where the business community forged extremely cooperative relationships with the mayoral regimes of Maynard

Jackson and Andrew Young. See Clarence N. Stone, *Regime Politics*, op. cit., pp. 191–99.

80. Aldon D. Morris, *The Origins of the Civil Rights Movement* (New York: The Free Press, 1984), p. 282.

81. Ibid., p. 284.

82. William Julius Wilson "Inner-City Dislocations," in Dennis Judd and Paul Kantor (eds.), *Enduring Tensions in Urban Politics*, op. cit., pp. 191–99.

83. Georgia A. Persons, op. cit., p. 61; also see Clarence N. Stone, *Regime Politics*, op. cit.

84. Ira Kantznelson, op. cit.

85. Terri Sewell, op. cit., pp. 50–51.

86. A. Sivanandan, op. cit., p. 120.

87. See Conrad W. Worrill, "Beyond the Million Man March," in Haki R. Madhubuti and Maulana Karenga (eds.), *The Million Man March / Day of Absence: A Commemorative Anthology* (Chicago: Third World Press, Los Angeles: University of Sankore Press, 1996), pp. 80–82.

88. Thomas Byrne Edsall and Mary D. Edsall, *Chain Reaction* (New York: W. W. Norton and Company, 1991), pp. 3–31.

89. John Solomos, op. cit., pp. 56–57.

90. Ibid., pp. 55–63.

91. See Monte Piliawsky, "The Clinton Administration and African Americans," in Theodore Rueter (ed.), *The Politics of Race* (Armonk, New York: M. E. Sharpe, 1995), pp. 385–98; also see Kalbir Skukra, "Black Sections in the Labour Party," in Harry Goulbourne (ed.), *Black Politics in Britain* (Aldershot, England: Avebury Press, 1990), pp. 165–89).

92. Ira Katznelson, op. cit., pp. 24–25.

93. Ibid., p. 23.

94. Gideon Ben-Tovim, John Gabriel, Ian Law and Kathleen Stredder, *The Local Politics of Race* (London: Macmillan Education LTD, 1986), p. 23.

95. Ibid., pp. 108–11.

96. Ibid.

97. Ibid., pp. 139–40.

98. Ibid., pp. 144–45.

99. Ibid., pp. 100–104.

100. Ibid., pp. 65–66.

101. Terri Sewell, op. cit., p. 55.

102. Robert C. Liberman, "Race and Political Institutions: The United States in Comparative-Historical Perspective," paper prepared for the Annual Meeting of the American Political Science Association, Washington, D.C., August, 1997.

103. Ibid., pp. 2–3.

104. Ibid., p. 24.

## Chapter 2. Boston and Liverpool: A Tale of Two Cities

1. For an assessment of local politics in Britain, see Brian N. Jacobs, *Black Politics and Urban Crisis in Britain* (Cambridge: Cambridge University Press, 1986); also see Gideon Ben-Tovim, John Gabriel, Ian Law, and Kathleen Stredder, *The Local Politics of Race* (London: Macmillan Education, LTD), 1986.

2. Frederic Cople Jaher, "The Politics of the Boston Brahmins: 1800–1860," in Ronald P. Formisano and Constance K. Burns (eds.), *Boston 1700–1980: The Evolution of Urban Politics* (Westport, Connecticut: Greenwood Press, 1984), p. 41.

3. Ronald P. Formisano, "Boston, 1800–1840: From Deferential-Participants to Party Politics," in Ronald P. Formisano and Constance K. Burns (eds.), ibid., p. 41.

4. J. Brian Sheehan, *The Boston School Integration Dispute: Social Change and Legal Maneuvers* (New York: Columbia University Press, 1984), p. 41.

5. Steven P. Erie, *Rainbow's End* (Berkeley: University of California Press, 1988), p. 33.

6. Peter Eisinger, *The Politics of Displacement* (New York: Academic Press, 1980), p. 34.

7. Thomas H. O'Connor, *The Boston Irish: A Political History* (Boston: Northeastern University Press, 1995), p. 170.

8. Ibid.

9. Ibid, p. 183.

10. J. Brian Sheehan, op. cit., p. 25.

11. Steven P. Erie, op. cit., p. 76.

12. J. Brian Sheehan, op. cit., p. 26, Steven P. Erie, op. cit., pp. 7–8.

13. Boston Urban Study Group, *Who Rules Boston?* (Boston: Institute for Democratic Socialism, 1984), p. 12.

14. Thomas H. O'Connor, op. cit., p. 226.

15. Ibid., p. 231.

16. Ibid.

17. See Tony Lane, *Liverpool: Gateway of Empire* (London: Lawrence and Wishart, 1987), pp. 125–57.

18. Alan Harding, "Recent Public Policy Approaches to Urban Economic Development in Britain: The Politics of Centralisation," Working Paper Number 5 (Liverpool: University of Liverpool Centre for Urban Studies 1989), p. 2.

19. Peter Fryer, *Staying Power* (London: Pluto Press, Ltd, 1984), p. 41.

20. Michael Parkinson, *Liverpool on the Brink* (Hermitage, England: Policy Journals Publication, 1985), p. 10.

21. Ibid., p. 11.

22. Liverpool interview.

23. Andrew Buni and Alan Rogers, *City on a Hill: An Illustrated History* (Boston: Windsor Publications, Inc., 1984), p. 49.

24. Ibid.

25. Ibid.

26. Robert C. Hayden, *African Americans in Boston: More Than 350 Years* (Boston: Trustees of the Boston Public Library, 1991), p. 17.

27. Ibid.

28. Ibid., p. 19.

29. Ian Law and June Henfrey (eds.), *A History of Race and Racism in Liverpool, 1660–1950* (Liverpool: Whitechapel Press, 1981), p. 9.

30. Ibid.

31. Douglass R. Manley, *"The Social Structure of the Liverpool Negro Community With Special Reference to the Formation of Formal Associations,"* Ph.D. Dissertation, Department of Sociology, University of Liverpool, 1959, p. 69.

32. Ibid.

33. Peter Fryer, op. cit., p. 299.

34. Douglass R. Manley, op. cit., p. 69.

35. Robert C. Hayden, "A Historical Overview of Poverty among Blacks in Boston: 1850–1990," occasional paper (Boston: William Monroe Trotter Institute, University of Massachusetts Boston, 1994), p. 7.

36. Ibid., pp. 7–8.

37. Ibid.

38. Boston interview with Robert C. Hayden.

39. Ibid.

40. Paul Watanabe (ed.), *A Dream Deferred: Changing Demographics, Challenges and New Opportunities for Boston* (Boston: University of Massachusetts Boston, 1996), p. 15.

41. Phillip Hart, "A Changing Mosaic: Boston's Racial Diversity, 1950–1990," in Phillip L. Clay (ed.), *The Emerging Black Community in Boston* (Boston: Institute for the Study of Black Culture, University of Massachusetts Boston, 1985), p. 116.

42. Paul Watanabe, op. cit., p. 5.

43. Ibid., p. 9.

44. Ibid., p. 15.

45. Margaret Simey, *Democracy Rediscovered: A Study in Police Accountability* (London: Pluto Publishing LTD., 1988).

46. Granby Toxteth Community Project, *Statistical Analysis of the 1991 Census* (Liverpool: Poverty 3, N.D.), p. 8.

47. Interview with Gideon Ben-Tovim.

48. The issue of who is Black and who is not is a highly controversial one. Application of the term *Black* to refer to all African Caribbeans and South Asians has not been universally accepted.

49. Paul Wantanabe, op. cit., p. 18.

50. Ibid.

51. Ibid., p. 19.

52. Ibid.

53. Ibid.

54. Quoted in James Blackwell, "Jobs, Income and Poverty: The Black Share of the New Boston," in Phillip L. Clay, op. cit., p. 17.

55. Ibid., p. 19.

56. Ibid.

57. Ibid., p. 24.

58. Ibid., 27–38.

59. Russell Williams and Sue Kim, *Overview of Minority Owned Businesses in the Boston Metropolitan Area* (Boston: William Monroe Trotter Institute, University of Massachusetts Boston, 1995), p. 1.

60. Ibid., p. 10.

61. James Blackwell, op. cit., p. 62.

62. See Lord Gifford, Wally Brown, and Ruth Bundey, *Loosen the Shackles* (London: Karia Press, 1989), p. 40; Merseyside Community Relations Council, the Liverpool Black Caucus, and the Merseyside Profile Group, *Racial Discrimination and Disadvantage in Employment in Liverpool* (Liverpool: Merseyside Area Profile Group, 1986), p. 19; Granby Toxteth Community Project, op. cit., p. 19.

63. Merseyside Community Relations Council, ibid., p. 19.

64. Granby Toxteth Community Project, op. cit., p. 19.

65. Ibid.

66. Merseyside Community Relations Council, op. cit., p. 19.

67. Michelle Connolly and N. P. K. Torkington, "Black Youth and Politics in Liverpool," unpublished paper, Department of Sociology, University of Liverpool, 1990, p. 7.

68. Granby Toxteth Community Project, op. cit., p. 20.

69. Merseyside Association for Racial Equality in Employment and the Merseyside Area Profile Group, *Equal Opportunities and the Employment of Black People and Ethnic Minorities on Merseyside* (Liverpool: Merseyside Association for Racial Equality in Employment and the Merseyside Area Profile Group, 1983), pp. 116-123.

70. Merseyside Community Relations Council, op. cit., pp. 9-12.

71. Liverpool Interview.

72. Massachusetts State Advisory Committee to the United States Commission on Civil Rights, Report on Racial Imbalance in the Boston Public Schools. (Boston: United States Commission on Civil Rights, 1965), p. 4.

73. Ibid.

74. Ibid., pp. 34-35.

75. Boston Interview.

76. Merseyside Area Profile Group, *Racial Disadvantage in Liverpool: An Area Profile* (Liverpool: Merseyside Area Profile, Group, 1980), p. 25.

77. Lord Gifford, Wally Brown, and Ruth Bundey, op. cit., p. 117.

78. Liverpool Interview.

79. Liverpool Interview.

80. "A Murderous Hoax," Newsweek Magazine, January 22, 1990, pp. 18-21.

81. Boston Interview.

82. Boston Interview.

83. N.P.K. Torkington, The Racial Politics of Health: A Liverpool Profile (Liverpool: Merseyside Area Profile Group, 1983), p. 25.

84. Phillip L. Clay, "Housing, Neighborhoods and Development," in Phillip L. Clay (ed.), op. cit., p. 186.

85. Ibid., pp. 184-195.

86. Ibid., p. 182.

87. Lord Gifford, Wally Brown, and Ruth Bundey, op. cit., p. 102.

88. Boston interview.

89. Mel King, *Chain of Change* (Boston: South End Press, 1981), p. 23.

90. See John F. Stack Jr., *International Conflict in an American City* (Westport, Connecticut: Greenwood Press, 1979). See also Ronald P. Formisano, *Boston Against Busing* (Chapel Hill: The University of North Carolina Press, 1991).

91. See Herbert J. Gans, *The Urban Villagers*. (New York: The Free Press, 1982). The concept "urban villagers" has been developed by Herbert J. Gans.

92. Boston interview.

93. Mel King, op. cit., pp. 19–22.

94. Boston Urban Study Group, op. cit., pp. 17–18.

95. Liverpool interview.

96. Liverpool interview.

97. Liverpool interview.

98. Liverpool interview.

## Chapter 3. Boston: City Governance and Black Political Empowerment

1. Barbara Ferman, *Governing the Ungovernable City: Political Skill, Leadership and the Modern Mayor* (Philadelphia: Temple University Press, 1985), p. 25.

2. Steven P. Erie, *Rainbow's End: Irish Americans and the Dilemma of Urban Machine Politics, 1840–1985* (Berkeley: University of California Press, 1988), p. 178.

3. See the discussion in chapter 4 of the transfer to the mayor's office of the power to appoint members of the Boston School Committee. Many

activists in the Black community have labeled this transfer a "takeover" of Boston Public Schools by Mayor Flynn and Mayor Menino.

4. Barbara Ferman, op. cit., pp. 19–23.

5. See Herbert J. Gans, *The Urban Villagers* (New York: The Free Press, 1982).

6. On the role of the press in Boston politics, see William E. Alberts, "What's Black, White and Racist All Over?" in James Jennings and Mel King (eds.), *From Access to Power: Black Politics in Boston* (Cambridge, Massachusetts: Schenkman Books, Inc., 1986). See also Barbara Ferman, op. cit., p. 31.

7. See Martha W. Weinberg, "Boston's Kevin White: A Mayor Who Survives," in Ronald P. Formisano and Constance K. Burns (eds.), *Boston 1700–1980: The Evolution of Urban Politics* (Westport, Connecticut: Greenwood Press, 1984), p. 219.

8. Barbara Ferman, op. cit., pp. 31–36.

9. Mel King, *Chain of Change: Struggles for Black Community Development* (Boston: South End Press, 1981), pp. 23–24.

10. Thomas H. O'Connor, *The Boston Irish: A Political History* (Boston: Northeastern University Press, 1995), pp. 226–31.

11. Ibid., pp. 236–37; Mel King, op. cit., pp. 19–23.

12. Thomas H. O'Connor, op. cit., p. 249.

13. Barbara Ferman, op. cit., p. 57.

14. Ibid., p. 68.

15. Ibid, p. 163.

16. Ibid., p. 69.

17. On the abandonment of the race strategy by Kevin White, see J. Anthony Lukas, *Common Ground* (New York: Alfred A. Knopf, 1985), pp. 30–31; also see Barbara Ferman, op. cit., p. 69.

18. Tilo Schabert, *Boston Politics: The Creativity of Power* (Berlin: Walter de Gruyter, 1989), pp. 171–77.

19. Ibid., p. 33.

20. Ibid., pp. 33–34.

21. Ibid., pp. 33–37.

22. Ibid., p. 139.

23. Barbara Ferman, op. cit., p. 74.

24. Ibid.

25. Boston interview.

26. Toni-Michelle C. Travis, "Boston: The Unfinished Agenda," in Rufus P. Browning, Dale Rogers Marshall, and David H. Tabb, (eds.), *Racial Politics in American Cities* (New York: Longman Press, 1990), p. 114.

27. When Doris Bunte, head of the Boston Housing Authority, refused to cooperate with the mayor's office, White attempted to have her dismissed from her position. Bunte was found guilty of insubordination after a hearing before the mayor and city council; this action was reversed in court in the wake of an appeal by Bunte of the mayor's efforts to dislodge her from city government.

28. Boston interview.

29. Tilo Schabert, op. cit., p. 215.

30. Thomas H. O'Connor, op. cit., p. 275.

31. Boston interview with Professor Robert Dentler.

32. Boston interview.

33. Boston interview with Charles Yancey.

34. Boston interview.

35. Boston interview.

36. Boston interview.

37. Boston interview.

38. Boston interview.

39. Rufus P. Browning, Dale Rogers Marshall and David H. Tabb, *Protest Is Not Enough: The Struggle of Blacks and Hispanics for Equality in Urban Politics* (Berkeley: University of California Press, 1984).

40. Boston interview with Bruce Bolling.

41. Ibid.

## Chapter 4. Black Political Linkage: The Search for Alternative Sources of Power

1. J. Anthony Lukas, *Common Ground* (New York: Alfred A. Knopf, 1985), p. 12.

2. J. Brian Sheehan, *The Boston School Integration Dispute: Social Change and Legal Maneuvers* (New York: Columbia University Press, 1984), p. 60.

3. Ibid., p. 178.

4. Boston interview with Jean McGuire.

5.  James Jennings, "Race and Political Change in Boston," in Phillip L. Clay (ed.), *The Emerging Black Community in Boston* (Boston: Institute for the Study of Black Culture, University of Massachusetts Boston, 1985), p. 320.

6.  Boston interview.

7.  Boston interview.

8.  Boston interview.

9.  Boston interview.

10. *Massachusetts Black Caucus Handbook for New Members and Legislative Staff* (Boston: Massachusetts Black Caucus, 1989), p. 1.

11. Boston interview with Byron Rushing.

12. Mel King, *Chain of Change: Struggles for Black Community Development* (Boston: South End Press, 1981).

13. The concept of 'competitive establishment' is derived from the theoretical work of William Gamson. It connotes the existence of a collection of represented groups and authorities that exercise considerable control over the American political process. One hallmark of these groups and authorities is their efforts to keep unrepresented groups such as Blacks from developing solidarity, becoming politically organized, and entering into effective arenas of policy making. See William Gamson, "Stable Unrepresentation in American Society," *American Behavioral Scientist,* Volume 12, 1968; also see Doug McAdams, *Political Process and the Development of Black Insurgency, 1930–1970* (Chicago: University of Chicago Press, 1982), p. 38.

14. Boston interview.

15. Boston interview.

16. Sheehan, op. cit., pp. 44–45.

17. Ibid.

18. Stephan Thernstrom, *Poverty, Planning and Politics in the New Boston: The Origins of ABCD* (New York: Basic Books, Inc., 1969), p. 22.

19. Mel King, op. cit., p. xxiii.

20. Boston interview.

21. Phillip L. Clay, "Housing, Neighborhoods and Development," in Phillip L. Clay (ed.), *The Emerging Black Community in Boston* (Boston: Institute for the Study of Black Culture, University of Massachusetts Boston, 1985), pp. 185–87.

22. Boston interview.

23. Boston interview.

24. Sheehan, op. cit., pp. 52–53.

25. Mel King, op. cit., pp. 111–115.

26. Peter Dreier, "Urban Politics and Progressive Housing: Ray Flynn and Boston's Neighborhood Agenda," in W. Dennis Keating, Norman Krumholz, and Phillip Star (eds.), *Revitalizing Urban Neighborhoods* (Lawrence: University Press of Kansas, 1996), pp. 73–74.

27. Ibid., pp. 74–75.

28. Ibid., p. 75.

29. Ibid, p. 80.

30. Peter Dreier, "Economic Growth and Economic Justice in Boston: Populist Housing and Jobs Policies," in Gregory D. Squires (ed.), *Unequal Partnerships: The Political Economy of Urban Redevelopment in Post-War America* (New Brunswick: Rutgers University Press, 1989), pp. 48–50.

31. For a discussion of the funding strategies of CDCs, see Avis C. Vidal, "CDCs as Agents of Neighborhood Change: The State of the Art," in W. Dennis Keating, Norman Krumholz and Phillip Star (eds.), *Revitalizing Urban Neighborhoods* (Lawrence: University Press of Kansas, 1996), p. 153.

32. Ibid., pp. 150–54

33. Working document of the Dudley Street Neighborhood Initiative, "Dudley Neighbors, Inc.: Our Community Land Trust."

34. Working document of the Dudley Street Neighborhood Initiative, "The Introduction to the Dudley Street Neighborhood Initiative."

35. Avis C. Vidal, op. cit., p. 152.

36. Peter Dreier, "Urban Politics and Progressive Housing: Ray Flynn and Boston's Neighborhood Agenda," op. cit., p. 71.

37. Avis C. Vidal, op. cit., pp. 151–52.

38. Presentation by Reginald Nunnally, director of the Boston Empowerment Center, delivered at a conference on small business development sponsored by the William Monroe Trotter Center of the University of Massachusetts Boston, 16 May 1997.

39. Ibid.

40. Boston interview.

41. Boston interview.

## Chapter 5. Boston: Strategic Dimensions of Black Politics

1. Andrew Buni and Alan Rogers (eds.), *Boston: City on a Hill* (Boston: Windsor Publications, Inc., 1984), p. 75.

2. Benjamin Quarles, *Black Abolitionists* (London: Oxford University Press, 1969), pp. 16–17.

3. Ibid., pp. 23–41.

4. Ibid., p. 149.

5. Robert C. Hayden, *Faith, Culture and Leadership: A History of the Black Church in Boston* (Boston: Boston Branch of the NAACP, 1983), p. 19.

6. Benjamin Quarles, op. cit., pp. 111–12.

7. Robert C. Hayden, op. cit., p. 29.

8. Ibid., p. 20.

9. Ibid., pp. 30–35.

10. The Niagara Movement was an early twentieth-century campaign for civil rights lead by W. E. B. Du Bois and William Monroe Trotter. It derived its name from the site of the first organizing meeting, Niagara Falls, Canada. This initial meeting was held in June 1905. See John Hope Franklin and Alfred A. Moss Jr., *From Slavery to Freedom: A History of Negroes in America* (New York: Alfred A. Knopf, 1988), sixth edition.

11. Robert C. Hayden, op. cit., p. 24.

12. Andrew Buni and Alan Rogers, op. cit., p. 120–21.

13. Boston interview.

14. Boston interview.

15. James Jennings, "Black Politics in Boston 1900–1950," in James Jennings and Mel King (eds.), *From Access to Power: Black Politics in Boston* (Cambridge, Massachusetts: Schenkman Books, Inc., 1986), p. 18.

16. J. Brian Sheehan, *The Boston School Integration Dispute: Social Change and Legal Maneuvers* (New York: Columbia University Press, 1984), pp. 50–51.

17. Mel King, *Chain of Change: Struggles for Black Community Development* (Boston: South End Press, 1981), p. 129.

18. Ibid, pp. 130–31.

19. Ibid, pp. 96–97.

20. Ibid., pp. 96–99.

21. Boston interview.

22. Mel King, op. cit., p. 193.

23. Boston interview with Hubie Jones.

24. Boston interview with Paul Parks.

25. Mel King, op. cit., p. 44.

26.  Boston interview with Jean McGuire.

27.  J. Anthony Lukus, *Common Ground* (New York: Alfred A. Knopf, 1985), p. 130.

28.  Boston interview with Paul Parks.

29.  Quoted in J. Brian Sheehan, op. cit., pp. 64–65.

30.  Ibid.

31.  John Hillson, *The Battle of Boston* (New York: Pathfinder Press, 1977), p. 27.

32.  Ibid., pp. 23–36.

33.  Quoted in John Hillson, ibid., p. 17.

34.  Ibid.

35.  Boston interview.

36.  Boston interview.

37.  John Hillson, op. cit., pp. 63–64.

38.  Ibid., p. 71.

39.  James Q. Wilson, *Political Organizations* (New York: Basic Books, 1973).

40.  Mel King, op. cit., p. 79.

41.  Boston interview.

42.  Boston interview with Bill Owens.

43.  Ibid.

44. Ibid.

45. Boston interview with Dianne Wilkerson.

46.  Boston interview.

47.  James Jennings, "The Mel King for Mayor Campaign," in Rod Bush (ed.), *The New Black Vote* (San Francisco: Synthesis Publications, 1984), p. 281.

48.  Boston interview.

49.  Boston interview.

50.  Boston interview.

51.  William E. Alberts, *The Role of Mainstream Media in Discrediting Black Candidates: The Boston Mayoral Campaigns of 1983* (Boston: William Monroe Trotter Institute, University of Massachusetts Boston, 1995), p. 28.

52. Boston interview.

53. Boston interview with Bruce Bolling.

54. Hubert E. Jones, "Boston Update 94: The State of Black Boston: A Snapshot," in Joseph R. Barresi and Joseph S. Slavet (eds.), *Boston's Update '94: A New Agenda for a New Century* (Boston: The John W. McCormack Institute of Public Affairs, University of Massachusetts Boston, 1994), pp. VII–14.

55. William E. Alberts, op. cit., p. 40.

56. Quoted in William E. Alberts, ibid., pp. 40–41.

57. Toni-Michelle C. Travis, "Boston: The Unfinished Agenda," in Rufus P. Browning, Dale Rogers Marshall, and David M. Tabb, (eds.), *Racial Politics in American Cities* (New York, Longman, 1990), p. 117.

58. Boston interview.

59. Boston interview.

## Chapter 6. Resource Mobilization and Black Political Linkage

1. For analyses of Black political developments in these cities, see Rufus F. Browning, Dale Rogers Marshall, and David H. Tabb (eds.), *Racial Politics in American Cities* (White Plains, New York: Longman, 1997), second edition; see also Michael B. Preston, Lenneal J. Henderson Jr., and Paul Puryear, *The New Black Politics* (White Plains, New York: Longman, 1982 and 1987), first and second editions.

2. See Philip Hart, "A Changing Mosaic: Boston's Racial Diversity, 1950–1990," in Phillip L Clay (ed.), *The Emerging Black Community of Boston* (Boston: Institute for the Study of Black Culture, University of Massachusetts Boston, 1985).

3. Ibid., pp.121–22.

4. Interview in Washington, D.C. with Carol Hardy-Fanta.

5. Ibid.

6. James Jennings, "Black Politics in Boston, 1900–1950," in James Jennings and Mel King (eds.), *From Access to Power: Black Politics in Boston* (Cambridge, Massachusetts: Schenkman Books, Inc., 1986), p. 12.

7. Hubert E. Jones, "Boston Update 94: The State of Black Boston: A Snapshot," in Joseph R. Barresi and Joseph S. Slavet (eds.), *Boston Update '94: A New Agenda for a New Century* (Boston: The John W. McCormack Institute of Public Affairs, University of Massachusetts Boston, 1994), pp. VII–14.

8. Boston interview.

9. James Jennings, "Urban Machinism and the Black Voter: The Kevin White Years," in James Jennings and Mel King (eds.), op. cit., pp. 67–68.

10. Boston interview.

11. James Jennings, "The Black Voter in Boston 1967–1983: Myths and Realities," in Rod Bush (ed.), *The New Black Vote* (San Francisco: Synthesis Publications, 1984), p. 228.

12. Boston interview.

13. Boston interview with Leonard Alkins.

14. Ibid.

15. Boston interview.

16. Hubert E. Jones, op. cit., pp.VII–13.

17. Boston interview.

18. The financial situation of Freedom House is so severe that most of its staff has been dismissed, and a serious search has been launched to arrange some form of organizational merger with another more fiscally viable community agency.

19. Boston interview.

20. Boston interview.

21. Boston interview.

22. Boston interview.

23. Boston interview.

24. Boston interview with Reverend Eugene Rivers III

25. Boston interview.

26. Boston interview with Reverend Eugene Rivers III.

27. Ibid.

28. Ibid.

29. Ibid.

30. Wendy Murray Zoba, "Separate and Equal," *Christianity Today*, 5 February 1996, p. 23.

31. Eugene Rivers III, "The Challenge Before the Churches, *Sojourners*, February–March, 1994, p. 13. This version of the Ten Point Plan was co-authored by Jeffrey L. Brown, Union Baptist Church; Ray A. Hammond, Bethel African Methodist Episcopal Church; Susie Thomas, Mt. Olive Temple of Christ; Gilbert A. Thompson, New Covenant Christian Center;

Bruce H. Wall, Dorchester Temple Baptist Church; and Samuel C. Wood, Lord's Family African Methodist Episcopal Church.

32. Boston interview with Jean McGuire.

33. Boston interview.

34. Boston interview.

35. Boston interview.

36. Boston interview with Professor Martin Kilson.

37. Ibid.

38. Ibid.

39. See Don Aucoin, "Raising the Stakes," *The Boston Globe Magazine*, 19 May 1996, pp. 24–39.

40. Boston interview.

41. Boston interview.

42. Boston interview.

## Chapter 7. Liverpool: Local Governance and Black Political Empowerment

1. Lord Redcliffe-Maud and Bruce Wood, *English Local Government Reformed* (Oxford: Oxford University Press, 1974), pp. 10–11.

2. Liverpool interview.

3. These figures were provided by the office of Alan Chape, deputy chief executive of the Liverpool City Council.

4. *Powers and Duties of Committees and Sub-Committees* (Liverpool: City of Liverpool, 1989/90), pp. 9–13. Distributed by the office of W. I. Murray, city solicitor, secretary to the council.

5. Ibid.

6. Liverpool interview with senior council officer.

7. Redcliffe-Maud and Wood., op. cit., pp. 19–22.

8. Liverpool interview with senior council officer.

9. Liverpool interview with senior council officer.

10. Liverpool interview with senior council officer.

11. Liverpool interview with John Hamilton.

12. Liverpool interview with senior council officer.

13. Liverpool interview.

14. Liverpool interview with senior council officer.

15. Liverpool interview with senior department officer.

16. F. F. Ridley, "Liverpool Is Different: Political Style in Context," *The Political Quarterly*, Volume 57, No. 2, April–June, 1986, p. 131.

17. See Michael Parkinson, *Liverpool on the Brink* (Hermitage, England: Policy Journals Publication, 1985).

18. Ibid., p. 20.

19. This view of Militant was strongly articulated in notes on an early draft of this study supplied by Sam Semoff.

20. Liverpool interview with Gideon Ben-Tovim.

21. In 1997 the distribution of seats was forty nine Regular Labour, forty five Liberal Democrats, three Militant (or Broad Labour) and two Conservatives.

22. Liverpool interview with Gideon Ben-Tovim.

23. Gideon Ben-Tovim, John Gabriel, Ian Law and Kathleen Stredder, *The Local Politics of Race* (London: Macmillan Education LTD), pp. 100–128.

24. Liverpool Black Caucus, *The Racial Politics of Militant in Liverpool* (Liverpool and London: Merseyside Area Profile Group and Runnymede Trust, 1986), p. 23.

25. Ibid.

26. See Lord Gifford, Wally Brown, and Ruth Bundey, *Loosen the Shackles* (London: Karia Press, 1989).

27. Liverpool interview.

28. This line of analysis was stimulated by extensive conversations with Noel Boaden, Senior Lecturer at the University of Liverpool.

29. Liverpool Black Caucus, op. cit., pp. 31–32.

30. Ben-Tovim, Gabriel, Law, and Stredder, op. cit., p. 75.

31. Liverpool Black Caucus, op. cit., pp. 44–45.

32. Ibid., pp. 44–68.

33. Liverpool interview with Christine Duala.

34. Liverpool interview.

35. Liverpool interview.

36. Liverpool Black Caucus, op. cit., pp. 85–87.

37. Liverpool interview.

38. Liverpool Black Caucus, op. cit., p. 121.

39. Paul Taaffe and Tony Mulhearn, *Liverpool: A City That Dared to Fight* (London: Fortress Books, 1988), p. 266.

40. Liverpool interview.

41. Liverpool interview.

42. Liverpool interview.

43. Liverpool interview.

44. Liverpool interview.

45. "Secret Past of Our Next Mayor," *Liverpool Echo*, 9 August 1994.

46. Liverpool interview.

## Chapter 8. The Toxteth Riots and the Race Policy Agenda

1. John Solomos, *Race and Racism in Contemporary Britain* (London: Macmillan Education LTD, 1989), pp. 46–47.

2. Ibid., p. 48.

3. John Rex and Sally Tomlinson, *Colonial Immigrants in a British City: A Class Analysis* (London: Routledge and Kegan Paul, 1979), p. 49.

4. Ibid.

5. Quoted in Solomos, op. cit., pp. 55–56.

6. Ibid., p. 58.

7. John Solomos, *Black Youth, Racism and the State: The Politics of Ideology and Policy* (Cambridge, England: Cambridge University Press, 1988), pp. 219–27.

8. See Institute of Race Relations, *Policing Against Black People* (London: Institute of Race Relations, 1987).

9. On the Bristol riots, see Martin Kettle and Lucy Hodges, *Uprising: The Police, The People and Riots in Britain's Cities* (London: Pan Books, 1982), pp. 22–38.

10. Ibid., pp. 104–06.

11. Lord Scarman, *The Brixton Disorder* (London: Her Majesty's Stationery Office, 1982).

12. Liverpool interview.

13. I am grateful to Sonia Bassey for providing me with a record of official reports of riot events. Bassey's diary of the riots, including personal observations, pictures, and newspaper clippings, was an invaluable source of data for this chapter.

14. Liverpool interview.

15. Liverpool interview.

16. Report of the Merseyside County Fire Brigade, July 1981.

17. "Police Open Fire on Civilians," *New Statesman*, 17 July 1981, p. 43.

18. Ibid., p. 44.

19. Bassey diary. Information compiled from riot reports.

20. "Riot Police 'Lose' Killer Van," *Morning Star*, 1 August 1981.

21. Liverpool interview.

22. Liverpool 8 Defence Committee, Community Bulletin No. 1, 25 September 1981.

23. For a summary of the Defence Committee's case against Chief Constable Oxford, see ibid.

24. Statement from a press release by MCRC, 15 July 1981.

25. *Ten Years On: 1981–1991*. A Liverpool Profile compiled by Dave Clay, p. 6.

26. "Time to Abandon Political Divisions," *The Daily Mail*, 11 July 1981.

27. "Toxteth Hit by New Riots," *The Guardian*, July 1981.

28. MCRC Internal Research Report.

29. Ibid.

30. Liverpool interview with Margaret Simey.

31. "MPs in Cry for Peace," *The Daily Star*, 7 July 1981.

32. Ibid.

33. See Merseyside Area Profile Group, *Racial Disadvantage in Liverpool: An Area Profile* (Liverpool: Merseyside Area Profile Group, 1980); Merseyside Association for Racial Equality in Employment and Merseyside Area Profile Group, *Equal Opportunities and the Employment of Black People and Ethnic Minorities on Merseyside* (Liverpool: Printfine LTD, 1983); Ntombenhle Protasia Khotie Torkington, *The Racial Politics of Health: A Liverpool Profile* (Liverpool: Merseyside Area Profile Group, 1983).

34. See Commission for Racial Equality, *Race and Housing in Liverpool: A Research Report* (London: Commission for Racial Equality, 1984).

35. Lord Scarman, op. cit., p. 132.

36. Lord Gifford, Wally Brown, and Ruth Bundey, *Loosen the Shackles* (London: Karia Press, 1989), pp. 93–96.

37. Liverpool interview with Dave Clay.

38. See the company brochure, *MST: Positive Action for Positive Results.*

39. Among the studies completed by EOI were the following: *General Survey of Adult Education in Liverpool,* April 1992; *The Educational Needs of Chinese Adults,* May 1992; *Education and Skills Attainment pf Black Small Business Owners,* September 1992; *Black Ex-Offenders in Liverpool,* April 1993; *Educational Attainment and Occupation Aspiration of Young Black Women in Liverpool,* June 1993.

40. For a cogent analysis of the concept of symbolic reassurance, see Murray J. Edelman, *The Symbolic Uses of Politics* (Urbana: University of Illinois Press, 1964).

41. Lord Gifford, op. cit.

42. Liverpool interview with senior council officer.

43. Liverpool interview.

44. Liverpool interview.

45. Liverpool interview with senior department officer.

46. Liverpool interview.

47. Liverpool interview.

48. Liverpool interview.

49. Liverpool interview.

50. Liverpool interview with senior department officer.

51. Gideon Ben-Tovim, John Gabriel, Ian Law, and Kathleen Stredder, *The Local Politics of Race* (London: Macmillan Education LTD, 1986), p. 101.

52. An interesting discussion of clientage relations in Black politics can be found in Matthew Holden, *The Politics of the Black "Nation"* (New York: Chandler Publishing Company, 1973).

53. Liverpool interview.

54. For a discussion of anticipatory reaction in the decision making process, see Michael J. Parenti, "Power and Pluralism: A View from the Bottom," in Alan Shank (ed.), *Political Power and the Urban Crisis* (Boston: Holbrook Press, Inc., 1973), second edition. Permissive dimensions of race policy in Britain are discussed in Gideon Ben-Tovim, "Race Politics and Urban Regeneration: Lessons from Liverpool," in Michael Parkinson, Bernard Foley, and Dennis Judd (eds.), *Regenerating the Cities: The U.K.*

*Crisis and the US Experience* (Manchester: Manchester University Press, 1988).

55. Liverpool interview.

56. Liverpool interview.

57. Alan Harding, "Recent Public Policy Approaches to Urban Economic Development in Britain: The Politics of Centralisation?" University of Liverpool, Centre for Urban Studies, working Paper No. 5, 1089, p. 6.

58. Ibid., p. 11.

59. Ibid., p. 12.

60. Michael Parkinson and Richard Evans, "Urban Regeneration and Development Corporations: Liverpool Style," University of Liverpool, Centre for Urban Studies, Working Paper No. 2, 1988.

61. Ibid.

62. Liverpool interview.

63. Ben-Tovim, Gabriel, Law and Stredder, op. cit., pp. 144–45.

64. Liverpool interview with James Warnock, director of the Merseyside Task Force.

65. Ibid.

66. Ibid.

67. Ibid.

68. Liverpool interview with Paul Wilson, director of the Granby Toxteth Task Force.

69. Michael Parkinson, "A New Strategy for British Cities," in *Policy Studies*, "City Challenge," Summer 1993, Volume 14, No. 2, p. 8.

70. Michael Parkinson, "Urban Leadership and Regeneration in Liverpool: Confusion, Confrontation and Coalition?" University of Liverpool, Centre for Urban Studies, Working Paper No. 14, 1989, pp. 20–26.

71. Liverpool interview.

72. Final Report, Granby Toxteth Community Project, pp. 15–22.

73. Liverpool interview with Audrey Young, director of the Granby Toxteth Community Project.

74. These figures are derived from an interview with Ray Quarless, director of the Steve Biko Housing Association.

75. Liverpool interview.

76. Liverpool interview.

77. Interview with a member of the Liverpool City Council.


Chapter 9. Liverpool: Political Strategies and Political Empowerment

1. Mark Christian, "An African-Centered Approach to the Black British Experience with Special Reference to Liverpool," in the *Journal of Black Studies*, Volume 28, No. 3, 1998, p. 302.

2. Ian Law and June Henfrey (eds.), *A History of Race and Racism in Liverpool, 1660–1950* (Liverpool: Merseyside Community Relations Council, 1981), p. 13.

3. Ibid., p. 19.

4. Peter Fryer, *Staying Power* (London: Pluto Press, 1984), p. 108.

5. Ibid.

6. Law and Henfrey, op. cit., p. 18.

7. Ibid., p. 27.

8. Fryer, op. cit., p. 301.

9. Ibid.

10. Christian, op. cit., pp. 297–98.

11. Law and Henfrey, pp. 31–32.

12. Ibid.

13. Liverpool interview.

14. Liverpool interview.

15. D. R. Manley, *"The Social Structure of the Liverpool Negro Community With Special Reference to the Formation of Formal Associations,"* Ph.D. Thesis, Department of Sociology, University of Liverpool, 1959, pp. 269–70.

16. Ron Ramdin, *The Making of the Black Working Class in Britain* (London: Gower Publishing, 1987), p. 389.

17. Manley, op. cit., pp. 227–28.

18. Ibid, pp. 231–35.

19. Ibid., p. 207.

20. Ibid., p. 206.

21. Ibid., p. 207.

22. A. Sivanandan, *A Different Hunger: Writings on Black Resistance* (London: Pluto Press, 1987), p. 11.

23. Merseyside Anti-Racialist Alliance, *First Annual Report of MARA* (Liverpool: Merseyside Anti-Racialist Alliance, 1979), p. 2.

24. Gideon Ben-Tovim, John Gabriel, Ian Law, and Kathleen Stredder, *The Local Politics of Race* (London: Macmillan Education Ltd., 1986), p. 86.

25. Liverpool interview.

26. Liverpool interview.

27. Liverpool interview with Shaun Deckon.

28. Liverpool interview.

29. Liverpool interview.

30. Liverpool interview with Shaun Deckon.

31. Ibid.

32. Liverpool interview.

33. Liverpool interview with Chief Ben Agwuna.

34. Liverpool interview with Gideon Ben-Tovim.

35. Liverpool interview with Wally Brown.

36. Liverpool interview with Chief Ben Agwuna.

37. See Larry Bennett, *Neighborhood Politics: Chicago and Sheffield* (New York: Garland Publishing, Inc., 1997).

38. Liverpool interview.

39. Liverpool interview.

40. Liverpool interview.

## Chapter 10. Linkage Politics and Political Resources

1. James Jennings and Mel King (eds.), *From Access to Power: Black Politics in Boston* (Cambridge, Massachusetts: Schenkman Books, Inc., 1986).

2. Harbhajan Brar and Michael Keith, "The Politics of Blackness," presented at the seminar New Issues in Black Politics, sponsored by the Centre for Research in Ethnic Relations, University of Warwick, 16 May 1990.

3. Liverpool interview.

4. Brian D. Jacobs, *Black Politics and Urban Crisis in Britain* (Cambridge: Cambridge University Press, 1986), p. 38.

5. Ibid. pp. 71–72.

6. Liverpool interview with Wally Brown.

7. Liverpool interview with Maria O'Reilly of the Liverpool 8 Law Centre.

8. Ibid.

9. Liverpool interview with an officer of the Liverpool Black Sisters.

10. Liverpool interview with a staff member of Mary Secole House.

11. Liverpool interview with a member of the Management Committee of Mary Secole House.

12. Liverpool interview with Clair Dove.

13. Liverpool interview with Carleton Benjamin, chief executive, Toxteth Activities Group.

14. Ibid.

15. Liverpool interview.

16. Liverpool interview.

## Chapter 11. Boston and Liverpool: The Comparative Context of Black Politics

1. See Ira Katznelson, *Black Men, White Cities* (Chicago: The University of Chicago Press, 1976), Phoenix edition.

2. See Lucius Barker, Mack H. Jones, and Katherine Tate, *African Americans and the American Political System* (Saddle River, New Jersey: Prentice Hall, 1998), fourth edition.

3. Ira Katznelson and Margaret Weir, *Schooling for All* (New York: Basic Books, 1985), p. 204.

4. Michael Parenti, "Power and the Powerless: A View from the Bottom," in Alan Shank (ed.), *Political Power and the Urban Crisis* (Boston: Holbrook Press, Inc., 1973), second edition.

5. Ira Katznelson, *Black Men, White Cities*, op. cit., p. 24.

6. Liverpool interview with John Hamilton.

7. Liverpool interview with Ray Quarless.

# Index

protest organizations of the
1940s and 1950s, 239–240
Black Sisters, Liverpool, 216, 272
Black United Front, 131
Black Youth in Liverpool: conflict
with police, 203–204;
involvement in Toxteth riots,
204–207; problems of unemployment, 48; the issue of crime;
201–202
Blacks in Boston: conflict with
police, 53; changes in demographic patterns, 41–43; educational segregation, 51–52;
employment and occupational
mobility, 45–47; encounters with
discrimination, 40–41; levels of
poverty, 45; limitations on housing opportunities, 54–55;
patterns of business development, 47; political dilemmas,
55–57; settlement  patterns,
38–39
Blacks in Liverpool: deprivation of
health services, 54;  discrimination in education, 52; limitations
on housing opportunities, 55;
political dilemmas, 57–59;
problems of unemployment, 48
Blair, Tony, 224
Blyden, Edward, 238
Bollin, Bruce, 79, 81, 82, 83–84,
131; criticism of by *Boston Globe,*
127; decision to run for mayor,
125–126; obstacles to election in
the 1993 mayoral contest, 128,
131; opposition to candidacy in
the Black community, 126–128;
strategies employed in 1993
mayoral campaign, 126
Bollin, Royal Jr., 92
Bollin, Royal Sr., 92, 119, 121
Bond, Sampson, 182, 213, 217, 243,
246, 267, 291; controversy over
appointment as race adviser to
the Liverpool City Council,

182–185; violent reaction to
Bond's politics in the Black
community, 185
Boston Black Political Assembly,
83
Boston Brahmins: conflict with
Irish mayors, 32–33; participation in local politics, 3
Boston City Council: conservative
ideology of, 79–81; control
by dominant White coalition, 79;
dilemmas of countervailing
power, 85; discontinuous interaction with the Black community,
83; impact of nondecision
making on effective Black
linkage, 84–85; marginalization
of Black interests in, 293–294;
racial impact of the committee
system on Black interests, 293;
role of Black councillors in,
80–82; structural distribution of
council seats
Boston City Government:
allocation of power by the city
charter, 63–64; mayoral patronage resources, 64; political
culture, 64
Boston Empowerment Center, 101,
102
Boston Housing Authority, 100
Boston Irish: early registration and
voting patterns, 31–32; election
of politicians to public office.
32–33; immigration and social
development patterns, 31
Boston Jobs Coalition, 110
Boston People's Organization, 124
Boston Redevelopment Authority
(BRA), 96, 98
Boston School Committee: conflict
with NAACP, 113–114; mayoral
control of committee appointments, 90–91; opposition to committee policies in the Black
community, 115; opposition to

Liverpool Community College,
254–256
Liverpool Educational Authority,
251
Liverpool 8 Defence Committee,
207–209, 211, 242, 243, 251–252,
267, 291
Liverpool 8 Law Centre, 208, 216,
242, 259, 264, 270–71, 272
Liverpool Housing Trust, 232
Liverpool Port, 37–38
Liverpool Training and
Management Consultants, 278
Liverpool Women's Hospital, 234
Local Authorities in Britain: color-
blind policy objectives, 24; efforts
to dilute minority power, 24; pol-
icy-making practices and power,
24
Local Government Act (1966), 215
Logan, William D., 106
Logue, Ed, 96
Lopes, Diane, 76
Lord Mayor of Liverpool, 36, 166,
288
Lower Roxbury Community
Development Corporation, 100

Madison Park Community
Development Corporation, 100
Major, John (British Prime
Minister), 35, 224
Mandela Referendum, 128–130
Malcolm X, 131, 241
Manpower Services, 252
Maritine Museum, 225
Martin, Ralph, 157
Marshall, Dale Rogers, 14–15, 78
Massachusetts Black Legislative
Caucus, 91–94
Massachusetts Black Political
Assembly, 120, 123
Massachusetts Citizens for Human
Rights, 115
Massachusetts General Colored
Association, 105

Mattapan Community Health
Center, 146
Mau Mau, The, 121
McGinnis, Hattie, 153
McGuire, Jean, 88, 113, 153–154
Menino, Thomas (Mayor of
Boston), 64, 81, 90–91, 102, 137;
assessment of mayoral style, 75;
Black leadership co-optation,
76–78; consolidation of city
departments, 64; political
linkage with the Black commu-
nity, 76
Merseyside Action Group (MAG)
185
Merseyside Anti-Racialist Alliance
(MARA), 241–243, 267, 291
Merseyside Community Relations
Council (MCRC) 203, 209, 211,
216, 242, 266–270, 272, 280,
292, 297, 299, 300, 302; coordina-
tion of Black organizational
interests, 266–267; creation of
Black Caucus, 266; decline of
leadership capacity, 269–270;
role as political broker, 266–267
Merseyside Area Profile Group,
212
Merseyside Development
Corporation, 36, 211, 225, 226
Merseyside Docks and Harbor
Company, 36
Merseyside Fire Brigade, 205
Merseyside Improved Housing, 232
Merseyside Left Forum, 241
Merseyside Race Equality Council,
269
Merseyside Skills Training, 215,
219, 292
Merseyside Task Force, 226–227
Merseyside Training and
Enterprise Council (MTEC),
277–278
Merseyside West Indian
Association (MWIA), 240
Methodist Youth Centre, 216